THE RULE OF
BENEDICT

THE RULE OF
BENEDICT

Pope Benedict XVI and His Battle

with the Modern World

DAVID GIBSON

HarperSanFrancisco
A Division of HarperCollinsPublishers

HarperCollins books may be purchased for educational, business, or sales promotional use. For information please write: Special Markets Department, HarperCollins Publishers, 10 East 53rd Street, New York, NY 10022.

HarperCollins Web site: http://www.harpercollins.com

HarperCollins®, ®, and HarperSanFrancisco™ are trademarks of HarperCollins Publishers.

FIRST EDITION

Library of Congress Cataloging-in-Publication Data
Gibson, David.
    The Rule of Benedict : Pope Benedict XVI and His Battle with the Modern World /
David Gibson. — 1st ed.
        p.   cm.
    ISBN-10: 0–06–085841–9
    ISBN-13: 978–0–06–085841–4
    1. Benedict XVI, Pope, 1927– .   I. Title.
BX1378.6.G53   2006
282.092—dc22   2005055087

06 07 08 09 10   RRD(H)   10 9 8 7 6 5 4 3 2 1

For Josephine,
who makes it all possible.

CONTENTS

Introduction

BLACK SMOKE,
WHITE SMOKE, AND
SHADES OF GRAY

T here may be nothing as supremely disorienting, or as profoundly emblematic of what it means to be a Catholic today, than the experience of standing in St. Peter's Square waiting for the identity of a new pope to be revealed.

The sensation goes beyond the merely historic, which in these high-speed days can mean most anything that hasn't happened more than twice in the past week. Of course, History was an interested onlooker, along with the rest of us filling the huge oval piazza in the late afternoon of April 19, 2005. Just seventeen days earlier, Pope John Paul II had died after years of infirmity and a grim last-ditch struggle against a massive blood infection. The outcome was inevitable, and a long time coming. And yet the world was stunned by the passing of the aged hero. "John Paul the Great," as he was being acclaimed even before his death, reigned as pope for more than twenty-six years, the third-longest pontificate in the two-thousand-year history of the papacy (Saint Peter himself comes in at number one), and it had been so long since the College of Cardinals had gathered to elect a successor that the whole exercise seemed like the first time it had ever happened. In fact, it was a first for most of the tens of millions of people watching the events transpire on television, for most of the thousands of journalists—like myself—on hand to cover the event, and, more to the point, for 113 of the 115 cardinals assembled in the strictest secrecy in the conclave inside the Sistine Chapel. So there was the plain strangeness of it all to contend with.

Beyond the unfamiliar, however, was the disconnect, bordering on the bizarro, of staring intently at a rustic stovepipe poking above the terra-cotta tile roof that covered the world's most glorious frescoes and trying to figure out if smoke was really emanating from the chimney and, if so, whether it was black smoke or white, and then periodically checking those impressions against the glowing electronic version of the image on huge television monitors a few yards in front of our faces. Was there smoke or wasn't there? Was it white or was it black? This back-and-forth, squinting first at the stovepipe—surprisingly small given its task of announcing the election of a new Roman pontiff to the world—and then at the Vatican's Jumbotron, seemed to embody the whipsaw of the ancient and the modern, the eternal and the evanescent, firm belief and pervasive doubt, that can provoke vertigo in the mind of a Catholic in the front end of the third millennium.

Central to the Catholic dilemma was the fact that the man who was to emerge on the balcony of the massive basilica in front of us would have an unparalleled authority over the religious lives of more than one billion Catholics across the globe, not to mention an audience with just about any world leader at just about any time he pleased. In an era in which authority and institutions are automatically suspect, a Supreme Pontiff with no real check on his power, chosen by a cadre of elderly celibate men behind closed doors, presents an imposing challenge to the conscience of Catholics. The puff of white smoke we were looking for would signal a selection affecting the lives of Catholics everywhere, and the course of the church itself, for years, even generations to come, and it would arrive at one of the most critical junctures in the church's history. Dogged by scandal and controversy in North America, debilitated by religious indifference in Europe, booming in Africa, buckling to Protestant competition in Latin America, an overwhelmed minority in Asia, Catholicism was at a crossroads, and everyone in the piazza, everyone in the world, sensed it.

Yet even as the modern world was moving faster than ever, the Catholic Church was taking its own medieval time about choosing a leader to deal with that changing reality—someone who could somehow reconnect the past and the future in the "eternal present," as Saint Augustine described our condition.

What would the cardinals decide?

Anything was possible, and no one had a clue. Rarely had there been so many different issues pressing in on the church and the cardinals at one time, and rarely had there been so little consensus on at least a handful of frontrunners. Commentators had speculated for months, spinning so many scenarios that Top 10 lists expanded into Top 20 and even Top 40 lists of *papabile,* as potential candidates are known, literally "pope-able." News services took their best guesses and prepared dozens of extensive profiles of prospective popes. All but one would go in the trash as soon as the winner walked out. Then again, maybe none of the preselected would win, and we'd all be starting from scratch. With no overt politicking and no reliable polling possible, and with the proceedings of the conclave cloaked by solemn oaths and an unprecedented electronic shroud of jamming devices, there was precious little intel to go on. The reality is that whether a single cardinal whispered musings to a reporter before the conclave began, or whether twenty did, or even forty, they all entered the locked room as free men, able to vote as they liked for the first, and perhaps only, time in their lives, for the man among them who would lead the Holy Roman Church.

To translate the moment into American political terms, imagine an entire marathon presidential campaign distilled into a single announcement, a split second when hundreds of millions of people with an enormous stake in the outcome suddenly find out the identity of their new leader. No primaries and no stump speeches, no boring conventions and scripted debates winnowing the field to a manageable pair of candidates, and no daily surveys, all of which serve to habituate the mind to one of two possibilities. With a conclave there was no real idea at all of what was happening, or why, or above all, who. The result is like an arranged marriage: Here is the person you'll have to live with. Now fall in love.

With a papal election, there isn't even the fallback position of "better luck next year." Popes do not serve for fixed terms, they do not have term limits, and they do not retire. Moreover, the steady advances in medical technology, especially in geriatrics, mean that the notion of a "transitional" papacy, once a favorite consolation for Catholics disappointed when the cardinals decided to choose an elderly "caretaker" pope, seems forever obsolete. Today even a seventy-five-year-old cardinal—and there were plenty of them in the college—could reign for fifteen or twenty years, though perhaps not terribly effectively. The length and breadth of John Paul's papacy conditioned us to many ideas, one of them being that the papacy was a lifetime job—our lifetime as much as the pontiff's.

In fact, the young adults around me in the square had never known a pope other than John Paul, and in a sense I hadn't either. I had converted to Catholicism some fifteen years earlier, at the ripe age of thirty, right around the corner from where I now stood, in the Chiesa di Sant'Anna, the small Baroque parish church of Vatican City. (St. Peter's is not a parish church, except to the wider world perhaps, which is why a separate church was needed to serve the spiritual needs of the 2,500 or so employees and citizens of the 108-acre protectorate.) I had left the employ of the pope standing there in the piazza. I still meant John Paul II when I said "the pope," as if the title were his alone and needed no elaboration—a few days before my conversion, believing that the requirements of free will would be better met if I was not taking a paycheck from the man who ran the religion to which I was about to entrust the care of my soul.

I had worked at Vatican Radio for most of the five years I lived in Rome, traveling occasionally with John Paul to exotic locales and, more regularly, covering the daily roll call of papal events at the Vatican, which alternated between the quirky—a visit to the pope from Frank Sinatra Jr., for example—and the oddly routine, such as his audience with the Third World Rabbit Congress, an organization whose purpose seemed to change depending on which word in the title I stressed during the broadcast. Through it all, the idea of John Paul as *the* pope imprinted itself on my generically Christian brain, as it did in the minds of much of the rest of the world, even those who did not swim the Tiber. How much John Paul himself had to do with my conversion remains a puzzle to me. But whatever the truth, the fact is that in Catholic terms, I was a bit like a newborn animal in a behavioral study, who attaches itself to the first thing it fixes on, believing whatever it sees to be its progenitor because it knows nothing else.

For me, as for so many of the more than 100,000 people who had streamed into St. Peter's Square, John Paul was still the pope.

Now, all of that was about to change, and in the most dramatic fashion possible.

And yet, at a moment designed to produce clarity and renewal, confusion reigned. Was the smoke white or was it black? This had happened in earlier conclaves, and the Vatican had taken great pains to avoid such problems by giving the cardinals special coloring cartridges to toss in the stove with the ballots. One cartridge would produce black smoke, the other white. Or not, it seemed. As a wise backup plan, the Vatican announced that the bells of St. Peter's would ring out when a pope was elected. The problem was that the bells ring every quarter hour, and on the hour—just at the moment when the smoke was supposed to rise—they ring for an extended time.

Uncertainty had been a problem from the start of the conclave twenty-four hours earlier. The evening before, on Monday, the cardinals processed into the Sistine Chapel, with every solemn footfall broadcast in the piazza on a live video feed until the papal master of ceremonies, Archbishop Piero Marini, announced "*Extra omnes!*"—"Everybody out"—and sealed the princes of the church from the outside world. Under the conclave rules, the cardinals, after a bit of administrative housekeeping and extensive recitations of secrecy oaths, had the option of taking a first vote or waiting until the next morning to start the balloting.

At least one European cardinal confidently assured aides that no vote would be taken the first evening, and that the cardinals would settle in for the night and take up the business first thing the next day. Other sources suggested there might be a shake-out ballot that first night, while some Vatican officials indicated that either way, the cardinals would let the world know so that we all wouldn't stand around on the cobblestones in the cooling evening. Which is just what we wound up doing. And around 8:00 PM, after an hour's wait, just as frustrated onlookers started to drift away, there it came, the first puffs of smoke and a huge roar from the crowd, which surged en masse toward the Vatican wall to see if indeed we had a new pope.

The smoke looked black at first but then turned a suspicious gray. "I started calling people at home," said Stephen Wisniew, an army captain based at Fort Bragg, North Carolina. "It was amazing to be there—I was saying on the phone, 'Hey, we're not sure yet.'"[1] Then the smoke turned black again, and the crowd let out a collective groan. But with the negative vote, I found that the reality of what was happening suddenly hit me in the gut, the awareness that if not that evening, then soon, we would have a new pope, and everything in the church could be dramatically different, or, perhaps worse, nothing at all would change.

It was a sobering moment and, perhaps, in the way that first impressions tell an underlying truth, a sign of my own trepidation at what could result, and a distinct lack of faith in the cardinals and the conclave system—and in the Holy Spirit, the *grande elettore*. The one name that had been emerging from the pack of contenders in the days leading up to the conclave was that of Cardinal Joseph Ratzinger, the late pontiff's longtime theological enforcer and arguably the man with the worst press in the entire College of Cardinals. (Excepting the former Boston archbishop, Cardinal Bernard Law, who resigned in disgrace in 2002 over his role in the sexual abuse cover-ups. But Law got a cushy ceremonial post in Rome, and because he was still a cardinal under eighty years old, he retained the right to vote in the conclave, which his successor, an archbishop back in Boston, did not enjoy.) As head of the Congregation for the Doctrine of the Faith, the former Holy Office of the Inquisition, Ratzinger held the second-most powerful job in the Vatican and was responsible for maintaining discipline and excluding dissent. By nature and job description, he was the "bad cop" to John Paul's "good cop." He had silenced theologians, censured books, and offended women, homosexuals, and other Christian churches with his unvarnished descriptions of what he saw as their inherent shortcomings. As a reward for all his hard work, Ratzinger was labeled everything from God's Rottweiler to Cardinal No to *Der Panzerkardinal* and, of course, the Grand Inquisitor. Yet it was a testament to how polarized the church had become under John Paul and Ratzinger that his supporters saw the epithets as merit badges. The Web site of the Ratzinger Fan Club boasted of their man: "Putting the smackdown on heresy since 1981."

Apart from his track record, Ratzinger was also seventy-eight years old and had not been the most vigorous of men even in his halest days. Moreover, his retiring, bookish mien would be such a come-down from the mediagenic John Paul that there was no way he would be elected pope. Also, he was German, of all things, and his list of nicknames showed that even in an age of ostensible political correctness, Germans remained the one nationality no one really feared offending. A German pope coming in as Bishop of Rome after the long tenure of a Pole who was the first non-Italian in more than 450 years seemed beyond unlikely. Moreover, there hadn't been a German pontiff in a thousand years, which was no surprise given the terrible history of disputes and misalliances between the Germans and the Italians over the centuries. A German pope standing on the balcony of the basilica whose gaudy construction lost Germany to the papacy back in 1517? Not likely. Moreover, no cardinal had ever gone from the Holy Office to the Throne of Saint Peter—Grand Inquisitors were no more popular among the cardinals than they were with anyone else. Ratzinger would take a bloc of votes on the first ballot, a kind of gold watch for his lengthy service to the Holy See. Then the real conclave would start, and Joseph Ratzinger would be sent toddling back to a scholarly retirement in his native Bavaria. That was what he wanted anyway, as he had told everyone, including the late pope, who always persuaded Ratzinger to stay on.

Ratzinger would certainly have an important voice in the conclave, but there was no way he would be elected or accept the job. His friends had said as much in the days leading up to this moment.

That scenario seemed to be confirmed by the unsuccessful ballot the first evening. Whatever momentum Ratzinger might have started out with that Monday night would be spent by the morning. About noon Tuesday, the smoke came out black again, indicating two unsuccessful ballots that morning, but the bells started tolling and cheers went up, only to fade into a collective sigh within a couple of minutes as people realized what was happening, or not happening. So the game was still on.

And yet, there was that niggling suspicion that something unexpected could be in store. Despite the many proclamations that the election of a pope is purely the work of the Holy Spirit, as if it moves cardinals like a pointer on a Ouija board, the reality is far more complex, both theologically and historically. If the cardinals are simply channeling the Holy Spirit in some kind of closed-door séance, then how does one account for the run of scandalous, murderous, and villainous popes who have alternated with genuine saints on the Throne of St. Peter?

The best explanation of the process is that given by one of the few surviving veterans of a conclave, a cardinal who was asked in a 1997 television interview if the Holy Spirit chooses the pope. "I would not say so, in the sense that the Holy Spirit picks out the pope," he said. "I would say that the Spirit does not exactly take control of the affair, but rather like a good educator, as it were, leaves us much space, much freedom, without entirely abandoning us. Thus the Spirit's role should be understood in a much more elastic sense, not that he dictates the candidate for whom one must vote. Probably the only assurance he offers is that the thing cannot be totally ruined."[2]

The cardinal was Joseph Ratzinger.

By late Tuesday afternoon, whatever the Holy Spirit, and the cardinals, decided at this conclave finally appeared close to revelation. It was 5:49 PM when smoke began issuing from the stovepipe, wisps at first, then growing clearer both to the naked eye and on the huge TV screens. This had to be a confirmation, since smoke at this hour would have meant that the first ballot of the afternoon had been successful. The second ballot would not have wound up until 7:00 PM.

So much would depend on the choice, so much would be clarified by the result.

"*É bianco! É bianco!*"

"It's white! It's white!" some yelled.

Then consternation set in when the wisps turned blackish.

"What are they doing?" a Roman behind me complained. A boisterous crowd of Brazilians in front of us started chanting "*Habemus papam,*" the Latin phrase used to announce "We have a pope." Then their yelling tailed off as the uncertainty continued. The background of the overcast gray sky didn't help, and the vaunted technology wasn't doing so well. Cell networks were jammed, and the huge TV screens just made the images fuzzy. The Roman fellow behind me started joking that the smoke was both white and black. "*É Juventino!*" he laughed, meaning the new pope was a fan of the Turin-based soccer team Juventus, whose colors are black *and* white. The smoke tailed off after a few minutes, causing further uncertainty.

Then the bells rang and everyone roared.

But we realized the bells were tolling the six o'clock hour and everyone sighed.

Then, at 6:04 PM, the bells of the basilica started ringing back and forth, insistent, certain. There was no doubt. The crowd roared as one, "*Habemus Papam!*"

This was it. But who was it?

The moment was here, but it would take some forty-five minutes, judging by past conclaves, to vest the pope in his new white cassock and get him out of the chapel and up to the balcony. Thunder rolled ominously behind the church, and it looked as though it would rain. "*Fuori, fuori!*" shouted a group of teenage girls nearby, growing impatient along with everyone else. "Come out! Come out!" Another woman kept singing "Alleluia," and various national groups chanted "*Viva il Papa!*" fully expecting that the scenario favoring their compatriot would be realized. All was still possible, and hopes and prayers flew in every direction until 6:40 PM, when a marching band tromped out in their Gilbert and Sullivan military uniforms ready to play for the new pope. Cardinals in red birettas and lace-edged rochets over scarlet capes started filling the balconies on either side of the central loggia where the new pope would stand. Two minutes later, the huge glass doors leading onto the balcony opened and out stepped Cardinal Jorge Medina Estevez, an elderly Chilean prelate whose seniority gave him the honor of announcing the new pope to the world.

Medina was clearly relishing the moment of suspense. He began by saying, "Dear brothers and sisters" in five languages—Italian, Spanish, French, German, and finally English, underscoring the universality of the crowd and the church but giving no clue as to the nationality of the new pope. Then he began the ancient Latin formula, ever so slowly:

"*Annuntio vobis gaudium magnum,*" he said, "I announce to you a great joy." Applause and a long pause . . .

"*Habemus papam!*"

More applause, then silence, awaiting the name of the cardinal who was now pope. Medina waited, saying nothing for a full thirty seconds. For the church, that was an eternity. He was milking it—taking "pompous delight," as one commentator put it.[3] And it worked. The crowd was on its toes, straining forward. Finally Medina spoke: "*Eminentissimum ac Reverendissimum Dominum*"—pause—"*Dominum Iosephum. . . .*"

Joseph? Could it be? Six cardinals in the Sistine Chapel had variations on the name Joseph, but there could be only one who was elected. Sure enough, Medina finished the announcement and the choice was confirmed: "*Sanctae Romanae Ecclesiae Cardinalem Ratzinger . . .*"

Ratzinger? *Ratzinger?*

That's what Medina said: "The Most Eminent and Reverend Lordship, Lord Joseph Cardinal of the Holy Roman Church Ratzinger."

Cheers went up, but the hosannas were clearly tempered by surprise, even shock. A woman next to me looked stricken. Another plunged her face into her hands in tears. "It's Ratzinger," Silvie Genthial, a French pilgrim, barked into her cell phone before hanging up. "We were all hoping for a different pope—a Latin American perhaps—but not an ultraconservative like this," she told the Associated Press. The cell phone of an aide to Cardinal Cormac Murphy-O'Connor, who was considered something of a progressive, buzzed with a text message. It was from Sir Stephen Wall, formerly public affairs adviser to the cardinal, and it simply said, "Shit."

An elderly Italian woman, wiping away tears, expressed her doubts while talking to someone on her cell phone, but her daughter reassured her, patting her on the back and saying, "You'll like him, you'll see."[4]

Of course, many already did. Huzzahs and cheers went up from the crowd that surged closest to the balcony for the best view. A group of seminarians were beside themselves with joy, and a contingent from Christendom College, a strongly conservative Catholic school in Virginia, shouted and waved a Vatican flag that they had fixed above the American Stars and Stripes. In the studio above the square, Raymond Arroyo, anchor for the retro-conservative Evangelical Word Television Network, the Alabama-based Catholic cable giant started by the redoubtable Mother Angelica, fought back tears of joy. "We are all misty-eyed and a bit beside ourselves up here in the studio," he said.

(Back in Germany, Benedict's brother, Father Georg Ratzinger, was not quite as upbeat. "I'm not very happy," Georg told the AP. "He's okay, and his health is good. I just wish for him that his health holds out and that his office isn't a worry and a nuisance to him.")

Cardinal Medina finished his announcement, telling the crowd that Ratzinger would now be known as Pope Benedict XVI, and a moment later Ratzinger—or rather, Benedict—emerged and clasped his hands together over his head in exultation. This was a stunning moment for so many reasons, not the least of which was that Joseph Ratzinger was probably the least demonstrative of churchmen, a shy man with an almost diminutive physical presence who rarely moved his arms beyond what was required for invoking a blessing. A bigger shock to me, however, and to many others, was the simple, stark realization that John Paul II was no longer the pope. Yes, I realized, the papacy really was about an office rather than a man, and Joseph Ratzinger was not doing a bad impersonation of John Paul. He *was* the pope. Most of all, I couldn't help thinking—dreading—that given his well-publicized past, this could not be good news for those of us, the silent majority of Catholics, who were hoping, praying, for the vibrancy and openness that would herald a new chapter in the history of the church. Would our worst fears be realized?

"Dear brothers and sisters," Benedict began, speaking Italian fluently, as he does several languages, though all with the same German inflection. His audience hung on his words to see what they would tell us about the man who was suddenly the Supreme Pastor of the world's largest Christian body.

"After the great Pope John Paul II"—applause erupted at the dead pope's name—"the cardinals have elected me, a simple and humble laborer in the vineyard of the Lord.

"The fact that the Lord knows how to work and to act even with inadequate instruments comforts me, and above all I entrust myself to your prayers.

"Let us move forward in the joy of the Risen Lord, confident of his unfailing help. The Lord will help us, and Mary, his Most Holy Mother, will be on our side. Thank you," he concluded before giving the traditional *Urbi et orbi* blessing, to the city of Rome and to the world.

The new pope's first message was spare and delivered almost flat. He was still suffering the effects of a head cold that had run through the conclave, but clearly the church had entered a different era. Gone was the magnetism of John Paul. Benedict did not offer greetings in any other languages, as John Paul always did, nor did he offer any warm fuzzies for the folks in the square and those watching on television. When Karol Wojtyla was elected John Paul II, he was a complete unknown, even to many of the cardinals. He came from behind the Iron Curtain, with no public record to speak of in the West, in the days before Google catalogued every utterance for everyone to read at a mouse click. At the announcement of Wojtyla's name, people in the square were stunned into silence, thinking at first that the cardinals had elected "*un Africano*," as many whispered. Others thought an Asian by the sound of his name, pronounced "voy-TEE-wah." John Paul immediately sought to put the crowd at ease by speaking their mother tongue. "I don't know whether I can explain myself well in your . . . *our* Italian language," he said, breaking the ice and winning over the crowd in a single phrase. "If I make a mistake, you will correct me."

Pope Benedict, on the other hand, hardly needed to define himself. Joseph Ratzinger was the most prolific author in the entire College of Cardinals. Since Vatican II in the 1960s, he had been the church's most prominent theologian, producing dozens of articles, treaties, and books, and he was also the subject of several biographies and book-length interviews. Since 1981 he had held the most visible post in the church, apart from the pope, and the most controversial by far. Everyone knew what Cardinal Ratzinger thought about most anything, and everyone had their opinion. Ratzinger was the most polarizing figure in modern Catholicism, and there was no middle ground when it came to opinions on him.

"He'll correct the lackadaisical attitudes that have been able to creep into the lives of Catholics," an exultant Father M. Price Oswalt, an Oklahoma City priest, told the *New York Times*. "He's going to have a German mentality of leadership: either get on the train or get off the track. He will not put up with rebellious children." Likewise, Maria Piscini, an Italian grandmother, toasted the new pope with a paper cup filled with dark red wine. "A clear and true voice of faith," she told the Associated Press. Others had a different view. A woman named Eileen from Boston said, "As soon as I heard the name, I had a letdown, a sinking feeling that this man is not going to be good for the church." She was afraid to give her last name because she did not want to cause problems for her pastor back home, or jeopardize her daughter's imminent church wedding.[5]

The headlines were just as stark. "The Iron Cardinal," blared the Italian daily *La Repubblica*. "Ratzinger is the Counter-Reformation personified," wrote the *Frankfurter Allgemeine Zeitung*. The *Berliner Zeitung* called him "autocratic, authoritarian" and "as shrewd as a serpent." *Die Tageszeitung* described him as a "reactionary churchman" who "will try to seal the bulkheads of the Holy Roman Church from the modern world." In Britain, the *Daily Mirror* said, "He was known as 'God's Rottweiler.' . . . Now he is Pope Benedict XVI," and the *Daily Mail* echoed with "Cardinals pick 'the Rottweiler.'"

A text message went out on Italian cell networks that was a parody of a famous off-the-cuff talk the beloved John XXIII gave to a Roman crowd in 1963, in which John broke protocol by speaking to the people extemporaneously and not in formal Latin. Good Pope John famously told them to go home and "hug your children and tell them that this hug is from the pope." The Benedict version was quite different, complete with idiosyncratic spelling to underscore his German accent: "When you go back home, slap your children and tell them this slap is from the pope" (*Kuando tornerete alle vostre kase tate un ceffone ai fostri pampini e tite questo è il ceffone del papa*).

An Irish priest who had been standing next to me, arms crossed as he watched the spectacle, finally turned to leave. "Well," he said, "I hope the Holy Spirit knows what he—or she—is doing."

The odd thing is that the very uncertainty that the white smoke, and the election of a man like Joseph Ratzinger, was supposed to dispel only grew in the hours and days after Benedict's election. In an unprecedented public relations move, many cardinals emerged to talk to the press that very evening, in an effort to redefine the cardinal who easily had the most baggage of any of them going into the conclave—and coming out of it.

"He's a very loving, lovely person, very unassuming, and shortly you will see this," explained New York's Cardinal Edward M. Egan, one of many cardinals eager to head off criticism of the new pope, at a news conference the day after the conclave. "You need to be slow in making judgments. Sometimes it's good to watch for a while and see if what you've heard is true." Cardinal Aloysius Ambrozic of Toronto said that because of the nature of Pope Benedict's position as the church's head theological enforcer, people did not see other facets of his personality. "There's a real difference between the image and the reality. The media doesn't really know the man," he said. Cardinal Roger M. Mahony of Los Angeles agreed. "Much of the baggage that goes with anyone who is given a responsibility is hard to overcome," he said. "But his job was preserving the doctrine of the church against dilution or errors. That was his job; that is what Pope John Paul II asked him to do, but that is not his job now. I think you will see emerge his far more spiritual and pastoral sides," Mahony said. "I have seen him in those roles, and I think people will be very, very surprised in a good sense."[6]

Could it be that a cardinal who was the paladin of orthodoxy to conservatives and the Darth Vader of the Vatican's Death Star to liberals was actually something different? Would the kinder, gentler Joseph Ratzinger that the cardinals knew personally project his private self onto his new public stage? On that chilly spring evening in the piazza, Pope Benedict's image on the giant video screen was so pixelated as to be indistinct—deconstructed by modern technology, as it were, beyond recognition. Were we simply too close to it all to make considered judgments about the man? Would the demands of the papacy bring a new Joseph Ratzinger into focus?

The church had fed off the galvanic presence of John Paul as its chief pastor for so long that many questioned whether a retiring, almost monastic man like Benedict could maintain the necessary momentum. John Paul II may not have changed the Catholic Church the way he wanted, but he certainly transformed the papacy. Would Benedict grow into that leading role? Or was he destined to die the death of a character actor, an interesting fellow because of his regular display of one or two salient virtues—or vices—but one who inevitably bows out in service to a larger plot whose central actor remains John Paul II? Would he be a bridge to the past or to the future?

Moreover, no matter who walked out on that balcony at St. Peter's that evening, the circumstances of the contemporary church and the world today would present Catholics with more questions than answers.

The polarization of the church is such that Catholicism is ripping itself apart from within. Can Benedict provide the neutral territory necessary for combatants to find rapprochement and greater individual sanctity? Does he want to? Judging from Benedict's lengthy record of sharply criticizing the modern world, it seemed plausible that he would be happier with a "smaller-but-purer" church, one shriven of its contentious elements—mainly on the left—a Fortress Catholicism that would wall itself in and guard the *depositum fidei* until the arrival of a more congenial era for the conservatives, or the Second Coming, either of which could be the preferred exit, depending on what strain of traditionalism one subscribes to.

Similarly, can he find a way for Catholics to perform the tricky mental bilocation that people of faith need to live in the modern world? Again, does he even want to? If faith and modernity are to coexist in Christianity's third millennium, or even collaborate, the laboratory for Benedict's experiment would seem to be the United States, which is by far the most religiously observant and spiritually pumped society in the industrial world. Yet nowhere is the crisis of Catholicism more acute than in America, where scandals and bankruptcies and internal disputes and anger at Rome have left many Catholics more willing than ever to join the country's teeming religious marketplace as spiritual freelancers. What about Europe? Religious observance in the ancestral home of the Roman faith is close to collapse. Will Benedict's push to challenge that decline be the tipping point that leads to inexorable decline or will his forcefulness be the gut-check that Europeans are looking for?

In the developing world, the Southern Hemisphere, where more than two-thirds of the world's Catholics live and where many believe the future of the church resides, the questions are just as pressing. Could a pope so single-mindedly focused on promoting—or just preserving—the Catholic faith in the modern world afford to let Third World Catholicism languish? While Catholicism in Africa is booming, the young church there needs tending. In Asia, the tiny church needs a freer hand to adapt to a culture so foreign to Western Christianity. And how long will the worsening situation of the church in Latin America be allowed to continue? Nearly half the world's Catholics live there, but desperate priest shortages, ecclesiastical infighting, inroads by conservative Protestants, and endemic poverty and human rights concerns make inaction untenable. Problems that existed, and even worsened, during the reign of John Paul II remain unresolved but cannot go unaddressed by the new pope.

Religious allegiances are far more tenuous today than ever before, and the days when the church could elect a "placeholder pope" while waiting for the Holy Spirit to clarify its intentions are over. If Benedict tries to stand pat, the next pope could find himself walking out on that balcony and discovering the piazza below deserted.

It is one of the many paradoxes of Benedict's surprise election that the choice of the best-known cardinal in the college could prompt so much uncertainty. By picking Joseph Ratzinger, the College of Cardinals took a huge gamble at a perilous time for the Catholic Church, and their overriding message in the days after his election was one of reassurance, that Benedict would "surprise" the church and world.

But how exactly?

With the reign of Benedict now well under way, several things have become clear, some surprising, some not, most of them unsettling for those looking for a vigorous, hope-filled church to emerge from the inertia of scandal and papal infirmity.

One surprise is that Benedict's presence in the public square is far different from that of his predecessor and from what many fans of Joseph Ratzinger may have expected. With his low-key style and low-wattage personality, not to mention his understandably slow pace at almost eighty, Benedict is deliberately downsizing the profile of the papacy in keeping with his laudable desire to emphasize Christ over the person of the pope. Yet that is a signal departure in emphasis and one that may have unintended consequences for the Vatican's influence in a zeitgeist driven by the cult of personality, in the field of religion as well as entertainment and politics. Also, in stressing the call to personal holiness over all else, Benedict risks pulling the church back from its mission of working for social justice in the world, once a hallmark of Catholicism. By this strategy, Benedict may wind up reducing not only the visibility of the papacy but also the presence of the Catholic Church in the world at a time when such a witness is not only needed but demanded as external evidence of the church's inner renewal.

Nor is Benedict particularly concerned about, or open to, the structural reforms of the institutional church that so many Catholics, especially in the United States, are demanding in the wake of the horrific revelations of clergy sexual abuse. While Benedict has been—as Ratzinger was   a patient listener, he will always form his own conclusions. And those conclusions seem to preclude changes in church teachings or internal reforms. For example, transparency and collaboration in nondoctrinal areas like finances and governance have received no boost from the pope, who has opted for purging the priesthood rather than holding accountable the bishops whose actions turned the crimes of some clerics into a churchwide scandal. At the same time, the years of pent-up demands for greater dialogue and openness on sensitive issues like clerical celibacy and the role of women and communion for divorced and remarried Catholics also seemed destined to be thwarted, and to produce greater frustration that could eventually spill out in a wave of resignation.

Internal reform for Pope Benedict tends to focus on matters of liturgy, for example, which is undeniably vital, as the Eucharist remains the "source and summit" of Catholic life. But his is a self-described "reform of the reform," a return to past rites and Latin prayers rather than innovations or improving the experience of the mass for worshippers. In the context of the other challenges facing the church, Rome's fetish for the minutiae of rubrics, for dictating new, supposedly more liturgically correct, translations of beloved communal recitations, seems to Catholics like a kind of nano-theology that shrinks to irrelevance compared with the larger pastoral crises swirling about.

In short, what should not be surprising from his freshman year as pope is that Benedict XVI is not so different at all from what Cardinal Ratzinger was. Joseph Ratzinger was always convinced not only of the rightness of his own ideas but also of his unvarying constancy in those beliefs.

Ratzinger's new papal alter ego does not need to be the public "enforcer" that he was as a cardinal, but he is also not about to embrace compromises that he would not have considered before, or permit the church to change its teachings or traditions, or allow the free debate that Catholics want. Benedict's role in the forced departure of the editor of a leading Catholic journal in the United

States, his new policy restricting the ordination of seminarians with a homo-sexual orientation, and the Vatican inspection of more than two hundred U.S. seminaries and houses of priestly formation to root out hints of dissent were reminders of the pope's cramped definition of catholicity. On communion for divorced and remarried Catholics, or optional celibacy for priests, he also endorsed the status quo. At the same time, he seemed determined to promote liturgical reforms that "reformed the reforms" of Vatican II, such as making the familiar vernacular sound more like a direct translation from Latin.

Even on his stated priority of promoting Christian unity, Benedict has been less accommodating than John Paul was. Benedict always encourages dia-logue—more so with other Christians than within the Catholic Church, in fact—but he consistently reminds his partners that Catholics can only prac-tice ecumenism from a position of strength—that is, by asserting the Catholic Church's own unique identity as expression of the fullness of Christian truth. His greatest concern in interreligious dialogue seems to be soliciting allies who will join in an "ecumenism of the barricades," putting aside differences of be-lief in order to form a united front in the public square on moral issues of common concern. That goes for his outreach to secularists as well, whom he asks to behave "as if God exists," thereby providing strange bedfellows with a common platform for public action without compromising the beliefs of either side.

What all this points to is the "smaller-but-purer" church that Joseph Ratzinger has predicted for years, but which is not necessarily about num-bers or sanctity. Rather, that vision of the church amounts to privileging one segment of the faithful—namely the self-declared orthodox—over another, thus encouraging some to remain active in a church that gives their views an imprimatur, while alienating others, who will see their beliefs and practices marginalized or even prohibited. Many of the former will be no holier for their pious practices or their self-satisfaction in being part of the in-crowd in Rome. And many of the latter may leave, or drift about the shadowlands of the faith, or simply practice on their own terms. Catholicism may grow in some places and shrink in others, but it will everywhere be afflicted by a par-tisanship that is the inevitable result of a campaign of purification and an in-version of the traditionally expansive view of what it means to be Catholic.

Where the practice of the faith declines quantitatively, conservatives will hail the development as a leap forward in quality and a vindication of the providence of Benedict's election and, not coincidentally, of their own views about who is a good Catholic. In reality, however, that scenario would be more akin to a self-fulfilling prophecy, an enforced winnowing resulting not from the defection of faithless believers who did not march to the Vatican's tune, but from the actions of church authorities who succumbed to the temptation to use their power to tailor a church to their own tastes. Where the practice of the faith increases quantitatively, conservatives will also hail it as a triumph for their side, even though in other contexts they disparage numbers as a reliable indicator of spiritual health.

We are witnessing a struggle for the soul of Catholicism. That battle has been going on for decades, but the election of Benedict brought the conflict to a head. Where will it all lead? In the end, Benedict's election is a X-ray of the state of Catholicism—every conclave is a statement about where the church is at that moment on its pilgrim path through history—but it is also very much the story of a person, Pope Benedict XVI, whether he wants to be the center of attention or not. As a consequence, understanding Benedict himself is crucial, because his character, as much as his enormous body of theological writings, will set the tone in the church for the coming years and will be key to forecasting how he will act in whatever time remains to his papacy.

As with anything in the Catholic Church, however, we cannot understand the present circumstances or divine the future possibilities without first delving into the past. And for the past generation, that history was all about Pope John Paul II. That is where the papacy of Benedict was born, and that is the legacy that will shape its future.

Chapter One

THE SHADOW OF
THE PONTIFF

Ligh above St. Peter's Square, inside the warren of apartments that make up the imposing complex of the Apostolic Palace, the old pope sat slumped in a wheelchair as aides tried to pretend they weren't completely preoccupied with his every move. Over the previous weeks, as the silver jubilee of this historic pontificate approached, Parkinson's disease, which had afflicted John Paul II for years, was also advancing, just as inexorably. The question seemed to be which would arrive first, the anniversary or the angel of death.

As often happens in such cases, the affliction that was steadily paralyzing synapses in the pontiff's brain passed through phases, with good days and bad. Sometimes the pope looked to be on the edge of death, to the point that newsrooms hit the panic button and started mobilizing for the funeral. At other times, and for long stretches, he would rally and become animated to such a degree that one thought he might go on forever. Vatican insiders said that the swings were due to changes in his medications. Some suggested that John Paul disliked taking them because they dulled his famously agile mind and made him too sleepy to engage the crowds that energized him. So for major events, such as the jubilee of his election, he would cut back on the pills. Others said the pope's doctors had to periodically flush the powerful drugs out of his system so they would not harm his organs.

In those unmedicated times, the pope's death seemed imminent. As his health worsened, the circle around him grew tighter, and even officials who had once enjoyed regular access to the pope were cut off. Information became speculation. At one point, the talk around the Vatican was that John Paul was being given some kind of mixture that included a cocaine-like stimulant to keep him going. The rumor had some basis in history. A nineteenth-century pope, Leo XIII, whose papacy John Paul would eventually surpass, enjoyed a sparkling red wine laced with opium, called Vin Mariani, which kept him going until the ripe age of ninety-three. Leo liked it so much he endorsed the tonic in ads; it was also favored by Queen Victoria and President McKinley.

In any case, medical care was never the Vatican's forte. The quack remedies of Pius XII's personal physician may have hastened his death in 1958, and the mysterious sudden death of John Paul I in 1978 after just thirty-three days as pope instilled no great confidence in the Holy See's health care system.

Whatever the rumors, however, it was clear that as the twenty-fifth anniversary of his election approached, on October 16, 2003, John Paul II was struggling just to get through each day alive. The pontiff who considered an acting career as a young man could barely make himself understood, his voice a guttering flame, his face a frozen mask. John Paul struggled for breath and winced with pain, as even the slightest movement aggravated the arthritis that afflicted his hips and knees without respite.

Like worried offspring, the prelates hovering about the Holy Father struggled for words of comfort and produced only the usual non sequiturs that come to even the most well-intentioned at such times.

Then suddenly, the old man himself spoke, stirring from beneath the cope of senescence and blurting out, *"Non omnis moriar."*

The phrase sounded like some stray fragment from the old Latin Mass, a Tridentine reverie plucked from the memory of a long-ago Polish seminarian casting back to the beginning of his religious life as he faced the twilight of his earthly days. Instead, the pope's words were those of Horace, the pagan poet from a Rome of two millennia before John Paul, from the odes that Karol Wojtyla, a bright young student from Krakow, had memorized ages earlier on his way to earning his school's Latin prize.

Non omnis moriar (I shall not wholly die).[1]

In the mouth of the dying pope, the ancient words may have been a declaration of the Christian faith in the Resurrection that triumphed over the pagan world. Or perhaps they were simply an effort to ease the concern of those around him. Then again, Horace's poem, read in its entirety, also alludes to a more temporal reality of which the pope, himself a poet of no small renown, was undoubtedly aware:

I have achieved a monument more lasting
than bronze and loftier than the pyramids of kings,
which neither gnawing rain nor blustering wind
may destroy, nor innumerable series of years,
nor the passage of ages. I shall not wholly die,
a large part of me will escape Libitina, the goddess of Death:
while Pontiff and Vestal shall climb the Capitol Hill,
I shall be renewed and flourish in further praise.[2]

Indeed, whatever John Paul intended by his muttered recitation, nothing could state more clearly the imposing legacy of his quarter-century on the Throne of St. Peter, nor the daunting task facing the man who would become his successor. Only 3 other popes in history—out of 264—reigned longer than John Paul, one of them St. Peter himself. For years, Catholics had acclaimed him as John Paul the Great, granting him an honorific that history has conferred on just three other pontiffs, all of whom lived in the fifth and sixth centuries and gained renown by preserving Rome from barbarian invaders. One of his many biographers, Jonathan Kwitny, called John Paul the "Man of the Century." As the pope passed his silver jubilee, many would have extended the time frame to the past millennium.

With John Paul II, it seemed that the Fates, out of folly or perhaps from boredom with the routine of elderly Italian men shuffling through the Petrine office, had decided to shake up the Catholic Church at the end of the second millennium and pump some life into the wheezing Great Man theory of history. In Cardinal Karol Wojtyla of Krakow they found their protagonist, a romantic Pole with a captivating life story plus an intellect and spirit that worked in tandem rather than at odds, and they placed him in a geopolitical scenario that was, given the threat of nuclear annihilation, as dramatic as anything since the Dark Ages. Rather than casting up a general or statesman to drive the plot, however, the Fates chose the papacy to stage their play and thrust Wojtyla out front to play the lead. His was such a dynamic personality, driven by a deep conviction in the workings of Providence both in history and in the smallest events of his own life, that he needed no further encouragement to see his choice as a divine mandate.

Elected in October 1978, after the slow decline of Paul VI and the ill-starred, monthlong papacy of the fragile and overtaxed John Paul I, the fifty-eight-year-old Wojtyla resurrected the name of his immediate predecessor and immediately electrified the Catholic Church and the world. Within a year, he had traveled to the United States and Latin America, to Muslim Turkey, and most important, behind the Iron Curtain, to his Polish homeland, directly challenging the Communist authorities by drawing millions to public masses and joining them in thunderous chants of "We want God!" The reverberations from those cries, plus John Paul's support of the Solidarity trade union movement and his insistence on returning to his homeland again and again, would help lead a decade later to the fall of the Berlin Wall and the end of the Cold War.

But if those trips launched his greatest triumph, they were only the start of his papal peregrinations. By the time his traveling days ended, John Paul would log more than 773,000 miles—the equivalent of thirty-one trips around the world—on 104 apostolic voyages outside Italy to 129 different countries. He made 145 trips inside Italian territory (including sixteen vacation trips to the Italian Alps), in which he visited 259 different towns. He spent some 6 percent of his entire pontificate on the road—the figure was nearly 10 percent before the infirmity of his later years curtailed his travel. In contrast, Paul VI, the pontiff originally known as the "Pilgrim Pope" because he was the first pope in modern times to venture outside Rome, spent a total of thirty days abroad. John Paul II was on a whole different plane. "He saw himself as the pastor to the world," said Father Peter-Hans Kolvenbach, head of the Jesuit order.[3]

He kissed the ground each time he arrived in a new country, as if to claim it as his own parish, and that's how the flock saw it, too. A poll of American Catholics conducted in 2004 revealed that just four in ten said they knew the name of their own bishop; they were not checked to see if they actually did know, so the real figure could have been much lower.[4] Yet everyone—Catholic and non-Catholic—knew who the pope was, and by name. "Pope John Paul II overshadowed the bishops of every country, including the United States. If one wanted to find out where the Church stood on a given issue, one hardly had to consult the bishops' conference, since the Pope himself made the evening news more often than national prelates. This was a pontiff with a public vision, ubiquitous in his travels, indefatigable in meeting with his fellow bishops, tireless in issuing his own pastoral letters and statements, and enthusiastic about the conciliarism of world synods and extraordinary regional assemblies," Archbishop Timothy Dolan, who had worked for years in Rome before John Paul named him to the archdiocese of Milwaukee, said in an October 25, 2004, lecture.[5]

That enthusiasm, combined with the length of years given to him, resulted in a body of work that by itself would have ensured John Paul's relevance well into the third millennium.

Over the course of his tenure, John Paul promulgated fourteen encyclicals, fifteen apostolic exhortations, eleven apostolic constitutions, forty-five apostolic letters, and twenty-eight *motu proprios,* letters written on his own initiative to the whole church. It was calculated that he pronounced, wrote, and transmitted more than ninety thousand pages of text, which are compiled in fifty-five volumes by the Vatican Library. While a prolific writer himself, the demands of John Paul's public appearances required an entire new office to keep up with his speeches and homilies, headed by an archbishop with the title of Apostolic Nuncio with Special Tasks. By way of comparison, Pope Pius XII gave on average seventy speeches a year, totaling less than five hundred pages of text; John Paul II's average annual output was 746 talks, totaling more than 3,600 pages.[6]

Beyond their quantity, John Paul's pronouncements were also given—in a deliberate strategy overseen by his theological right hand, Cardinal Joseph Ratzinger—a weight of authority that no other pontiff had enjoyed. In document after document, on issues from bans on women priests to birth control and the validity of Anglican ordinations, Ratzinger declared that John Paul's teachings were to be "definitively held" by the faithful to be matters of infallible church doctrine, an unprecedented invocation of powerful language on behalf of a single pope, which critics denounced as a "creeping infallibilism" that was out of step with centuries of church tradition on the development of doctrine.

Whatever the controversy, the effect was to reinforce John Paul as the final word on anything and everything Catholic. As he said on a visit to Assisi little more than two weeks after his election, the church "speaks with my voice." The crowds cheered, and continued to do so for decades.

But John Paul also cemented his legacy by being the first pope to shatter so many precedents. He reigned for twenty-six years and, somehow, in an office whose raison d'être is the conservation of tradition, never seemed to copy any of his predecessors or even to repeat himself.

He was the first Slavic pope ever and the first non-Italian pontiff in 455 years. He was the first pope to visit a synagogue and the first to visit a mosque. He was the first to visit Canterbury since the excommunication of the divorce-happy king, Henry VIII, and the first to visit Eastern Orthodox countries where Catholics, not to mention Roman pontiffs, had long been persona non grata. He apologized for the Inquisition's condemnation of Galileo—not to affirm the obvious fact of the astronomer's heliocentric theory, but to foster a "loyal recognition of wrongs" by church authorities. With unprecedented regularity he issued mea culpas to different audiences—to indigenous peoples in Santo Domingo in 1984, to Muslims in 1985, to Africans in 1986, and, most memorably, to the Jewish people at Rome's synagogue in 1986 and at several other points. In Madrid he referred to the "errors and excesses" of the Inquisition, and in Vienna in 1983 he apologized for the wars of religion that had scarred Christendom. He also pushed the Catholic Church further than ever in undoing the mutual anathemas leveled between Christian denominations.

He was just the second pope in history to preside over the turning of the millennial clock, a grand occasion that he also used as an opportunity for formal penance. "Only the courageous admission of the faults and omissions of which Christians are judged to be guilty" can lead the church forward, John Paul said in announcing the coming jubilee. In his book, *When a Pope Asks Forgiveness,* Vatican correspondent Luigi Accattoli toted up no fewer than ninety-four occasions at which John Paul apologized for some past action of the church and for their legacy in the present. John Paul oversaw the first revision of the Catholic Catechism—the comprehensive handbook to all church teachings—since 1566, the height of the Counter-Reformation. He promulgated the first update of the entire Code of Canon Law—the church's exhaustive legal corpus—since 1917, and only the second such compilation in church history. He added mysteries to the traditional Marian prayer of the Rosary, altering the formula for the first time in centuries.

John Paul's devotion to popular piety was reflected in his zeal for making new saints. In his pontificate he canonized more saints—483 all told—than the combined total of all the previous popes since the system was regularized in 1588 after the Council of Trent. He beatified 1,342 people, more than the previous total of 1,000 beatifications in the preceding four centuries. He even streamlined the process for sainthood and reduced the number of miracles needed to be elevated to the Altar of Saints. When Mother Teresa of Calcutta, whom many considered a "living saint" (a contradiction in terms, actually), was asked how one becomes a saint, she liked to quip, "Die now—the pope's canonizing everybody."[7] Indeed, after her death in 1997, John Paul waived the mandatory five-year waiting period before a cause of sainthood could begin and gave her process a jump start.

During his pontificate, John Paul held 1,165 general public audiences on Wednesdays, drawing a total of 17.7 million people. He received some thousand state and government leaders in private audiences at the Vatican, and during his pontificate 83 countries established diplomatic relations with the Holy See, raising the total to 174.

John Paul named more than three-quarters of the world's bishops, whose numbers increased during his tenure from 3,400 to 4,600. He also called fifteen synods of bishops (special monthlong meetings at the Vatican) and created a record-setting 231 new cardinals, of whom 117 were under eighty and thus eligible to vote at the time of his death.

No other pope in modern times had such a profound impact in shaping the leadership of the church or in harnessing the media and popular culture to advance his message.

The first pope to publish books commercially, John Paul wrote five memoirs, the last of which was published weeks before his final illness. His poetry, from before and after his election (while pope he continued to write verse under a pseudonym, which few knew until late in his papacy), sold better than almost any other modern poet. His poems were even recorded by musicians, in one case set to a disco beat by a Polish singer, Stanislaw Soyka, and in another sung by the American jazz singer Sarah Vaughan. He allowed his voice and prayers to be marketed on CDs, and his plays, written as a young priest, were produced on stage and screen. He was the subject of several long biographies and untold coffee-table books, calendars and thought-for-the-day devotionals, as well as countless tchotchkes. He even achieved the elusive immortality of a Pope-on-a-Rope soap.

On the first anniversary of his pontificate, the *Time* magazine cover—the same magazine that in the previous decade had wondered, "Is God Dead?"—used three quite different words that described how dramatically the scene had changed: "John Paul—Superstar." After the pope visited Great Britain in 1982, the *Times* of London said that if there were such a title as First Citizen of the World, John Paul would win it. Later that year, Marvel Comics added him to the pantheon of superheroes, along with Spider-Man and the Hulk, by adapting the story of his life into a sixty-four-page biography with full-color images, called "The Life of Pope John Paul II."

The pop cultural apotheosis was not just fitting but perhaps inevitable. John Paul arrived on the world scene in the late 1970s along with the blockbuster movie and the cult of celebrity, for both of which his personality and his biography seemed tailor-made.

Born in Poland in 1920 in the ruins of the Austro-Hungarian Empire and the old world shattered by World War I, Karol Wojtyla would soon be swept up in the atrocities and industrialized barbarity of Nazism. A sister died before he was born, and his beloved mother died before he was nine, an agonizing loss that would mark him for life. One of his early poems, "Over This, Your White Grave," was dedicated to her:

Over this, your white grave
the flowers of life in white—
so many years without you—
how many have passed out of sight?
Over this your white grave
covered for years, there is a stir
in the air, something uplifting
and, like death, beyond comprehension.
Over this your white grave
oh, mother, can such loving cease?
for all his filial adoration
    a prayer:
Give her eternal peace.[8]

His older brother Edmund, a doctor, died three years later from scarlet fever he caught while attending to patients. At twelve Karol was alone with his
father, a retired military officer and devout Catholic whose health was rapidly
declining. Karol was twenty when his father died, and friends say he knelt for
twelve hours in prayer at his father's bedside. The youthful Wojtyla enjoyed
sports and hiking, and he had a gift for acting and playwriting that naturally
drew him into the theater. But he was also a contemplative young man who
spent many hours in church, an "apprentice saint," as friends came to call him.
No one was surprised when Wojtyla left his forced labor post at a rock quarry
and entered an underground seminary, a decision that could have cost him his
life if the Nazis ever found out. On November 1, 1946, the Feast of All Saints,
Karol Wojtyla was ordained a priest.

Yet there was no respite for him or his homeland. As soon as the Nazi trials ended, the shadow of communism fell over Poland and over the Catholic
Church, which was the lone bulwark against total cultural and political annihilation. A brilliant priest with an engaging pastoral presence, Karol Wojtyla
was quickly marked for promotion. When he was thirty-eight he was made
a bishop, the youngest in Poland's history, and nine years later Paul VI made
him a cardinal, one of the youngest in the entire Catholic Church. He was a
brilliant philosopher, a profound moral theologian, and a modern-day politician whose talents with the masses quickly impressed—and concerned—the
Communist authorities. When he was elected pope on October 16, 1978, the
world was stunned; the Soviets were worried.

On the eve of John Paul's return to his homeland a few months later—
"Nine days that changed the world," as Weigel put it—the Polish Commu-

nist Party sent out secret instructions warning about what was to come: "The Pope is our enemy. . . . Due to his uncommon skills and great sense of humor he is dangerous, because he charms everyone, especially journalists. Besides, he goes for cheap gestures in his relations with the crowd, for instance, puts on a highlander's hat, shakes all hands, kisses children, etc. . . . It is modeled on American presidential campaigns."[9]

The Communists got that part right.

John Paul was to the papacy what John F. Kennedy was to the presidency—so new, so attractive, so *cool* for someone in what was supposed to be an uncool job that he made Catholics proud to be Catholic even if they didn't agree with him. So great was their affection that most Catholics didn't bother to let such disagreements, when they thought about them, trouble their relationship with the church and the Holy Father. Nothing could shatter the aura created by the events of John Paul's life and the universality of his charisma. John Paul epitomized that bridge between what cultural critic Neal Gabler, writing in another context about John F. Kennedy Jr., described as the confluence between the classical hero and the modern celebrity. "The hero," Gabler wrote, "has to negotiate between the ordinary and the godly, the temporal and the otherworldly, keeping a foot in each camp so that he can show us how to adapt ourselves to a world that is half spiritual, half material—a world of wonder but also of pain. . . . Half god, half man, the celebrity, like the hero, is always poised between our identification with him, which makes him one of us, and our idolatry of him, which makes him better than we. If he lists too far in either direction, he loses his Olympian perch: too far toward the godly and we must reel him back in; too far toward the ordinary and we lose interest."[10]

In the midst of a ravenous celebrity culture, John Paul managed to maintain that balance, and he did so while surviving the martyrdom that claimed the Kennedys, *père et fils.* Tragedy largely insulated the Kennedys (at least for some years) from the inevitable dents that a long life in the public square is bound to bring. John Paul somehow survived both an assassination attempt and a long and often controversial career with his prestige enhanced rather than diminished.

Indeed, the 1981 attempt on John Paul's life only reinforced his image as a unique pope who enjoyed the mantle of divine protection. He was shot on May 13, the feast day marking the appearance of the Virgin Mary to three shepherd children in 1917 in the Portuguese village of Fatima. The site of the appearances has become one of the great Marian shrines in the world, drawing millions each year in search of healing and answers to prayer. It was thus no surprise that John Paul, with his intense devotion to the Holy Mother (his

papal motto was a vow to the Virgin Mary: "*Totus Tuus*" [I am all yours]),
would later see in his narrow escape from the grievous wounds—he lost six
pints of blood and required hours of surgery that was touch-and-go at several
points—the intervention of the Virgin. A year later, finally recovered from his
injuries, John Paul traveled to Fatima to place the fragments of the bullet into
the gilt crown set on the head of the statue representing the Virgin who appeared to the three children, just one of whom, Sister Lucia, was still alive, a
nun in a nearby monastery. John Paul told the faithful that the hand of Mehmet Ali Agca, his assailant, guided the gun, but it was another, "a motherly hand,
that guided the bullet millimeters away from vital blood vessels, and halted
him at the threshold of death."

More far-reaching than this intervention, however, was the revelation eighteen years later, in the millennial year of 2000, of the so-called Third Secret
of Fatima. Decades earlier, Sister Lucia had vouchsafed to the Vatican three
"secrets," or prophetic visions, that the Virgin Mary had granted the three children. Two were published during World War II and were interpreted as relating to the terrible conflicts of the twentieth century. One was an apocalyptic
vision of hell, which seemed to foretell the Second World War. The second was
a warning to consecrate Russia to the Virgin so that it would stop spreading
"errors throughout the world, causing wars and persecutions of the Church."
That was widely seen as a reference to the Soviet Union, whose collapse in 1994
was hailed by Fatima supporters as a fulfillment of the second secret.

But the third secret remained a mystery until John Paul decided to publish it in 2000. The text was stunning, relating not to an apocalyptic prophecy
about the end of the world but to the apparent death of a pope—a "Bishop
dressed in White" who "passed through a big city half in ruins, and half trembling with halting step, afflicted with pain and sorrow, he prayed for the souls
of the corpses he met on his way; having reached the top of the mountain, on
his knees at the foot of the big Cross, he was killed by a group of soldiers who
fired bullets and arrows at him." A month after the revelation, Cardinal Ratzinger published a commentary directly linking the most explosive prophecy of
the past century to Pope John Paul himself. Ratzinger wrote, "When, after the
attempted assassination on 13 May 1981, the Holy Father had the text of the
third part of the secret brought to him, was it not inevitable that he should see
in it his own fate?"[11]

Much of the world agreed, or at least saw in the assassination attempt the
irrefutable sense of a cosmic drama in which John Paul was a major player.

In short, for an entire generation, the story of Catholicism was essentially the drama of a single man—a pope "from a faraway country," as he told the crowd in St. Peter's Square the evening of his election, who came to define not only the papacy but, to many, the church itself. It was as if he refounded the papacy, as if he were the first pope, and everything that followed would flow from what he did.

Yet even as John Paul transformed the papacy, it was also just as clear, if little noted, that he had not changed the church, at least not in the way he would have wanted. In fact, by personalizing the papacy so thoroughly, John Paul may actually have diverted attention from many internal structural and political problems that grew worse, or grew up, during his reign. So intense was the focus on the person of John Paul that his consistently strong popularity came to be seen as the barometer for the health of the church itself. The reality on the ground, however, was often very different, despite the liberation of Eastern Europe and the popularity of John Paul. As Cardinal Ratzinger wrote in 2000, "Anyone who expected that the hour had come again for the Christian message was disappointed. . . . Christianity failed at that historical moment to make itself heard as an epoch-making alternative."[12] The "springtime of faith" that John Paul predicted for the new millennium was an illusion, Ratzinger said.

The numbers seemed to confirm the German cardinal's dark view. Vocations to religious life, for example, continued to decline despite John Paul's priority on drawing more men to the priesthood, and men and women to religious orders.

According to data in the *Statistical Yearbook of the Church* 2003, published by the Vatican, the number of priests decreased between 1978—the year of John Paul's election—and 2003 by 3.8 percent. Combined with the 40 percent rise in the number of Catholics in the world during that time, from 757 million to more than 1.1 billion, the ratio of Catholics to priests went from 1,800 to 1 in 1978 to nearly 2,700 to 1 in 2003—a hefty jump in the workload for priests and a corresponding decrease in access to the sacraments for the faithful. While the numbers of vocations rose in some areas, such as parts of Africa and Asia, their overall impact on the shortage has been negligible, especially considering that the increase in Catholics in those areas far outstrips the vocations. In fact, by 2005 some 25 percent of parishes around the world had no resident priest. Moreover, the 40 percent jump in the Catholic population was actually less than the 45 percent increase in the overall global population.

The situation was even worse in the United States and Canada, where the number of priests dropped more than 25 percent during John Paul's reign, with the remaining priests growing considerably older while, again, serving an ever-growing population. The number of American seminarians—the future priest corps—also declined 40 percent, and the number of nuns in the United States continued to plummet, from 135,000 in 1975 to just 70,000 in 2004.

Church attendance, one of the slipperiest statistics in data collection, was clear on one point: participation at Sunday Mass, a Catholic's central religious obligation, continued to erode, especially in North America. After falling sharply in the 1960s from a weekly attendance rate of about 70 percent, mass participation leveled off in the early years of John Paul's papacy to just above 50 percent, according to self-reported annual surveys by the Gallup Poll. By 2004 the figure hovered around 40 percent, and some polls put the figure significantly lower, at closer to 30 percent. In some areas, such as the once–rock-solid Catholic precincts of Boston, the actual annual census in 2003 showed just 16 percent of registered Catholics at Mass on any given Sunday.

Even Latin America, a once monolithic Catholic continent that remains home to nearly 45 percent of the world's Catholics, showed significant erosion despite John Paul's persistent and popular efforts there. According to a 2005 survey by the Chilean polling firm Latinobarometro, the number of South Americans who identified as Catholic dropped over the previous decade from 80 percent to 71 percent. At the same time, the percentage who consider themselves evangelical or Protestant rose from 3 percent to 13 percent, seeming to bolster the pope's fear of Protestant missionaries as "rapacious wolves." Only 40 percent of self-identified Catholics said they practiced their faith, and in Mexico that figure fell by half in a decade, from more than 60 percent in 1995 to 31 percent in 2005.

In Europe the numbers were even worse. In Germany just 21 percent of respondents in a 2002 Pew Research study said religion "plays a very important part in their lives," and 12 percent attended religious services weekly, according to the 1999–2000 European Values Study. In France just 11 percent said religion was important and 5 percent attended weekly services. In Italy, the seat of the papacy, the numbers were 27 percent and 15 percent, respectively. Contrast that with nearly 60 percent of Americans who consider religion a very important part of their lives.

Still, Catholic beliefs and behaviors in the United States, long regarded by Rome as the best indicator for the future of faith in the modern world, did not seem to change significantly despite John Paul's great popularity. Polls around his twenty-fifth anniversary showed that nearly nine in ten Catholics supported the use of birth control, two-thirds thought premarital sex was okay, and nearly half thought homosexual relations between consenting adults were acceptable. Several polls at the time of John Paul's death, when papal nostalgia was feverish, showed that more than 33 percent of American Catholics wanted a more "liberal" pope, and just 4 or 5 percent wanted someone more conservative. A Gallup survey showed that 63 percent wanted the Vatican to allow priests to marry and 55 percent wanted the ban on women priests lifted, positions that John Paul decisively rejected. All those numbers were higher than they had been when John Paul was elected, and they were much higher among young Catholics, whom the pope had made a special focus of his exhortations.

Even priests themselves were ambivalent about John Paul's legacy. An extensive survey of American priests by the *Los Angeles Times* in 2002 showed that 40 percent of the clergy thought John Paul would be remembered above all for his travels, and 30 percent for his role in defeating Soviet communism. Just 15 percent said he would be remembered chiefly for his "moral and spiritual" leadership.

Clearly, while Catholics loved the singer, they were not in love with the song. That would have been true even absent the terrible clergy sexual abuse scandals that battered the church starting in 2002, but the impact of the crisis touched off by the scandals in the United States and much of the influential English-speaking world cannot be overstated. As the bishops themselves said in the charter they passed to stanch the bleeding, "Since 2002, the Church in the United States has experienced a crisis without precedent in our times. The sexual abuse of children and young people by some priests and bishops, and the ways in which we bishops addressed these crimes and sins, have caused enormous pain, anger, and confusion. As bishops, we have acknowledged our mistakes and our role in that suffering, and we apologize and take responsibility again for too often failing victims and the Catholic people in the past. From the depths of our hearts, we bishops express great sorrow for what the Catholic people have endured."[13]

The apologies were repeated but did not seem to take hold. Though many Catholics continued to attend church and contribute to their local parishes, their anger at the hierarchy, whom they saw as responsible but unaccountable for the actions that led to abuse, did not abate. A large majority of Catholics in the United States demanded institutional reforms, and lay groups, most notably the Boston-based grassroots organization Voice of the Faithful, continued to push for greater transparency. John Paul's own teflon approval ratings, usually in the high 70s or better, slipped somewhat as the Vatican's hesitant and ultimately tepid response to the crisis alienated even some of his greatest loyalists on the Catholic Right.

The Vatican's tin ear for the anger in the pews was confirmed in the most sensational way possible in May 2004 when Cardinal Bernard Law was given a plum position in Rome as archpriest of the Basilica of Saint Mary Major, one of the four principal basilicas in the Catholic world and one of the oldest and most beautiful churches in Christendom. Law had been archbishop of Boston when the scandal erupted, and revelations of his misdeeds in shuffling predatory priests around and stifling victims' complaints made him the villain of the drama. He was also the only prelate to step down because of his role in the cover-ups, and that move was accepted only with great reluctance by Pope John Paul. At first Law "retired" to a monastery in Maryland, although he continued to travel regularly, always first-class, and spent a great deal of time in Rome, often taking a prominent place at major Vatican events. Law's promotion to Rome, little more than a year after his resignation, came with the perks of a spacious apartment in the basilica and a generous monthly stipend to support a personal staff. It also came just two days after the Boston arch-diocese announced that it would be forced to shut at least sixty-five parishes in large part due to the financial shortfall caused by lawsuits stemming from Law's mishandling of the abuse cases. Catholics were as outraged as they were stunned by the Vatican's insensitivity. "It's an utter disgrace and the people of the archdiocese are being burdened by this," said Father Bob Bowers of St. Catherine's Church in Charlestown.[14]

But it is important to understand that the anger over the scandal went much deeper than the sexual abuse itself—horrific as it was—and centered princi-pally on the abuse of authority that had allowed such crimes to go unchecked for years, even decades. In that sense, the sexual abuse scandals were symp-tomatic of a larger crisis afflicting the church, one that centered on how au-thority—and the power that authority conferred—was wielded in the church of John Paul II.

Almost from the start of his papacy, John Paul made it clear that while he would be an evangelist to the wider world, engaged with modernity and ex-ploiting it wherever possible, he would also demand an almost lockstep loyalty within the church itself. John Paul remained deeply affected by his experi-ences under first Nazism and then as a churchman under the heel of Soviet communism, and for him a divided church was a weak church whose fissures could be exploited by ruthless opponents. Moreover, John Paul was a cultural conservative in Catholic terms. This was something not many of his backers understood in 1978 when they supported him in the conclave, imagining that his main thrust would be as a champion of human rights for the politically oppressed and an advocate for the economically subjugated masses in the rest of the world. There was perhaps an assumption that Karol Wojtyla's focus on justice and pastoral concerns would translate into a pontificate characterized by flexibility within the church as well. But it was a sign of how little-known Wojtyla was that when he became Pope John Paul II he immediately set out to rein in what he saw as liberalizing tendencies among bishops and theologians and to quash the voices of those who publicly dissented from Vatican positions. The record of theologians silenced and bishops disciplined became part of the public persona of the first decade of John Paul's papacy, mentioned in the same breath as his heroic journeys and near-martyrdom.

As John Paul grew older and infirm, however, the taskmaster was gradually eclipsed by the universal grandfather who became so beloved that the earlier controversies echoed faintly, if at all. Besides, after a quarter-century, much of the "wet work" of punishing offenders had been accomplished, and far fewer bishops, priests, or theologians were inclined to cross Rome. Others were content to wait out the pope, knowing that death was approaching and hoping that a new, less restrictive, papacy was in the offing.

Still, unease, even resentment, over the centralization of power in Rome—the "papalization" of Catholicism, as the Jesuit church historian John O'Malley termed it—ran so deep that church officials continued to chafe under what they saw as the Vatican's excessively interventionist bureaucracy, the Roman Curia. On issues ranging from adapting the liturgy for local use to policing Catholic universities and even allowing national hierarchies liberty to implement their own policies, bishops around the world grew increasingly upset at being micro-managed by Rome, and they began to speak out as if in anticipation of a coming conclave.

The clearest and most public sign of the discontent—and one that would have immediate repercussions after the conclave—was an exchange between two German prelates, Cardinal Walter Kasper and Cardinal Joseph Ratzinger. Kasper was a former theology professor who had for years been the bishop of Rottenburg-Stuttgart. In February 2001 he was made a cardinal and soon after was appointed president of the Pontifical Council for Promoting Christian Unity, the Vatican's ecumenism office. In April 2001, *America* magazine, a prestigious Jesuit weekly based in New York, published an essay by Kasper that was actually the latest in a series of exchanges with Ratzinger over the nature and direction of the contemporary church. Most of the back-and-forth had been in German publications, but when Kasper's piece appeared in English, the fissures within the hierarchy were exposed to the media machine. In unusually frank language, Kasper critiqued Ratzinger's views on the exercise of authority by Rome. "The right balance between the universal church and the particular churches has been destroyed," Kasper wrote, adding that this was not just his own perception but the experience and complaint of many bishops from all over the world. Even more significantly, he spoke of "a mental or practical schism" between the universal church—by which he meant Rome—and local practice: "Many laypersons and priests can no longer understand universal church regulations, and simply ignore them."[15]

"No bishop should be silent or stand idly by when he finds himself in such a situation," Kasper wrote.

> *He faces, however, an awkward dilemma. While his task is to be a bond of unity between the See of Rome and his people, he is pulled in two directions. On the one hand, he is a member of the universal episcopal college in solidarity with the pope and his brother bishops; he must therefore protect the unity of the Catholic Church. On the other hand, he is the shepherd of a local church; he must, therefore, take care of his own people, respond to their expectations and answer their questions. . . . If the bishop attempts to enforce the general norms ruthlessly—as his Roman superiors sometimes expect—his effort is likely to be useless, even counterproductive. If he remains passive, he is quickly judged disobedient. He seems to be caught in an impasse. Yet there is a solution: the bishop must be granted enough vital space to make responsible decisions in the matter of implementing universal laws.*

After some hesitation (he did not want to encourage the appearance of a public dispute, he said), Ratzinger responded a few months later in *America* with an essay so characteristically erudite that it initially seemed to indicate that the two men had no real differences, while making it clear that poor Cardinal Kasper was completely wrong. Then, warming to the debate, Ratzinger concluded that Kasper's argument, "objectively speaking, makes no sense."

The two Germans came to embody the tensions of the latter days of John Paul's reign—the hard-line *Panzerkardinal* on one side, and "Kasper the Friendly Pope" for those looking to a different future.

The laments over Roman centralism only grew as the pope's frailty increased. In 2003 Cardinal Godfried Danneels of Brussels, considered a leader of the hierarchy's shrinking progressive wing, called for a moratorium on the avalanche of paper coming to bishops from Rome. "We are always inundated with very long documents, instructions, and manuals," he said, which "come without any organization which would indicate to us which are important and which are less so." In the same interview, Danneels also lamented the intense focus on the person of the pope, arguing that "the identification of a role and a particular personality is not a good thing." Danneels said that early in the second millennium the papacy modeled itself after national monarchies, a template that should be dropped, so that the church "emphasizes the essential characteristics of the Petrine ministry."[16]

The unrest was not limited to the more liberal side of the church spectrum. Many conservatives bridled at the Vatican's overweening ways, and the irritation seemed to grow with the geographic distance from Rome. In 2003, for example, Japanese cardinal Stephen Fumio Hamao gave an interview in which he criticized the Roman Curia for behaving as if their role was "to instruct, to teach, and to correct" local diocesan bishops. In fact, he argued, Vatican officials should understand that their role is "to listen, to help, and to encourage." Hamao said he favored convening a new council, a worldwide meeting of all Catholic bishops, to discuss "the necessity of greater autonomy for the local churches."[17]

The debate was hardly academic, or a question of power politics of interest largely to ecclesiastical pundits. The Vatican's unprecedented level of oversight was undermining the morale of the bishops, priests, and church workers in the parishes and dioceses where the real work of propagating the faith is done. The human toll was illustrated by a poignant episode in December 2003, at a Rome conference on changes in the liturgy that was attended by Cardinal Francis Arinze, head of the Vatican office that is the church's top liturgical watchdog. Arinze is a fascinating character, a Nigerian who converted from his native animism early in life and went on to become a cardinal and a fixture in the Roman Curia, where he worked for more than twenty years on interfaith issues before being transferred to the Congregation for Divine Worship and the Discipline of the Sacraments.

The translation of liturgical texts might sound like a dry topic to most Catholics, but adapting the language of the Mass for local use is one of the most sensitive issues in the church, with the Vatican increasingly using heavy-handed tactics in its efforts to maintain control of any changes. At the 2003 conference celebrating the fortieth anniversary of *Sacrosanctum Concilium,* the Vatican II document that opened the way to enormous changes in the Mass that are today taken for granted, one speaker, an elderly Catalan priest named Father Ignacio Calabuig, OSM, spoke movingly about the "greats" of the liturgical reform movement whom he had known. In an account later circulated to friends by another participant, Jesuit Father Robert Taft, Calabuig then departed from his prepared text, looked at Cardinal Arinze, and in a trembling voice said: "I feel I must tell the prefect that the devastating impression the congregation seems to be spreading throughout the church, that men of great culture in their own lands are not capable of translating liturgical texts into their own mother tongue, is causing great discontent and concern in the church."

At that point, Taft recounted, "the entire audience, some 600 strong in the basilica, spontaneously exploded into prolonged, enthusiastic applause that thundered on for about three minutes. It was a historic moment, the message was crystal clear, and even His Eminence himself felt finally constrained to join— albeit timidly—in the applause that went on and on and just would not stop. I hope the reporters were there to record that one for posterity! This is my 39th year in Rome and I never saw anything like it before. I could not have been more delighted, and have told the story to anyone willing to listen."[18]

It was an extraordinary, and courageous, act of honesty by Calabuig, and by Taft for passing the story along. For years the Vatican had quietly fostered tactics to quash disagreements and intimidate objectors before they could make their views known. The chief tactic in this battle was known as "delation," an old-time practice coined by the Inquisition, but one which Rome found handy even after the Inquisition was relegated to history, at least in theory. Delation is basically a McCarthyite stratagem by which angry Catholics denounce a priest or professor or some Catholic groups they dislike to Rome, which then passes the complaints—always anonymous—on to the local bishop and demands an explanation for why he is allowing such deviance in his own backyard. With conservatives holding the reins of power in Rome in recent decades, and with conservative Catholic lobbies by far the best funded, best organized, and most generously funded groups in the church, delation became a highly effective weapon against anyone viewed as less than trenchantly orthodox.

In fact, the Vatican at times seemed to openly encourage the practice. A sharply worded document on liturgical abuses released by Arinze's office in 2004, called *Redemptionis Sacramentum*, explicitly stated that any Catholic could report concerns directly to the Holy See. That was a further green light to conservative groups who were already masters at letter-writing campaigns, and it drew criticism from others who saw in the tactic a disturbing echo of the *Sodalitium Pianum*, a secret society set up a century before, with the encouragement of the anti-Modernist Pope Pius X, to report any suspect Catholics to Roman authorities.

So powerful were these conservative activists that bishops would rarely challenge them, or the practice, in public. That explains why, when an English prelate, Bishop Crispian Hollis of Portsmouth, spoke out against delation at a conference on church communications in the summer of 2004, his words drew applause and made headlines in the leading English Catholic journal, the *Tablet.* Hollis confessed to his listeners that he at first did not want his remarks taped, because "the difficulty with recordings is that they get out, and get into all sorts of hands, and I would have felt very inhibited if any session—or indeed this session—had been taped." He added, "There are plenty of people who would accuse us of selling our past, being liberal with our doctrines, or careless with the way we formulate things."[19]

But, he continued, "I've stopped looking over my shoulders." Yes, he said, "There are those who delate us to Rome. We get letters from Rome. But I've really got to the stage in life where it really doesn't terribly matter." Hollis said the whispering campaigns once depressed him, submerging him in the negative aspects of church life. "You get letters from Rome and you scratch your head and say, 'Why are people in the Roman Curia wasting their time . . . ?'" Hollis said in exasperation. "I've had complaints arising out of a parish newsletter. What sort of world is this?" But during a recent sabbatical, he told the *Tablet,* "I rediscovered something in my own self, and that's good." He said he realized that "I don't owe a living to anybody or anything except Christ and the Gospel and the best traditions of the Church. And if Rome don't like it, then that's tough."

Unfortunately, while Hollis made his peace with the situation—and ended any possibility of advancement in the hierarchy—life in the Catholic Church he so aptly described continued to be tough on many priests and nuns and other church professionals who did not have the protection afforded by a higher office.

A remarkable article published in the November 2003 *Testimonio,* a Chilean Catholic periodical, articulated the view of the church from the bottom rungs of the ladder in stark terms. The article, "Violence in the Church," was written by a Carmelite priest, Father Camilo Maccise, who served both as head of his own worldwide Carmelite order and for two terms as president of the Union of Superiors General (USG), an umbrella group representing thousands of order priests, nuns, and brothers doing church work on all five continents. In it, Maccise made the stunning revelation that for nearly a decade, since 1995, he and other representatives of the church's religious orders had tried to get an audience with Pope John Paul to voice their concerns but had been turned away. "The centralist control of the Roman Curia," he wrote, "prevents the access of these qualified groups to direct dialogue with the Pope." Maccise spoke about the "violent forces of centralism," the "violent forces of authoritarianism," and the "violent forces of dogmatism" that he saw represented in the contemporary Vatican.

Centralism, he explained, "is a refined form of violence since it concentrates the decision-making power in an ecclesiastical bureaucracy which ignores the challenges confronted by believers in different socioeconomic and ecclesial environments" and treats believers as if they were "minors needing overprotection." He said the "violent forces of authoritarianism" operate by using "sacred power" and the cover of secrecy. Finally, he wrote, the "violence of dogmatism" imposes "a single theological perspective, that of traditionalism, which takes on the form of philosophical and cultural conditioning of a past era." In grievances involving the Congregation for the Doctrine of the Faith that end in favor of the accused, that person "receives no letter of acquittal" and "worse, the accuser receives no admonition or canonical sentence for having lied or slandered."

If all was not well in the Catholic Church, the deepening infirmity of John Paul and the increasing uncertainty over just who was in charge at the Vatican, if anyone, only exacerbated the problems. As the pope's grip on the reins weakened, the Roman bureaucracy began to assert itself in the pope's name, while the Curia's own myriad factions began elbowing each other to claim various bits of church turf.

Part of the problem was endemic to John Paul's papacy and grew out of his character; always an evangelist more than an administrator, John Paul was more than content to leave the details of church government to the Curia while he went barnstorming for Christ across the continents. When a reporter on the papal plane once referred to the Vatican as a prison, John Paul's response was telling: "You have to have experienced *that* prison in order to enjoy *this* freedom." Such disdain for the home office did not sit well with many church leaders, especially the Italians who stressed the *Roman* part of Catholicism and believed the church was not only their birthright but existed to be governed. "John Paul II has revived the religious sense of the world, and that is no small thing," Cardinal Giuseppe Siri, the late Genoese prelate who finished second to Wojtyla in the 1978 conclave and never got over it, said in 1993. "But enough now! There is the Curia and there is government; and in order to govern, one must be at his desk."[20]

John Paul paid Siri no more heed than he did any of his other detractors, and while he was healthy the pope did not have to worry too much about the curialists back home undercutting him because he, and they, knew that his personal popularity, undergirded by his global travels, gave him an authority that they dared not cross. But when age finally did begin to do what the Curia could not—to keep John Paul homebound more than on the road—the dynamic was already set, and John Paul was too feeble and too disinterested to change things. The Curia had the upper hand.

A story recounted by Cardinal Paulo Evaristo Arns of Brazil offered a telling insight into the situation. Among many other things, Arns was a champion of the poor and of the liberation theology that many Latin American priests were espousing as an answer to the intractable problem of economic injustice and violence on the continent—and which conservatives saw as a Trojan horse for Marxism. It was a stance that made him a hero to millions in the southern hemisphere but suspect to conservative curialists in Rome and to John Paul, whose memories of the Marxist-Leninist legacy in his native Poland made much of liberation theology anathema to him. Over the years, the Vatican steadily undercut Arns, at one point carving his enormous archdiocese into several smaller dioceses and appointing conservative bishops who allied against him. His battles with the Curia were legendary, and he dreaded every visit to Rome. When John Paul finally accepted Arns's retirement in 1998, the grand old man of the Latin American church made a last visit to the pope. The two men always remained on good terms personally, chatting in German—a second language to both—and with great frankness.

As Arns told it in a February 2005 interview with a Brazilian newspaper, as he stood to take his leave of John Paul, the pontiff stopped him.

"Just a minute, Paulo," the pope said. "I have a letter for you. . . . They"—the pope indicated curial officials—"gave me the text and I only have to sign it."

Arns said he suggested that he and the pope read it together. "It was a three-page memorandum with different topics, written in Portuguese, and very critical of me," Arns said. "I started to read it to him, translating it into German. When we got to the third paragraph, the pope became indignant and said: 'I am not going to sign this! I never said this about you, Paulo, and neither do I want it stated in a document.' He threw the paper on the floor. I picked it up. Then he decided that I should write two lines saying that I had answered all the questions satisfactorily. He signed it and it must be filed somewhere."

The document, Arns said, "had to be written by someone who wanted me to leave the archdiocese as a failure or as a bishop who did not have a good relationship with the pope." He suspected that the document, "full of rebukes and signed by the pope, would be divulged to the four corners of the church. But the plan did not work."[21]

But over time the papal lieutenants did grow more powerful, or rather the vacuum at the top allowed them to pursue their respective agendas without fear of oversight or contradiction.

There was no clearer indication of the problem than the comments that emerged at an extraordinary three-day meeting of all the church's 155 cardinals, called a consistory, that John Paul convened in May 2001, ostensibly as a way to get the leadership in unison as Catholicism embarked on its third millennium. The meeting, however—the first since 1994—only revealed that there were many issues facing the global church and little coordination, or sensitivity, from Rome. Several cardinals called for more frequent dialogues between the bishops resident in dioceses around the world and Vatican officials, and one, Brazilian Cardinal Aloisio Lorscheider of Brazil, put the matter bluntly: "The decisions of Vatican Council II are not being applied, and we all suffer, on the ground, from a distant bureaucracy that is increasingly deaf." Lorscheider elaborated on his concerns to a French newspaper, *La Croix:* "The Pope is a prisoner of those who surround him and who undermine him."

A few years after that consistory, a regular visitor to the papal apartments told me the problem had worsened. "Ah, they've finally got him right where they want him," said the priest, referring to the curialists. "They can control him. They've been looking forward to this for years."

It was in many respects a typical *fin de régime* scene, with various courtiers jockeying for rewards and position while the king lay unawares or too ill to do anything.

√　The most powerful man in the church, however, may well have been a Polish priest, Monsignor Stanislaw Dziwisz, John Paul's personal secretary and irreplaceable confidante for more than four decades. As John Paul grew steadily weaker, unable to care for himself or even speak in public, Dziwisz, whom John Paul affectionately called "Stasiu," became the papal gatekeeper to a greater extent than he ever had before. An exceedingly gracious man with visitors, "Don Stanislao," as he was known to the Italians and Vatican-watchers who came to know him over the years, was also a fierce loyalist to the man he considered a father figure. Yet as the pope's health deteriorated, there was increasing worry about where John Paul ended and Dziwisz began. Dziwisz would often attend meetings in place of the pope, taking questions from participants, shuttling them back to the pope, and later returning with what he said were the pope's responses. In John Paul's final months, even senior church officials, many of them cardinals who had once had regular access to the Holy Father, were left waiting in anterooms, only to be told, eventually, that they would not be able to see the pope that day. "Don Stanislao is the pope," a Vatican official told me the last time I saw the pope alive, in September 2004. The veteran Vaticanista Sandro Magister called Dziwisz "the *éminence grise* of the circle that governs the Church in the shadow of pope Wojtyla." It was widely rumored that John Paul had in fact secretly made Dziwisz a cardinal. (The speculation was moot, as Benedict promoted Dziwisz to archbishop of Krakow just two months after John Paul's death and in March 2006 made him a cardinal, almost ensuring that John Paul would have eyes and ears in the next conclave.)

Bishops who visited John Paul in these final years found that the pontiff could not recall where they were posted, and these were some of the most senior leaders in the church. Dziwisz would step in and remind the Holy Father, and the meeting would go on. Various dignitaries and heads of state would return from audiences with the pope completely uncertain of what he said or whether he understood them. A theologian in Rome recounted the many times that he saw John Paul given a document of signal import to sign, only to wave his pen over the paper because the tremors in his hands had robbed him of the ability to write his name. Yet the document would later emerge with a perfectly legible papal signature, raising the hypothesis that there was a signing machine somewhere in the Vatican, much like those that politicians regularly use. But congressional signature machines are for generic constituent mail rather than key documents promoting church teachings or appointing bishops and creating the cardinals who would eventually elect the pope.

In 2004 the pope's personal spokesman, Joaquin Navarro-Valls, finally admitted that the pontiff could barely write, but in a nifty bit of flacking added that John Paul "remedies [this] by giving his instructions verbally, thus accomplishing more in less time."[22] At another point Navarro-Valls argued that despite the pope's infirmity and the lack of any major initiatives coming from the Holy See, the church was not adrift. He told the *Los Angeles Times* that John Paul's will continued to be executed, whether or not he personally conveyed it, because his aides could anticipate and project his thoughts. "His goals and ideas are there. They are impregnated in his collaborators," Navarro-Valls said. "Even though the physical energy is declining, what is coming out of the Holy See is John Paul II. It is his thinking. His intellectual product is so large that even after [his death], that body of ideas will be very much present."

Navarro, a suave Spaniard and lay member of the conservative Opus Dei organization, was the pope's longtime aide and also a key figure in interpreting the pope's wishes to the outside world.

Divining exactly what those wishes might be, however, became increasingly complex. Internecine spats among curial officials, which were usually just an amusing source of ecclesiastical gossip, began to descend into serious turf wars that sowed confusion and concern about the public image and internal governance of the church. The Vatican reaction to America's preemptive war in Iraq was a salient example. While John Paul voiced—or had read for him—general laments against the invasion, many of his top aides and other church leaders voiced varying degrees of opposition, much of it far stronger than the pope's own statements. Compounding the situation was that some of the Vatican officials who were against the Iraq invasion had supported the American intervention in Afghanistan, and the U.S. bishops as a whole condemned both the Afghan war and the Iraqi invasion. At one point, in November 2002, *Civiltá Cattolica,* a Jesuit journal in Rome that is vetted by the Vatican so that it represents the Holy See's thinking, opined that an American attack could be legitimate if Saddam Hussein represented an imminent threat—a position the Bush administration espoused—and a month later Cardinal Renato Martino, the Vatican's top human rights official, stated bluntly that "a preventive war is a war of aggression." So it went for months.

The religious battle over John Kerry's 2004 political campaign was another episode that seemed to highlight the lack of a strong central command. The first Catholic presidential candidate since John F. Kennedy in 1960, Kerry inherited a far different world than the one JFK had moved in. Kennedy's task had been to distance himself from Rome enough to assuage Protestant America; he could pretty much take the Catholic vote for granted. Kerry did not realize until it was too late that his challenge was almost the opposite. Kerry, also a Catholic Democrat from Massachusetts, had to convince the Christian Right that he was Catholic enough. He also had a strong and well-organized right flank within the church that was his sworn enemy and a staunch supporter of President George Bush, an evangelical Protestant who only a few years earlier would have considered most anything connected with Roman Catholicism an abomination. One reason for the Catholic opposition to Kerry was his uncompromising support for abortion rights. That position led a number of conservative bishops to challenge the right of Kerry, and other Catholic politicians who supported the right to an abortion, to receive Holy Communion, the most sacred duty of every Catholic.

The so-called wafer watch—would Kerry take communion?—roiled the presidential campaign and the Catholic Church, which was split by fierce debates over the proper course of action. In April 2004 Cardinal Francis Arinze, head of the Vatican department patrolling worship and liturgy issues, made headlines when he seemed to indicate, in response to a reporter's question, that a public supporter of abortion should not take communion. "Yes. Objectively, the answer is clear," Arinze said. "The person is not fit. If he shouldn't receive it, then it shouldn't be given." The headlines blared that the Vatican wanted to deny Kerry communion, but in fact when asked specifically about Kerry, Arinze said, "The norm of the church is clear. The Catholic Church exists in the U.S. There are bishops there. Let them interpret it."

The problem was that the bishops in the United States were interpreting the norms differently in different dioceses, which was a disturbing bit of confusion on such a central issue. The bishops appealed to Rome for guidance, which arrived in the form of a letter from Cardinal Ratzinger. But even that letter was a source of dispute within the American hierarchy, prompting a follow-up from Ratzinger that affirmed the authority of the local bishops to decide the matters prudentially. This provoked still more debate and uncertainty. The low point of the saga came when a right-wing canon lawyer in Los Angeles, Marc Balestrieri, announced on his Web site and in an October 15 interview on the arch-conservative Eternal Word Television Network, that he had "received a written response prompted by the Vatican's Congregation for the Doctrine of the Faith affirming that Catholic politicians who persist in supporting the right to abortion are 'automatically excommunicated,'" meaning, he said, that Kerry was a "heretic." A top aide to Ratzinger, the U.S. Dominican Father Augustine DiNoia, had to clarify that the letter to Balestrieri, which he had sent by another theologian, was only a "private" response and not an official "Vatican response." Still, the controversy only added to the appearance of disarray.

On a range of other issues, from who would be allowed to speak at Catholic campuses to which lay groups would be permitted to use church facilities to which groups would be given communion, different Catholic bishops were giving completely different answers and the Vatican seemed unable to provide clear direction. One day John Paul would praise Father Marcial Maciel Degollado, the founder of a controversial conservative religious order called the Legionaries of Christ, and the next day the Vatican would announce that long standing charges of corruption and sexual abuse by Maciel were being reinvestigated. Meanwhile, some bishops in the United States were giving Maciel's order a warm welcome while others were banning it as a divisive force.

Even something as simple as a papal thumbs-up—or down—on a movie became a farce worthy of Feydeau. In the intensive publicity campaign for his neo-gothic film version of Jesus's death, *The Passion of the Christ,* the breakaway traditionalist Catholic Mel Gibson managed, through the kind of back channels opened up by the institutional inertia of recent years, to get a DVD to the papal apartment for a private screening by Pope John Paul. It was Advent of 2003, and the pontiff was barely able to make pronouncements on some of the most pressing issues of the day. But over two days he watched the film in his private apartment along with Dziwisz, his personal secretary. A few days later, Dziwisz met Gibson's coproducer on the film, Steve McEveety, who said Dziwisz relayed the pope's review of easily the most controversial and troubling film of recent years: "It is as it was." Gibson and his promoters ran with the endorsement, bannering it everywhere they could in an effort to blunt the rising criticism of the movie, much of it based on its allegedly anti-Semitic depictions.

Stunned by the reaction to an unprecedented papal movie promo, some Vatican officials let it be known anonymously that the pope had not said anything, while others insisted he had. In January, Dziwisz himself broke his usual press silence to tell Catholic News Service that the purported review by John Paul was a fabrication. "The Holy Father told no one his opinion of this film," Dziwisz said. "He does not make judgments on art of this kind; he leaves that to others, to experts." But Gibson's allies on the Catholic Right insisted the pontiff had endorsed the film, and produced an e-mail allegedly from papal spokesman Navarro-Valls testifying to that effect. Navarro issued a noncommittal statement that copped to nothing but allowed wiggle room for the endorsement to have been uttered, and Gibson's company continued to ride the publicity wave all the way to a blockbuster release on Ash Wednesday 2004. (Whatever John Paul's real view of the film, Gibson got a real thumbs-up a few months later when the pope beatified Anne Catherine Emmerich, the German nun and mystic whose nineteenth-century visions of the Passion—complete with bloody flourishes and Jewish caricatures—provided inspiration for Gibson's celluloid version.)

In the end, the real loser in the sorry episode was the pope himself, who came off looking like the crazy uncle locked in the Vatican's attic.

Amid all of the competing agendas and mixed signals, one voice that remained a constant was that of Joseph Ratzinger.

If the pope left politics and temporal affairs up to his powerful secretary of state, Cardinal Angelo Sodano, then Ratzinger, as head of the Congregation for the Doctrine of the Faith, was the pope's man on internal church discipline, as well as his all-around go-to guy.

That John Paul had always relied heavily on Ratzinger was never in question. One U.S. ambassador to the Holy See, former Boston mayor Raymond Flynn, recalled presenting his credentials to the pope, who said that Flynn would largely work with Archbishop Tauran, who was still the Vatican's foreign minister at the time. But John Paul then told Flynn that "if I had any problems I was to talk to Ratzinger—that's how he said it," Flynn recalled.[23] Cardinal Arns also indicated that Ratzinger was the chief stand-in for John Paul. "John Paul II has left his mark, especially in his earliest documents," Arns said in a 2005 interview. "Today it is Cardinal Ratzinger . . . who leaves his mark."

Ratzinger's influence had grown especially noticeable since August 2000, when he issued a blunt pronouncement on the status of other Christian churches, in a document titled *Dominus Iesus*. In it, Ratzinger—whose brief did not include ecumenical dialogue—declared that followers of other religions are in a "gravely deficient situation" compared to Christians, who alone "have the fullness of the means of salvation." He added that "there exists a single church of Christ, which subsists in the Catholic Church, governed by the successor of Peter and by the bishops in communion with him," and for good measure said that many Protestant churches cannot be considered churches "in the proper sense."

✓ The document drew sharp protests from Protestants and other believers, and unusual public criticism from many of Ratzinger's fellow cardinals, who questioned the timing and wording of the document. Despite the public debate, Ratzinger claimed to have John Paul's imprimatur, and the powerful prefect of the Congregation for the Doctrine of the Faith continued to issue important church statements under his own name, including pronouncements on Catholic politicians, the role of women in church and society, and a document denouncing gay marriage that also descried adoption by gay couples as tantamount to "doing violence to these children." Issued at the height of the scandal over the hierarchy's cover-up of decades of clerical child abuse, that document did not get a warm reception in many quarters.

In October 2004, Sandro Magister wrote that Ratzinger "exercises unprecedented power. Before him, the heads of the Holy Office responded to inquiries on individual doctrinal cases, and questioned unorthodox theologians. Ratzinger does this, and much more. He releases doctrinal documents that customarily are produced by the pope. He writes encyclicals, circular letters to the bishops of the whole world, another typical papal prerogative." In 2002, when Ratzinger turned seventy-five, the usual age at which curial officials step down, John Paul instead reconfirmed him without an age limit. In other words, the pontiff said, Ratzinger has been here nearly as long as I have, and he is staying until the end.

Overlooked amid all these public controversies was a seemingly insignificant bit of hierarchical housekeeping prompted by the decision by Cardinal

Bernard Gantin, an African from Benin who had spent decades in Rome, to step down as dean of the College of Cardinals when he turned eighty. The dean's duties are largely ceremonial, consisting mainly of presiding at various formal functions during the interregnum that follows a pope's death. Indeed, the previous dean of the college was an eighty-five-year-old Italian cardinal, who presided during the two papal funerals and conclaves of 1978. But Gantin wanted to leave the post, so in December 2001, in keeping with protocol, a group of ten cardinals, mainly curialists living in Rome, elected one of their colleagues, Cardinal Ratzinger, as the new dean.

It was a fateful move, but one that was given no notice outside the Vatican. Too much else was afoot as the church and the world watched the agonizing, slow-motion finale of the papacy of Pope John Paul II. For an organization like the Catholic Church, which exists because of a unity of beliefs and practice, the situation at the end of John Paul's reign was unsettling. Uncertainty was the hallmark of Catholicism early in the third millennium, and the state of the Catholic Church at the twilight of this indisputably historic papacy was far more problematic than most observers recognized. Issues needed to be addressed, and while no one wanted to criticize a beloved pope who was entering the final stages of life, there was a growing sense of anticipation and an increasing buzz of sub rosa discussions about what should come next. In other words, the conclave to elect John Paul's successor had already begun.

But before he left the stage, John Paul had one more act to play out. In some ways it would turn out to be his greatest performance ever, and perhaps his most important legacy. And its dramatic power would be so great that it would thrust almost every other issue into the background and recast the dynamics of the conclave that would follow one of the most poignant curtain calls in modern history.

Chapter Two

THE PASSION
OF THE POPE

Pope John Paul II projected such a galvanic image of action and vigor that it is easy to forget that his pontificate was a long-running saga of physical suffering and decline as much as a triumphant crusade around the globe. When he was elected in October 1978, John Paul was quickly dubbed "God's athlete" because of his fondness for hiking, skiing and almost anything that would put him out and about. Indeed, a major factor behind the cardinals' choice was the fact that this fifty-eight-year-old mountain climbing churchman was not likely to drop dead in a month, as had happened to his predecessor, John Paul I. The death of the first John Paul, coming so quickly after the passing of Paul VI, whose physical frailty in his later years seemed to underscore his reputation as an anguished, Hamlet–like pope, traumatized the cardinals, who wanted the world to see a vibrant papacy and a sure hand guiding the Barque of St. Peter.

Karol Wojtyla gave them all that and more, and faster than they could ever have expected. John Paul I, pressured from the start by the awesome task before him, had quickly signaled that he would not attend a major gathering of Latin American bishops planned for early 1979 at Puebla in Mexico. The decision was no surprise but something of a disappointment, though not inside the Vatican. In 1978 papal trips were still unusual—Paul had made nine journeys outside Italy during his fifteen-year pontificate, the first foreign travel by a pope in the modern era. These apostolic journeys, as they came to be known, were major undertakings that could not be thrown together in a few weeks. Besides, John Paul I was just getting his bearings as pope. "I'm sure in the back of his mind was, 'What the Hell am I going to say to those bishops over there in Latin America?'" later recalled Father Diego Lorenzi, Luciani's closest aide. The disorientation of the papal office overwhelmed Albino Luciani, who was known as a sensitive man and caring pastor during his tenure as cardinal-archbishop of Venice, and apparently aggravated his circulatory problems. He was stricken in the middle of the night and discovered the next morning, dead just thirty-four days after his election.[1]

When John Paul II took office the following month, the change in approach was immediate, the energy level ratcheted up to a point that the curialists who normally set the pontiff's agenda were instead running hard to keep up with their new boss. John Paul quickly announced plans to attend the Mexico meeting just three months hence, and that was just the beginning. Even at home he was in motion. He had the Vatican build a swimming pool at Castelgandolfo, his summer residence in the Alban hills outside Rome, to help him stay in shape. When the cardinals in charge of the Vatican's always precarious finances worried about the cost, John Paul told them that the pool would be cheaper than holding yet another conclave.

Then, less than three years after this Polish dynamo captivated the world, it all nearly came to a sudden, tragic end.

Shortly after 5:00 PM on May 13, 1981, John Paul's open-topped popemobile was making its way through the crowd that had gathered in St. Peter's Square for the Wednesday public audience. The people-loving pope had just returned a little girl to her parents' arms after giving her a hug when a Turkish assassin, Mehmet Ali Agca, fired two shots from a Browning 9-millimeter semiautomatic pistol. One shot grazed the pope's elbow and then struck and wounded two American pilgrims. The other deflected off his finger and tore through his abdomen. John Paul groaned and fell backward into the arms of Monsignor Dziwisz, an iconic image that evoked the Deposition from the Cross as it was beamed around the world to a stunned global audience. Others recalled Karol Wojtyla's last poem, written in the hours after the death of John Paul I and before Wojtyla became pope. Titled "Stanislaw," the verse was a wrenching exaltation of martyrdom that told of a bishop of Krakow who had died at the hands of King Boleslaw, declaring that if "the word did not convert, blood will convert."[2] There, on a spring afternoon in St. Peter's Square, it seemed the word had turned to blood.

The pontiff was rushed to Gemelli Hospital, given last rites, and underwent five hours of surgery. The bullet perforated his intestines and his colon but missed, barely, his spinal cord and his abdominal artery. A fraction of an inch closer and John Paul never would have made it to Gemelli alive. Thanks to his surgeons, John Paul would not be a martyr that day. But in retrospect the shooting presaged a series of health problems that would make for a slow-motion martyrdom over the next two decades.

John Paul struggled to recover from the shooting, in part because the same stubborn determination that endeared him to the public also made him a difficult patient who chafed at remaining in the hospital. He left as soon as he could, but subsequent infections required further rehospitalizations over a full year. Eventually the pope seemed to regain his energy, and the 1980s witnessed some of his papacy's most historic moments—the triumph of the Solidarity trade union in Poland and the crumbling of Soviet communism, as well as the suppression of liberation theology in Latin America, clashes with American Catholics, and the disciplining of theologians and bishops. Still, by 1986 some medical experts thought they detected the first signs of the neurological disease—tremors and a growing hunch to his posture—that would define John Paul's image for the last dozen years of his papacy and finally lead to his death.

√   By 1992, the stiffening of the pope's facial muscles, the unceasing tremor in his left hand and his shuffling gait were undeniable signs that something—probably Parkinson's disease—was wrong. But the Vatican at first tried to chalk up what were patently neurological problems to simple arthritis and residual complications from the shooting. Other problems mounted. In July 1992, surgeons removed an intestinal tumor that was the size of an orange and beginning to turn malignant; many were surprised that the pope was not undergoing the regular medical tests that should have found the tumor much earlier. At the same time, they removed John Paul's gall bladder. In November 1993, John Paul fell down the short steps from his throne during an audience, dislocating his right shoulder. He wore a soft cast and a sling for several weeks and later joked about the accident and the growing speculation as to his true condition: "It's a slightly deficient Pope," he said, "but still in one piece and not dead yet." (It was actually a rare but amusing—to the Italians—malapropism by the Polish pope, since the usual connotation of *deficiente* is "stupid.") In April 1994 John Paul slipped in the bath and broke his right thigh bone, requiring hip replacement surgery and a month's hospital stay. He began to walk with a cane and was forced to cancel a trip to the United States that year and to forgo the outdoor activities that he loved. In December 1995 he missed Christmas Mass for the first time ever, and later in the day suffered a severe bout of fever and stomach pain that dramatically halted his live Christmas television address from the loggia of St. Peter's Basilica. During 1996 the pope had to cancel several events due to what the Vatican said were problems of a "digestive nature," and finally in October his appendix was removed. In June 1999, during a twelve-day visit to his homeland, his longest trip there, John Paul fell and had to cancel a huge open-air Mass.

All the usual vulgarities associated with the deathwatch of a famous person began to appear. Web sites were taking bets on when the pope would die, with one site based in the Netherlands running a sweepstakes that offered a free trip to Rome to anyone who correctly guessed the date of John Paul's death, the length of the conclave that would elect his successor, and the successor's name. Naturally, suggested remedies and treatments poured in. Luc Montagnier, the French researcher who helped discover the AIDS virus, met with the pope in June 2002 and gave him some of his own designer antioxidant tablets based on a papaya extract that he said would help the pope live for years, results he claimed the supplement had achieved for AIDS patients in his care. Montagnier also offered his services as a papal medical consultant on several occasions but never received a response. At one point it was reported that John Paul was undergoing dialysis, which one Vatican official confirmed privately and another denied publicly. The speculation was only fueled by the lack of any solid information about the pope's treatment. It was widely assumed that John Paul was taking levodopa, a standard Parkinson's treatment, but in 2004 it was reported that before public appearances he also received a shot of a drug called apomorphine hydrochloride, which provides a quick energy boost.[3]

John Paul himself was as stubborn as ever, refusing to slow down or take himself out of the media spotlight. Italian government officials who dreaded the security arrangements that the pope's funeral would entail were frustrated at John Paul's stubborn refusal to abide by his doctors' insistent advice that he slow down to preserve his health. "It's a question of activity versus prolonging his life," one official told reporters.

However obvious John Paul's health problems, the Vatican continued to downplay them, even though John Paul's neurological disorder was clearly worsening. During a papal visit to Hungary a month before his 1996 appendectomy, Navarro, the papal spokesman, made a rare slip by saying that the pope was suffering from an "extra-pyramidal syndrome"—a nonspecific term that refers to the part of the motor system that controls nonvoluntary movement. That was widely interpreted as confirmation that the pope had a degenerative, Parkinson's–like disorder. Navarro stayed mum after that, and John Paul tried to triumph over his ailments, burnishing his heroic image and reassuring the faithful that the church remained in good hands. But after the millennial celebrations of 2000, the pope could no longer hold back the onslaught of what was obviously Parkinson's disease. Soon what was once a courageous battle against age and illness became a painful, often voyeuristic deathwatch. Slumped in a wheelchair, he could barely raise his head, and drool poured from the sides of his mouth. Vatican photographers who had once enjoyed the easiest job in journalism—shooting the most photogenic world leader around—now struggled to get anything useable. "You work harder now for a good shot, to make him look okay, and you still don't get one," a veteran Vatican photographer told me in September 2004.

When Wojtyla was elected pope in 1978, his mentor and compatriot, Cardinal Stefan Wyszynski, told him, "If the Lord has called you, you must lead the church into the third millennium." John Paul saw that mission as the mandate of Providence, and almost like a dying parent who endures to see one final holiday with the family, he soldiered on through the extensive preparations for the year 2000. But after the great jubilee, the pope appeared more exhausted than ever, worn down to his essence—a "soul leading a body," as biographer George Weigel put it.

His official writings over the last years of his pontificate more than ever reflected the profound interiority that was always at the center of John Paul's persona. From the death of his mother and his other family members, to the rape of his homeland by the Nazis and then the Communists, to his physical travails and the burdens of the papacy, John Paul saw his personal suffering, and its redemptive power through the reality of the Cross, as the unifying thread of his life. But for years the Vatican publicly ignored that emphasis while keeping the focus on the pope as a successful politician and actor.

Now that persona was being stripped away, so there was nothing to obscure the mystical soul that always existed just beneath the surface. "While the strength of my body declines, I feel even more strongly the strength of prayer," John Paul said in 2004. He wrote about the spiritual life of the church, about the liturgy and the sacraments, and he meditated at length on personal devotions such as the Rosary. The days of the great social encyclicals—elaborated texts on a single topic that define a pope's record—were long behind John Paul, and his philosophical writings were increasingly to be found in his memoirs and related musings. His final encyclical was characteristic of this late period. *Ecclesia De Eucharistia* (On the Eucharist in Its Relationship to the Church), was issued on Holy Thursday in 2003 and commemorated the institution of the Eucharist, which embodies the mystery of Christ's sacrifice on the cross.

He declared 2003 the Year of the Rosary, and 2005 the Year of the Eucharist, to be concluded with a special synod, or Vatican meeting of the world's bishops, on the Eucharist—an event he would not live to see.

In 2003, John Paul visited Slovakia and appeared so weak that speculation about his health drowned out any coverage of the substance of his remarks, and television networks mobilized for his death. The pope could not finish his speeches, and emergency medical equipment, including defibrillators and oxygen tanks, appeared at papal venues and on the plane, setting off alarm bells in newsrooms. Despite hydraulic lifts and custom-built conveyances, events ran behind schedule as Vatican officials struggled to get John Paul from one venue to another. John Paul was a prisoner in his own body. "I believe that had it not been for the assassination attempt in 1981, the pope would easily have the force to lead the church until he was 90 or beyond," Bishop Rudolf Balaz of Slovakia told reporters.

By his twenty-fifth anniversary a month later, John Paul no longer walked in public, and, a few months after that, he was permanently confined to a wheelchair, unable to walk at all or even to speak intelligibly. Medical equipment was installed in the papal apartments, and Gemelli Hospital became known as the "third Vatican" (the summer residence at Castelgandolfo being the "second Vatican"); John Paul would eventually spend close to five months as a patient there, a record that became nearly as distinctive as his travels outside Rome.

In a way, John Paul in his final years was a man caught in a trap of his own construction. By becoming a media star and a jet-setting evangelizer, John Paul thrust himself into the public spotlight and raised the stakes for what the papacy meant to the church and to the world. Once he became a celebrity, there was no retreat. In previous decades and centuries, pontiffs could toddle off into their dotage—one that would likely not last too long given the state of medicine in those days, especially in Italy—with hardly anyone noticing, or minding. Popes did not leap the Berlin Wall or even kibitz with pilgrims in the piazza on a regular basis. Mostly they had to appear a couple of times a year on the balcony of St. Peter's to utter a few Latin benedictions and that was enough. Everyone knew that the pope was on his throne—he was Italian and he wore white—and so all was right with the world. We know now that many popes were senile in their later years, a fact everyone surmised but few would admit. Leo XIII, who died in 1903 at the age of ninety-two, was a near-senile recluse the last two years of his life, and Pius XII reportedly saw visions of the Virgin Mary everywhere the last three years of his life, during which his only communication with the outside world was through an aide.

But it hardly mattered, as the faith's ship of state was on virtual autopilot in a world that ran at a far slower pace. Besides, in that more willfully naïve age, to even bruit the idea that a pontiff was less than 100 percent was considered heterodoxy. The famous Roman quip "The pope is never sick until he's dead" was given life by an episode in 1914, when the Vatican's official newspaper, *L'Osservatore Romano*, blasted commentators who had suggested that Pius X was suffering from a head cold. Less than twenty-four hours later, Pius was dead. Faith in the Vatican's transparency on papal health matters was further weakened decades later, when it finally emerged that the death of John Paul I in 1978 did not unfold according to the "official" Vatican version, which had it that the corpse of poor Luciani was discovered in bed in the morning by his personal secretary, Monsignor John Magee, a beatific look on the dead pope's face and personal notes in his hands—working for the Kingdom until the end. As the fabricated story started to break down, discrepancies turned up over who found the pope and when, over the cause of his death and the state of his health. The truth was that the "smiling Pope" was actually found on the floor, perhaps by a nun, his face a rictus mask of pain, and that he had probably been there for hours unattended. The effort to elide the facts of his all-too-human end fueled all manner of wild conspiracy theories, which were finally unraveled in John Cornwell's 1989 investigative book, *A Thief in the Night*.

Karol Wojtyla was determined to end such deceptions, and his opportunity to do so came in characteristically mediagenic fashion with his recovery from the 1981 assassination attempt. John Paul II allowed himself to be photographed in his hospital bed, dressed only in a patient's gown and with tubes running from his nose and arms. He also insisted on taping a message to be played at his usual Sunday noontime Angelus prayer encounter with pilgrims in St. Peter's Square. The recording was delivered in a pained voice, but both the words and the photo showed the world that while the pope might be sick, he was not dead. The precedent of not hiding the pontiff's condition was set, but it would lead to other complications for the Vatican more than two decades later, as Rome was forced to explain the pope's obvious debilitation while maintaining the company line that he was still in charge.

On one level, John Paul's identification with the suffering and elderly was truly a powerful testimony and, as many later agreed, perhaps his greatest legacy and most effective prolife statement.

"If you evaluate the situation in purely human terms, you see a great enterprise guided by an old, sick man," Cardinal Julian Herranz, the Vatican's top canon lawyer and a close aide to John Paul, told the Italian media. The pope "is carrying out a great evangelizing mission, showing that in a world that only seems to appreciate youth and strength and beauty and power and hedonism and wealth, that old age and sickness also have value." John Paul "can speak to the hearts of just as many people as when he was young and strong,"[4] he said, adding that the pope had a very clear sense of his own divine mandate to continue leading the church. As another Vatican official told the *New York Times*, "What he is saying is that life is worth living until its natural end. . . . It is an important witness, and I am sure he is conscious of it—that there is no kind of life which humanly speaking can be terminated because it seems not to be worth living."

As John Paul grew more frail, he made many moving efforts to underscore the value of the elderly and to encourage them by his example, much as he had invigorated the church with his energy in earlier years. "It is important to speak of suffering and death in a way that dispels fear," he told hospice workers in Austria in 1998. In a letter addressed to the elderly for the 1999 World Day of the Sick, he described the achievements of the aging Moses: "It was not in his youth but in his old age that, at the Lord's command, he did mighty deeds on behalf of Israel," he wrote. In August 2004, during a visit to the Marian shrine at Lourdes, which commemorates miraculous healings, John Paul directly addressed his own condition in speaking to the ill: "With you I share a time of life marked by physical suffering, yet not for that reason any less fruitful in God's wondrous plan."

But from this dynamic, two competing, and often contradictory, themes emerged that were difficult to reconcile: one depicted John Paul as the Suffering Servant of Isaiah, fulfilling his providential mission by undergoing a new kind of crucifixion; the other theme depicted John Paul as the heroic captain of the ship, in full command even as the storms of age and illness raged around him.

This conundrum was to a large degree forced on John Paul and the Vatican by the fact that since the Middle Ages popes have not retired. Apart from the Great Western Schism of the fifteenth century, when a council had to get rid of three rival popes, the last pope to resign his office was Celestine V, a hermit who was elected in 1294 at the age of eighty and resigned after a few months. He was imprisoned by his successor, who feared having a rival to the throne, and Dante later placed poor Celestine in the Inferno for what he termed his cowardly "Great Refusal." So, given the circumstances of history and Rome's penchant for giving such historical accidents the weight of tradition, John Paul II had little choice but to continue on, no matter what his condition. Canon law was also vague on how to deal with papal retirement or, even worse, mental or physical incapacitation. There is no vice-pope, and no one to whom the pope might submit his resignation. A senile pope would be a crisis of historic proportions for the church. As a result, the Vatican had to keep up the image—real or not—that John Paul had his wits about him and was in charge.

Beyond tradition, however, John Paul's vision of the divine sanction of his office and his role in history meant that he was not about to be the first modern pope to step down, despite speculation that the ever-innovative pontiff would contemplate such a move. After hip replacement surgery in 1994, he joked with his surgeon about the church law that would let him resign if he became incapacitated. "Doctor, neither you nor I have any choice. You have to cure me because there is no room for a pope emeritus." Above the administrative concern, however, was John Paul's theological justification for remaining in the saddle no matter what. Later in 1994, he told an audience: "I must lead her [the Church] with suffering. The pope must suffer so that every family and the world should see that there is, I would say, a higher gospel: the gospel of suffering, with which one must prepare the future."[5]

✔ Or, as he told aides repeatedly, "Christ did not come down from the cross."

The problem with this model was that Christ on the cross was not in control; the sacrifice at Calvary was about relinquishing the very thing that we—and many of Jesus's disciples—want, which is to take charge on earth. Yet governing a temporal body is what popes, the successors to Saint Peter, must do.

So even as John Paul and his closest aides exalted his status as a fellow sufferer of the lame and the halt, they always pulled back from a complete identification with the disabled. John Paul still had to be the pope, and thus his physical infirmity was carefully isolated from his mind and soul in ways that could lead to another form of mythologizing. "I don't govern the Church with my legs," John Paul would tell visiting bishops who asked after his health. To others he would point to his neck and say from that point up—motioning toward his head—he was feeling fine.

The Vatican wanted to have it both ways, alternating between defiance at the intensive coverage of John Paul's condition and hailing the display of suffering that had engendered so much media speculation. The situation created difficulties for anyone, in the media or the church, who sought to probe the potential downsides of the pontiff's health or the growing controversy over whether he should resign. Taking on a Roman pontiff was not something that anyone did lightly. "*Qui mange du Pape en meurt,*" Napoleon was reported to have said—"He who eats a pope dies"—reflecting concern about his kidnapping of Pius VII, who died in the emperor's custody. Monsignor Dziwisz, John Paul's personal custodian, was not shy about updating that maxim: "Many journalists who in the past have written about the pope's health are already in heaven," Dziwisz liked to say, referring to reporters whom John Paul managed to outlive. Even senior churchman who spoke out of turn about John Paul's health found themselves in hot water. In October 2003, Dziwisz brought the powerful *Panzerkardinal* to tears after Ratzinger told the German magazine *Bunte* that John Paul was "in a bad way" and that the faithful should pray for him. "Cardinal Ratzinger was crying yesterday, explaining that he never gave an interview but merely answered someone he met on the street, saying, 'If the pope is sick, pray for him,'" Dziwisz told reporters in a revelation that may not have been welcomed by the head of the Congregation for the Doctrine of the Faith.

As a consequence, the Vatican line continued to be that John Paul, despite his almost complete incapacitation, possessed a superhuman strength that set him apart from other senior citizens and allowed him to run the church, perhaps for years to come: "He surely will, because he is driven by an incredible strength, an extraordinary will and extraordinary clarity," Mexican cardinal Javier Lozano Barragan, president of the Pontifical Council for Health Care, said during one of the pope's final hospitalizations. The seventy-two-year-old Lozano Barragan said, implausibly, that John Paul had the energy of an ordinary man twenty years younger than himself: "The word 'resignation' is not part of the Pontiff's vocabulary." Even a month later, just a week before the pope's death, Cardinal Camillio Ruini said the pope's decline had created no problems for church governance. "His physical condition may be fragile, but his mental condition is absolutely sound," said Ruini, the pope's vicar for the Rome diocese. He said the Holy Father "continues to carry out acts of government, to make the big decisions, as he always has."

This line of argument—that the pope was mentally clear whatever his physical limitations—would be devoutly followed up to the moment of John Paul's death, creating a new spin on the old maxim. Before John Paul, a pope was never sick until he was dead. Now, a pope is never senile until he is dead.

Up to the end, the Vatican would maintain this dual story line, even if it became untenable at times. In the end, the Christological pope would win out, and in moving, powerful fashion.

In a sense, the drama had to play out this way. By the last year or two of John Paul's life, it was too late for him to resign. His condition was so compromised that any resignation would be suspect, and the questions such a move would raise would bedevil any successor: Who really made the decision? What would happen to the "former" pope? How would he be decommissioned? How would a new pope be elected? Would the church be thrown into schism by competing claims? There were rumors that John Paul had left instructions, as Paul VI did, about what to do in case of his incapacitation. But the letter, which—astonishingly, given the stakes—did not exist, would only have produced more uncertainty if it had suddenly popped up.

As a result, the church was left with a mute, immobile pope, and the cardinals had no option but to recognize his example of suffering, and pray that John Paul did not slip into a coma.

"I ask myself, why am I not concerned?" Chicago's Cardinal Francis George told *NCR* in March 2005. "I just don't think it will happen, and I don't really know why. I suppose it has something to do with the providence of God. This is a holy man, and somehow if God keeps his promises regarding the good of the church, it won't come to that. . . . It could be foolish, but I'm just not concerned." Added London's Cardinal Cormac Murphy-O'Connor: "We believe in the providence of God, that it won't come to this, that the pope will come to his natural end."

It was a prayer that would be answered within a month.

The final agony of the pope began, and ended, in a manner so mundane as to pass unnoticed were it anyone else—a frail, elderly man catching the flu in the middle of an unusually frigid winter and failing to fight off the infections that ensued. But this was not just anyone's grandfather.

The precipitating event of the pope's final illness was, fittingly, a Sunday noon appearance at his study window above St. Peter's Square. John Paul had made the space, temporally and physically, a signature of his pontificate, and he was loath to miss the twenty minutes or so he spent reciting the prayer with the faithful, and perhaps offering a few remarks. On Sunday, January 30, 2005, the pope appeared at the open window despite the cold, and although his voice was especially hoarse and weak, he seemed in good spirits and good form, relatively speaking. With two Italian children by his side, he released two white "peace doves" and then smiled broadly as one of the doves thought better of the weather and tried to fly back into the papal apartment. John Paul laughed and tried to shoo the dove outside, to the delight of the crowd. But the cold air apparently aggravated an incipient case of influenza, which was rampant in Italy that winter, and that evening Navarro-Valls announced that John Paul, too, had come down with the flu.

Two days later, on the evening of Tuesday, February 1, the flu became a full-blown crisis as John Paul suffered a breathing crisis and was rushed to the hospital, dangerously close to choking to death. The Vatican insisted all was well, but John Paul's appearance the following Sunday, February 6, for the Angelus only complicated matters. The pope appeared at the window and seemed reasonably alert and comfortable, despite the cold air outside. The *sostituto*, who acts much like a White House chief of staff, was Archbishop Leonardo Sandri, and he read the pope's brief remarks, as he often did, and John Paul then tried to recite the last phrases of the Angelus prayer in Latin. But during those recitations the pope's voice seemed to change abruptly, and many watching a live feed on big screens two miles away at St. Peter's thought they heard the click of a tape recording at one point. Sandri was holding up a sheet of paper in front of the pope's mouth, ostensibly with the prayers that John Paul knew by heart. These clues, combined with the pope's insistence on remaining in public view, the public's fascination with the pope, and suspicion about the pope's condition, led to reports that the Vatican had arranged a "Milli Vanilli" moment and that John Paul was lip-synching the prayer. Navarro and others dismissed the reports as absurd, though suspicions lingered and contributed to the strange atmosphere surrounding those final days.

That strangeness was heightened when the pope was finally released from the hospital on Thursday, February 10. It was 7:30 in the evening in a darkened Rome when Navarro arranged for John Paul to be seated in a glass-enclosed popemobile with the ceiling light switched on to bathe the pontiff in an ethereal glow. The popemobile then traveled slowly down the boulevard leading to the Vatican, as well-wishers lined the streets to wave to the mute pope, who waved back feebly. Television carried the procession live. It was the kind of theater John Paul usually excelled at, but this time it seemed odd, as though John Paul were a kind of papal El Cid, propped up on his charger to reassure the faithful that they would carry the day. "That was a big mistake by Navarro," one Vatican insider, a priest, told me later. It was a view shared by many, though not all, in the Vatican.

With the start of Lent and the pope's usual retreat from public view, little information was available on John Paul for the next two weeks. Speculation continued and was just as regularly dismissed, until Thursday, February 24, when John Paul was taken back to the hospital and given a tracheotomy to help his breathing. Navarro described the procedure as elective rather than emergency, and said the thirty-minute operation under anesthesia went fine. After the pope's relapse, Dr. Corrado Manni, his former anesthesiologist, told an Italian newspaper, *La Stampa,* that John Paul should have "definitely" stayed hospitalized longer after his first crisis, but he added that was a problem after the 1981 attempt on his life. "He [John Paul] told me: 'The pope is either well, and then he must leave, or he is not well, and then he must stay.' I answered him: 'Your Holiness, there is a state of illness and of well-being, but in the middle there is a third state, that of convalescence.' Words spoken to the wind. I understand the difficulties his aides must have in dealing with such a situation. The Holy Father is difficult."

The tracheotomy relieved many of the immediate symptoms, and the Vatican portrayed John Paul as once again in command, holding meetings and issuing statements as he had done for decades. It was as if John Paul had built a humming engine but forgot to give it a lower gear setting, much less an off switch. As a result, dozens of speeches and proclamations and documents and homilies continued to stream forth almost daily in the pope's name, even as it became increasingly clear that John Paul had little if anything to do with them. News coverage of the documents usually began with the formulation, "Pope John Paul II said today . . . ," which fed the illusion of an active, acting, speaking pope.

Some of the statements seemed oddly timed, given his condition. During John Paul's first hospitalization, for example, he issued a statement calling on the medical community to ascertain with "moral certainty" that a patient has died before removing organs for donation. A few weeks later, as he was convalescing, he issued a statement saying that human dignity does not depend on "quality of life," and extends to those "who are still not capable or are no longer capable of understanding and loving." That statement followed a papal pronouncement a year earlier that had seemed to throw years of Catholic teaching into uncertainty when John Paul declared that feeding tubes for seriously ill patients in a "persistent vegetative state" were "morally obligatory." Catholic teaching until then had seen such tubes as extraordinary measures that could be refused or withdrawn. John Paul now termed such actions "true and proper euthanasia by omission," and he also raised concerns about what that could mean for his own eventual care.

The February 2005 statement was widely interpreted to refer to severely brain-damaged and comatose patients, and came against the backdrop of the case of Terri Schiavo, a forty-one-year-old American woman who had been in a persistent vegetative state for fifteen years. The legal fight within her family over whether she was brain-dead and whether to withdraw her feeding tube created a media storm for weeks and provided a poignant, and sometimes bizarre, parallel to the pope's own public decline. "The right-to-life types want to renounce brain death and keep everyone going forever," Father John Paris, a Jesuit theologian at Boston College and expert on end-of-life issues, told *Newsweek*. "It seems that Lenin's mausoleum will be the model for the future. The entire enterprise is mischief-making at the Vatican."

The emergence of this iconic pontiff, like a frieze from the Stations of the Cross, had been gradual and inevitable. Still, it raised serious questions, which were never resolved. For many months, John Paul had only "presided" at Mass in "concelebration" because he, the church's top priest, was unable to lead the celebration himself. The Vatican finessed the matter by comparing the pope's new situation to the practice of Eastern-rite Catholic churches, which had presiders rather than celebrants. Cardinal Francis Arinze, the Vatican's top liturgist, in October 2004 insisted, "You really can't measure the number of decibels necessary for a valid Mass."

On Sunday, March 13, after eighteen days at Gemelli, twice as long as his first stay, John Paul returned to the Vatican, this time in somewhat less spectacular fashion. He rode in a gray Mercedes minivan, but Vatican officials did install a video camera behind the pope's shoulder so people watching the live television feed could see the pope's view of the crowds as he returned in the twilight to St. Peter's, blessing the people a week before Palm Sunday. At the end of the procession, the pope disappeared behind the Vatican walls, and so did any news of his condition. Immediately rumors circulated that he was worsening, or even that he had died. The Vatican denied all of this, and in fact said he was growing stronger and raised the possibility of a miraculous recovery. But the advent of Holy Week brought fresh gossip and reports revealing that John Paul had lost more than forty pounds since his surgery, a gauntness that was visible to all and an ominous sign for his stamina. John Paul delegated his top lieutenants to preside at the key Holy Week celebrations, which were normally the liturgical highlight of John Paul's year.

On Good Friday, the Vatican broadcast a video image of John Paul from behind, sitting in his private chapel, his back to the camera and watching a television monitor in front of him as Cardinal Ratzinger offered the Good Friday meditations at Rome's Coliseum, where John Paul had always given them. John Paul never moved, and a message was read on his behalf: "I also offer my sufferings so that God's plan will be realized and his word spread among peoples," said Cardinal Ruini, who carried the symbolic cross for the pope. Ratzinger made a stir with the force and darkness of his own Good Friday words. "How much filth there is in the Church, and even among those who, in the priesthood, ought to belong entirely to him!" Ratzinger declared in his lament. "How much pride, how much self-complacency!" He decried a Christianity that "has grown weary of faith, has abandoned the Lord: the great ideologies, and the banal existence of those who no longer believe in anything, who simply drift through life, have built a new and worse paganism, which in its attempt to do away with God once and for all have ended up doing away with man. And so man lies fallen in the dust."

At the last station, back in his chapel, John Paul held a crucifix in his hands.

It was vintage Ratzinger, and vintage Wojtyla.

In 1984 John Paul devoted an apostolic letter, *Salvifici Doloris,* to "the Christian meaning of human suffering." Said Father Raymond Helmick, professor of theology at Boston College, "He understands his sickness and mortality, revealing to us all the importance of living it out in front of a world public. Communication has been his strong suit all these many years he's been pope, and basically he's doing it still."[6]

Not everyone agreed. The conservative columnist and prominent Catholic William F. Buckley shocked many when he wrote that he refused to join his congregation at Mass in praying for the pope to recover. "I hope that he will not recover," Buckley wrote. Buckley said he detected "an element of vanity" in John Paul's struggle to remain in the public eye, and he said that "clinging to the papacy as a full-time cripple" did not serve the church.[7]

But the end for John Paul was so poignant and so irrefutably faith-filled that for the vast majority it shunted aside all such qualms and became an experience unto itself, independent of all Vatican spin and media machinations.

On Easter Sunday, March 27, John Paul appeared at his apartment window determined to impart his *Urbi et orbi* blessing. He had missed Mass that morning for the first time in his twenty-six-year papacy, and he was desperate to show himself to the thousands of people in the square below. Aides readied a microphone, but the pope struggled mightily to utter even a sound. He was frustrated and grimaced in pain. He lifted his hand to his throat at one point, shook his head, and seemed to wave off aides who tried to help him. For twelve agonizing minutes he stayed at the window. The pontiff who drew millions with his actor's baritone now drew tears from a crowd that realized something had changed irrevocably.

The end was inevitable, and sensing it, crowds began to gather beneath the pontiff's window. They held candles and many prayed the Rosary.

On Friday, April 1, Navarro announced that John Paul's condition was "very grave." His circulatory system was collapsing, with his blood pressure spiking and crashing. John Paul was given the Anointing of the Sick, which used to be known as Last Rites, and he decided he would not return to the hospital. At his own insistence, John Paul would die in his bed, the way popes always did. Given that it was Friday, the day Christ was crucified, the pope, "conscious and serene," the Vatican said, asked that the fourteen stations of the cross, representing Jesus's path to Calvary, be read to him. He crossed himself at each station. "This is surely an image I have never seen in these twenty-six years," Navarro said, losing his legendary composure as tears fell. John Paul had prepared his entire life for this moment, and he seemed to be the only one ready for the inevitable. News crews began a hurried mobilization as if for a military operation. Television coverage went 24/7, and there was even a Friday evening report that John Paul was dead. That turned out to be wrong, but not by much. "The Holy Father can already touch and see the Lord," Cardinal Ruini said at a Mass for the pope that evening. "This evening or this night, Christ opens the door to the pope," said another Italian prelate, Archbishop Angelo Comastri.

By Saturday morning, John Paul was slipping in and out of consciousness, and his organs were failing in an inevitable downward spiral. Navarro-Valls said the pope struggled repeatedly to make out a phrase, which he said aides parsed together as "I have looked for you. Now you have come to me and I thank you." Navarro-Valls said the words were apparently directed at the young people below the pope's window. As evening approached, various aides and collaborators stopped by the deathbed, blessing the pope and later recounting his efforts to bless them. Cardinal Achille Silvestrini, a close friend of the pope for decades, said that when he and Archbishop Jean-Louis Pierre Tauran entered the bedroom the pope responded but was unable to speak. "He gave us a look of recognition," Silvestrini said. "He had a relaxed expression on his face. He didn't have to make an effort to breathe. I kissed his hand. I caressed his brow, and I said, 'Thank you, Holy Father, for all you have done for the church.' He seemed to have understood."

In September 2005 the Vatican released a detailed, 223-page account of John Paul's final illness, from January 31 to his death. The report was unprecedented, and calculated to scotch any rumors or conspiracy theories, such as the one that claimed he actually died on Friday. The report said John Paul slipped into a final coma at 7:00 PM, Saturday, April 2, and "according to a Polish tradition, a small lighted candle illuminated the gloom of the room, where the pope was expiring."

John Paul was on his side, his head elevated on pillows. He was dressed in white bedclothes, surrounded by medical equipment, doctors and nurses, and the Polish nuns who had always cared for him. At 8:00 PM, Archbishop Dziwisz presided over a Mass for the Feast of Divine Mercy in the pope's room. The feast day was to be Sunday, though it was considered to have officially begun at sundown. The feast was associated with a Polish saint, Faustina Kowalska, whom John Paul had made the first saint of the third millennium in April 2000. Dziwisz was assisted by several Polish prelates, and Polish religious songs were sung. During the Mass, the pope received the Anointing of the Sick for the second time in three days. Outside, the crowd of 70,000 in the chilly piazza was singing hymns, and some chanted, "Stay with us. Don't leave us."

As the Mass in the pope's sparsely furnished room ended, so too did the earthly life of Pope John Paul II. Various accounts of John Paul's last moments emerged in the year after his death, reflecting the different perspectives of the mourners, and the inevitable emotions that inform any eyewitness account, especially of the passing of so great a figure. Some in the room stressed that John Paul was "serene" throughout, and that at the end the pope raised his right hand as if in blessing, then with his last effort uttered the word "Amen." A nun who was near John Paul in the pontiff's final hours said she heard the pope say, "Let me go to the Lord." According to the official Vatican report, his last comprehensible words were "Let me go to the house of the Father," pronounced "with a very weak voice and mumbled words" in Polish at 3:30 PM, six hours before he died. Dziwisz said his beloved mentor's last words were "*Totus tuus,*" his pledge of trust to the Virgin Mary. "He heard everything. He heard the square, he heard the prayer, the presence of the young people. The Holy Father heard, because he was conscious right to the end, almost to the end, even the last day," Dziwisz told an Italian television station in August, just before he was installed as the archbishop of Krakow, John Paul's former see, to which Pope Benedict promoted him within weeks of John Paul's death. Dziwisz said the pope "had not one bit of fear. . . . For him, death was really a passage from one room to another, from one life to another. In the last hours of his life there was a great tranquility and peace." In an alternate account, Dr. Renato Buzzonetti, John Paul's personal physician, said that the pontiff "passed away slowly, with pain and suffering," and that he "could not utter a single word before passing away."[8]

Whatever the exact story, it was all over at 9:37 PM Rome time.

Almost unfathomably, this great life had ended. Several cardinals immediately arrived to pay their respects. The Polish prelates, priests, and nuns who had maintained the death watch at the bedside did not recite the usual requiem for the dead, but sang the *Te Deum,* a solemn hymn of thanksgiving. "The religious sisters, the secretary, and the few others who were present spontaneously intoned it to thank God, not for his death of course, but for those 84 years that were so fruitful," Navarro-Valls said a few months later. "I myself found it extraordinarily difficult in that moment to recite the usual prayers on behalf of the deceased."

Yet, as if by instinct, the Catholic Church knew it had to go on. Within moments, the necessary, comforting rituals of death took over, both ancient and modern. The Vatican *camerlengo,* or chamberlain, Cardinal Eduardo Martinez Somalo, was summoned, as was Ratzinger, who as dean of the College of Cardinals would preside over the election. On the death of a pope, all top Vatican officials resign their posts and no important decisions may be made until a new pope is elected. The camerlengo is one of only three Vatican leaders to retain his job at the death of a pope; the camerlengo's function is essentially administrative, to organize the conclave and keep the Vatican's day-to-day operations running.

The camerlengo, Somalo in this case, was also to confirm the pope's death. In earlier years, though perhaps not since the early twentieth century, a silver hammer was used to tap on the pontiff's forehead while the camerlengo called out his baptismal name three times—the first time since his election that a pope is officially addressed by the name his parents gave him as a baby. It is believed that no soul can resist the call of their baptismal name. In John Paul's case, Somalo reportedly used an alternate rite, placing a veil of linen over the pope's face, then lifting it and saying softly, first "Karol," the pope's name in Polish, and then "Carolus," his Latin name.

There was no response.

Then an electrocardiogram was used for the first time to determine that the pope was indeed dead, and Buzzonetti signed the official death certificate, which was made public, also a first. It said that John Paul died of septic shock complicated by acute breathing problems, a benign enlarged prostate, and heart disease. Somalo then closed the papal apartments with ribbon and wax seals. They would be opened only by the successor.

At 9:55 PM a text message to journalists' cell phones relayed the news to the world: "The Holy Father died this evening at 9:37 PM in his private apartment. . . ."

About the same time, the Rosary prayer in the piazza ended, and Archbishop Sandri, who had been leading it with several other Vatican officials, broke the news to the thousands gathered in the square. "Our Holy Father, John Paul, has returned to the house of the Father," he said. "We all feel like orphans this evening."

The mourners fell silent, as if stunned. Then, as tears began to fall, they stared up at the fourth-floor papal apartment, at the window from which John Paul had addressed them so many times, still illuminated in the evening darkness, and broke into applause.

The ovation was just the beginning of a global tribute.

Encomiums and condolences came from every corner of the world, from Lech Walesa and Fidel Castro, from Israelis and Palestinians, Iranians and Americans, from all the continents that John Paul visited during his reign, and from friends and erstwhile foes. "What can I say—it must have been the will of God. He acted really courageously," said former Soviet president Mikhail Gorbachev. Billy Graham said John Paul was "unquestionably the most influential voice for morality and peace in the world during the last 100 years." He was mourned by Protestants and Orthodox, Arabs and Jews. "No Pope did more for the Jews," said Rabbi Marvin Hier, founder of the Simon Wiesenthal Center. The Dalai Lama praised the pope, whom he met several times, and the Hare Krishnas said his death was a great loss "to all people of faith."

But it was the popular reaction that made the aftermath of the death a stunning, historic event that surprised even those used to millions showing up for John Paul's appearances.

A requiem Mass in St. Peter's Square the Sunday morning after John Paul's death attracted 130,000, and that was a relative trickle that heralded a flood. Some 500,000 came to the square over the next twelve hours, more than 3 million over the next few days, with one estimate running as high as 5 million pilgrims visiting the Vatican. Overnight makeshift shrines sprang up, almost like lower Manhattan after 9/11, though in this case to recall the death of a single person rather than a massacre. The authorities, who were usually strict about removing any such displays, left them alone. "*Ciao Papissimo*" read a small sign that eight-year-old Francesco Monterisi tended next to a votive candle in the piazza.

The influx of mourners more than doubled the population of Rome. They found accommodations where they could, some taken in by Italian families, others sleeping in piazzas and parks, all told leaving thirty tons of litter a day. Untold millions more watched the wall-to-wall television coverage that began during the last days of John Paul's life and continued almost uninterrupted for the next week. The networks were finally able to use the pricey rooftop locations overlooking St. Peter's that they had reserved for years, at an unmentionable price.

Antenna trucks and scaffolding for mobile sets sprang up around the Vatican, as more than six thousand journalists, photographers, and radio and TV personnel were accredited to cover the events of the coming days.

"If it didn't happen on television, it didn't happen," John Paul liked to say, and the Vatican made sure his death and funeral were a happening.

When people around the world turned on their television sets the day after the pope died, on April 3, they saw his body lying in the Sala Clementina, where deceased popes are traditionally taken for private viewing before being moved to the basilica for public viewing. But it was not private this time. Not only was the Clementine Hall broadcast, but outside photographers were invited in along with journalists, diplomats, and various others. The mourners included one man wearing a backward baseball cap and several young people in jeans. John Paul lay on a flat catafalque, his head elevated by three gold pillows, his hands clasping a rosary, his pastoral staff next to him. He wore a white miter and vestments of dark red, the mourning color of popes, the scuffed oxblood loafers he preferred still on his feet, an incongruous reminder of the traveling pontiff who preferred movement and informality over potted ritual.

Swiss Guards in their striped Renaissance uniforms stood watch as organ music played softly. Members of John Paul's inner circle wiped away tears as they knelt in prayer. Cardinal Ratzinger sat leaning forward with his face buried in his hands.

The Romans like to say there is nothing deader than a dead pope—one of their famously irreverent but insightful quips, which are perhaps inevitable when living so close to such a potent neighbor for so many centuries. The saying is taken to mean that once a pope is gone, he can no longer exercise his almost limitless authority. Yet with John Paul, the contrast between the lifeless, waxy form on that bier in the Clementine Hall and the soul that inhabited the body, even at its most agonized, was especially sharp. The Vatican was intent on going old school, doing nothing to dress up the corpse. Just as John Paul died at home, his body, unlike those of some predecessors, had only been "prepared" for viewing, apparently not fully embalmed. It was believed that the corpse was injected with chemicals, not preserved in the usual manner.

The explanation evoked the odd and not always happy history of papal corpses. For centuries the organs and viscera of popes were removed and kept in a church near the Trevi fountain that had an ancient claim to be the parish of the pontiffs. That custom ended in 1914, and several popes were embalmed after that. But Pius XII had a fear of autopsies and even embalming. He also had a quack of a doctor, Count Riccardo Galeazzi-Lisi, who was in fact an oculist. Galeazzi-Lisi only got the job as papal physician because his brother, Count Enrico Galeazzi, was a friend of New York's powerful Cardinal Francis Spellman. Galeazzi-Lisi showed Pius the severed hand of an accident victim he had preserved with a home-brew of resins and oils applied topically, and the same process was used on Pius when he died—a demise likely hastened by bizarre treatments by Galeazzi-Lisi and a Swiss doctor. The preservation process was a disaster, with the corpse bloating on the trip from Castelgandolfo to the Vatican and popping the seals of the papal coffin at a most inopportune moment of the liturgy. Galeazzi-Lisi also went down in infamy for taking secret photos of his patient as Pius was dying and later selling them to *Paris-Match*. That made the Vatican's ban on photos of sick popes or their corpses understandable, and the introduction of television cameras into John Paul's death rites that much more unusual.[9]

On Tuesday, April 5, after two days in the Sala Clementina, John Paul's body was carried in a solemn procession to the basilica by the Papal Gentlemen, an honorary title given to select laymen acting as pallbearers. A long train of monks, priests, and bishops, with Cardinal Ratzinger bringing up the rear as dean of the College of Cardinals, made its way through the twisting passageways of the apostolic palace, from the Sala Ducale to the Sala Regia, down the grand staircase designed by Bernini, through the great bronze door, under the colonnade, into the piazza, and then to the basilica. Gregorian chant and the Litany of the Saints accompanied the procession. Every step was broadcast live, which had never been done before.

Lines for the public viewing, set to start late Tuesday afternoon, began forming before 9:00 AM Monday. The Vatican announced the basilica would close for three hours in the middle of the night, from 2:00 AM to 5:00 AM, but pressure from the crowds forced them to shorten the break for cleaning to just an hour, between 3:00 AM and 4:00 AM. By the time the "global Calvary," as one priest pundit put it, was done, the Vatican estimated that 21,000 people per hour entered St. Peter's Basilica to view John Paul's body, a rate of 350 people a minute. The average wait was thirteen hours, with some mourners, at the height of the crush, waiting an exhausting twenty-four hours in a line that snaked nearly three miles through the neighborhood around the Vatican. They came from all over the world, more than a million alone from Poland. The young and the old, Catholic and non-Catholic, believer and nonbeliever, everyone felt they had to be a part of the moment. Tens of thousands of volunteers and Italian security personnel helped out—the throngs were remarkably peaceful and orderly and needed little looking after. Some 3,600 portapotties were trucked in and set up around St. Peter's and some three million bottles of water were distributed free.

"This is the most extraordinary thing that ever happened," said Philadelphia's Cardinal Justin Rigali, who had witnessed three other papal funerals, all of them far smaller in scope.[10]

For the funeral of Pope John Paul II on Friday, April 8, more than half a million people filled St. Peter's Square and the Via della Conciliazione, with another 600,000 watching on twenty-nine giant screen TVs around Rome. The Vatican said 137 television networks in eighty-one countries on all five continents broadcast the funeral, and television executives believe it was the most watched event in broadcast history. The Holy See's Web site received almost 1.5 million visits during the papal funeral.

The funeral began after John Paul's body was placed in a cypress coffin. Dziwisz laid a white silk veil over his mentor's face, and a summary of his life in 842 Latin words was written on a small scroll called a *rogito,* inserted into a lead tube, and placed in the casket along with three bags of coins—gold, silver, and copper—marking each year of his reign. "The whole church, especially young people, accompanied his passing in prayer," the *rogito* read. "His memory remains in the heart of the church and of all humanity."

The casket was carried out onto the *sagrato,* the sloped esplanade in front of St. Peter's Basilica, in keeping with the simplified rites started by Paul VI. Pope Paul took the funeral out of the basilica and into the square, while prescribing a plain wooden coffin topped by a book of Gospels. John Paul did the same, with a cross and the letter "M" for Mary burned into the lid. The coffin rested on an oriental carpet, but there were no flowers or any other decoration.

The funeral drew not only millions of mourners but also an unprecedented array of dignitaries, many sworn enemies.

President Bush sat in the second row of dignitaries, and former president Clinton was there. Bush was the first American president ever to attend a papal funeral, and he was a member of the evangelical wing of Protestantism, which only a few years earlier would have abhorred any tribute to a Roman pope. King Juan Carlos of Spain sat in front of him, and nearby was Prince Charles. The heir to the English throne and future head of the Anglican Communion, formed when Henry VIII broke with Rome, Charles delayed his wedding to Camilla Parker-Bowles to attend. The archbishop of Canterbury was there, as was British prime minister Tony Blair, who once received communion from John Paul despite his own Anglican membership. Israeli president Moshe Katzav was there along with Syrian president Bashar Assad. The two shook hands—Atlanta archbishop Wilton Gregory joked that it was John Paul's "first miracle"—but Iranian president Mohammad Khatami denied reports that he shook hands and chatted with Katsav, whose country Iran considers its main enemy. There was a flight ban around the city during the entire service, and helicopters and fighter jets patrolled overhead.

The Vatican said that some two hundred delegations attended, representing 140 nations, including ten reigning sovereigns, fifty-seven heads of state, seventeen heads of government, and the heads of the United Nations, European Community, and Arab League. Orthodox, Anglican, and Protestant churches sent representatives, as did ten Jewish and ten Muslim groups, as well as Buddhist, Sikh, and Hindu communities.

Archbishop Piero Marini opened the Book of the Gospels and set it on the casket. A strong wind blew the pages while television cameras framed the shot for the worldwide audience. In keeping with John Paul's multilingual habits, the Bible readings were in Spanish, English, and Latin, and the prayers of the faithful were recited in French, Swahili, Tagalog, Polish, German, and Portuguese.

Cardinal Ratzinger, in his role as dean of the cardinals, presided over the funeral Mass with 164 of the world's 183 other cardinals arrayed behind him. Some 500 bishops and 3,000 priests, wearing red stoles, also concelebrated at the most watched Catholic liturgy in history.

Ironically, Ratzinger had always disdained the televised spectacles of John Paul's masses, as well as many other modern accommodations masterminded by the late pope's longtime master of ceremonies for the pontifical liturgies, Archbishop Marini. Since Marini began choreographing papal events in 1987, he freely incorporated novel elements of music and dance to make John Paul's appeal more universal. "The direction of the liturgy is obliged to harmonize itself with television direction," Marini said in a 2003 interview. If Ratzinger disliked such theatricality in the Mass, he now benefited from it. The Vatican cameras that provided the feed to other networks intentionally avoided close-ups of mourners in the pews in order to focus on Ratzinger and his role as the principal celebrant speaking to the entire assembly. Detailed production preparations aimed at making John Paul's funeral a first-class broadcast had been in the works for years under the direction of Marini and two other

Vatican officials, Marco Aleotti and Father Silvano Maggiani. Both men had trained with well-known Italian movie director Ermanno Olmi in producing Vatican broadcasts during the great Jubilee of 2000.[11]

ν Using Jesus's exhortation to Peter to "follow me" as a refrain, Ratzinger repeatedly punctuated his funeral oration with the gentle reminder of how John Paul had always heeded God's call, finding suffering, yes, but above all a joy that the multitudes who gathered around the square, spilling into the adjoining neighborhoods, recognized in their beloved pope.

The church's renowned doctrinal watchdog, a cardinal with a reputation as a cold academic, showed a warm, almost poetic side, using the drama of John Paul's life as a way to connect with the huge crowd in a way that Cardinal Ratzinger never had.

In personal terms, he spoke of how the young Karol Wojtyla answered an irresistible call to the priesthood despite the dangers, and later answered the appointment to become a bishop just as he was embarking on a pastoral and academic career. "Leaving the academic world, leaving this challenging engagement with young people, leaving the great intellectual endeavor of striving to understand and to interpret the mystery of that creature which is man and of communicating to today's world the Christian interpretation of our being—all this must have seemed to him like losing his very self, losing what had become the very human identity of this young priest."

He then recalled Wojtyla's election as pope, and his exile from his beloved Poland. "To the Lord's question, 'Karol, do you love me?' the archbishop of Krakow answered from the depths of his heart: 'Lord, you know everything: you know that I love you.' The love of Christ was the dominant force in the life of our beloved Holy Father. Anyone who ever saw him pray, who ever heard him preach, knows that.

"The Holy Father was a priest to the last, for he offered his life to God for his flock and for the entire human family, in a daily self-oblation for the service of the Church, especially amid the sufferings of his final months," Ratzinger said. "The Pope who tried to meet everyone, who had an ability to forgive and to open his heart to all, tells us once again today, with these words of the Lord, that by abiding in the love of Christ we learn, at the school of Christ, the art of true love."

Ratzinger was interrupted thirteen times by applause, and he even seemed moved to tears at one point, an unusual public display by a man who normally played it straight as an arrow, reading his homily from behind large glasses.

In his most affecting touch, Ratzinger concluded by recalling John Paul's final days, and giving the late pope the unofficial seal of sainthood.

"None of us can ever forget how in that last Easter Sunday of his life, the Holy Father, marked by suffering, came once more to the window of the Apostolic Palace and one last time gave his blessing *Urbi et orbi*," Ratzinger said. "We can be sure that our beloved pope is standing today at the window of the Father's house, that he sees us and blesses us. Yes, bless us, Holy Father. We entrust your dear soul to the Mother of God, your Mother, who guided you each day and who will guide you now to the eternal glory of her Son, our Lord Jesus Christ. Amen."

The Mass lasted nearly two and a half hours, but the grandest flourish came at the end.

As the white-gloved pallbearers carried the wooden coffin toward the basilica's entrance, to its final resting place in the crypt, they stopped in front of the red velvet curtain covering the entry, turned the coffin to face the crowd, and raised it, tilted as if for one final bow.

Just as there was spontaneous applause at the announcement of John Paul's death, now too came a thunderous ovation, rolling through the oval drum of the piazza and then down the grand boulevard in front of the basilica. Across Rome, across Europe and the world, in homes around the United States, where untold numbers of people, Catholic and non-Catholic, had gotten up in the predawn hours to watch the funeral, Pope John Paul II took a curtain call that sent chills up the spine and tears down the cheeks. The pallbearers turned and carried the grand old man's remains into the darkened church, toward the grotto where they laid him to rest in the ground, as he had requested.

For a full fifteen minutes the applause continued, punctuated by chanted acclamations for John Paul's canonization—"*Santo, santo!*"—or a formal recognition of his greatness—"*Magno! Magno!*"—which rocked the square.

The applause finally died away, but its echo would reverberate over the next two weeks. The cardinals who followed the coffin into the basilica were also swept up in the emotion of the moment, but they were also looking ahead to the task before them. Choosing a successor to John Paul had been a daunting prospect before the pope died. Now it seemed inhuman. Who could follow such a man? Who would want to?

The focus of the world's affections and emotions remained John Paul. But the eyes of the cardinals had already started shifting to the man who surprised them by ushering John Paul into the next world with such grace and eloquence: Joseph Ratzinger.

Chapter Three

THE RATZINGER
SOLUTION

A papal conclave is to Roman Catholics what the Book of Revelation is to conservative Protestants: a chance for all our hopes and dreams of redemption to finally come true, for the wicked to be cast down and the righteous to be lifted up, and exactly in the way that we ourselves would want. Like the Messiah arriving with a blast of heavenly trumpets, a new pope seems divinely endowed with the power and sanctity to undo the many wrongs that we and the world have endured. So powerful is that image that Catholics—like biblical literalists on the other side of the Reformation divide—happily indulge in the cognitive dissonance necessary to explain away the fact that the eschatological horizon always seems to be receding into the distance.

With every natural disaster or Middle Eastern conflict, with every "secret code" discovered in Bible texts or every turn of the millennial calendar, certain Christians find confirmation of the impending Apocalypse and then turn to the skies in great expectation, only to discover that the Second Coming never arrives. Similarly, with every papal election, Catholics look to the balcony of St. Peter's Basilica, praying that the man who emerges as the Heir to the Fisherman and Vicar of Christ's church on earth will be "their" candidate—and then they go on about their lives of faith when the result turns out to be, as it usually does, far more prosaic than expected.

Still, few can resist the temptation to fantasize about the possibilities. Readers keep buying apocalyptic prophecies in spite of their perennially unfulfilled promises, and seers and novelists work ceaselessly to satisfy that demand by coming up with new and increasingly overwrought scenarios for the conclave.

The elements are so inherently dramatic and conspiratorial—a super-secret election by the select leaders of a global religion—that no plot device is out of bounds. As John Paul's health faded and speculation about the coming conclave grew, Dan Brown, author of the megaselling *The Da Vinci Code,* followed up his fanciful thriller by reissuing an earlier drama that he had written about the conclave. Called *Angels & Demons,* it was even more over the top than most examples of the genre—an antimatter time bomb set to go off just as the conclave gathered to elect a new pope. Brown's description of conclave procedures and routinely murderous church politics turned out to be as imaginative as his theories on physics.

To be fair, Brown had to be creative given that the "pope fiction" genre has been cranking out plots since at least as the thirteenth century, when a community of Italian hermits became famous for predicting the advent of a *papa angelicus,* an unworldly holy man who would become pope and miraculously pull the church from the pit of vice into which it had sunk. In the sixteenth century, Nostradamus forecast much the same thing, and his writings proved so popular that a few decades later some clever forgers came up with a set of papal prophecies that they backdated to the twelfth century and attributed to an Irish reformer named Saint Malachy.

In more recent times, novelists from Father Andrew Greeley (*White Smoke*) to former U.S. ambassador to the Vatican and Boston mayor Raymond Flynn (*The Accidental Pope*) have built on the market that was given new life in 1963, when Morris West wrote *The Shoes of the Fisherman.* In West's novel, a Russian priest released from a Siberian prison camp goes to Rome and stuns the world (and himself) by being elected pope and preventing a nuclear war. In 1968 the book was made into a film starring Anthony Quinn, and a decade later life seemed to imitate art when an unknown Polish cardinal named Karol Wojtyla was elected the first non-Italian pope in 450 years and helped end the Cold War—providing enough true drama to keep papal fantasies spinning in the minds of readers and writers alike. John Paul's reign was the reality show of papacies; thereafter no drama could be too far-fetched.

In fact, the conclave field was so open that *Third Secret,* a novel published in the spring of 2005, envisioned the almost unthinkable election of Jakob Volkner, an elderly German cardinal, of all things, as a caretaker pope who took the name of Clement XV.

It could only happen in fiction.

. . .

Certainly, for more than a decade before John Paul's death, the burgeoning corps of *Vaticanisti*—the journalists and commentators whose full-time job is reading the Roman tea leaves—had often seemed to be as creative as novelists in their papal prognostications. They had to be. The Vatican beat had been a discreet deathwatch for so long that reporters covering the Holy See were in a state of perpetual agitation, waiting for the middle-of-the-night tip that John Paul was dead and trying to keep up with the byzantine politics and the ever-changing gallery of personalities who would determine his successor once he was gone.

It wasn't easy, given that John Paul kept chugging along, creating a new batch of cardinals every few years, while aging cardinals (more than a few of whom were mooted as potential successors) kept dying or passing the eighty year threshold at which they lost the right to vote in the conclave. It was a kaleidoscope of candidates that even the actuarial tables could not winnow down to a manageable number. In past centuries there were often as few as a dozen members of the College of Cardinals, but as the system of papal elections grew more regularized, the number of electors also increased, and in 1586 Pope Sixtus V set the maximum number of cardinal-electors at 70 (the number of elders of the Tribe of Moses). Over his brief pontificate, Pope John XXIII ignored the ceiling and let the college grow to more than 80 cardinals. In 1970, Pope Paul VI formally raised the limit to 120 electors, and at the same time he excluded those over eighty years of age from voting. Pope John Paul II was never one to be restrained by legalisms, and several times he exceeded the limit by as many as 15, pushing the college to 135 cardinals.

Because so many of them were elderly, however, death and age steadily reduced their numbers, so that by the time John Paul died and the conclave began there were 117 electors—still the largest number in history and more than twice the size of the 1958 conclave. Only three of them were not John Paul appointees; one of the three, Cardinal Jaime Sin of Manila (yes, the conclave almost had a Cardinal Sin, as well as a Cardinal Law), was too ill to attend. The other two were resident in Rome: American cardinal William Wakefield Baum and German cardinal Joseph Ratzinger.

Apart from the sheer number of potential candidates, another wild card created by the constant turnover in the College of Cardinals was that few of the electors knew each other very well. In 2001, John Paul created the largest number of cardinals ever at a single consistory, 44, and in 2003 he created another 30 cardinals at once. (A consistory is the service at which the pope formally creates cardinals and gives them their signature three-cornered red biretta.) Although not all were electors, this large number of new members meant that nearly half the cardinals voting in the Sistine Chapel had only been electors for a few years, and most of them had not met since their elevation.

Moreover, the internationalization of the College of Cardinals, which started in earnest under Pius XII in the mid-twentieth century, was given a big boost by John Paul. Up until Pius, the College of Cardinals had for centuries been the almost exclusive province of the Italians, with French and Spanish cardinals periodically claiming smaller stakes. (There were rarely any German cardinals, since Germans controlled the Holy Roman Empire; that was more than enough, in the minds of the popes.) In 1875 New York archbishop John McCloskey became the first cardinal named from the Western Hemisphere, but even at the 1903 conclave some 97 percent of the college was still composed of Europeans. And when Pius was elected in 1938, well over half the cardinals (57 percent) were still Italian. Pius appointed the first cardinals from India and China, and Latin American electors went from 3 percent to 16 percent of the college under his reign. Paul VI continued that globalization trend, and the appointments of John Paul II reduced the Italian presence even further.

At the time of John Paul's death, in fact, just 17 percent of the cardinals were Italian, down from nearly 24 percent when he was elected in 1978. Not surprisingly, the percentage of Eastern Europeans doubled under the Polish pope, from 5 to 10 percent. Latin America increased just slightly, from 16.7 percent in 1978 to almost 18 percent in 2005. African and Asian representation remained almost the same at 10 and 9 percent, respectively. U.S. cardinals made up almost 10 percent of the college, also almost the same as in 1978. All told, European cardinals in the 2005 conclave accounted for just under 50 percent.

While the growing diversity of the college is undeniably praiseworthy, it is also making the College of Cardinals more geographically dispersed than ever, which introduces a different set of complications. Despite jet travel and the instant communication afforded by the Internet, these men rarely get together as a body to form personal relationships or learn about each other. The Europeans and Americans tend to be the most prominent cardinals, because they can afford to travel and their speeches and interviews and writings have a major platform in the Western-dominated media. But there is no real group dynamic, and no opportunity to develop one. At the consistory of 2003, the new cardinals had to wear name tags for each other's benefit—a custom that could have been useful at the 2005 conclave. "There are too many of us to really know each other," Cardinal Lubomyr Husar, a plain-speaking Ukrainian who had spent many years in the United States, said before entering the conclave.[1] Moreover, since the cardinals are forbidden from discussing the pope's successor while the pope is alive, there is no way to get a sense of who might be a favorite, except from Roman cocktail chatter, whispered rumors, and reading between the lines of some cardinal's homily.

√ Add to the mix the fact that there were so many diverse challenges facing the church at the 2005 conclave—no single issue stood out, such as resisting Soviet communism or implementing Vatican II or safeguarding the church in wartime—that the permutations seemed infinite, both to the cardinals themselves and to the *Vaticanisti*. "You cannot come up with a profile, then look around the room to see who fits," Husar said.

In this informational vacuum, the Vaticanologists did a remarkable job.

In several books and in his "Word from Rome" columns, the most prominent English-language Vatican-watcher, John Allen of the *National Catholic Reporter*, a liberal, widely honored U.S. weekly, elaborated any number of scenarios in the years leading up to John Paul's death. At one point Allen identified four ideological camps within the College of Cardinals, each reflecting its respective priorities: the Border Patrol, focused on maintaining Catholic identity; the Reform Party, intent on advancing the reforms of Vatican II; the Social Justice bloc; and the hard-line culture warriors in the "Integralist" camp. Allen also cited several criteria the cardinals would use to measure a cardinal for the papacy, among them age, nationality, linguistic talents, vision of the issues, and not least, someone who was *not* a member of the Roman Curia. Using these factors, Allen produced a general Ident-A-Kit image of a pope who would be between sixty-five and seventy-five years old, not from Rome but able to speak Italian, possessed of a strong public presence, and willing to loosen the reins of Vatican authority.

Naturally, there were so many factors and ideological blocs and different combinations, all of them in a constant state of flux, that over the years Allen came up with dozens of possible candidates based on the unending permutations of characters and camps. Although Allen is the author of a fine 2000 biography of Cardinal Ratzinger, he rarely included the prefect of the Congregation for the Doctrine of the Faith—whom he placed in the Border Patrol camp—in the *papabile* pool, for all the same completely understandable reasons that everyone else excluded Ratzinger.

Other Vatican observers tried to avoid the horse race and instead focused on issues more than personalities, yet with about as much success.

Writing a papal "job description" in the January/February issue of *Foreign Policy* magazine, Notre Dame church historian R. Scott Appleby cited three principal challenges for the church, and thus for the coming conclave: a "new and aggressive secularization" aided by globalization and hostile to traditional faith; the religious competition between Islam and Catholicism, as well as the potential for collaboration between the two traditions; and the revolution in biotechnology and the unforeseeable moral quandaries that genetic engineering will pose.

Papal biographer George Weigel cited almost the same trinity, which he said would determine the conclave's outcome: the collapse of Catholic practice in Europe (and the demographic collapse resulting from plummeting birthrates); the "clash of civilizations" between the Catholic West and radical Islam; and biotechnology. In the end, Weigel predicted, "the next conclave is going to be complex, difficult, probably lengthy—and perhaps quite surprising."[2]

Perhaps the most prescient analysis, however, was also the most parsimonious. In an *Atlantic Monthly* essay in September 2004, Paul Elie, the editor and writer on things Catholic, reviewed the boom in the Vaticanology field (and just among English-language pope-watchers; the Italian Vatican industry adds an almost impenetrable layer of fact and myth). Elie's lament was that all of the prognosticating by all these *Vaticanisti* was "a triumph of process over character" that missed the question that would outstrip all others in the minds of the cardinal-electors—the men who "will ask first of all how authentic the faith of that man of faith is—how high his hopes, how deep his thoughts. They will ponder his character, mindful that John Paul's character has shaped the Church worldwide for a quarter of a century. They will ask, What kind of believer is he?"

As Allen noted in his rejoinder to Elie, "My experience is that when I ask a cardinal, 'What are the criteria you will use to pick a candidate?' most don't respond in terms of 'how high his hopes, how deep his depths.' It's more common to start with whether or not the next pope should be an Italian, or what kind of background he's had as a diocesan bishop, or what approach he would take to the relationship with Islam." In other words, holiness was a given.

At that point, it didn't much matter. The welter of issues was so daunting, the roster of *papabile* so long, that one could focus on almost any cardinal and not be wrong.

Many naturally spoke of a turn to a Latin American pope, who would be the first pontiff from outside Europe since several African popes who ruled in the first centuries of the church. A modern-era African was also a favorite hypothesis—imagine the headlines!—with Nigerian cardinal Francis Arinze being the most likely possibility. Others hoped for an "Italian restoration," in the belief that Italians have a unique talent for governing the church, having done it for so long. There were also plenty of European neo-con candidates, several of them allies or former students of Ratzinger. (Americans are never considered *papabile* chiefly because of America's superpower role in the world—the same concern that helped keep Germans off the Throne of Saint Peter for the previous thousand years. The cardinals would prefer that the pope come from a smaller, less influential, country, so that the universal pastor is not overidentified with a particular national power. That is why, apart from the Italian home field advantage in the college, having Italian popes made geopolitical sense. It is also why the choice of a pope from Poland, which was subjugated by the Soviet Union at the time, was an attractive non-Italian alternative.)

And so it went. Betting agencies and office pools got into the act, which was nothing new. In the sixteenth century, gambling on the conclave was epidemic, to the point that in 1591, shortly after he was elected pope, Gregory XIV issued a bull, *Cogit Nos*, forbidding wagering on the papacy under pain of excommunication. It didn't work then, or in 2005. Several bookmakers and Web sites posted odds on dozens of candidates. One of the most entertaining examples was a graphic of tournament brackets modeled after the recently completed NCAA college basketball playoffs in the United States. The "Popapalooza 2005" tournament featured the "Sweet Sistine" of cardinal finalists in four brackets—Europe, Latin America, Africa-Asia, and Italy. The United States had no bracket, nor any candidates. Oddly, Cardinal Oscar Andres Rodriguez Maradiaga of Honduras was placed in the "Italy" bracket, and Duke University was in "Africa-Asia."

By the time the conclave began, such silliness may have been as insightful as any other prediction.

Through it all, rarely did Ratzinger merit a mention—until his homily at John Paul's funeral. That was Friday, April 8. From then until the cardinals went into conclave on Monday, April 18, Joseph Ratzinger would increasingly emerge on the radar screens of the cardinals, first as a viable candidate, then as a likely candidate, and finally as an inevitable candidate. Some of this momentum leaked out to the newspapers, but it was most obvious to the cardinal-electors themselves. Still, many of them did not believe it would happen, up to the moment Joseph Ratzinger crossed the threshold of votes. Nor did they necessarily want it to happen.

. . .

When a pope dies, the complex machinery of the papal transition automatically kick-starts a process carefully engineered over the centuries to maintain the propriety and sanctity of the election process.

All of the heads of the dicasteries, or Vatican departments, immediately resign their posts, with the support staff continuing on to maintain the necessary functioning of the bureaucracy. Only the cardinal camerlengo (Cardinal Eduardo Martinez Somalo), the vicar of the Diocese of Rome (Italian cardinal Camillo Ruini, who governs the diocese on behalf of the bishop of Rome), and the major penitentiary (American cardinal J. Francis Stafford), who must ensure that confessional matters are always attended to, retain their offices. No major decisions are made during the interregnum, and all decisions are considered provisional until a new pope confirms them.

It is the camerlengo who essentially runs the Holy See during the interregnum, summoning all the cardinals to Rome and organizing the conclave. At the death of Paul VI in 1978, the camerlengo was the imposing French cardinal, Jean-Marie Villot, who sent telegrams that read simply, "The Pope is dead. Come at once." In 2005, most of the cardinals heard about John Paul's death first from news reports, and a few were already in Rome, having been tipped that there would be no miraculous recovery for the pope. The College of Cardinals—often referred to as the Senate of the Church—has the power of governance during the *sede vacante,* but their authority is carefully prescribed. They cannot change the rules of the conclave, for example, or name new cardinals, or take any other important decision affecting the election process.

According to standing decrees, the pope is to be buried between the fourth and sixth day after his death, "except for special reasons." The huge crowds for John Paul's monumental wake almost caused the funeral to be delayed, but he was buried on the sixth day, just under the wire. At that point, the Catholic Church begins the *novemdiales,* or nine days of official mourning, with a requiem Mass for the deceased pontiff celebrated each day in St. Peter's Basilica by one of the cardinals.

In modern times, the conclave starts no sooner than fifteen days after a pope's death—that is, the day after the final requiem Mass—and no later than twenty days after the death. In the past, cardinals who were resident in Rome often used their proximity to engineer the papal election, convening the conclave before rivals or undesirable candidates could arrive.

The principal reason for instituting the delay in recent times was to allow far-flung cardinals to arrive in time, something that was difficult to do before intercontinental air travel. In 1878 the cardinal of Dublin did not even make it to Rome before Leo XIII was elected. Only at the conclave of 1903 did Baltimore cardinal James Gibbons become the first U.S. cardinal to cast a vote for pope, and that was only because he happened to be in Rome when Leo XIII died.

At the 1914 conclave, six of the sixty-five cardinals did not reach Rome in time (the interval between the death and the conclave was just ten days then). Two of the absentees were Americans, Cardinal Gibbons and Cardinal O'Connell of Boston. They sailed for Italy the same day they heard of the death of Pius X, and rented a car as soon as they embarked at Naples. But as they raced toward Rome, they heard the church bells ringing in the villages and realized that a new pope had already been elected. O'Connell was determined not to be denied the next time, and when Benedict XV died in 1922 he took a plane from Boston to New York (he was probably the first cardinal ever to fly) and jumped aboard an ocean liner that had delayed its departure to wait for him. He then took a fast boat from Brest, in France, bound for Naples, where a special train waited to take him to Rome. As he sped from the station in Rome, however, he was informed that the conclave had just ended. O'Connell was known for his temper, and his rage over this second missed opportunity was volcanic. As a result, the new pope, Pius XI, established a fifteen- to eighteen-day window for a conclave to start, which was later extended to twenty days.[3]

(Americans have never had great luck in papal politics. Detroit's Cardinal Edward Francis Mooney was the only American cardinal to make it to the 1958 conclave, but he died an hour before the cardinals entered the Sistine Chapel.)

Today, though most cardinals can get to Rome in a day, the two-week delay between the death of a pope and the conclave is perhaps more important because it is then that all of the cardinals, including those over eighty years old, take part in the daily closed-door meetings known as "general congregations." These general congregations begin almost immediately, as soon as a critical mass of cardinals are in Rome. In 2005, the general congregations began on Monday, April 4, two days after John Paul's death.

The general congregations take place in the synod hall inside the Vatican, a lecture hall with amphitheater seating, and they are designed to allow the cardinals to discuss anything they like regarding the priorities and challenges for the church. It is a way of talking about the next papacy without talking directly about the next pope, even though the last pope is dead. There is no overt politicking allowed, nor would it be considered proper. But these general congregations are crucial for letting the cardinals get to know each other, sound each other out about their chief concerns, and size up the *papabile* among them. They can do this by talking about issues that would obviously play to the strengths of a certain cardinal, or they can talk to each other at meals or during coffee breaks in the kind of conclave code that telegraphs a favorite without naming the candidate.

As it happens, the person delegated to run the general congregations is the dean of the College of Cardinals, who in 2005 was none other than Joseph Ratzinger.

So it was that, during the thirteen preconclave sessions, the entire college was called to order by Ratzinger, who then monitored their discussions and kept the meetings moving. By all accounts, Ratzinger did an excellent job. It was not surprising. He could speak so many languages so well that he could converse with most cardinals in their native tongue and help sort through any translation difficulties. He was also the one cardinal that almost everyone knew, and the one cardinal who knew almost everyone there—and he remembered their names—because they had all come through his office several times during their periodic visits to Rome. Ratzinger was the hub of the cardinals' fragile network, and thus the cardinals constantly looked to him for guidance.

As capable as Ratzinger was, however, there were serious problems with the general congregations that also redounded to Ratzinger's advantage, although not by his intent. One difficulty was that in John Paul's 1996 apostolic constitution updating the rules for the conclave, *Universi Dominici Gregis* (Shepherd of the Lord's Whole Flock), the pope wanted to be certain that the cardinals understood the conclave rules completely. Always one to follow the letter of the law, Ratzinger had the entire 14,000-word document read aloud, which took up many hours, especially since more than a few cardinals insisted on requesting a clarification on some arcane aspect or other of the constitution. This was apparently a great temptation for the over-eighty cardinals—more than fifty of them who, perhaps realizing they would not participate in the actual conclave, wanted to have their say when they could. In any case, it left many of the electors frustrated and drove a couple I spoke with to distraction. They felt the precious time could have been spent much more productively.

Moreover, at the 1978 conclave the general congregations had been organized more efficiently, with each day dedicated to a theme—such as relations with the communist countries, the challenges of Third World poverty, changes in the liturgy, and so on. In 2005, once the procedural housekeeping was finally over, the cardinals were allowed to speak for seven minutes each on whatever topic they felt important. While that was an admirable bit of openness,

several cardinals said it meant that the discussions were arbitrary and unfo-
cused, jumping from topic to topic without much chance for give-and-take
on a subject or a chance to reflect deeply about any particular issue. Also, the
octogenarian cardinals once again took the floor with great regularity, and did
not seem to feel bound by the seven-minute limit.

Of greatest concern, however, was the lack of adequate translators for the
general congregations. The internationalizing of the College of Cardinals, plus
the decline in the use of Latin in seminary training, has meant that Latin is no
longer the lingua franca of the church, even among the princes of the church.
Today, a hodgepodge of English and Spanish is the favored medium, but those
who know Italian—the "power language" of the Vatican and thus of church
politics—are the ones who can really negotiate their way through the Babel
of such gatherings. That leaves a lot of churchmen frozen out, however, especially prelates from the Third World. For much of the interregnum, the Vatican
was scrambling to find trustworthy clerics and religious who could provide
translations for the confidential meetings, but it was a case of too little, too
late. "About half of them understood what was being said, about half of them
didn't," one translator estimated. That hardly seems fair, or adequate to the
importance of the task of electing a pope.

That was also the case for the *prattiche*, an Italian word for the unofficial
kibitzing that goes on among cardinals over drinks or dinner. The *prattiche*
are indispensable to the politics of a papal election, and are where the nitty-
gritty takes place—where candidates are most likely to be named and their
pros and cons debated. And yet cardinals from Africa and Asia, in particular,
were cut out of much of this informal talk because they often had to stay in
religious houses far from the city center and the Vatican. They often were not
familiar with Rome, and they could not afford to stay in pricey hotels near the
Vatican, the way the European and North American cardinals could. This was
a source of great frustration to many of these cardinals, a de facto segregation
that should be corrected at the next conclave.

One simple solution would have been to lodge all the cardinals in the
Domus Sanctae Marthae, the $20 million motel-like residence built inside the
Vatican walls next to St. Peter's in 1996. The Domus Marthae was constructed
specifically to house the cardinals in a conclave, though since the only retirement route for a pope is death, raising any issue related to the conclave with a
living pontiff can become dicey. In presenting the idea for the Domus Marthae
to John Paul, the cardinal in charge of the Vatican city-state operations reportedly found himself bumbling about for alternate rationales for the residence

other than the obvious one: to make the cardinals more comfortable once John Paul was dead. The poor cardinal was rescued by Don Stanislao, who cut to the chase for the sake of the pope and the cardinal. John Paul was happy to endorse the idea.[4]

That a housing upgrade was necessary was beyond argument. The impression of the Vatican as a sumptuous residence where cosseted prelates sup on peacock brains is a persistent one, continually resuscitated by the mistaken equation of great art with comfy accommodations. But museums are great for touring, not living. Much of the Vatican is actually made up of large, drafty rooms often (though this is changing) afflicted with bad plumbing and balky elevators—charming but not surprising given the antiquity of the place. Ironically, the situation has always been worse when the cardinals gather in conclave. Since the conclave system and location has actually been an ad hoc affair for much of its existence—it was fixed at the Vatican and the Sistine Chapel only in the late nineteenth century—no thought was given to fixed accommodations for the cardinals. Moreover, for much of the past couple of centuries the Vatican has struggled to pay its bills, and the cost of a conclave forced economizing wherever possible.

The result was that every time a pope died there was a mad scramble to jury-rig cots and hang curtains so as to create some sort of sleeping arrangements for the cardinals in the alcoves and corridors around the Sistine Chapel. It was a miserable existence. So little forethought was given to the next conclave once a pope was elected that sometimes the Vatican donated the bedding and other furnishings to the poor, and the camerlengo for the next conclave had to start from scratch. As late as 1978 the facilities were insufficient. The first 1978 conclave, in August, was "an airless tomb," according to the late Cardinal Giuseppe Siri of Genoa. And the other amenities were lacking, from decent reading lamps to bathrooms. "The cardinals are almost all old, with prostate problems, tired—with a bathroom for every 10 people," Cardinal Silvio Oddi, who died in 2001, once told an Italian magazine. "I slept near the toilet, but I saw these poor old people crossing 70-meter corridors to get to the bathroom, which they found occupied. Such pain, and what a humiliation."[5]

As always, the beds were a trial of the back and the spirit, and the food was usually terrible. There was a certain esprit de corps created by the dormitory experience, but that was too often outweighed by the potentially severe discomforts. "Off we go to prison," Cardinal Achille Ratti said as he headed into the conclave of 1922 that would see him elected Pius XI.[6]

With the Vatican's finances finally stabilized in the 1990s, and with the College of Cardinals growing to the point that the previous housing arrangements would have been simply unworkable, the pope's advisers finally got smart and built the Domus Marthae, which features 105 two-room suites and 26 single rooms. As conclaves are so rare, the residence serves as a kind of Vatican hotel for important guests most of the time, but it is vacated for the cardinals and sealed, like the Sistine Chapel, when the pope dies.

The problem was that the cardinals did not go to the Domus Marthae until Sunday evening, April 17, twenty-four hours before the conclave, so in the end they wound up spending forty-eight hours inside a residence expressly built to enhance their deliberations. (The rooms are distributed by lottery, and Joseph Ratzinger was one of the few cardinals who wound up with a single room, on the fourth floor, and not a full suite. He did not seem to mind.) Many cardinals from the developing world and from Europe and North America did not understand why better use was not made of the Domus Marthae by having everyone live together for the two weeks of the general congregations *and* the conclave itself. Nor was any explanation given by the Vatican. By not housing all the cardinals in the Domus Marthae, it reinforced the hometown influence of those cardinals, namely the curialists, who lived at the Vatican and continued to stay in their own apartments and serve as hometown hubs for the college's networking system.

Another factor aiding local cardinals and the cardinals who frequent Rome and speak Italian was their contacts with the Italian media and the Vatican's permanent press corps. This relationship resulted in a disproportionate amount of news coverage highlighting the comments or leaks from American and European cardinals and Vatican officials, especially the Italians. While the cardinals were not to talk directly about the content of the general congregations, they could put their message out to the public by talking to reporters about their own agendas and interests for the next papacy. After several days of this, complaints from the cardinals reached the point that many of them—reportedly led by those from Africa and Asia who felt their voices were being drowned out—asked the entire body of cardinals to declare a self-imposed press blackout for the rest of the general congregations. (The conclave would be secret as a matter of course.) The cardinals agreed, and from John Paul's funeral on Friday, April 8, until after the election on April 19, they did not speak to the media—at least not on the record. But it was telling that the blame for the self-censure was initially placed by Italian media at Ratzinger's feet. In reality, it seems Ratzinger did not push for the ban, and in fact, according to Cardinal Danneels of Belgium, Ratzinger objected on the grounds that speaking to the press should be considered a human right.

But the cardinals voted for the ban, and Ratzinger went along, following the rules, as he always did. Indeed, so scrupulous was Ratzinger that one morning after John Paul died, Ratzinger's second-in-command at the Congregation for the Doctrine of the Faith, Archbishop Angelo Amato, arrived at the Holy Office as usual but was surprised to find Cardinal Ratzinger waiting patiently in the antechamber of his own office. A perplexed Amato hurried to greet his boss, who explained to Amato that upon the death of the pope, Ratzinger, like all heads of the Vatican offices, had resigned his office to await reconfirmation by a new pope. "With admirable humility he asked my permission to enter his office," Amato recalled, adding that from then on he made sure he arrived early in the morning so that he could accompany Cardinal Ratzinger inside without Ratzinger having to ask to enter the office he had held for nearly twenty-four years.[7]

On Monday, April 11, Cardinal Bernard Law provided a couple days of unfavorable headlines when he was selected by the Vatican to celebrate the fourth requiem Mass for John Paul at the papal altar in St. Peter's Basilica. Despite his awful baggage, church sources said Law apparently gave no thought to ceding the prestigious role to another cardinal. He was the only American so honored. "We should be able to focus on the Holy Father's death, but Cardinal Law's presence is putting the sex abuse scandal front and center," Barbara Blaine, a victim of clergy abuse and president of the Survivors Network of Those Abused by Priests. "When he puts himself out in that public position, it's rubbing salt in open wounds." When Blaine and another victim spoke with media in St. Peter's Square while the Mass was going on inside, police pushed them off the Vatican's grounds.

Despite the restrictions on speaking to the media, news of course filtered out, usually to the Italian press, which sometimes seems like an unofficial congregation in the Roman Curia. As Cardinal Theodore E. McCarrick of Washington joked after the conclave, "It was the newspapers that were telling us how Ratzinger was a favorite, so we knew. . . . The Holy Spirit may even speak through newspapers." For several days leading up to the conclave, the Italian newspapers were citing a firm bloc of support for Ratzinger at forty and perhaps fifty votes. On Saturday, April 16, which was also Joseph Ratzinger's seventy-eighth birthday, the Rome newspaper *Il Tempo* had his vote count up to fifty-nine cardinals—a remarkably precise figure, if indeed it had any meaning at all. Bergoglio was cited as a strong alternate, "even though he is a Jesuit." (No member of the large and influential Society of Jesus has ever been elected pope.)

The rumor mill was also whirring, as it always does during the conclave, with last-minute gossip planted in last-ditch efforts to influence the cardinals one way or another. Most stories were little more than preconclave pasquinades, but some were more dangerous. Cardinal Scola was said to have been treated at a psychiatric clinic in Switzerland (not true), while Cardinal Schönborn of Vienna, an acolyte of Ratzinger and a man never known for his personal touch, suddenly found his distant temperament described as "mood swings" symptomatic of clinical depression (also false). Much was made of Scottish cardinal Keith O'Brien's description of Cardinal Dionigi Tettamanzi of Milan as "that wee fat guy"—even though poor Cardinal O'Brien was only repeating an observation by his late compatriot, Cardinal Thomas Winning.

At one point, news reports announced that Cardinal Ivan Dias of Bombay, one of the most prominent of the Asian *papabile,* was suffering from diabetes—which was news to Cardinal Dias. "I am surprised to find I have diabetes," the cardinal told a friend. One cardinal was reportedly being downgraded because he was said to wear a surgical corset.

A common and slightly less Machiavellian way to doom a papal candidacy is simply to boost a cardinal as a front-runner—which there was plenty of time to do given the long decline of John Paul II. Cardinals do not like presumptive nominees: "He who enters the conclave a pope, leaves a cardinal," as the Roman adage goes. Cardinal Arinze, who was repeatedly mentioned by friends and foes alike as the best African candidate—he is Nigerian but worked for more than twenty years in the Roman Curia—was incensed at what he saw as a campaign by those who continually threw his name into the ring. "It is really vicious, the way the cardinals are doing this, and on purpose!" an indignant Arinze told a friend a year before John Paul's death. "They want to 'burn' me by calling me *papabile.*" Arinze did not exactly tamp down the speculation, however, with his frequent travels around the world, his widely covered lectures, and the 2003 publication of a glossy autobiography, titled *God's Invisible Hand,* that struck some as uncomfortably akin to a campaign pitch.

To be sure, some do campaign, in their subtle ways. Like princes of a royal house, cardinals have been described as men in a state of "splendid waiting," and there is no doubt that some don't like to wait, instead finding ways to put their name out there, yet without appearing to campaign. Cardinal Rodriguez Maradiaga, a mediagenic, multilingual Honduran, was so popular at one point that the satirical American weekly, *The Onion,* ran a preconclave photo of a smiling Maradiaga under a headline that read, "Cocky Pope-Hopeful Ready To Make Some Changes Around Vatican."[8]

Such machinations and rumors made it all the more difficult to interpret the growing media reports on the eve of the 2005 conclave that claimed Ratzinger had the conclave virtually wrapped up. Was this a show of force by the Ratzinger camp to scare off pretenders? Or was it a counterstrategem to rally opposition?

In retrospect, that Ratzinger emerged as a favorite in the run-up to the conclave was not as surprising as it seemed at the time.

As John Paul grew weaker and less visible, Joseph Ratzinger was the voice of the Vatican who stood out by standing to the side. He was not spending all of his time in the papal apartment or at Gemelli Hospital, having his picture taken for the evening newscast or talking to reporters about the pope's health or speculating about the pope's fate. Instead, he was presiding at major church events or giving lectures that elucidated the challenges for the church in the third millennium—and his vision of what the church needed to do to address those challenges.

One of the first signs of his ascent came six weeks before the pope's death, on February 24, at the funeral of Monsignor Luigi Giussani, the founder of Communion and Liberation. CL, as the group is known, is one of a number of so-called movements that emerged in the postwar, post-1960s era of European Catholicism. Ratzinger was tabbed to preside over the funeral Mass in Milan's huge cathedral, instead of the archbishop of the city, Cardinal Dionigi Tettamanzi, a roly-poly eminence who tried to model himself on Pope John XXIII, which he was not, and who was seen as having done all but declare himself as the great Italian hope of the conclave. Ratzinger's homily was a beautifully rendered homage to Giussani and the faith, and it brought great applause from the enormous crowd of mourners. When Tettamanzi added his own remarks, the congregation was silent.

A month later, on Good Friday and nine days before John Paul died, Ratzinger was given the signal honor of standing in for John Paul at the traditional Way of the Cross procession around the Coliseum—an occasion he used for a striking and dark denouncement of the "filth in the church," which he said, "often seems like a boat about to sink." The day before John Paul died, on April 1, Ratzinger gave an important speech at the village of Subiaco in the mountains outside Rome, where in the sixth century Saint Benedict founded his first monastery, the seed of the community that would do so much to preserve Christendom and Western civilization. Speaking in a chilly convent there, Ratzinger said the "disdain" for God in the West today has led civilization once again "to the edge of the abyss." The Subiaco address was naturally forgotten amid the mourning for John Paul, but Ratzinger's profile with the public and the cardinals only elevated further with his April 8 funeral oration for the deceased pontiff.

Then, on Monday April 18, the cardinals emerged from the isolation of their general congregations for one last public event, the Mass for the Election of the Roman Pontiff, celebrated at the papal altar in St. Peter's Basilica. The chief celebrant and homilist would once again be the dean of the College of Cardinals, Joseph Ratzinger. As the cardinals began arriving for the Mass, I stood off to one side in the press pen, watching as each of the prelates passed in front of the altar, giving a brief genuflection before going off to vest for the liturgy. When Cardinal Ratzinger entered, wearing a long black trench coat, he stopped before the altar and stood in intense contemplation for a full minute, even as several other cardinals passed behind him. Then he made the sign of the cross and walked quickly into the sacristy.

The Mass was as solemn as the occasion. As the great liturgy unfolded with resplendent processions and sublime chants, so ornate yet at its core so familiar, there was a recognition among the cardinals and the congregants that the future of the church would be in play in the coming hours and days. And there was an expectation that Cardinal Ratzinger would try to put the moment in perspective, to offer the church and the world a sign of comfort amid the tension.

Yet as his homily proceeded, Ratzinger's words grew increasingly, almost alarmingly, forceful. Wearing his large reading glasses and coughing periodically, Ratzinger maintained his even, almost academic tone, reading his text in a voice that was slightly higher and thinner than normal. But his words were uncompromising, as he cited Saint Paul's warning against being "carried about by every wind of doctrine."

"How many winds of doctrine have we known in recent decades, how many ideological currents, how many ways of thinking?" Ratzinger asked ominously. "The small boat of the thought of many Christians has often been tossed about by these waves—flung from one extreme to another: from Marxism to liberalism, even to libertinism; from collectivism to radical individualism; from atheism to a vague religious mysticism; from agnosticism to syncretism and so forth. Every day new sects spring up, and what Saint Paul says about human deception and the trickery that strives to entice people into error comes true."

You could see the surprise on the faces of the cardinal's listeners, and also a question: Where was he going with all this? Would he find some sense of joy or hope? But Ratzinger barreled on, undeterred: "Today, having a clear faith based on the Creed of the Church is often labeled as fundamentalism. Whereas relativism, that is, letting oneself be 'tossed here and there, carried about by every wind of doctrine,' seems the only attitude that can cope with modern times. We are building a dictatorship of relativism"—the sharp phrase was like the crack of a whip in the huge sanctuary—"that does not recognize anything as definitive and whose ultimate goal consists solely of one's own ego and desires."

What Ratzinger offered was a challenge to his listeners to live an "adult faith" worthy of Christ. He offered no solace, no resting place for the emotions, and his line about the "dictatorship of relativism" became the media's "money quote," as he knew it would.

As I stared at Ratzinger, I was dumbfounded by the language and tone of his sermon. Whether he was campaigning or not, his words were so dark, so full of foreboding, that they seemed to confirm the caricature that his allies took such pains to dispel. That he was correct in many of the ills he diagnosed became almost irrelevant. Yes, there was a great deal of shallow belief in modern life, and too many pseudo-religious ideologies had produced more ruin than redemption. But the church also bears burdens of history that require honest self-reflection. Moreover, there was also much good in the world, and in the church. Was this jeremiad the sum of the Christian message? As a surprised colleague remarked when Ratzinger finished, "Where was the Easter in that?"

Good question. Behind us, under a side altar in a sealed glass case, lay the earthly remains of John XXIII, "Good Pope John," the pastoral peasant who forty-three years earlier, from the same spot where Joseph Ratzinger was speaking, opened the Second Vatican Council with one of the most memorable homilies ever heard in the great church. "In the daily exercise of our pastoral office," Pope John said, "we sometimes have to listen, much to our regret, to voices of persons who, though burning with zeal, are not endowed with too much sense of discretion or measure. In these modern times they can see nothing but prevarication and ruin. They say that our era, in comparison with past eras, is getting worse, and they behave as though they had learned nothing from history, which is, none the less, the teacher of life."

"We feel," he said, "we must disagree with those prophets of gloom, who are always forecasting disaster, as though the end of the world were at hand."

Everything, Pope John concluded, "even human differences, leads to the greater good of the Church."

They were inspiring, life-changing words, and yet as I glanced now at the corpse of Pope John lying behind me, his fingers clutching a Rosary, his waxy face seemed more lifeless than ever.

Even Australian cardinal George Pell, a bully supporter of Ratzinger, was a bit startled by the "blunt and provocative" words from the German cardinal, particularly the "dictatorship of relativism" line. "It is an evocative phrase which frightened some and provoked confusion in others," said Pell, a former Australian league footballer with an enormous frame and a presence—many say an ego—to match. "When I heard these words . . . my first instinct was to think that Cardinal Ratzinger obviously did not want to be pope. I wondered whether he thought a few home truths would not go astray on this final occasion when he was at center stage."[9]

If Pell felt that way, it was no wonder that many others looked at Ratzinger's sermon as the political equivalent of the "scream" speech that doomed Howard Dean after his bitter loss in the 2004 Democratic primary in Iowa. Now another dean, this time of the College of Cardinals, seemed to be taking the same exit line. Yet this time the campaign would take a different turn, and within just a few hours, when the cardinals solemnly proceeded into the Sistine Chapel.

Now "the Ratzinger solution," as the long-standing campaign was called by his supporters, could finally be put into effect.

Chapter Four

SECRETS OF THE
CONCLAVE

The history of papal elections can be read most simply as the story of a centuries-long effort to make a papal election safe for the Holy Spirit, the *grande elettore* who ideally guides the choice of the pope. And for most of Catholicism's two millennia, that process had nothing to do with either cardinals or conclaves.

During the church's first thousand years, the pope was elected like any bishop, usually by the local clergy, often with input from laypeople—which usually meant the city's ruling families. Even into the Middle Ages the new bishop was often approved (or rejected) by the vox populi when he introduced himself to the masses. On at least two occasions, the election was decided when a white dove landed on the right hand or shoulder of a cleric, who was then acclaimed as the choice of the Holy Spirit. With such obvious approbation from on high, how could he not be the pope?[1]

In time, the Bishop of Rome, the successor of Saint Peter, came to be recognized across Western Christianity for his primacy over the entire church (the once-common title of "pope," from the Greek word for father, was not reserved exclusively to the Bishop of Rome until Pope Gregory VII did so in the eleventh century), and as the pope became more important, the temptation for secular powers to control the papal election naturally increased. That led the church to gradually restrict the papal electors first to the clergy of Rome, and then to a select group of Roman priests and bishops known as cardinals (the name may have come from the Latin *cardo*, meaning "hinge," indicating their important administrative functions). Only in 1059 did Pope Nicholas II rule that cardinals have the primary right to elect a pope, and a century later, in 1179, the Third Lateran Council set a two-thirds vote as the minimum threshold for a valid papal election.

The conclave (the word comes from the Latin *cum* and *clavis*, "with a key," as in "to lock up") was not instituted until the thirteenth century, and the reasons were essentially twofold: to keep the cardinals locked in and to keep everyone else locked out.

As with so many sacred traditions in the church, the conclave was a pragmatic solution to a messy crisis. For nearly three years, from 1268 to 1271, the church was without a pope because the fractious cardinals could not agree on a candidate. The election was being held in Viterbo, a town near Rome, and after such a long time without a pontiff, the townspeople got fed up, locked the cardinals in a house, and then removed the roof, exposing them to the elements in order to hasten their decision. (The idea for removing the roof supposedly originated with an English cardinal, who joked that it would make it easier for the Holy Spirit to enter. That was the first time the Holy Spirit was mentioned in connection with the papal election.)

After two cardinals died under the harsh conditions, a makeshift roof was installed, but the coercion had the desired effect, and the cardinals finally chose a pope, Gregory X. Pope Gregory was as scandalized as everyone else by the delay and confusion associated with his election, so he called a council at Lyons that formalized the procedure of a conclave, in which the cardinal-electors would be locked up, with no communication with the outside world, until they fulfilled their duty. As a further spur to their deliberations, the council decreed that the cardinals would be given a single plate of food and bowl of soup each per day, and that after five days without a successful outcome, the rations would be reduced to bread and water, and of course a little wine.

This basic template for choosing a pope—an election by cardinals enclosed in a conclave who must reach a two-thirds supermajority—has remained in place ever since, with a few tweaks and travails here and there.

One of the more recent traditions, oddly enough, is that of holding the election in the Vatican, and precisely in the Sistine Chapel. Of 265 popes, in fact, just 24 were elected in the surroundings that usually come to mind when one thinks of a conclave, though all popes since 1878 have been elected inside the chapel. The thirteenth-century decrees of the Council of Lyons stated that an election was to be held in the city where the pope had died (popes often journeyed around southern Europe in those days), and in later centuries wars and political upheavals frequently forced the conclave to be held outside Rome.

The last conclave to take place outside the Eternal City was in 1800, on the island of San Giorgio in Venice. For much of the nineteenth century, conclaves were held in the Quirinal Palace in Rome, built as a residence for the popes. After the establishment of Italy as a nation-state in 1860, and the subsequent takeover of Rome from the papacy in 1870, Italy's secular leaders took over the Quirinal, forcing the popes to confine themselves to the Vatican and to find a better site for the conclave.

The Sistine Chapel hosted conclaves as soon as it was redone by Pope Julius II and repainted by Michelangelo in the early 1500s. The chapel was actually a fortress—a telling detail—named for the uncle of Julius II, Pope Sixtus V, who commissioned its construction in 1475. Michelangelo painted the famous Old Testament frescoes in the vault in the first decade of the sixteenth century, and two decades later he returned to paint the *Last Judgment* on the altar wall. In 1513 Leo X became the first pope elected in the Sistine Chapel, and then no conclave was held there until Urban VIII was chosen in 1623. There was also a century-long gap between 1775 and 1878.

The Sistine Chapel seemed like a natural location when Pius IX died in 1878. But so uncertain were relations between the Vatican and the Italian government that some consideration was given to holding the conclave in Malta, the island nation off the coast of Sicily, or even of floating the cardinals into the Vatican city-state in hot-air balloons so they would not have to touch the soil of the anticlerical Italian nation.[2]

In the end, the conclave was held in the Sistine Chapel, where it has been held ever since. In his 1996 decree on the papal election system, Pope John Paul II declared that every conclave should be held there henceforth. But in one of his last poems, simply titled *Judgment,* John Paul went further than any mere decree, virtually consecrating the chapel as the sacred site for conclaves and, with his powerful verse and reminiscences of the 1978 conclaves, reiterating in words for the cardinal-electors the fear of God that Michelangelo depicted in the frescoes of the Last Judgment:

> *Those entrusted with the legacy of the keys*
> *Gather here, letting themselves be enfolded*
> *By the Sistine's colors,*
> *By the vision left to us by Michelangelo—*
> *So it was in August, and again in October,*
> *In the memorable year of the two Conclaves,*
> *And so it will be once more, when the time comes,*

After my death.
Michelangelo's vision must then speak to them.

John Paul concludes with the potent reminder to the cardinals that "*Omnes nuda et aperta sunt ante oculos Eius*" (all is bared and open before the eyes of God). And in his closing words, the dying pontiff assures them that God will direct their minds to the one who is to be chosen: "He will point him out."

The actual voting also proceeds according to a well-defined system. Once the cardinals are inside the Sistine Chapel, they place their hand on the Gospels and "promise, pledge and swear" to support whoever is elected pope, and above all to maintain secrecy regarding the proceedings on pain of excommunication. The cardinals then listen to a final meditation on their solemn duty by an over-eighty cardinal—in 2005 the task fell to Czech cardinal Tomás Spidlík—who then departs, leaving the cardinals to finally get down to the work of electing a pope.

In past centuries popes were elected by acclamation, a now rarely used option by which the cardinals, possessed by the Spirit, unanimously declare one of their number the new pope. There was also an option of having a deadlocked conclave delegate authority to a committee of cardinals who would choose the successor. Pope Gregory XV banned acclamation in 1621, and in his 1996 decree Pope John Paul II reaffirmed that ban and also ruled out the option of election by delegation. Significantly, John Paul also restated a rule, apparently begun by Paul VI, of allowing for election by a simple majority if the conclave remains deadlocked after a certain number of ballots—thirty-four under John Paul's rules. Because the conclave rules stipulate that there can be two ballots in the morning and two in the afternoon, with a day off for meditation and prayer every three days, the option of moving to a simple majority (which the cardinals would decide with a majority vote) would not be possible until more than two weeks had passed, an exceedingly long time for a modern conclave. (The average length of the eight conclaves in the twentieth century was three days.)

Given the amount of time cardinals spend away from home after counting up the time for the pope's funeral plus the general congregations, it was generally assumed that the 2005 conclave would be shorter rather than longer. Also, the cardinals prefer to move quickly because a lengthy conclave might signal a divided conclave, which could be seen as undermining the authority of whoever is elected pope. Still, the complexity of the issues facing the cardinals and the lack of a clear favorite seemed to favor a conclave of at least several days.

Moreover, the conclave of 2005 was unlike any other. With the cardinals living comfortably in the Domus Marthae, and with the possibility of a simple majority being able to control the conclave in time, there was speculation that the conclave could go for two weeks, with a determined minority preventing a two-thirds threshold and thereby forcing the majority to grant concessions. The other, more likely, scenario, in light of the simple majority option, is that a candidate who attracted a cohesive bloc of voters could lead the rest of the electors to jump on board once they realized that dislodging such a bloc would take an extraordinary effort, which could seriously divide the conclave and weaken the next pope.

In short, the election of a pope is less a divine system and more of an evolving process that has by popular legend become fixed in the public imagination as a tradition as eternal as the papacy itself.

One challenge that has remained constant is maintaining the secrecy of the conclave. As church historian Christopher M. Bellitto has written, during the Middle Ages and the Renaissance, servants who were allowed inside to attend to the cardinals' needs were known to scribble vote tallies on the bottoms of dirty dishes, which they smuggled outside to the waiting crowd (and to bookies). "In 1549," Bellitto notes, "the emperor Charles V bragged that he was so well informed on what was happening in the conclave that he knew when the cardinals used their chamber pots."[3] Such intelligence was crucial because European monarchs often influenced, or at times even rigged, the conclave to ensure the outcome most advantageous to them politically. The most common and enduring tactic was to invoke the "right of exclusion," by which a monarch would have a friendly cardinal announce to the conclave that a certain candidate was unacceptable to that king or emperor, a move that usually doomed the prospective candidate. Popes banned the secular blackball in the nineteenth century, but remarkably, the practice endured up to the conclave of 1903, when the cardinal-archbishop of Krakow—a predecessor of Karol Wojtyla—excluded an Italian *papabile* who was unpalatable to the Austro-Hungarian emperor, Franz Joseph. The tactic worked, barely, but the empire collapsed in World War I, and it is almost inconceivable that exclusion would ever work again.

Still, governments take a keen interest in the outcome. The CIA learned the outcome within minutes of the election of Pope Paul VI in 1963, well before anyone else outside the conclave. Today, the media probably poses as great a challenge. Even in 1922 a photographer was discovered just before the conclave was sealed, and a reporter's scheme to masquerade as a waiter was also foiled at the last moment.[4]

At the 2005 conclave, the Vatican went to unprecedented lengths to stop information from leaking out. Apart from barring the cardinals from bringing in cell phones, pagers, and other electronic devices, the Vatican also built a temporary false floor in the Sistine Chapel that was chockablock with sophisticated jamming equipment. On a preconclave tour for reporters, security officials challenged the journalists to try their cell phones, which in fact didn't seem to work. Jamming signals were broadcast around the Domus Marthae, which sits on the other flank of St. Peter's Basilica (on the left, as you face the basilica) from the Sistine Chapel (on the right). As the cardinals arrived at the Domus Marthae on Sunday evening, several of them tried to open the blinds that shut out all light, only to find that the windows and shutters were sealed with the same ribbons and wax seals that had been placed on the papal apartments after John Paul's death. ("With the lack of regular light, I caught a cold," grumbled Toronto's Cardinal Aloysius Ambrozic, who apparently did not appreciate the significant upgrades in the accommodations from 1978.)[5]

The minibuses that shuttled the cardinals to and from the Sistine Chapel were accompanied by security officials who made sure no service workers on the Vatican grounds made any contact with the electors. (A few cardinals—Cardinal Walter Kasper among them, reportedly—liked to walk to the Sistine Chapel, perhaps showing off their robust health, but also making the security forces nervous.)

All the security in the world can only do so much, however. Up until the early twentieth century, cardinals frequently recorded their memories of the conclave in diaries that found their way into the newspapers, often after the cardinal's death.

Recent popes have tried to halt that practice as well, with varying degrees of success. John Paul II explicitly banned any release of vote tallies, even after the conclave, by any elector—a ban whose value is questioned by many who feel that the secrecy feeds as many rumors as it stops, as well as leaving history the poorer. But the priority for the Vatican is to bolster the new pope's aura of authority and sense of divine inevitability, so there is a concerted effort to make any election appear as close to universal acclamation as possible. That was the case after the election of Cardinal Ratzinger, as many of his allies intimated that he had received more than 100 out of 115 votes, perhaps close to 110, in an overwhelming victory that they argued should put the progressives to flight for good. Such a tally would also portray the handful of holdouts as sore losers who were out of step with the will of the Holy Spirit.

Yet information always leaks out, even from a conclave, and my own interviews with several cardinals and Vatican insiders, as well as other journalistic accounts, indicated a more nuanced election than either the speed of the vote or the public comments from cardinals afterward indicated.

But it was the emergence in September of a detailed diary of the 2005 conclave that seemed to definitively recast the election, fleshing out what had been educated guesses and pointing toward some interesting scenarios for the next election.

For all the drama that everyone outside the conclave gins up about the election, the actual process inside the chapel can be so ritualized that the cardinals struggle to keep busy. In fact, the book detailing all the procedures for electing a pope, the *Ordo Rituum Conclavis* (Rites of the Conclave), runs to 343 pages. "Actually, if you could watch what happens inside, you'd be bored to tears," the late Austrian cardinal Franz König once said.[6] Contrary to popular mythology, a conclave is not a partisan caucus; there is no politicking or debating inside the chapel. The atmosphere is one of prayer and reflection, with some quiet small talk. "I can only say that I recall a climate of intense recollection—almost mystical—that was present at those sessions," said Argentine cardinal Jorge Mario Bergoglio. "We were all conscious of being nothing but instruments, to serve divine providence in electing a proper successor for John Paul II." But it is also a laborious procedure, since each elector (especially with the record number in 2005) must walk up with his ballot, pray briefly and recite an oath, and then all wait while the votes are counted and triple-checked and the results announced.

After the conclave of August 1978, Cardinal Karol Wojtyla was ready when he returned in October, bringing into the Sistine Chapel several academic journals, including one on Marxist thought, which he was reading when he was elected.[7] In 2005, Cardinal Murphy-O'Connor must have been expecting a long conclave, because he planned on packing a Victorian novel or two. "It'll be a sort of Brontë. Or Jane Austen."

Cardinal Ratzinger undoubtedly had books to read, which is his favorite hobby after piano playing, a diversion that was not possible. But he also has a sweet tooth, one of his few weaknesses, if it could be called that. In fact, every year on his birthday, members of Memores Domini, a small community of laymen and -women who have consecrated to lives of virginity and prayer, make strudel for the prefect. With all the transition hubbub, and with the cardinals cut off from most contact and about to enter the enclosure of the conclave, the community forgot all about the strudel until they received a phone call late on the night of April 16, the cardinal's seventy-eighth birthday and two days before conclave. It was Cardinal Ratzinger, wondering if he could still get the strudel. The community mobilized in the middle of the night, and Ratzinger took strudel with him into the conclave. (After he became pope, Benedict rewarded the community by asking Memores Domini to look after his needs in the papal household.)[8]

Following the morning's Mass and Ratzinger's electrifying sermon, the cardinals proceeded into the chapel at 4:30 PM. They took their assigned seats and sang the ninth-century hymn *Veni, Creator Spiritus* (Come, Creator Spirit), and then collectively, and finally individually, took an oath of secrecy. For the first time, this was all broadcast live on television. Then, at 5:24 PM, Archbishop Piero Marini, the papal master of ceremonies, ordered everyone out with the traditional formulation, "*Extra omnes*"—a phrase that is usually written with a declarative exclamation point, but which Marini spoke quite softly. The death of John Paul, whom Marini had served so closely and devotedly for so long, had deeply grieved the good-natured liturgist, and it was fitting that after he closed the door on the conclave, the assembled cardinals gave him a round of applause.

Then, with everyone out and the TV cameras off, they got down to business. The cardinals in their crimson cassocks sat at twelve tables arranged in two rows on each side of the chapel. Three cardinals are chosen by lot each morning and afternoon to act as "scrutineers," or vote-counters. Three others are chosen to act as *infirmarii* to collect the ballots of any cardinals in the conclave who are too sick to come to the Sistine Chapel. (None were needed this time.) Finally, three others are chosen to act as "revisers," who review the work done by the scrutineers.

Each cardinal-elector has paper for noting the tallies as they are read out, and for every *scrutinio* they are given a small rectangular ballot on which the words "*Eligo in summum pontificem*" (I elect as supreme pontiff) is printed at the top with a space below to write the name of the man they think should be pope. The cardinals are instructed to disguise their handwriting so that the vote-counters will not know who voted for whom. After writing the name, the cardinals fold the ballots in half and march up to the front of the chapel in order of seniority, holding the papers up so that they can be seen. At the altar beneath Michelangelo's fearsome Christ separating the damned from the saved, each cardinal kneels in brief prayer, then rises and says, "I call as my witness Christ the Lord who will be my judge, that my vote is given to the one who before God I think should be elected." He places his ballot on a small plate called a paten that sits atop an urn, and then tips the plate so that the ballot falls in—a procedure designed to keep a cardinal from casting two ballots.

The scrutineers then go through a lengthy process of checking and rechecking and counting the ballots, reading the name on each ballot aloud. (With 115 electors in the 2005 conclave, a cardinal needed 77 votes to become the next Roman pontiff.) Only one written record of the vote total of each session is allowed. It is prepared by the camerlengo and approved by three cardinal assistants at the end of the conclave, and is given to the new pope, who places it into the Vatican secret archives where it remains sealed unless opened with the express permission of the pontiff.

The final task of the cardinal-scrutineers is to pierce each ballot with a threaded needle so that all the used ballots can be bundled together. At the end of a morning or afternoon session of voting—usually two rounds, if no one is elected on the first ballot of the session—all the ballots and any notes the cardinals have taken are bundled together and burned in the chapel's special stove.

Traditionally, wet straw was mixed in the stove with the ballots to produce black smoke, which told the expectant crowd that no pope had been elected and they would have to wait a bit longer. When a pope was elected, dry straw was mixed in to produce white smoke.

Interestingly, though the white smoke signal is probably the best-known tradition associated with a papal election, to the point that it has become a universal cliché, it is apparently a relatively recent addition to conclave rituals. Ballots have been burned since the 1417 conclave, but not to signal an election. That was generally done—when the election was held in Rome—by the ringing of church bells and cannons firing from nearby Castel Sant'Angelo. In fact, smoke was only referred to as a conclave signal in nineteenth-century accounts, and then only as the sign of an unsuccessful ballot because the votes were being burned. When there was no smoke at the appointed time, the crowd then assumed a pope had been chosen.

The first mention of white smoke indicating a successful outcome was at the 1914 conclave, but the method has always been more unreliable than helpful. In every conclave thereafter, the wet straw/dry straw trick produced confusion, and for the 1963 conclave the Vatican used black flare cartridges obtained from the Italian military that the cardinals threw into the stove. But in the first 1978 conclave, Vatican officials forgot about the flares, and the election of John Paul I was announced with black smoke that only later turned white.

It is rumored that for the second 1978 conclave the cardinals used chemical additives.[9]

That such a recent development as the white smoke could become so firmly implanted in the collective imagination is in one sense a tribute to the creative influence of the Catholic sensibility. But in another sense it is a cautionary tale of how that same sensibility can quickly transform ad hoc solutions into hallowed rites that cannot be questioned without incurring accusations of dissent.

In any event, by 2005 the Vatican was determined to get the smoke thing right. They had a newfangled attachment for the stove and separate canisters to produce either black or white smoke. Leaving it to the cardinals, however, would have been like leaving a new VCR with no directions to your grandfather and his buddies. So the Vatican arranged for technicians to come in after the votes and fire up the stove. On the first ballot Monday evening, no one received the necessary two-thirds—no surprise—and so they burned the ballots with the black cartridges. But not only did the smoke come out more gray than black, the flue apparently didn't draw very well and smoke wafted through the Sistine Chapel—and up to Michelangelo's glorious frescoes. "It's a good thing there were no art historians inside," Austrian cardinal Christoph Schönborn told an Italian newspaper. "They should have practiced this," agreed Los Angeles cardinal Roger Mahony.[10]

The smoke troubles would continue until a pope was elected, and with the speed of the conclave, the cardinals wouldn't have many opportunities to get better at that aspect of the process.

On the first ballot that Monday evening, Cardinal Ratzinger received forty-seven votes, according to the diary of the anonymous cardinal—thirty short of the two-thirds needed for election. The diary was most likely penned by an Italian, as it was written in Italian, and it was published in the respected Italian foreign affairs journal, *Limes,* in September. The magazine said the diary-writer knew he was breaking the oath of secrecy but felt it was more important that history get the story straight. Naturally, the anonymous cardinal could have any number of motives for publishing the conclave details, not least of which is bringing the new pope down a notch by showing that his vote total was not as high as assumed.

But the *Limes* editors said they confirmed the details with other cardinals, and the diarist's version of events also comports with other reports, both at the time and that emerged in the months after the conclave, often in snippets dropped here and there. The diary is valuable for confirming what I and others were hearing, but also for providing the internal atmospherics of the conclave and debunking some other myths about the votes.

One of those was the persistent report that the great hope of the progressive wing, Italian cardinal Carlo Maria Martini, received as many or more votes than Ratzinger on that first ballot. That scenario seemed dubious at the time. Martini was a Jesuit and seventy-eight at the time of the conclave. He was afflicted with Parkinson's disease and had pressed John Paul to allow him to retire as archbishop of Milan when he reached seventy-five. Since then he had been living in Jerusalem, doing the biblical studies that were his passion. Martini was nonetheless still a galvanizing presence for progressives. But doubts were quickly cast on the reliability of his first ballot showing—his age and health and the fact that he truly did not want the job made it unlikely that any showing for him would be more than a farewell tribute to a grand figure of the twentieth-century church.

Those doubts later proved correct. According to the conclave diarist, Martini received nine votes on the first ballot, the touted Cardinal Rodriguez Maradiaga received just three, and Cardinal Tettamanzi only two. Cardinal Ruini and Cardinal Sodano received six and four votes respectively, a respectable showing for their prominence but no indicator of future potential. The rest of the thirty-four votes were scattered among individual cardinals. It is a custom of the conclave that on the first ballot, the electors vote for a friend or to honor someone who will never be pope but who can at least know that they received a vote in a conclave. Cardinals joke that they vote for who they want on the first ballot, then they let the Holy Spirit guide them. In the conclave of 1829, a bon vivant and decidedly non-*papabile* cardinal named Vidoni was shocked to hear his name read out as receiving a vote. "Is the Holy Ghost drunk?" he exclaimed.[11]

The real surprise of the first ballot was that the Argentine, Cardinal Bergoglio, was the apparent pretender, with ten votes. That was a far cry from Ratzinger's forty-seven, but it made him a real prospect because his Latin American experience would make him a rallying point for those opposed to Ratzinger or those who wanted the Church of Rome to look to the developing world for the first time.

Back at the Domus Marthae after the tense first ballot, some of the cardinals had a light dinner and retired early. Cardinal José da Cruz Policarpo of Portugal, who was known as a habitual smoker (these days a strike against him as *papabile*) was spotted sneaking outside for a cigar since the Domus banned smoking. But many others spent the evening gathering in groups of two or three to talk about the day's vote and the prospects for candidates and the church. This is where the conclave's real politicking, if it can be called that, takes place—the *murmuratio* between meals and small talk over coffee or cocktails.

The next morning, Tuesday, after Mass and breakfast and a shuttle (or stroll) over to the Sistine Chapel, the cardinals resumed their voting, and the results of the night's private colloquiums became apparent. According to the anonymous diarist, Ratzinger's total went from forty-seven to sixty-five (a dozen short of election) and Bergoglio jumped from ten to thirty-five votes. Other reports confirmed a similar shift. It was clear that Bergoglio was becoming the rallying point for the cardinals who, for any number of reasons, did not want Ratzinger to be pope. Many of them were likely Europeans and Americans and Latin Americans who would have liked to see a Latin American pope, a first, who might energize Catholics in the developing world, even if he was unlikely to be the doctrinal reformer many liberals wanted. Martini's nine votes disappeared that morning and likely went to Bergoglio, while Ruini's went over to his colleague in the Curia, Cardinal Ratzinger. There would be no Italian restoration; Sodano still had four votes, and Tettamanzi was stuck at two. There were just nine votes dispersed among other candidates. The camps had formed.

But Ratzinger's bloc was daunting. His partisans already controlled enough votes—more than half—to prevent another candidate from winning, and they could conceivably prolong the conclave the necessary thirty-four ballots until the cardinals could opt for a simple majority vote. But that was highly unlikely, since no one wanted to see a protracted conclave.

Also, Bergoglio was seen as something of a risk. Like Martini, the sixty-eight-year-old cardinal was a Jesuit, which would make many cardinals nervous, but his relations with his own order were not the best. As leader of the Jesuits in Argentina during the dark days of the government's human rights abuses of the 1970s, Bergoglio was often at loggerheads with his confrères over his reluctance to be as socially and politically active as they were becoming. To be sure, Bergoglio was known for his humble lifestyle and his deep piety, and he was outspoken on issues of globalization and social justice. But the Latin American church was often so divided along political and theological lines that it was unclear how popular he would be on the continent.

Moreover, according to the conclave diarist, there was uncertainty as to whether Bergoglio would accept if elected. As Bergoglio went up to cast his vote before Michelangelo's Last Judgment, the cardinal wrote, "He had his gaze fixed on the image of Jesus who judges souls at the end of time. His was a face of suffering, as if imploring: God, please do not do this to me."

Still, by the second ballot of the morning, Bergoglio had gained five more votes, for a total of forty. But Ratzinger gained seven to reach seventy-two votes, just five shy of election. It was a two-man race; everyone else had disappeared. If Bergoglio's camp wished, they could hold tight and prevent Ratzinger from reaching seventy-seven. There were only three stray votes in play, which would have given Ratzinger just seventy-five, two short. Then the cardinals broke for lunch, an interval when the conclave would be decided. As the diarist noted, even before leaving the Sistine Chapel, "there were the first comments and contacts. There was great concern among the cardinals who hoped for the election of Cardinal Ratzinger."

"The outcome of the conclave, for several hours after the third ballot of Tuesday morning, April 19, still seemed in doubt," he wrote.

Through it all, Joseph Ratzinger struck several cardinals who ate at his table or chatted with him as a picture of calm. In a revealing episode that he spoke about after his election, Ratzinger said that at one point a friendly cardinal pressed a note into his hand reminding him of the words of Jesus to Saint Peter that Ratzinger had cited at John Paul's funeral a few days earlier: "When you were younger, you used to fasten your own belt and to go wherever you wished. But when you grow old, you will stretch out your hands, and someone else will fasten a belt around you and take you where you do not wish to go." His friend told Ratzinger that "if the Lord addressed that 'follow me' to me, I could not refuse the call."

While some were busy persuading Ratzinger to accept the election, should it happen, other allies were working hard to make sure he got over the top. Historically, many cardinals have come close to election, only to disappear, just a footnote to church history. In the dynamics of a conclave, when the tide crests, it never returns. If Ratzinger did not win in the afternoon, there was a strong possibility the conclave would start looking at other candidates, which could effectively put them back at square one. Ratzinger's supporters, especially in the Curia, began working their colleagues during the lunch break. "No outcome was ruled out," the diarist recorded.

But the Ratzinger forces, and the momentum of the conclave, would not be stopped. When the cardinals returned for the first ballot of the afternoon, which started at 4:00 PM, the numbers started to pile up again for the German and the Argentine, until Ratzinger's total climbed above his previous high of seventy-two. A moment later he reached the threshold of seventy-seven votes. The cardinals seemed stunned by what had happened. It was 5:30 PM, almost twenty-four hours to the minute since they had begun their deliberations—one of the fastest conclaves in modern history. The cardinals had elected a successor to Pope John Paul II, and it was Joseph Ratzinger.

Many cardinals described a collective gasp when it was clear Ratzinger had taken the required minimum, followed by applause. Ratzinger's fellow Germans recalled joy and tears. "When the numbers worked there was spontaneous clapping," said Cardinal Joachim Meisner of Cologne, one of Ratzinger's closest friends in the German hierarchy and an ally in his battles with more reform-minded German prelates like Kasper and Lehmann. But none of the Germans was about to let past disputes cloud this astounding moment of German glory. "I covered my face. I cried. I wasn't the only one," Lehmann said.

A Spanish cardinal said Meisner, normally "a very, very serious man," was "crying like a child, and then blowing his nose like a child, overwhelmed." Meisner was not apologizing: "I am a man and not a machine. And a man with a heart can weep," he said. Ratzinger himself later said that as the vote neared the magic threshold, he felt as if a guillotine were descending on him, and he prayed to be spared. But throughout it all he appeared calm, perhaps aware that this moment was coming, but also deeply convinced that this was the will of God and that he could do no other.[12]

Normally the dean of the college would ask the new pope if he would accept the burden of the office—a tradition because the dean is usually an older man who is not in the running. But since Ratzinger was the dean, the task fell to the vice-dean, Cardinal Sodano, who put the question to Ratzinger in Latin.

Joseph Ratzinger did not hesitate: "In obedience with the Holy Spirit, to the vote of the cardinals I respond: Yes." As soon as he pronounced the Latin "*Accepto,*" Joseph Ratzinger was the pope. Sodano then asked him by which name he would like to be called, and the new pope also answered without hesitation: Benedict XVI.

According to the diary of the anonymous cardinal, Bergoglio lost fourteen votes in that final round, finishing at twenty-nine. A dozen of them switched to Ratzinger. But Ratzinger apparently did not win as convincingly as recent popes had. At the first 1978 conclave, Luciani won with 92 votes out of 111; at the October conclave, Karol Wojtyla won 97 votes out of 111.[13] In 2005, Ratzinger apparently finished with 84 votes out of 115, just 7 more than needed for victory. In the days after the conclave, several church insiders told me that Ratzinger did not reach 90 votes, and Bergoglio was the educated guess for the second-place finisher. John Allen quoted an unnamed African cardinal as saying the conclave was "something of a horse race" between Ratzinger and Bergoglio, and several other sources confirmed that.

Perhaps the most shocking revelation in the anonymous cardinal's diary is that the disgraced Cardinal Law received a single vote on the last ballot. It was apparent that Ratzinger was to be the victor, so the vote for Law came off as a final slap in the face to American Catholics and especially the victims of sexual abuse. (A favorite barb in Boston was that Law voted for himself.)

Now that he was elected and had accepted, the first thing Joseph Ratzinger —or rather, Pope Benedict XVI—had to do was to dress the part. The Holy Spirit may choose the pope, but the uniform makes the man a pope in the eyes of the public. A white cassock equals Holy Father, even though the *simar,* as this special soutane is formally known, only became a settled tradition after the 1566 election of a Dominican, Pope Pius V, who decided to keep the traditional white habit of the order. Now the outfit seems as integral to the papacy as infallibility.

When elections have been held in the Sistine Chapel, the new pope is immediately ushered into an adjoining sacristy known as the Salla della Lacrime, or Hall of Tears, because so many popes have broken down at the realization of their fate. There he is vested in the papal whites, which for most of the past two centuries have been tailored by Gammarelli's, a family-run business of clerical tailors whose shop sits near the Pantheon, in Rome's ecclesiastical garment district. The job is of course a great honor, but it is also as great a challenge as it is for *Vaticanisti* to pick the pope. With so much uncertainty over the winner and in view of the corporeal diversity of the cardinals, the *sarti* of Gammarelli's bring at least three cassocks to the Sistine sacristy—small, medium, and large, so that the new pope, like Goldilocks, can see which fits best. (The Gammarellis have been known to sniff out a winner; in 1963 they correctly guessed that Cardinal Montini would be elected Paul VI, and prepared a fourth cassock to his exact measurements.)[14]

Unfortunately, even the prêt-à-porter solution doesn't always work. In 1914, Pope Benedict XV was so slight that all of the cassocks were too large. In 1958, the robust Angelo Roncalli had the opposite problem when he was elected, in a surprise to everyone, as Pope John XXIII. Pope John was so portly that the papal tailors had to slit the soutane up the back and jury-rig buttons for his first appearance on the balcony.

Joseph Ratzinger was also unlucky in his sartorial debut as pope, though it was another indicator of his outwardly tranquil nature that he didn't let the fuss bother him. As the Gammarelli brothers went thought their rack of soutanes, they couldn't find any that fit, which seems unusual given that Cardinal Ratzinger is a slight man but certainly not undersized. The tailors were feverishly trying to alter one of the simars to fit—this was something of a *brutta figura,* as the Italians say, since a papal election is the Gammarelli's moment to shine—and the new pope finally told them not to worry about it because he couldn't keep the people outside waiting to find out what only the cardinals of the conclave knew.

("The main tailor is young and this is the first time she's had to cut for a new pope," Lorenzo Gammarelli said of the tailor, whose name he gave only as Monica a few days before the conclave. "So she is very, how do you say, emotional." She may have felt worse after the election.)[15]

They pondered the options. He couldn't use a red cassock, because he wasn't a cardinal any longer, and the confusion if he walked onto the balcony looking like a cardinal would have been an inauspicious start. "Well, what have you got that's white that'll fit?" the new pope asked the Gammarellis. They looked around and could find only an alb, which is the plain white cotton vestment that clerics wear under the more ornate chasuble. It is the most ordinary liturgical garment, and Benedict thought it was just fine.

Then he asked about the weather. The new pope had a bit of a cold, and he was always careful about taking a chill, especially as he grew older. The word came back that it was rather brisk (any one of us in the square could have told him that). So he told them he was going to keep his black sweater on, too, to be safe. The tailors all looked at each other—this wasn't what they had in mind for their first Sistine Chapel fitting in twenty-six years—but Joseph Ratzinger was the pope.[16] (As pope, he could also find another tailor, a prospect that set off a fashion war months after the conclave, when it was rumored that Benedict was set to dump Gammarelli's after two centuries of sartorial service to the pontiffs.)

Even his shoes were too big, the traditional red leather slippers with buckles that he opted for over the plain oxblood loafers that John Paul preferred. When Benedict came back into the chapel, his friend Cardinal Meisner of Cologne noticed the odd fit of everything, and he even thought they had forgotten the *zucchetto* until he realized that the white papal skullcap disappeared against the new pope's white hair.

The new pope—he was Benedict XVI now, no longer Joseph Ratzinger—then received the cardinals, who knelt before him one by one, congratulating him and pledging obedience. John Paul insisted on standing for this moment—a pope receives his fellow brothers standing, he said—but Benedict, either out of tradition or understandable fatigue, sat on the throne as the electors proceeded past. Meisner was the first German to greet his countryman, but he was too choked up to speak. Benedict eased his friend's nerves by assuring him that he would travel to Cologne for the long-planned World Youth Day in August, at which up to a million Catholic young adults were expected. "I am going to Cologne and I am happy to go to Cologne," the pontiff said.[17]

When Cardinal Justin Rigali of Philadelphia had his turn with the pope, Benedict actually remembered that Rigali had turned seventy that day and wished him a happy birthday. "With all the things he had to think about, he had a very human touch," Rigali said. Cardinal Napier of South Africa told Benedict, "Congratulations and thanks for accepting." The pope replied, "Please pray for me and support me."[18]

The new pope then invited the cardinals to stay with him for dinner at the Domus Marthae, where they shared champagne and sang Latin hymns after a simple meal of thick bean soup, dried beef salad, and a meat dish. The atmosphere was quietly celebratory. "A burden had been offloaded," said Cardinal Lehmann.[19]

Not everyone was ecstatic, however. Cardinal Danneels skipped the post-election dinner, preferring to speak with the media and attend to unspecified other events. (It seems unlikely Pope Benedict missed him. The two men were on different sides of almost every controverted issue. So great was the divide that in an interview a few months after his brother's election, Georg Ratzinger said that Danneels was one of several liberal cardinals who are "no longer in accord with a Catholic understanding." He added that Danneels had been "taken over by the loss of substance"—a loaded phrase indicating that he considered Danneels a virtual apostate.)[20]

Others were disappointed as well, or simply stunned that after so much buildup and with so much at stake, the conclave was over so fast. "I think a lot of us were surprised it went so quickly," one cardinal told me.

So how and why did Cardinal Joseph Ratzinger come to be elected Pope Benedict XVI?

For all the conspiracy theories (and novels) that sprout like weeds in the post-conclave period—the *dietrologia* that is the stock-in-trade of *Vaticanisti*—the obvious answers to the "why" of a papal election are usually the most accurate. And when a conclave goes as rapidly as it did in April 2005, some of the obvious answers are clearer than ever.

The principal factor was that the choices of the conclave largely came down to Joseph Ratzinger and "Everybody Else." Ratzinger was a renowned figure, effectively the right-hand man of the beloved late pope. He had a superior intellect, an obvious and profound spirituality, and the bearing and self-mastery to shoulder the terrible burden of the papacy—an even heavier weight given that he had to follow a superstar pontiff. Everyone else in the college either didn't want the job (who would, at that point?) or were seen as unknown quantities or simply not qualified for the job. Joseph Ratzinger had an outstanding résumé, and he spoke many languages fluently. For the second conclave in a row, the cardinals had picked the smartest man in the room. "They tried to find an alternative to Ratzinger, but they couldn't," said a Vatican official close to several cardinals.

But Ratzinger's visibility and comportment were also so impressive throughout the emotional tumult of the interregnum that enough cardinals were reassured that, while Ratzinger wouldn't be breaking any papal longevity records, he was up to the strenuous job. "We all felt like he was a brother with superior qualities," Cardinal Christoph Schönborn of Vienna, a devoted former student of Ratzinger, told Catholic News Service. "Age isn't important," Brazilian cardinal Cláudio Hummes, who was on the short list of Latin American hopefuls, told the Associated Press. "There were some very short papacies which did great work."

Above all, Ratzinger's performance in the interregnum reassured cardinals who were nervous about his terrible press clippings that he could be a pastor rather than an enforcer. "You could see this in the way he interacted with the crowd at Pope John Paul's funeral—for example, when he patiently allowed the crowd to keep chanting during the Mass instead of cutting it off. We could see that this was the kind of person who was able to read situations and respond to them," said Cardinal Wilfrid Fox Napier of South Africa. Italian cardinal Tarcisio Bertone of Genoa, who was once Ratzinger's second-in-command at the Congregation for the Doctrine of the Faith (CDF), agreed: "It was a historic moment, in which he was able to touch the sensitivity and the vision of the universal church."[21]

A year before the conclave, a North American cardinal told John Allen, "Ratzinger may be the man for the job. But my concern is how I would sell this back home." By the time of the conclave, that concern had eased somewhat.[22]

Another factor in Ratzinger's favor was that the cardinals did not want to project the image of a divided church. In the wake of John Paul's long struggle with death, after the historic outpouring for his funeral, the cardinals—and the church—wanted stability. That, too, turned the thoughts of the conclavists to Joseph Ratzinger. In fact, Britain's Cardinal Murphy-O'Connor acknowledged that as Ratzinger gathered momentum during the conclave, some hold-outs changed their votes "for the unity of the church."[23]

Yet conclaves don't just happen; the Holy Spirit is not a campaign manager. Conclaves are won and lost by the men inside the Sistine Chapel, and there was a strong and organized campaign to elect Joseph Ratzinger.

Naturally, the official view, especially as ranks closed after the conclave, was that Ratzinger did not campaign to be pope and did not want to be pope, and to some extent that is true, although not quite as much as Benedict later assert-ed: "I never thought I would be elected, nor did I do anything to make it hap-pen, but when slowly the unfolding of the votes led me to understand that the 'guillotine' was coming closer and looking at me, I asked God to spare me this fate," he told an audience of German pilgrims a few days after his election.

Still, it is clear that in the months as John Paul grew weaker and the conclave whispers strengthened, Joseph Ratzinger was also willing to allow Providence to guide the selection of the next pope, and if the Holy Spirit wanted to come under the guise of Ratzinger's allies, so be it. He was content to be the person he always was, to speak his mind and let the chips fall where they might.

The first signs that the chips might be falling Ratzinger's way came with reports as early as November 2004, some five months before John Paul's death, when Bruce Johnston (a longtime Rome hand who died a few months after Benedict's election) wrote in the *Daily Telegraph* of London that Ratzinger's age was now seen as an advantage, turning him from a popemaker into "an important late entry for the papacy." In January 2005, *Time* magazine's Vatican correspondent, Jeff Israely, quoted Vatican insiders as saying, "The Ratzinger solution is definitely on." But the campaign may have been rolling as early as 2002. That is when, according to George Weigel, Monsignor Thomas Herron, an American priest who had worked with Cardinal Ratzinger for many years at the CDF, was telling friends that Ratzinger was *molto papabile*—a notion that apparently was met with some disbelief. (Herron did not live to see his wish fulfilled; he died in 2004.)

What seems clear on reflection is that the Ratzinger campaign was well under way by the end of 2003. As *Time* reported in a conclave postmortem, at John Paul's silver jubilee in October 2003, Ratzinger seemed rejuvenated even as John Paul was failing. The cardinal was publishing and lecturing as much as he ever did, and he was especially visible in the Italian media, which reassured Italians who were bent on recapturing the Throne of Saint Peter. Ratzinger "had become the darling of the [conservative] Italian intelligentsia," a senior Vatican official told the magazine. Influential movements, such as Opus Dei and Communion and Liberation (CL), also began working for Ratzinger's candidacy on the Italian front.

Ratzinger's homily at the funeral for Giussani—the CL founder—plus his Good Friday meditations, his homily at John Paul's funeral, the visible role he chose to take in the preconclave meetings, and finally his powerful, uncompromising sermon just before the cardinals went into the conclave all served to show Ratzinger, as much as the electors, that perhaps he was being called—a final vocation. "Some inner fire was lit, like God had chosen him," a Ratzinger supporter told *Time*.

But the Roman Curia had also chosen Ratzinger, and it was their collective weight that threw the conclave so quickly and decisively to the German cardinal. "The Curia had the inside track, no doubt," one cardinal told me. Other accounts, including the very public satisfaction of many curialists with Ratzinger's election, certainly seemed to confirm that account.

Well before the conclave, it was assumed that a central political dynamic of the election would be a struggle between the center and the periphery—between the Curia and like-minded conservatives and the cardinals who head dioceses around the globe. But given the widespread irritation with Roman ways, and the fact that curial cardinals were outnumbered three to one, it was assumed that a pope would be chosen from outside the Roman orbit.

Yet that analysis neglected the reality that the curialists were a more compact and united bloc than the rest of the cardinals, and that their shared Roman perspective could be a stronger glue than nationality. Nine of the twenty Italians in the conclave were curialists, for example, and Cardinal Ruini was one of the most aggressive campaigners for Ratzinger. Likewise, several Latin Americans, Africans, and Asians were members of the Roman Curia and often more connected to the "Roman" part of Catholicism than to their national church. Two of the most insistent campaigners on behalf of Ratzinger were reportedly Cardinal Alfonso López Trujillo, a Colombian and head of the Vatican's Pontifical Council for the Family, and a Chilean, Cardinal Jorge Arturo Medina Estévez, former chief liturgist at the Vatican. The other cardinals had so many different agendas and were so diverse and unfamiliar with each other that organizing them under such conditions was impossible.

They also had no standout champion, as the curialists did. Ratzinger had had such a long and influential career that several of his former students were prominent churchmen. Cardinal Schönborn of Vienna was particularly keen to see Ratzinger elected. "When you talked to other cardinals about Ratzinger, most of them would say, yes, he's a good candidate, but there's also this man or that man," one cardinal told John Allen after the conclave. "Not Schönborn. For him, it was God's will that Ratzinger be pope, and that was it."[24]

The whole thing was over before anyone could mount a countercampaign. Ratzinger's allies knew they had to move quickly to elect their man, because any hesitation could cause second thoughts within the conclave, or in the public's mind if Ratzinger managed to survive a protracted battle. If it was to be Ratzinger, it must be quick and clear-cut, Montreal's Cardinal Marc Ouellet, a confidante of Ratzinger's, recalled thinking as the voting began. Otherwise, the reception would be disastrous, he said.[25] "The ease of Ratzinger's victory was proof of just how compact and well-prepared the Roman nucleus was," a cardinal-elector told *Time*. An aide to another cardinal told the *Los Angeles Times* much the same thing: "They didn't realize how strong Ratzinger was. The reformers have been out of touch with this growing tide around Ratzinger."

The efficiency of the curial campaign was also evidenced by the apparent surprise of many cardinals, especially Western Europeans and North Americans, who were clearly expecting a different outcome—or at least a longer and more intensive process of discernment in the conclave. "I went to Rome with the idea that an Italian will become Pope. And after four sessions Cardinal Ratzinger was elected," said Dutch cardinal Adrianus Simonis. "It was amazing."[26] Britain's Cardinal Murphy-O'Connor made an amusing slip of the tongue in postconclave interviews, telling reporters that "they chose this man"—referring to Ratzinger—before correcting himself by saying "*we* chose this man."

And what about the Third World candidates? On the eve of the conclave, Los Angeles cardinal Roger Mahony virtually ruled out a candidate like Ratzinger, telling Catholic News Service the cardinals would not elect a pontiff from a country like France or Germany where "practically nobody goes to church" and where the "churches are almost museums." He added, "What we are looking at is how to have the future pope be somebody who represents a dynamic part of the world," meaning where church life is "very vibrant," such as in "Africa or Asia or Latin America."

So why didn't the cardinals make the big shift?

One factor is surely the church's legacy of Eurocentrism. "Europe is the faith, and the faith is Europe," the French-born Englishman Hilaire Belloc famously declared in the early twentieth century, and one hundred years later the College of Cardinals still seemed to agree. Part of the reason is that many cardinals, some of them in the developing world, believe that the ills of modernity that afflict Western Christianity must be addressed or they could eventually infect the rest of the church. Ratzinger was clearly the cardinal who had addressed the challenge of secularism in the modern world and the need to restore a belief in transcendent, immutable truths, preferably as mediated by the Catholic Church. Ratzinger's choice of his papal name was telling: Saint Benedict of Nursia is Europe's patron saint and the founder of Western monasticism 1,500 years ago. Saint Benedict and his movement are credited with preserving the faith—and European culture—through the continent's Dark Ages, and his monastic model and deeply Christocentric spirituality always appealed to Joseph Ratzinger.

Those qualities also appealed to many cardinals.

"Twenty-six years ago, when Karol Wojtyla was chosen as the successor to Saint Peter, the most difficult challenges to the church's mission came from the East," Chicago's Cardinal Francis George said in explaining the choice, a day after the election of Pope Benedict XVI to succeed John Paul II. "Twenty-six years later the most difficult challenges to the church's mission come from the West. And there's a man now very well-prepared, who understands the society, and the history of the world and the place of the church within it, to be the successor of Peter."

Detroit's Cardinal Adam Maida, a Polish American and friend of the late pope, echoed that shift: "Just as Karol Wojtyla was called out of the East, this man was called out of the West to lead the church."

But there may have been other factors, too. Retired Brazilian cardinal Aloísio Lorscheider attributed the hesitancy of the cardinals to the "undeniable sense of superiority" of the European cardinals, who would not back a Latin American. "I know it well," Lorscheider told a Sao Paolo daily just before the conclave. (At eighty, he was not able to vote in the 2005 election.) "The election of Cardinal Ratzinger showed that it still wasn't the moment for a Latin American pope," said Cardinal Danneels, who declined to elaborate on his evident consternation with the election's outcome.

Some African electors apparently sensed the same attitude. Nigerian cardinal Francis Arinze told Italy's *Il Messaggero* daily before the conclave that "the West is not yet ready for a black pope." Cardinal Bernard Agré, from Ivory Coast, agreed. "Psychologically and spiritually, the West is not ready," he said. "An African pope would be a challenge for the church and for the world of the media."

There were other, more mundane, factors working against the Africans. Though the church in Africa is exploding, pushing toward 150 million, its cardinals made up just over 10 percent of the electors (versus 9.4 percent in 1978).

Moreover, if the cardinals were looking to Africa for a candidate, they had few candidates to choose from. The church in Africa is so young—the first native bishop there was consecrated in 1938, and they did not have a native-born cardinal until 1960—that is has not developed the depth of leadership necessary to produce a slate of viable candidates. "If people are disappointed that no strong candidate emerged enough to even have a realistic chance . . . of being the pope from the South, I think we've got to look at ourselves [and] ask if we are developing the kind of leadership that would make an impact on the rest of the Church," Napier told Vatican Radio after the conclave. "Are we working to the extent that prior to entering a conclave, others would say, 'There's a good candidate'?"

Also, Napier indicated that African church leaders tended to be less concerned with Roman politics than were their European and American confrères and more deferential toward Vatican bigwigs like Cardinal Ratzinger. "I suppose, in typical African style, as [Ratzinger] was one of the top cardinals, we left him, and them, to do the important business, while we went about the little business of giving reports on what was happening in our churches," Napier said of his earlier visits to Rome with fellow Africans.

Those same factors could have mitigated against the candidacy of a Latin American and might help explain why Bergoglio finished a distant, if strong, second in a conclave in which someone from the developing world was expected to do well.

Again, the numbers don't lie: while Latin Americans make up some 45 percent of the global Catholic population, Latin American cardinals still made up less than 18 percent of the cardinal-electors—21 of 115 eligible voters—just a single percentage point higher than the 1978 conclave. The solidarity of Latin Americans in the Curia also trumped regional loyalty, reflecting the fractured reality of the so-called Latin American bloc, which has serious divides over theology, social justice, the relationship between church and state, and evangelization. In fact, the glib references to Latin Americans (including my own, to be sure) as if they were one unit betrays a *norteamericano* bias that ignores the great differences among the countries. Brazilians certainly believed their country and culture to be worthy of the first Latin American pope; and as one Argentine journalist told me just before the conclave, if Bergoglio, the Argentine Jesuit, were elected, then the church in Chile might go into schism because of the long history of tension between those two nations. She was only half-joking.

The geopolitics of the College of Cardinals is certain to change in time, and probably sooner rather than later, with a Latin American candidate a likely successor to Pope Benedict XVI.

What may be of greater concern to Catholics, however, is the dynamic that the conclave of 2005 revealed—namely, that the bandwagon effect, which is often at work in conclaves, seemed to be the determining factor in electing Cardinal Ratzinger. Even before the latest conclave, in his 2004 book, *Heirs of the Fisherman,* former Vatican diplomat and papal historian John-Peter Pham, wrote that conclaves increasingly seem to be proving the social science theory that the larger the group, the greater the possibility of a little momentum carrying the entire group in one direction. As Spanish cardinal Vicente Enrique y Tarancón told an interviewer in 1984, "You know that your vote is important, but it is one, and you feel a little dominated by the blocs."[27]

The growth of the College of Cardinals plays into this dynamic while diminishing the influence of individual electors, especially those from countries far from the Roman nerve center. "We [cardinals] need to find ways to get to know each other better," Cardinal Thomas Williams of New Zealand said in his post-mortem of the conclave. "For example, I was staying with the Marists in Rome and saw an insert in [the French newspaper] *La Croix* that had pictures of all the cardinals, with their ages and nationalities. I took it with me to the General Congregation meetings, and whenever somebody would speak, I'd pull out the sheet and identify them. Before long, a number of other cardinals would come over to ask, 'Who's that speaking?'"[28] This hardly seemed like the best way to elect a pope, and the unfamiliarity of so many electors in the end gives greater power to the curial cohort, which could try to "run the table" at the next conclave as well.

"In many respects," Pham writes, "the equality of the electoral franchise with the College of Cardinals, coupled with the expansion of its membership, risks turning the venerable body into the ecclesiastical equivalent of the United Nations General Assembly: All are theoretically equal, but some enjoy greater 'equality' than others."[29]

Such a self-perpetuating dynamic could work to reduce the input of local churches even as the College of Cardinals grows more diverse, and it might also reduce the chance of the Holy Spirit "blowing where he will," as has been his wont in the past. One practical change that some cardinals are apparently considering in order to thwart a curial monopoly on the papacy is to require that the dean of the College of Cardinals—the platform that gave Ratzinger such a lift—be restricted to an over-eighty cardinal who would not be allowed in the conclave.

In his examination of conscience after the conclave, the *NCR*'s John Allen argued that the reason he and so many other Vaticanologists missed the

Ratzinger dynamic is that they overanalyzed all the many factors at work. Yet another way to look at the conclave of 2005 is that the College of Cardinals may have underanalyzed the situation, preferring to go with a safe and sure bet in Joseph Ratzinger rather than spending all the time it might take to sort through the many issues and the many other candidates that a different agenda might require.

It is a truism that popes never succeed themselves. The church does not believe in cloning, as Cardinal Walter Kasper said in a homily just before going into the conclave. Indeed, in just looking at the portraits of popes since the nineteenth century, one can quickly see how fat popes follow thin popes. The same often goes for the pendulum of papal styles. But sometimes there are transitional popes. People often forget that Karol Wojtyla did not succeed Paul VI; he came after John Paul I, whose thirty-three-day reign is seen as a footnote today. True, John Paul I did not live long enough to have a great impact. But Papa Luciani was the man chosen by the conclave—a sixty-three-year-old Italian with a down-to-earth, pastoral manner. He was different from Pope Paul, but not too different. And only after Luciani did the cardinals take the Great Leap beyond Italy.

To the many fans of Joseph Ratzinger—now Pope Benedict—he represents a courageous and reassuring leap in his own right, one that will fulfill many of the dreams that they felt were deferred even during the reign of the man they call John Paul the Great.

Yet the man who became Pope Benedict XVI on April 19, 2005, is far more complex than many of his friends, or his even more numerous critics, acknowledge, and that made predicting what kind of pope he would be especially problematic. Only now that he is pope is he able to freely exhibit that character, which cannot be understood without returning to the divided heart of wartime Germany, where the future pontiff was born.

Chapter Five

A GERMAN SOUL

The German soul often seems at war with itself, a psyche divided between the head and the heart, alternating between reason and instinct in a single-minded effort to figure out where the truth about the world and themselves lies, and in the process unnnerving anyone unlucky enough to run afoul of their imperial introspection. "The Germans," Goethe once said, "make everything difficult, both for themselves and for everyone else."[1] That fierce inner energy has, of course, fueled so many masterworks in philosophy, theology, history, music, poetry, and the sciences that by sheer volume the German intellectual output—"*la patrie de la pensée*," as Madame de Staël called it—has become the bibliography upon which much of the Western academic and creative opus rests.

An underlying reason for the ubiquity of German thought stems from the fact that to be German is to be so many different things that one can find an argument in the German canon to bolster almost any thesis or found any new style of art. "It is characteristic of the Germans that one is rarely completely wrong about them," wrote Friedrich Nietzsche, whose unclassifiable work epitomizes his own aphorism. The Protean quality of the German people—so different from the contemporary stereotype of lockstep Prussians marching off to war or churning out high-end goods from hyperefficient industries—has for centuries mystified outsiders. In *The Europeans*, Luigi Barzini calls them "the mutable Germans," a people who veer between the poles of imperialism and provincialism, obedience and rebelliousness, absolutism and relativism, the national and the individual, the concrete and the abstract, tradition and innovation.

The debate over what it means to be German stems largely from the nation's fragmented tribal history as a sprawling assemblage of peoples who were

forever disintegrating and recombining in unexpected ways, and thus forever intriguing and terrifying their neighbors. In 98 AD the Roman historian
Tacitus characterized his sketch of the northern tribes, already "a source of
vague terror to the Roman world," as an ethnography of "the various peoples
of Germany." Tacitus mentions forty different "peoples" in his *Germania;*
Ptolemy counted nearly seventy. It is sometimes a shock to realize that it wasn't
until 1870 that Otto von Bismarck was finally able to realize the elusive German dream and forge the various German states—at one point numbering
some three hundred principalities, free cities, and ecclesiastical provinces of
Lutherans, Calvinists, and Catholics—into a modern nation. Indeed, the tri-
partite division of the shattered country after World War II into East and West
Germany, with Austria regaining its independence, was perhaps closer to the
historical German reality.

During the long centuries of factionalism, the Germans seemed to embrace
any new ideology or belief that came along, even, or especially, if it undermined the previously held verities. The legacy of brilliance and paradox runs
the spectrum from an ordered Classicism to the turbulence of the Sturm und
Drang and Romanticism, from the cosmologies constructed by great German
theologians to the various obituaries of God penned by great German philosophers, from the exquisitely balanced sonatas of Brahms to the crashing
"Twilight of the Gods," the *Götterdämmerung* of Wagner.

The thread running through all things German, however, is an obsessive
quest for the *authentic*—the authentic German, the authentic emotion, the authentic philosophy, the authentic esthetic, the authentic faith. Germans want
to know where the truth is to be found, and they will risk anything and betray
anyone, even themselves, to get it. "Two souls, alas, are dwelling in my breast,
and one is striving to forsake his brother," lamented Faust before he made the
infamous bargain that gained him knowledge at the mere price of his soul. The
irony is that eternal damnation aside, the Germans usually wind up frustrated
by their endeavors, left only with themselves and their questions.

The "search for the historical Jesus" is a typical example. The pursuit was
begun by Enlightenment rationalists in Germany in the eighteenth century
and was later taken up by liberal Protestants trying to find a human Jesus,
rather than a divine Christ, they could live with. In 1906 Albert Schweitzer
declared that they were all simply looking down a well and seeing their reflection staring back up at them. (He then went off to become famous as a Nobel
Prize–winning missionary in Africa.) Such disregard for the facts could only
last so long, however, and beaverlike German scholars were soon back to dig-
ging up ancient papyri to ascertain just what Jesus said and when he said it.

Though the German forensic approach to Christianity remains popular, so too does the countervailing Pietist tradition, also something of a German legacy. For instance, just as Protestant-led German historicism was deconstructing Jesus in the early nineteenth century, a bedridden Catholic nun and stigmatic from Westphalia named Anne Catherine Emmerich (d. 1824) began having baroque and bloody visions of Christ's final hours. Her transcribed revelations became popular as *The Dolorous Passion of Our Lord Jesus Christ*, a text that later provided the extrabiblical glosses at the heart of Mel Gibson's 2004 blockbuster, *The Passion of the Christ*, one of the most successful movies of all time.

In fact, more than anything else, it may be Germany's Christian history that best reveals the German character. The search for religious truth, the conviction that comes with religious belief, and the sense of betrayal when that belief is challenged, as it always is, are hallmarks of German history. And the religious history of Germany is fundamentally the history of Germany's relationship to Rome—a relationship that alternated between admiration and fear, envy and hatred. As early as the first century, Tacitus was toting up the German virtues, such as their valor in battle and their unusual dedication to monogamy, as well as their vices, such as their tendency to drunkenness and "their strange inconsistency—at one and the same time loving indolence and hating peace."

Germany's relationship to Christian Rome was no less problematic. "From their first appearance in the history of the world the Germans represented the principle of unchecked individualism, as opposed to the Roman principle of an all-embracing authority," as the *Catholic Encyclopedia* (1913 edition) puts it. After the northern tribes helped bring down the cultured world of Tacitus and his progeny, the Catholic Church, as the Western successor to the empire, claimed the next round for Rome, winning Germany's pagan souls for Christianity. "The well-knit organization of the Church, the convincing logic of dogma, the grandeur of the doctrine of salvation, the sweet poetry of the liturgy, all these captured the understanding of the simple-minded but fine-natured primitive German," the encyclopedia continues. "It was the Church, in fact, that first brought the exaggerated individualism of the race under control and developed in it gradually, by means of asceticism, those social virtues essential to the State."

Characteristically, it was actually a heretical form of the faith that the Germans liked at first, an Arianism that argued that Jesus was less than divine. Rome would have none of that, and eventually the powerful Franks, who confessed an orthodox Catholicism, converted the German peoples in the Saxon Wars, which culminated with victories by Charlemagne in the late eighth century. In that conquest, they were aided by some remarkable Anglo-Saxon missionaries, most notably St. Boniface, who was especially successful in converting the southern German region of Bavaria, which would remain Rome's most loyal German tribe. (Boniface was martyred by the faithless Frisians.)

The breakdown of the Carolingian empire, however, inaugurated a perilous and violent age for Christendom and for the papacy, one that was only saved by the emergence, near the threshold of the second millennium, of a reconstituted German imperium that Otto the Great (d. 973) dubbed the Holy Roman Empire—later called the First Reich. It was famously neither very holy nor very Roman, but Otto's empire became the salvation of the papacy and, quickly thereafter, the bane of the church's existence. In a foretaste of a millennium of German–Roman conflict to come, Otto deposed Pope John XII for not acceding to the emperor's wish to control church affairs in Germany, and Otto asserted that every future pontiff would have to swear loyalty first to the emperor. It was no coincidence that the only five German pontiffs in history—before Ratzinger's election—served in the century following Otto the Great. It was also no coincidence that there were no German popes for almost a millennium after Victor II of Swabia (d. 1057), given the problems the papacy began causing for the emperor, and vice versa. In 1077, for example, Otto's successor, Henry IV, was forced by Pope Gregory VII to kneel in the snow at Canossa begging forgiveness for his transgressions in trying to manipulate the Holy Roman Church. But Henry would have his revenge, later driving the pope into exile and a miserable death.

The jousting between Germany—or the various Germanies—and the popes would continue even as their respective fortunes waxed and waned. By the fourteenth century, the decline of the empire gave rise once again to the priority of local sovereignty in Germany, even as the papacy was becoming increasingly imperial, and corrupt. But a German national consciousness was also emerging, in a common language and culture, and that emerging German identity—and its demand for a religion in keeping with its temperament—would contribute to the greatest crisis in German and Catholic history, the Protestant Reformation.

The Augustinian monk famous for touching off Western Christianity's schism was in many ways the quintessential German, or at least that is how Heinrich Heine saw him. Martin Luther was "not merely the greatest but also the most German man in our history, so that in his character all the virtues and failings of the German were united in the most magnificent way," Heine wrote in his *History of Religion and Philosophy in Germany*. Luther was "a cold scholastic word-cobbler and an inspired, God-drunk prophet who, when he had worked himself almost to death over his laborious and dogmatic distinctions, in the evening reached for his flute and, gazing at the stars, melted in melody and reverence."[2]

Luther may also have been the quintessential modern man, with his courageous declaration of personal liberty unleashing the grand and awful power of the individual: "Unless I am convinced by proofs from Scriptures or by plain and clear reasons and arguments, I can and will not retract, for it is neither safe nor wise to do anything against conscience," Luther told the Diet of Worms in 1521. "Here I stand. I can do no other. God help me. Amen."

Excommunication followed, as did bloody conflict. If Luther was a religious revolutionary, he was—yet another characteristic paradox—profoundly conservative politically, and he was dismayed by the popular rebellion his confrontation fomented. He sided with the secular powers in crushing the Peasants' War, prefiguring a Lutheran obeisance to the state—whoever happened to be in charge of it—that would haunt German Protestantism in the moral reckoning that followed World War II.

To be sure, the Reformation was likely inevitable. But the toll on Western Christianity, and the German body and soul, was unforeseen and unprecedented. Despite a century of efforts to find a truce, the latent religious strife erupted in 1618 into the conflagration that would become known as the Thirty Years War. Rampaging armies, Catholic and Protestant pawns in a larger duel among European powers such as France and Spain, devastated the German countryside for decades, sometimes reducing the peasants to cannibalism in order to survive. The Palatinate lost four-fifths of its inhabitants. Bohemia's population of 3 million in 1618 was down to 780,000 at the end of the war, and only 5,000 of its original 35,000 villages remained. Overall, Germany lost more than a third of its population, from 21 million people to 13.5 million, and most of its economic resources and vitality.

The Peace of Westphalia, which ended the conflict in 1648, left Germany atomized politically, culturally, and religiously. Richard Wagner said that the war destroyed the German *Wesen,* or "essence," which he tried to re-create through music. The treaty reduced Catholicism, which constituted what historian Gordon A. Craig called "the one shadowy semblance of unity in Germany" before the war, to a minority faith. Within a few decades of Luther's Reformation, nearly four-fifths of Germany was Protestant—Bavaria was one of the few Catholic holdouts—and though the Counter-Reformation, under the inspiration of the Council of Trent and the ministrations of the Jesuits, won back some of the lost territory, Catholics in Germany from the seventeenth century on were acutely conscious of their inferior status. Lutheranism became the dominant faith, or at least ethos, and the growing dominance of Prussia sealed the minority role of the Catholic princes. The conquests of Napoleon further eroded Catholic power—which Protestant Germany viewed with mistrust anyway—by dethroning bishops and putting large swaths of Catholic populations under Protestant rulers. Church property was confiscated, monasteries were dismantled, and Catholic schools and clergy became dependent on the state for support.

But the same German Catholics who were suspect at home for their ties to Rome actually posed as much of a challenge to the papacy as did the Protestants. Motivated in part by a desire to adapt to the regnant Protestant culture, German Catholicism took on many attributes of Protestantism, and in the eighteenth century a national Catholic movement known as Febronianism sought to form a quasi-independent German Catholicism. Named after tracts penned by Febronius, the pseudonym of Nicholas von Hontheim, Febronianism rejected papal infallibility and the right of popes to intervene in German Catholic affairs, and sought a simplified, primitive Catholicism that could more easily pursue reunification with other Christians. Local irritation with the papacy was so strong that sixteen of Germany's twenty-six bishops refused to publish Rome's condemnation of Febronianism, and the movement nearly succeeded, until Germany's hierarchy decided they could not sacrifice fidelity to Rome.

The nineteenth century continued to see a problematic—for the Vatican—Catholic ferment as Catholic scholars in Germany, like their Protestant and secular counterparts, boasted an academic excellence unrivaled in the rest of the Catholic Church—an intellectual pedigree they wanted to put at the service of liberalizing the increasingly revanchist Vatican. "As the only Catholic community in the world with theological schools located in the secular universities, they [German Catholics] were forced to keep in touch with scientific developments and so were more acutely aware of the need of the Church to face realistically the problems raised by modern culture," writes church historian Father Thomas Bokenkotter. "They saw that the Church could only deal effectively with the arguments raised by the rationalists by emulating their spirit of scientific impartiality. And so the German Catholic scholars broke away from the obsolete Scholastic texts and developed new scientific methods to defend the faith, with intellectual freedom presupposed as a sine qua non."[3]

That freedom, and the concomitant effort to engage modernity, did not sit well with the pontiff of the time, the reactionary Pius IX. This German-inspired push for greater openness—and the German-inspired counter-reaction that it provoked—would remain the central challenge for the Catholic Church, and the papacy, up through the present German pope, Benedict XVI.

In the nineteenth century, Pius was under siege and in no mood to liberalize. Napoleon's exiling of two previous popes and the destruction of the ancien régime, which had provided an altar-and-throne stability for centuries, were still fresh in the mind of Pius, as was his undignified escape from Rome just ahead of the anticlerical revolutionaries of 1848. Pius was restored to his see, but in 1860 Italian nationalists finally won out, uniting Italy and seizing the papal states that formed the basis of the pope's temporal kingdom. Then in 1870 a war with Bismarck's surging Prussia caused France to pull its troops from Rome, where they had served as protectors of the papacy, and Italian troops stormed the defenseless Eternal City. That forced the sudden adjournment of the First Vatican Council—which had just defined the dogma of papal infallibility, a decision anathema to the German bishops, who had lobbied hard against the measure—and the imprisonment of Pius in the Vatican city-state.

Pius took his revenge on the liberals, especially in Germany, excommunicating many of their most outspoken leaders and further dividing the new nation's Catholics. Ironically, German Catholicism was rescued by the persecution of the church in Bismarck's ill-fated *Kulturkampf*, or "struggle for civilization." Otto von Bismarck was the Prussian *Junker* and Pietist who as the "Iron Chancellor" forged the new German Empire through his ruthless policies of realpolitik. A focus of Bismarck's strategy was to eliminate the Catholic Church's political and social influence in the Prussian-dominated German state. In 1866 he succeeded in excluding Catholic Austria from his coalescing Second Reich—he defeated Austria's allies, the Bavarians, in the process—and once German unification was completed in 1870 (Bavaria was able to retain its own military, postal, rail, and diplomatic service for some years in the federation), he launched the *Kulturkampf* in order to destroy the rest of Catholicism's sway in the new Germany. Bismarck expelled religious orders, shuttered seminaries and religious schools, and imposed state controls on internal church life. But for once Bismarck miscalculated. The plan backfired badly, resulting in a doubling of the strength of the Center Party, the Catholic lobby Bismarck sought to thwart, and in an unprecedented wave of sympathy for the Catholic minority throughout Germany.

Bismarck's dedication to realpolitik was greater than his distrust of the Catholic Church, and he soon abandoned the antichurch campaign. But the *Kulturkampf* left yet another deep mark on the German Catholic psyche. For many, the era's injustices were epitomized by the drowning deaths of five

Franciscan nuns who had been forced to leave Germany by Bismarck's policies, embarking on a ship, the *Deutschland*, bound for America. The *Deutschland* left Bremen in the winter of 1875, struck a shoal in the mouth of the Thames while making for port in Southampton, and sank on December 6, claiming 57 lives among the 230 passengers and crew. The tragedy, and its legacy of Catholic exclusion, were immortalized a few years later in the poem "The Wreck of the *Deutschland*" by the English Jesuit Gerard Manley Hopkins, which memorialized the nuns, who were reported to have remained below, sacrificing themselves because there was so little space on deck:

> *Loathed for a love men knew in them,*
> *Banned by the land of their birth,*
> *Rhine refused them. Thames would ruin them.*

Hopkins also noted the internal paradox of German history that the *Deutschland* tragedy underscored: "O Deutschland, double a desperate name!" Both Gertrude, a thirteenth-century Catholic saint and mystic, and Luther the Protestant reformer were from the same small town, Hopkins wrote, but with starkly different legacies, at least from his decidedly Catholic point of view: One was "Christ's lily" and the other the "beast of the waste wood."

How is it, Hopkins asked, that Cain and Abel could suckle from the same breast yet turn out so differently?

That unfathomable darkness, the quest for certainty, and the bitter fruit of internal division are all questions that have dogged Germany and German Catholics for their entire history, and never more so than in the wake of the horrors that the Nazis inflicted on the world in the twentieth century. All those issues would cast a shadow on the life of the man who would become Pope Benedict XVI and, by extension, on the Catholic Church he led into the third millennium.

Joseph Aloysius Ratzinger was born in the Bavarian village of Marktl am Inn on April 16, 1927, just two weeks before a bumptious political upstart by the name of Adolph Hitler held the first Berlin rally of his resurgent *Nationalsozialistische Deutsche Arbeiterpartei*, the National Socialist German Workers Party, or what, in recognition of its growing prominence, was known simply as the Nazi Party.

The Nazis were originally centered in Munich, the capital of Bavaria, the country's most Catholic and most culturally and politically conservative region. The Austrian town where Hitler had been born almost thirty years earlier lay just a few miles from Marktl, across the River Inn, which separates Germany from Austria in eastern Bavaria, and the regions were similar in most respects, including the predominance of the Catholic Church. Like Ratzinger, Hitler was baptized and raised Catholic, and, like Ratzinger, Hitler was captivated by the power and spectacle of the Mass as a boy. But nationalism quickly displaced Catholicism as Hitler's religion, as it would for many in Germany, where Hitler moved shortly before the outbreak of the First World War. The country's devastating defeat in the Great War produced widespread unrest among Germans, who were saddled with the huge economic penalties imposed by the Treaty of Versailles—the *diktat*, as Hitler called it—and the Nazis were one of many *völkisch* movements that sprouted from the disillusionment that Hitler exploited so successfully.

But if there was one virtue Bavarians prized above all others, it was their tradition of internal stability. Throughout the centuries of war and turmoil and reformation, the *Land Bayern* remained an island unto itself, and revolutionaries tended not to fare well. In fact, in November 1918, when the last king of the Wittelsbach dynasty, which had ruled Bavaria since 1180, was deposed, a short-lived socialist government under Kurt Eisner came to power. A few months later, after Eisner's murder, Bolsheviks established a Soviet republic in Munich, inaugurating a violent period of unrest that included leftist thugs threatening at gunpoint the Vatican's nuncio—an archbishop named Eugenio Pacelli, who would later become Pope Pius XII. The communist experiment lasted three weeks. Returning German veterans were organized into a militia and quickly crushed the Red Brigades, executing more than one thousand people in the space of a week.

By that standard, Hitler got off easy. Authorities crushed his tragicomic Munich "beer hall" *putsch* in 1923, convicting him of treason and sending him to prison for eighteen months, which ironically afforded him time to write his political manifesto, *Mein Kampf*. After his release, Hitler relaunched the party, and the shift of the Nazis to Berlin and the northern power centers of Germany in 1927 presaged its coming national success. Ratzinger's family never bought into the Nazi line—Ratzinger contends his father was always critical of Hitler—but they did share in the burdens that roiled the entire Weimar Republic during the first decade of Joseph Ratzinger's life. "The time the family spent in Marktl was not an easy one: unemployment was rife; war reparations weighed heavily on the German economy; battles among the political parties set people against one another; endless illnesses visited the family," Ratzinger wrote in his 1997 memoir, *Milestones*.[4]

For anyone who is looking, there are any number of portents in Ratzinger's birth, the most obvious being that he entered the world early on the morning of Holy Saturday, the liturgical no man's land of the Christian calendar: the Crucifixion is over, but Easter has not yet arrived. Christ has descended into hell; the altars are stripped, and the statues are shrouded in dark purple. Into this borderland between death and life, the future pope was born. "The more I reflect on it, the more this seems to be fitting for the nature of our human life," he recalled. "We are still awaiting Easter; we are not yet standing in the full light but walking toward it full of trust."

This could be the mission statement for Joseph Ratzinger's entire world-view—living in darkness, seeking the light.

There are plenty of other signs. For those who prefer the Nativity angle, Ratzinger was the son of Maria and Joseph. His father was older, already in his fifties, with a thick gray moustache and close-cropped hair. He looked like the policeman he was, and the elder Ratzinger was a disciplinarian of "perhaps excessive strictness," as Cardinal Ratzinger later admitted—another omen, some would say, of things to come. For young Joseph, such an ordered existence was a godsend. "I always remember, with great affection, the goodness of my father and mother. And for me goodness also means the ability to say 'no,' because goodness that lets anything go can't be good for another," he told Vatican Radio in a 2001 interview.

The future "Cardinal No," as critics later dubbed him, was baptized that Holy Saturday, just hours after birth, but without his older sister Maria and his brother Georg in attendance. A bitter cold snap and heavy spring snows, not uncommon weather for that part of Bavaria, kept his siblings behind while he was baptized. "I have always been filled with thanksgiving for having had my life immersed in this way in the Easter mystery, since this could only be a sign of blessing." It was the first sacrament of a life that would be marked by the rituals of the church and an abiding love of the beauty of the liturgy.

The Bavaria of Joseph Ratzinger's youth was everywhere imbued with Catholicism, whose centuries-old rituals and customs found unquestioning support in an almost uniformly Catholic culture. Though then, as now, the rest of Germany was about a third Catholic and a third Protestant, Bavaria was 70 percent Catholic, and most of the Protestants—tradition-minded Lutherans—were concentrated in the northern Franconia area of Bavaria. For several centuries of its history, the region around Ratzinger's hometown was actually ruled by the archbishop of Salzburg rather than the Wittlesbach dukes, who reigned in the rest of Bavaria. Religion was a way of life for everyone, and everyone in Joseph's world was Catholic. "We let the steeple of our church continue to rise from the center of our village," as a Bavarian proverb has it.

For the Ratzingers and their neighbors, it was a life that was equal parts pastoral and devotional. The region is a picture book of lakes and rivers, and deep woods giving way to open fields worked by local farmers. As in Ratzinger's youth, Bavaria continues to be more rural than the rest of the country, with more than half the inhabitants living in villages of less than five thousand up through the 1990s. "The life of farmers was still organically structured in such a way that it enjoyed a firm symbiosis with the faith of the Church: birth and death, weddings and illness, sowing time and harvest time—everything was encompassed by the faith," he said. The alternative, he said, was "the void." Anyone who could not show a voucher proving he had fulfilled his Easter duty "would have been regarded as antisocial."

Ratzinger's vivid description of the annual Corpus Christi procession of his youth conveys the ache of nostalgia for small-town piety that would animate his later views of a starkly changed world: "I can still smell those carpets of flowers and the freshness of the birch trees; I can see all the houses decorated, the banners, the singing; I can still hear the village band, which indeed sometimes dared *more*, on this occasion, than it was able! I remember the *joie de vivre* of the local lads, firing their gun salutes—which was their way of welcoming Christ as a head of state, *the* Head of State, the Lord of the world, present on their streets and in their village. On this day people celebrated the perpetual presence of Christ as if it were a state visit in which not even the smallest village was neglected."[5]

The Ratzinger family went to Mass three times on Sunday, and most weekdays. They prayed the Rosary, and the parents saved from their meager income to send the children to Catholic schools, a financial sacrifice that instilled in Joseph an abiding appreciation for the purity of simplicity. "I often think back on how wonderful it was that we could be happy over the smallest things and how we also tried to do things for one another," Ratzinger recalled in *Salt of the Earth*. "How this very modest, sometimes financially difficult situation gave rise to an inner solidarity that bound us deeply together."[6]

Marktl, his birthplace, was a village of just three hundred to four hundred people, and the family lived on the second floor, above a dentist who had a motor car—a rare luxury—whose fumes are one of the future pope's few lasting memories of the town. The Ratzingers had to move several times during Joseph's childhood; when he was two years old, they moved from Marktl to Tittmoning, another small village. Tittmoning was his "childhood's land of

dreams," set on the Salzach River border with Austria, with grand old bur-
ghers' houses, shop windows illuminated at Christmastime "like a wonderful
promise," and two Baroque churches where young Joseph first found himself
enraptured by religious life and music.

Then in 1932 they moved again—his father "had simply said too much
against the brownshirts"—this time to the town of Aschau am Inn. In 1937,
when Joseph was ten and his father was sixty and had just retired, they moved a
final time, to a leaky old home in the Alpine style a half hour outside the town
of Traunstein (all these locales were within a few miles of each other). The roof
leaked and Maria Ratzinger had to carry water from a backyard well, as well
as cooking at a local inn to supplement their income. "But we experienced it
as a real paradise," Ratzinger said, the "beauty of an old house with its inner
warmth." They subsisted on whatever food his mother could find, and drank a
grain-based ersatz coffee but no wine or beer. That was beyond their means.

Culturally, Traunstein was very much in the orbit of Salzburg, Austria's musical capital, and the synchronicity of place and sensibility was perfect. "You
might say there Mozart thoroughly penetrated our souls," said Ratzinger, who
for the rest of his life loved to play classical piano, especially Mozart, and always
with the earnestness that marked everything he did. "His [Mozart's] music is
by no means just entertainment; it contains the whole tragedy of human existence."

Joseph Ratzinger's early life was the German experience of recent centuries—a "hometown culture" that was "provincial in the extreme," as Gordon
Craig puts it, but provided a warm and supportive environment for those fortunate enough to be born there.

The constant in all of the changes was the Catholic liturgy. Young Joseph
collected missals—the books a priest uses to say Mass—like other kids collect
baseball cards. (Another irony: his first missal was a vernacular German translation of the Latin rubric, given to the family by a "progressive" priest.) He was
enthralled by everything about the rituals and the ornamentation surrounding them. "Every new step into the liturgy was a great event for me. Every new
book I was given was something precious to me, and I could not dream of
anything more beautiful. It was a riveting adventure to move by degrees into
the mysterious world of the liturgy, which was being enacted before us and for
us there on the altar. It was becoming more and more clear to me that I was
encountering a reality that no one had simply thought up, a reality that no official authority or great individual had created. This mysterious fabric of texts
and actions had grown from the faith of the Church over the centuries."

The "wonderful edifice" of the Mass was "like one's own home," and church would be the place that Joseph Ratzinger settled for the rest of his life. But first this sensitive boy had to run the gauntlet of adolescence and Nazism. It was a test that would nearly compromise him, and even more so his beloved Catholic Church.

In 1933 Adolph Hitler took power in national elections that would leave the Führer as the unchallenged ruler of a Germany in which the Nazi ideology was the new faith. Catholic Bavaria was less amenable to the regime than were other regions, but closet Nazis began to emerge even in the towns where the Ratzingers lived. A teacher erected a maypole one spring in Aschau and composed a prayer for the event, in an effort to drive out Christianity and restore the pagan nature based religions of the great German past that Hitler loved to glorify. Looking back in his memoir, Ratzinger likened the anti-Christian Nazi propaganda of that time to modern secularist arguments against allowing Christianity a role in society, a parallel that many might question but that he would return to repeatedly.

Ratzinger said that back in the 1930s, however, the strength of Catholic culture was such that the locals were more interested in snatching the sausages that hung from the maypole than in buying into some old-time nature cult of the sacred groves. That view is supported by others. Gerd Evers, a local historian in Traunstein, says that the inroads the Nazi party was able to make in Bavaria early on were eroded in the 1930s as the party increased its anticlerical rhetoric, which offended Catholic sensibilities. At one point, Evers told the *New York Times,* some two thousand villagers signed a petition protesting a Nazi order to remove crucifixes from the schoolrooms. The Nazis complied.

Joseph Ratzinger's recollection of the advent of Nazism is an admixture of varying emotions and experiences. His reflections have a dreary tone at times, describing the dread of inevitable calamity as munitions plants and searchlights sprang up, and the military moved toward war. He occasionally concedes a bit of excitement at Germany's rediscovered national pride, and at other points he realizes that for a child in his relatively isolated circumstances, these years were something of an idyll, as he played in streams, built dams, and caught fish. "It was the kind of happy life boys should have."

But the "drama of history," as he called it, inexorably closed in on the Ratzingers' enclosed world. The 1938 *Anschluss,* or annexation of Austria, opened Salzburg's beautiful churches and the experience of its fabulous music to the Ratzinger boys, but Hitler's invasion of the Sudetenland in autumn of 1938 was "a mechanism of lies that even someone half-blind could see through." In September 1939 Germany invaded Poland. "The war was still far from us, but the future stood there—sinister, threatening, impenetrable." Yet with the German victories in Denmark and Norway, the Low Countries and France, Ratzinger admitted that "even people who were opposed to National Socialism experienced a kind of patriotic satisfaction." The postponement of the invasion of Great Britain prompted "doubts and disquiet," however, and the attack on the Soviet Union seemed to seal the nation's fate. Joseph's class was on a sunny Sunday's boating trip on a nearby lake when the news arrived, and it "hung over us like a nightmare and spoiled our joy. This could only take a turn for the worse. We thought of Napoleon; we thought of Russia's immeasurable distances where somewhere the German attack had to run aground."

Soon huge transports began rolling through town, often bringing "horribly wounded soldiers." Boys who had recently been classmates began to show up on the list of war dead. Every available space was used for hospital beds, and homes, including the Ratzingers', were confiscated. At fourteen Joseph was too young for the military, but Georg was seventeen and was drafted in the summer of 1942. Georg served in France, the Netherlands, and Czechoslovakia, and then in 1944 at the Italian front, where he was wounded. He was sent home to convalesce briefly before being sent back to Italy.

These developments would be traumatic for most any teen, but they seemed especially so for young Joseph Ratzinger, who was a sensitive and studious child, undersized and unathletic. As he would throughout his life, he tended to deal with unpleasantness by finding solace in the life of the mind and the faith.

He wrote poetry in grade school and would share everything he learned with his classmates, like the teacher he would become and remain. On moving to Traunstein, Joseph entered the *gymnasium,* or classical school, where he was the smallest and youngest child, but he immediately took to the Latin and Greek classes, which were "still taught with old-fashioned rigor." Ratzinger saw that a classical education, like classical Catholicism, "created a mental attitude that resisted seduction by a totalitarian ideology."

Soon, however, Nazi regulations imposed changes. Reluctant teachers were dismissed and replaced with promoters of the regime. Three years later, physical education and sports displaced much of the classics in the curriculum. With the encouragement of his pastor, at Easter 1939, when Joseph was twelve, he entered the minor seminary—a sort of prep school for aspiring priests, minor seminaries are largely extinct today—with joy and the expectation that the travails of the state school would be behind him. But it was even worse at first. What Ratzinger labels a "progressive" education included two hours of sports on the playground. "If this became such a complete torture for me, it was because, in the first place, I am not at all gifted at sports," he said. He was also younger and more frail than everyone else, and his are the painful memories of the last kid picked when teams choose up sides: "In the long run it is not very pleasant to have to live on others' tolerance, knowing that you are nothing but a burden for the team to which you are assigned."

It was a boarding school and Ratzinger hated it. He had to suffer the "torture" of a study hall with sixty other boys, so that learning, "which had always come so easily to me, now appeared almost impossible." The cocoon he had built for himself at home began to unravel, but with time he learned to get along with his classmates. He continued studying Greek and Latin, and he found real enthusiasm for mathematics and literature, especially Goethe. He began to write and to immerse himself in the liturgy. "This was a time of interior exaltation, full of hope for the great things that were gradually opening up to me in the boundless realm of the spirit."

But the daily liturgies also included the inevitable requiem for a fallen soldier, and the world of wonder and faith that had preserved Joseph Ratzinger began to crumble after 1941, when enrollment in the Hitler Youth became mandatory. Ratzinger was spared attending any *Hitlerjugend* meetings when a friendly math teacher told him he would sign him in once and thus obviate any further participation. As the war wore down the German resources, in 1943 it was decided that boys could do part-time duty manning anti-aircraft (flak) units. Seminarians were considered prime candidates because they were used to living in community boarding schools like soldiers in barracks. Ratzinger was enrolled and thrown together with other sixteen- and seventeen-year-olds, and realized for the first time how provincial his boyhood had been. He was able to create a world of his own, however, amid periodic bombing attacks—in his unit, one was killed and several wounded—and defending airstrips and airplane engine factories run by the Bavarian Motor Works, better known today as the automaker BMW. He told *Time* in 1993 that because of a badly infected finger he never learned to fire a gun, and that his weapons were never loaded, even while on duty. He secured a single room, which allowed him privacy to study, and found a network of Catholic friends to visit churches. "And so, paradoxically, this summer is inscribed in my memory as a wonderful time of largely independent living."

The war's destruction grew around them, however, and Ratzinger said he and his friends began to hope for an Allied victory to put an end to the fighting. But it was not to be. In September 1944, when he was seventeen, Joseph was drafted into an army labor battalion and endured "fanatical ideologues who tyrannized us without respite." In one episode, an SS officer tried to recruit the young men and boys by dragging them out of bed in the middle of the night, half-awake, and taking advantage of their drowsiness to make them "volunteer": "A whole series of good-natured friends were in this way forced into this criminal group. With a few others I had the good fortune to be able to say that I intended to be a Catholic priest. We were sent out with mockery and verbal abuse. But these insults tasted wonderful because they freed us from the threat of that deceitful 'voluntary service' and all its consequences."

Ratzinger would normally have been sent to a fighting unit, but in late November 1944, for some reason he and several others were given back their civilian clothes and sent home. A few weeks later he was recalled to Munich, but under the charge of weary veterans who knew the war was winding down, and they took it easy on the soldiers. The unit was never called to the front, and shortly after Hitler's suicide, in early May, he deserted his unit and made his way back home. Soldiers were under orders to shoot deserters, but when two guards spotted him they saw that his arm was in a sling from an injury. Although he had a moment's terror that he would be killed, they let him pass.

In the confusing days and weeks around the war's end, several German soldiers, including two SS officers with whom the elder Ratzinger argued, lodged themselves in the Ratzinger home, making for several unnerving days. Finally the long-awaited Americans arrived in Traunstein and chose the Ratzinger home as their headquarters. But they also sent Joseph to a prison camp as a POW, hands in the air, marched off with other defeated soldiers before his mother's eyes. For weeks he and the others subsisted behind barbed wire in open fields on a ladleful of soup a day and some bread. Joseph consoled himself by composing Greek hexameters and by attending Mass celebrated by imprisoned priests and theological conferences organized by seminarians and academics. The majestic spire of Ulm cathedral was visible on the horizon. "Day after day the sight of it was for me like a consoling proclamation of the indestructible humaneness of faith," he wrote in *Milestones*.

On June 19, 1945, he was released and hitchhiked the seventy miles home into the arms of his overjoyed parents and sister. The next month his brother, Georg, also showed up unannounced, and the joy was complete. Georg came in, sat down at the piano, and played the hymn "*Grosser Gott, wir loben dich*" (Holy God, We Praise Thy Name).

So what impact did the war exert on the future pope? Where did his responsibilities lie then, and what are the lessons he has learned for the church he would lead as pope?

First, it is clear that while neither young Joseph nor his family actively resisted the Nazi machine, it is hardly an apologetic to point out that an older father of three—or an undersized, studious boy in his early teens—would be unlikely to join a resistance that almost guaranteed death, or at best exile or imprisonment. At Ratzinger's election as Benedict, there were a few murmurings and some potshots about his military record; the headlines were almost too good to pass up. "White Smoke, Black Past," read the Israeli daily *Yediot Aharonot*. English newspapers, which developed a sudden case of amnesia about the Nazi costume that their own princeling, Harry, had worn at a "colonial and native" themed party two months earlier, seemed most dogged on the topic. "From Hitler Youth to the Vatican," said the *Guardian,* one of several British pieces on the topic that ran for a few days before finally losing steam.

The principal insults came from leftist groups and Web sites who exploited the Nazi horror for their own ends, or simply for the publicity of shock value. An Italian Web site proclaiming itself "a voice of the antagonistic Left" was shut down by authorities after posting a photomontage with Benedict's head superimposed on a figure wearing a Nazi uniform and standing in front of a large swastika. The site called him "Nazinger" and accused him of intolerance and misogyny, and said he would put homosexuals in ovens. An online magazine in Canada drew attention for posting an animated cartoon depicting Benedict giving a Nazi salute to the Virgin, with the caption "Heil Mary." In France, the satirical puppet show *Les Guignols de l'info* was reprimanded for depicting Benedict offering a blessing "in the name of the father, the son and the Third Reich." In Florida, an art show in Broward County called "Controversy" featured a work by artist Michael Friedman—a Messianic Jew who believes in Jesus—depicting Benedict on a Hitler Youth recruitment poster with the slogan *Jugend dient dem Führer* (Youth Serves the Führer). Oddly, Friedman had complained about what he saw as the inappropriateness of another work that showed President Bush being sodomized by an Arab sheik, intended to depict America's subservience to foreign oil. That picture was tucked away to a remote corner of the exhibit. His own Benedict-as-Nazi piece remained in a prominent position.

Mainstream Jewish groups did have periodic disputes with Ratzinger while he was a cardinal. That is not surprising given the Jewish community's great respect and affection for John Paul and Ratzinger's preference for unapologetically highlighting the primacy of Christianity, and particularly Catholic Christianity, over and above any other faith, no matter what its historical circumstances. In 1987, for instance, Ratzinger's remark that true Judaism exists only in the Catholic Church led Jewish delegates to a Catholic-Jewish conference in

Washington to cancel. The dispute was eventually patched up, and by the time he was elected pope, Jewish groups recognized that Ratzinger's long-standing record of dialogue with Judaism and his condemnations of Nazism and Christian anti-Semitism had absolved Benedict of any Nazi taint. An editorial in the *Jerusalem Post* the day after Benedict's election was representative: "As for the Hitler Youth issue, not even Yad Vashem has considered it worthy of further investigation," the *Post* wrote, referring to the Holocaust memorial and research center in Jerusalem. "Why should we?"

Even the Stasi, the East German secret police, were unable to unearth dirt on a Ratzinger connection to the Nazis. The Stasi opened a file on Ratzinger in 1974 as he began to rise to prominence, and after his promotion to Rome in 1981 the Communist spy unit scoured Nazi-era files and came up empty. "Documents on R. from the time before May 8, 1945 are not available," the files state, referring to him by his initial. Excerpts were released in a German newspaper in October 2005, with Benedict's permission.[7]

Yet there are aspects of Ratzinger's recollections of the war that bear heavily on his subsequent record as cardinal, and on the formation of his character and his later leadership as pope.

One is an understandable defensiveness regarding his family's role during the Nazi reign, and especially the responsibility of his father. Throughout his memoirs and in interviews, Ratzinger consistently depicts the elder Joseph as a staunch foe of the Nazis who presciently saw doom coming. "My father . . . was one who with unfailing clairvoyance saw that a victory of Hitler's would not be a victory for Germany but rather a victory of the Antichrist that would surely usher in apocalyptic times for all believers, and not only for them." His father subscribed to an anti-Nazi newspaper with cartoon caricatures of Hitler and "went into fits of rage" when he read it at home. "It mortified my father to have to work now for a government whose representatives he considered to be criminals." His father's opposition was based primarily on his traditional Bavarian patriotism, his son recalls, which saw Austria and France as historic allies rather than part of the "Prussianized Germany" of the loathed Bismarck. But the elder Ratzinger was "above all a committed Catholic," his son says. He quietly warned priests when neighbors were spying on them, and saved one priest from prison by doing so.

But the senior Ratzinger remained a crypto-dissident: "He made no public opposition; that wouldn't have been possible even in the village," Ratzinger said of his father. The future pope's brother agreed in an interview with the *Times* of London shortly before the 2005 conclave: "Resistance was truly impossible. Before we were conscripted, one of our teachers said we should fight and become heroic Nazis and another told us not to worry as only one soldier in a thousand was killed. But neither of us ever used a rifle against the enemy." How that last assertion squares with Georg's three years in combat is unclear. It would also be more accurate, and fair to the memory of so many martyrs, Catholic and otherwise, who did resist, often unto death, to admit that resistance was not impossible; it simply was not the Ratzingers' choice.

In fact, a small but significant number of the Ratzingers' neighbors spoke out, and it is important to recognize that fact. "It was possible to resist, and those people set an example for others," Elizabeth Lohner, now eighty-four and a Traunstein resident, told the *New York Times*. Lohner's brother-in-law was sent to Dachau as a conscientious objector. "The Ratzingers were young and had made a different choice."

There were others who engaged in active resistance, too, although it took an almost superhuman willingness to risk imprisonment or death and a personal determination to use violence. Underground partisans were found mainly among the Communists and students of the White Rose resistance faction, but there were some anti-Nazis whose resistance was drawn directly from their faith. The Ratzingers' own pastor in Traunstein, Father Josef Stelzle, preached a sermon on the Feast of the Epiphany in 1934 that led to his arrest. A police report detailed his incendiary homily: "Christ was born for all and died for all, white, yellow, and black. Today there are movements who do not want this to be true, who want a falsified Aryan Christ. These populist movements preach a so-called positive Christianity, a sham Christianity, a German Christianity which gives the overlords credibility, and which brings disease over the people. Beware these false prophets! Ask yourself whether they mean the real Christ, the child of Jews, who was born in Bethlehem."

Stelzle was expelled from Traunstein, returned in a year and continued to speak out, but managed to survive the war, dying in 1947. Ratzinger never mentions his pastor's experience.[8]

What the Nazi experience seems to have bred in Joseph Ratzinger, or the preexisting trait it reinforced in him, was a kind of distancing, a pattern of removing himself from unpleasantness, isolating the pure ideal—of the faith, the church, the family, the nation—from the inevitable corruptions of the world. This approach fosters a sense of remoteness in his remembrances, a detachment that may strike many as cold. In fact, it is problematic when a churchman who places such a high priority on personal rectitude and individual holiness appears unreflective about his own history. And it is even more problematic when that churchman becomes the Supreme Pastor of the Roman Catholic Church, the leader of the ongoing dialogue with Judaism. This crucial dialogue is not so much about examining theology—Ratzinger's forte—as it is about modeling interpersonal relationships, and Ratzinger's characteristic distance was evident during his visit to a synagogue in Cologne in August 2005 on his first visit abroad as Pope Benedict.

The visit was charged with meaning and emotion—the first German pope in a thousand years on his first trip abroad, making just the second papal visit ever to a Jewish house of worship, one that had been destroyed during Kristallnacht and the Nazi purge that briefly drew Benedict in, however tangentially. The synagogue dates to Roman times, the oldest temple north of the Alps, and the Germans nearly wiped out the 11,000-strong prewar Jewish community.

Though he was warmly welcomed by the five hundred Jews in attendance, Benedict never mentioned his own experience of the wartime era or sought to make any personal connection with his audience or, through them, to the wider Jewish community, for whom the moment was so freighted. He condemned the Holocaust as "the darkest period of German and European history" and called Nazism "an insane racist ideology, born of neopaganism," but he made no reference to Catholic self-examination and apology, which John Paul stressed in his meetings with Jews, or to the moral failings of German Catholics specifically. He repeated church condemnations of anti-Semitism in general but he was careful to distinguish between the Nazi war on the Jews and Christian-Jewish relations, which have had their own "complex and painful" history. Apparently referring to Jewish complaints about the Vatican's role during the war and the lack of access to some Vatican archives of the era, Benedict said that Jews and Catholics must work toward a "shared interpretation of disputed historical questions." He also signaled that though he wanted dialogue, he would not "gloss over or underestimate the existing differences."

Benedict's flat-footed tone at that momentous occasion—a contrast to the lyricism of his positive reminiscences of Germany—is a dismaying affect that understandably rankles many critics. In an often skewed attack on Ratzinger's youth during World War II, the literary critic Carlin Romano rightly points to the unsettling selectiveness in Ratzinger's memories of the horrific era as his primary fault: "Ratzinger never speaks of the slave-labor camp 12 kilometers outside of Traunstein. He never talks about Dachau, some 100 kilometers away, though contemporaries of Ratzinger have told reporters that townspeople knew of the camp, and even used 'Watch out or you'll end up in Dachau' as a warning," Romano wrote in the *Chronicle of Higher Education*. "Lack of indignation, rather than complicity, is the sin of omission in his reminiscences."[9]

In his indispensable 2000 biography, *Cardinal Ratzinger: The Vatican's Enforcer of the Faith,* John Allen makes a similar point: "One gets the impression that the Third Reich has meaning for Ratzinger today primarily as an object lesson about church and culture, and only the details consistent with that argument have passed through the filter of his memory."[10]

Allen and others cite many examples of this filter at work. Neither in Ratzinger's autobiography nor in *Salt of the Earth* or other expansive musings, for instance, does he mention the sign that hung in the *Stadtplatz,* or main square, of Traunstein, after 1933. It read, "Do not buy from the Jew. He sells you, farmers, out of house and home." Nor does he talk about the November 1938 *Kristallnacht* attacks on the homes of Jewish families in Traunstein, who were threatened with death and deportation. Instead, he points out that the day after *Kristallnacht* the archbishop's palace in Munich was stormed by a mob. The archbishop was not at risk of death, however. Traunstein's Jews, on the other hand, began leaving the next day; those who did not were forcibly removed and their homes confiscated. Many others died in the camps. On November 12, 1938, Traunstein was declared *Judenfrei,* or free of Jews. While the number of Jews in Traunstein were few, such events would have been common knowledge in a town of fewer than twelve thousand residents. Traunstein also had a number of leftist and student martyrs of Nazi violence, but they are all invisible in Ratzinger's recollections.[11]

When it comes to the guilt that has been the collective burden of Germany's postwar generations, Joseph Ratzinger tends to focus on the failings of individuals rather than on perceived defects in the national character. Then, as now, he does not like the notion of communal responsibility, or social sin, which can obscure personal guilt. When he does talk about the German character, he is defensive. In *Salt of the Earth,* for example, he argues that "we should also avoid an excess of German self-accusation," and he talks about the roots of Nazism as inadvertently nurtured by a surfeit of goodness:

Germany does have, of course, a historical burden all its own, which has grown heavy since 1933–1945. And the question of what actually happened to our people that something like that could take place is one we must ask with great seriousness. I think that the virtues of the Germans and their vulnerabilities are very closely connected. On the one hand, we are a people who value discipline, achievement, work, and punctuality, and so we really do get things done, a people who today are once again the strongest economic power in Europe and have the most stable currency. But that leads easily to a certain overrating of oneself and to a one-sided mentality that

values only things such as achievement, work, production, what we've pro-
duced by ourselves, discipline, and thereby allows many other dimensions of
human existence to atrophy. It can also lead time and again to a certain ar-
rogance toward other nations, so that people say that only what is German
is really any good, the others are all "sloppy," and so forth. This temptation
to self-righteousness, to a one-sided evaluation of things in terms of param-
eters of productivity, is doubtless a part of German or, at any rate, of recent
German history, and we have to set ourselves against it.

But an overdose of self-esteem by a high-achieving people, while perhaps
unseemly to one of Ratzinger's humble makeup, is hardly an adequate explanation for Germany's horrific twentieth-century legacy or a satisfying one
from a man in Ratzinger's position.

In discussing any specifically Catholic responsibility for the war and the Holocaust, Ratzinger also tends to be frustratingly elliptical, to say the least. When
the issue is raised, he notes first that Christianity, and most prominently Catholic Christianity, was a principal target of the Nazis. The Holocaust, he says, "was
not committed by Christians in the name of Christ but by anti-Christians who
also conceived of it as the first phase of the annihilation of Christianity. . . . The
fact that Hitler's annihilation of the Jews also had a consciously anti-Christian
character is important and must not be passed over in silence."[12]

He goes on to concede that some "baptized people were responsible" for
the Holocaust, but again he tries to separate the Nazi perpetrators from the
church, saying there were "hardly any believing Christians among them." He
agrees that it is "undeniable" that Christian anti-Semitism "prepared the soil to
a certain degree," but he adds that this anti-Semitism existed "in all European
countries." His family, by contrast, "really practised its faith. The faith of my
parents, of our Church, confirmed for me that Catholicism was a citadel of
truth and righteousness against the realm of atheism and deceit which nazism
[he refuses to confer a capital letter on Hitler's movement] represented. The collapse of the regime [the Third Reich] proved to me that the Church's premoni-
tions were right." Elsewhere Ratzinger has dismissed as "rash" any connection
between the rise of Nazism and the Catholic Church or his beloved Bavaria.
"The poisonous seeds of nazism are not the fruit of Austrian and Southern
German Catholicism but rather of the decadent cosmopolitan atmosphere of
Vienna at the end of the monarchy," he said. "In this atmosphere Hitler looked
with envy at the strength and resoluteness of the German North"—in other
words, Prussians and Protestants.[13]

But in 1934 Hitler also explicitly praised the famous—and famously anti-

Semitic—Passion play, which was the pride of the entire town of Oberammergau, a staunchly Catholic and quintessentially Bavarian town that had vowed to put on the play every decade after their prayers for deliverance from the plague in 1634 were answered. "It is vital that the Passion play be continued at Oberammergau; for never has the menace of Jewry been so convincingly portrayed as in this presentation of what happened in the time of the Romans," Hitler said.

That Ratzinger saw in Catholicism a heroic bulwark against the Nazis is not surprising given his investment in the German church, and his view is also not without merit given the historical record.

More than one thousand priests died at Dachau, and the *Martyrologium Germanicum*, published by the German hierarchy in 1999, lists some three hundred Catholics who are believed to have died for their faith at the hands of the Nazis.[14] "The Catholic Church does not have to be ashamed of its role during the course of this century," Cardinal Joachim Meisner of Cologne said at the presentation, reflecting a view widely held among German Catholics. The Nazis enacted all manner of egregious policies against the Catholic Church, confiscating property, harassing priests and nuns, suppressing Catholic organizations and publishing houses—a *Kirchenkampf*, or struggle against the church, that essentially re-created Bismarck's *Kulturkampf*, but at the point of a gun. German Catholics were less likely to back the Nazis in elections than in other regions, and in August 1932 the German bishops barred Catholics from membership in the Nazi Party.

Many German bishops spoke courageously against the Nazis, most prominently the bishop of Münster, Clemens August von Galen, an aristocrat known as the "Lion of Münster" for his fiery sermons against Nazi extermination policies and Gestapo tactics. His attacks were even distributed among the White Rose underground resistance. High-ranking Nazis for a time discussed the possibility of assassinating von Galen but decided his death would only rally Catholics against the Nazis. (In October 2005, von Galen was beatified in St. Peter's Basilica, the second step on the road to sainthood; he was the first German so honored by Pope Benedict.) Munich's Cardinal Michael von Faulhaber was also an outspoken critic of Hitler, denouncing Nazi efforts to recast Christianity as a *Judenfrei* Aryan religion. After *Kristallnacht*, Faulhaber loaned a truck to the city's chief rabbi so he could rescue religious articles from his synagogue, and he contributed to the 1937 encyclical of Pius XI, *Mit Brennender Sorge* (With Searing Anxiety), which condemned Nazi racism and anti-Christian attacks. The encyclical was smuggled into Germany and read from all pulpits, prompting further Nazi retribution.

That is only one side of the German Catholic story, however. The other side gets short shrift from Joseph Ratzinger.

For example, the March 1933 passage of the Enabling Act that gave Hitler dictatorial powers was achieved because it was endorsed by the Catholic Center Party and its leader, Monsignor Ludwig Kaas, in consultation with the German bishops. Four days later, the hierarchy rescinded the ban on Catholic membership in the Nazi Party, and the bishops began encouraging Catholics to acquiesce to state power. Church leaders apparently hoped their conciliation would moderate Hitler's antagonism. That was a tragic miscalculation, but the church kept trying.

In July 1933 the German church dissolved the Catholic Center Party, which was already losing popular Catholic support, and later that month came what many see as the quid pro quo when the Holy See's secretary of state, Cardinal Pacelli, signed a concordat with Hitler ostensibly guaranteeing freedom for Catholic institutions and religious activities. The ongoing debates over the judgment of Pacelli, later Pius XII, in this and other Nazi-era episodes continue to churn. But whatever the details, it is an undeniable, if unflattering, reality that the Catholic Church did much to aid the rise of Nazism. The church was always a politically conservative force antagonistic to the Weimar Republic, which Hitler unseated, and it was often more amenable to autocracies that favored church positions than to popular democracies that did not. Church leaders also saw Nazism as a defense against the atheistic Stalinist communism next door. The concordat gave Hitler international respectability at a critical juncture early in his regime. Moreover, it heralded the start of a policy of quiet diplomatic protests by the church—the "silence" that is so often cited against it—which was only broken with the 1937 encyclical, after the hierarchy saw how badly it had been deceived by Hitler.

German anti-Semitism and the role of the Christian churches, Catholic and Protestant, in fomenting its peculiarly virulent German strain, cannot be downplayed or diluted by contextualizing it with the anti-Semitism that was widespread at the time. Jews in Bavaria were regularly harassed or beaten by Catholics who accused them of being Christ-killers, a line they were fed in the liturgy of the time and in sermons. As Allen recounts, Catholic animus toward Jews was even encouraged by many priests and bishops. Archbishop Konrad Gröber of Freiburg was known as the "Brown Bishop" because of his support for the Nazis, and Cardinal Adolf Bertram of Breslau refused to aid Jewish victims of Nazi boycotts, saying they had "no very close bond with the church." Even Cardinal Faulhaber hedged his sermons on Judaism, clarifying that they were intended to defend the Jews of the Old Testament, not the Jews of the day. Faulhaber praised efforts to keep the German stock "as far as possible unadulterated," and he celebrated a special solemn Mass to give thanks for Hitler's escape from a 1939 assassination attempt. After the war, Faulhaber was instrumental in helping many former Nazis whom the church considered "good Catholics" to escape the American de-Nazification program and become leaders in the new civilian government, because otherwise the Allies would have promoted left-leaning politicians who did not favor church positions.

Ratzinger does not delve into these aspects of the church's record, and he tends to absolve ordinary churchgoing Germans of being soft on Hitler, pointing instead to Catholics "in academic circles" as those particularly responsible for being duped.[15] But it is important to note that relatively weak Catholic political support for the Nazis was tied to historical, regional, and cultural loyalties to local Catholic parties, which for decades had defended Catholic interests against whatever party was in power in Berlin. The political choices of German Catholics on behalf of their own party were hardly a pure application of Christian principles.

Clearly the Catholic Church's record in the Nazi era is complex and controversial, with rays of blessed light, but too often illuminating a pervasive darkness that Catholics and their leadership did far too much to create.

In the end, there is no real traction in the debate over whether Ratzinger did anything during the war or failed to do something extraordinary. What is important is the effect it had on his thought and future church career.

For Joseph Ratzinger, what the Nazi era demonstrated above all is that the internal unity of a loyal minority is vital to resisting wider societal deviations—be it Nazism or any totalitarianism. As John Allen puts it, Ratzinger learned from the war that only a pure church of unsullied belief and internal unity could resist oppression, whatever its source: "Having seen fascism in action, Ratzinger today believes that the best antidote to political totalitarianism is ecclesial totalitarianism." Allen says he has come to regret some of his judgments in *The Vatican Enforcer of the Faith,* and that may be one of them. But if he overstates the case, he gets at a truth about Ratzinger's hard-won lessons from his war experience.

In developing this view, Ratzinger points, with some justification, to the example of German Protestantism, which, because of its status as the country's virtual state religion and Lutheranism's legacy of almost uncritical support for state power, was susceptible to pressures from the Nazi regime, or at least a tempting target. Starting in 1933, Hitler sought to transform German

Protestantism into a nationalist *Deutsche Christen,* or German Christian movement, a state religion based on race and led by a *Reichsbishop* appointed by Hitler.

The *Deutsche Christen* movement did leave German Protestantism badly divided, and the Evangelical Church and other denominations never recovered. (Communist East Germany was four-fifths Protestant, and belief there did not survive more than four decades of official atheism.) But many German Protestants did rally against the Nazi campaign of co-optation and showed themselves to be among the most prominent foes of Hitler and Nazism. In May 1934, for example, the great Reformed theologian Karl Barth (he was Swiss but taught at German universities) and the Lutheran leader Hans Asmussen convened a meeting of 140 representatives of nineteen Protestant denominations. They issued a strong declaration rejecting any link between Nazism and Christianity and declared their independence from state oversight. The so-called Confessing Church that grew out of the Barmen Declaration and subsequent meetings led Hitler to largely abandon the *Deutsche Christen* effort, but also to widespread persecution of Confessing Church members. Martin Niemöller of Berlin was courageous in facing down Hitler and was sent to the Sachsenhausen; he survived, though many others did not. The Lutheran martyr Dietrich Bonhoeffer is perhaps the most prominent example.

Just as powerful as their record during the war was the statement of the Confessing Church immediately after the war, in the Stuttgart Declaration of October 1945: "We accuse ourselves that we did not witness more courageously, pray more faithfully, believe more joyously, love more ardently."

The Catholic Church in Germany in the immediate postwar era did not see itself in such terms. As Ratzinger himself recalls, "Despite many human failings, the [Catholic] Church was the alternative to the destructive ideology of the brown rulers [the Nazis]; in the inferno that had swallowed up the powerful, she had stood firm with a force coming to her from eternity. It had been demonstrated: The gates of hell will not overpower her. From our own experience we now knew what was meant by 'the gates of hell,' and we could also see with our own eyes that the house built on rock had stood firm."[16]

Ratzinger, while recognizing the heroic virtue of the Confessing Church, clearly sees the Catholic example as preferable. In the *Ratzinger Report* of 1985, he says, "The idea of a national, i.e., Germanic, anti-Latin Christianity gave a handle to Hitler, as did the tradition of State churches and the very strong emphasis on obedience to authority which is part and parcel of the Lutheran tradition. From these aspects German Protestantism, and Lutheranism especially, was far more liable to succumb to Hitler's attack. A movement such as the 'German Christians' could never have arisen within the Catholic concept of the Church.".

Ratzinger says that among "average Christians, Catholics found it easier to stand firm in opposition to Hitler's doctrines. That era showed us something that history has continually confirmed: while the Catholic Church can make tactical pacts, for the sake of the lesser evil, even with repressive States, in the last analysis she reveals herself as a bastion against totalitarian derangement. By her very nature, in fact, she cannot become tied up with the State."[17]

Indeed, the one aspect Ratzinger does find problematic about the church's war record was the hierarchy's temptation to negotiate with the Nazis to preserve the church's institutional perquisites. The German bishops' focus on maintaining Catholic schools, hospitals, and universities free of state control was their governing principle, and one they asserted in letters read from the pulpit as the Nazis increasingly deprived the church of those institutional controls. Ratzinger remembers them, and the lesson they imparted, even as a small boy: "Already then it dawned on me that, with their insistence on preserving institutions, these letters in part misread the reality. I mean that merely to guarantee institutions is useless if there are no people to support those institutions from inner conviction."[18]

Historians agree that the Catholic Church in Germany did compromise itself in protecting its assets rather than sacrificing for the Gospel, though their judgments would perhaps be harsher than those of Ratzinger. In her 2002 book, *Bishop von Galen: German Catholicism and National Socialism*, Beth A. Griech-Polelle writes that, during the Nazi era, "*religious* came to mean not supporting the universal values of brotherly love and equality but rather keeping Catholic confessional schools, organizations, and associations alive." The 1932 ban on Nazi Party membership, for example, was justified by the bishops because a Nazi takeover was likely to dim "the prospects for church interests."[19]

Ratzinger says there was a German core that did remain faithful to Catholicism, but as cardinal and pope he would return to the theme of the dangers of privileging institutional ties, emphasizing that the church would do better to shed bricks and mortar—universities, hospitals, parochial schools, and the like—rather than have them animated by anything less than a purely orthodox faith. This is an element in his oft-cited preference for a "smaller but purer" church of the holy remnant. This preference for the minimum, the creed of the classical conservative he remains, would manifest itself in many ways, notably in an ingrained suspicion of national bishops' conferences, which he saw in wartime Germany and later as acting in national self-interest rather than in the interests of universal Catholicism. That seed of suspicion would sprout decades later, when Cardinal Ratzinger led the Vatican's efforts to rein in episcopal conferences, especially in the United States, which he viewed as acting like autonomous national bodies.

The peril of institutionalism is a direct outgrowth of Ratzinger's personal reaction to the dangerous alliances of the Nazi era, or to even swimming in the same sea with such an ideology. Ratzinger's personality is the key to interpreting his later record, and indeed his sometimes abstruse thought and theology. The war instilled in Ratzinger the obvious imperative to condemn evil in his midst, but to do so in a way that would avoid unpleasant personal confrontations, which he always disliked. His preferred means of doing that would be through the academic routine of books and essays and disputation at a distance. Maintaining a safe distance from the messiness of the temporal world, and pledging allegiance only to the pure ideal, would be a leitmotif for the rest of his life.

The Joseph Ratzinger who emerged from the war remained a German but with the mind-set of the Israelites in the Babylonian captivity. He kept himself apart from the war and his family apart from the Nazis. He separated Bavaria from the rest of Germany, his Catholic Church from German Protestantism, and the failings of some Catholics from the inerrancy of the Catholic faith. Catholics who did make moral compromises did so either out of the best of motives (namely, the hierarchy) or they were "academics," intellectuals whose self-involved minds had clouded the judgment of their purer hearts. The "simple faithful" were the bearers of the true faith, but the war showed that that faith would need protection from the corruptions to which the human soul—especially, it would seem, the German soul—is all too vulnerable.

As Nietzsche wrote, "The German soul has its passageways and interpassageways; there are caves, hideouts, and dungeons in it; its disorder has a good deal of the attraction of the mysterious; the German is an expert on secret paths to chaos."[20] Ratzinger disdained Nietzsche but agreed with a similar sentiment voiced by another German radical. "Luther was right when he said that man must first be frightened of himself so that he can then find the right way," Ratzinger once said.[21]

For Ratzinger, the right way never seemed to be in doubt, and with the war over he got back to the predictable path whose ultimate destination would surprise everyone.

Chapter Six

COUNCIL, CRISIS, AND CONVERSION

J oseph Ratzinger's journey to the priesthood was as inevitable as his birth was providential—and nothing like the clamorous transformations of adulthood that so many of his heroes experienced. There was no blinding light like Paul's road to Damascus, no lifelong repentance for a misspent youth like that of Augustine, no terrifying lightning bolt like the one that sent Luther into the monastery. "I haven't had illuminations in the classical sense, if by that you mean something half-mystical," he once told an interviewer, in a tone that seemed shocked at the thought of such an emotional experience. "I am a perfectly ordinary Christian."[1]

But a Christian with an extraordinary intellect, and in typical fashion, God spoke to Joseph Ratzinger's heart by going through his head.

In November 1945, just a few months after returning from his army service, the eighteen-year-old Ratzinger arrived at the seminary at Freising along with his brother, Georg, who was three years older but at the same starting point in his studies because of the war. In fact, the 120 future priests studying with them covered a range of ages, some as old as forty, which was unusual in those days, when most priests entered as young men or teens. Many of the older seminarians were battle-scarred veterans who had had families or secular careers, and they looked down on Joseph and his contemporaries "as immature children who lacked the sufferings necessary for the priestly ministry, since we had not gone through those dark nights that alone can give full shape to the radical assent a priest must give."

Ratzinger freely conceded that he had discerned God's call to the priest-hood as a boy, though the inevitable flush of postconclave praise for Ratzinger as pope reached somewhat mythic levels. Anna Fischer, the last surviving neighbor of the Ratzingers' in Marktl, said that even as an infant "in his eyes lay a serene wisdom beyond his years."[2]

The future pope was always far more self-deprecating about his sanctity. At the presentation of his 1997 memoir, *Milestones,* Ratzinger was asked why he had made almost no mention of girlfriends in recounting his adolescence. "I had to keep the manuscript to 100 pages," he quipped. But Ratzinger appears to have been far more interested in books than girls, or much else outside the sanctuary. He wrote that while he was "touched by friendship" with girls as an adolescent, he never had any interest in a family or a vocation outside the priesthood. Indeed, when Ratzinger was five years old, the august Cardinal Faulhaber visited his town, arriving in a long black limousine and leaving a lasting image on the impressionable child: "With his imposing purple, he im-pressed me all the more, so that I said, I would like to become something like that." Recalled his brother Georg, "It wasn't so much the car, since we weren't technically minded. It was the way the cardinal looked, his bearing and the garments he was wearing that made such an impression on him."[3]

As a young seminarian, Ratzinger's enchantment with the "grand and ven-erable figure" of Faulhaber only deepened. "You could practically touch the burden of sufferings he had to bear during the Nazi period, which now envel-oped him with an aura of dignity." Ratzinger does not raise any doubts about Faulhaber's actions during the war, though in another context he revealed that Faulhaber once banned the ringing of church bells in Traunstein to appease the Nazis, a move greatly resented by Ratzinger's neighbors. Ratzinger saw in Faulhaber a powerful icon of the church, rather than the approachable pastor that others may have sought: "In him we were not looking for an 'accessible bishop'; rather, what moved me deeply about him was the awe-inspiring gran-deur of his mission, with which he had become fully identified."

The mission was pretty much all the church had left, since the glorious Ba-roque edifice Faulhaber once ruled lay in ruins. The old seminary was still being used as a military hospital for foreign prisoners, and for the first months the students had to bunk in makeshift accommodations in bombed-out buildings. Books were a rarity, and winter classes were curtailed because of a lack of heating fuel. But the almost complete destruction of what had been for so long a routin-ized system of priestly formation seemed to free the Ratzinger brothers and their fellow seminarians to explore the new world around them with a liberty that would have been unheard of in earlier days. "We wanted not only to do theology in the narrower sense but to listen to the voices of man today," Ratzinger writes in *Milestones*. The seminarians read novels by popular authors and caught up on the latest scientific breakthroughs by Einstein, Planck, and Heisenberg. They read widely in philosophy, the likes of Heidegger and Jaspers, Nietzsche and Bergson, and studied great Jewish writers like Martin Buber, as well as the writings—pre-Reformation—of Martin Luther, whom Ratzinger found particularly engaging. In non-Catholic authors he detected forgotten strains of the best of Catholic thinking, and in physics and philosophy he detected "a new openness to the unknown—and hence also to the Unknown, namely, God."

It was an exciting time to be a theologian. Theologians were the mind of the church at a time when Christianity was ready to do some hard thinking. They had none of the wartime baggage of the institutional church leaders, and they enjoyed the romance of radicals everywhere, tossing aside centuries of hidebound traditions to explore and formulate theology to speak to a twentieth-century people who would not reflexively accept the same old verities in the same old packaging.

Catholicism especially had a lot of ground to make up, and the evisceration of Christendom in two world wars helped spur the church—albeit with a little help from Rome—to heed the theological and liturgical renewal that had started between the wars and was now flourishing. In France and Belgium, the *Nouvelle Théologie* was upending the establishment and earning Roman reprimands for doing so, while the French theologian and paleontologist Pierre Teilhard de Chardin was incurring Vatican rebukes for his speculative connections between science and theology. The German-speaking world was, as always, at the center of the intellectual buzz. Protestant theologians like Karl Barth (a favorite of Ratzinger) and Rudolph Bultmann (less favored) were overturning liberal Protestant verities, but the ferment in Catholicism was especially ripe. German theologian Romano Guardini was leading the charge for modernizing the liturgy and establishing a theology centered on spirituality, and the Swiss theologian Hans Urs von Balthasar was pushing for a return to the teachings of early church fathers as an avenue to a more Christ-centered church.

Both men were heroes to Joseph Ratzinger, who, like so many other Catholic intellectuals of the time, was energized by the ferment that the postwar era permitted. "There was a great intellectual élan, and one got swept up with it," he recalled.

Entranced by the prospect of an academic career devoted to his beloved books, Ratzinger applied for admission to the Herzogliches Georgianum, a premier theology school associated with the University of Munich. It was a posting that would guarantee him access to the wider intellectual currents that so attracted him, and ensured the professor's life he wanted. In the fall of 1947 he began studies at the Georgianum, and in the study of theology and the intellectual repartee of the academy Ratzinger found "the drama of my life and above all the mystery of truth." The boy from small-town Bavaria had gotten a glimpse of the big city German *zeitgeist* and was never going back.

While the young Karol Wojtyla was treading the boards as an actor and writing poetry and plays, Joseph Ratzinger was exploring the life of the mind through the great systems of theology.

For Ratzinger, the new freedom meant "doing away with what was dusty and obsolete," as he later put it. In this process of reinvention, the chief obstacle was the old-fashioned Scholasticism that had been the philosophical framework for Catholic thought since the Middle Ages. Scholasticism was a method of inquiry that believed reason was a gift of God that could be used to make faith and the human condition intelligible to man, and thereby foster belief. This school of thought arose in the eleventh century, when theology was still the "queen of the sciences," a dominant mode of thought that encompassed faith and reason, philosophy and the emerging natural sciences. In the Middle Ages, all human activity was still oriented to God, and the church was the locus of intellectual exploration; the church's newly organized universities naturally drew the greatest minds of the day. And the greatest of these was Thomas Aquinas (1225–74), a Dominican friar and theologian whose voluminous treatises, scripture commentaries, and sermons were capped off by his magisterial *Summa Theologiae*, a masterwork that epitomized the ambition of the medieval mind. The *Summa* of Aquinas was to theology what the cathedral of Chartres was to architecture—a marvel of engineering whose beauty and harmony disguised the hard calculations that made it possible. Rather than appealing to authority (as most theologians did at the time), Aquinas set forth a more rigorous, almost scientific approach to theology, offering questions and answers, anticipating objections, carefully sifting the evidence, and finally offering a response.

Despite opposition from the still-dominant Augustinian school, Aquinas represented the unstoppable new breed, thinkers who ranged far afield in their efforts to elucidate the truth. They would eagerly scour the writings of Jewish thinkers like Maimonides, Muslims like Averroës, or pagans like Aristotle, believing that threads of truth were to be found everywhere; and, when woven together in the light of Christian faith, they would reveal a tapestry of eternal truth, as shown in Holy Writ. Aquinas "saw no opposition between nature and grace or between truths discovered by reason and those revealed by God," as the medievalist Walter Principe put it.

Within decades of his death, Aquinas was made a saint, and soon thereafter a Doctor of the Church, and still later the patron of all Catholic universities. The problem was that Scholastics after Aquinas extracted a dry Thomistic philosophy from his work, divorcing it from theology and leaving "a dessicated body of doctrines." His model suffered from its later interpreters and church leaders who co-opted Scholasticism (and the subset known as Thomism, after Thomas Aquinas) as a weapon to battle various movements that cropped up to challenge the church's authority in all spheres. Thus Scholasticism became infamous for a conceptual, sterile kind of theological argumentation over the minutiae of belief—the "angels on the head of a pin" school of theology. For example, scholars endlessly debated such pressing issues as whether the saved would be able to eat or drink after the resurrection. "We're taking due precautions against hunger and thirst while there's still time," was the response of the sixteenth-century humanist wit Erasmus.[4]

The Scholastic, text-driven mode of inquiry experienced periodic declines and resurgences, and after a long period of neglect, a movement known as neo-Scholasticism emerged in the early nineteenth century and flourished in the relatively bankrupt intellectual climate of Catholic thought left by the depradations of the Napoleonic era. In a hostile modern world that was impinging on the church from all sides, neo-Scholasticism functioned as a comforting one-size-fits-all answer.

But in the middle of the century another school of liberal Catholic thought arose to challenge the stuffy old ways, and nowhere was this school more vibrant or liberal than in Germany, and in Germany the liberal Catholic soul was centered in Bavaria. The unchallenged leader of this liberalizing movement was Johann Ignaz von Döllinger, a Munich professor whose studies in the new historical method moved him from his original ultramontane (literally, "beyond the mountains," as in across the Alps in Rome) view of authority to a more liberal attitude. Döllinger's optimistic view of modern developments, and his commitment to opening the borders between modernity and Catholicism, did not please the neo-Scholastics, based in the central Rhineland, who dominated seminaries and theology schools and who tended toward an authoritarian view of the church. The neo-Scholastics believed modern culture "was hopelessly rationalist and secular and inimical to the Church; they therefore favored a state-of-seige strategy and authoritarian methods," writes

Thomas Bokenkotter. "They wanted the Catholic faithful protected from contamination by secularism and rationalism and welded into a disciplined army led by zealous and pious priests trained in seminaries isolated from the pernicious influences of secular culture."[5] To achieve this aim, they favored a centralized Roman authority that would enforce adherence to every doctrine and statement from the Holy See, and they were especially tough on theologians who might stray from Rome's prescriptions.

Despite his outsider status, Döllinger's liberal influence extended across the continent, in part thanks to his famous student, Lord Acton, who would later become famous for his statement "Power tends to corrupt, and absolute power corrupts absolutely" and for his hard-line opposition to the doctrine of papal infallibility defined by the First Vatican Council in 1870. Acton also joined forces with the most famous Catholic convert of the century, John Henry Newman, soon to be Cardinal Newman.

The power of the liberals' ideas was no match for the Vatican's machinery, however, and the contest between the two camps became increasingly bitter as the embattled Vatican sought to crack down on Döllinger and his allies. In December 1864, Pius IX issued his *Syllabus of Errors*, which listed eighty errors of the modern world, including rationalism, naturalism, and religious freedom. One liberal proposition that was condemned was the idea that "the Roman Pontiff can and ought to reconcile and harmonize himself with progress, with liberalism, and with modern civilization." That was the final error, number 80.

Such language sounded like a declaration of war on the modern world, which it was, and the *Syllabus of Errors* sparked a furor. But it did succeed in halting the liberals' progress. It also provoked Döllinger to a growing shrillness in his critiques of Rome. In 1867, the year he was installed as rector of the University of Munich, he declared, "The papacy is based on an audacious falsification of history. . . . A forgery at its very outset, it has, during the long years of its existence, had a pernicious influence on church and state alike." In 1871 Döllinger was excommunicated and fired from the university.

Interestingly, Döllinger had a strong tie to Joseph Ratzinger's great-uncle, Georg Ratzinger, a priest who acted as Döllinger's assistant for several years in the 1860s and was the most famous Ratzinger before Joseph came along. Like Döllinger, Ratzinger's great-uncle Georg was an unapologetic liberal who, despite being a priest, decided to take his liberal views into politics, though with a decidedly populist and localized Bavarian cast. He championed the small farmers of the region against the wealthy special interests of the north, using the coalescing tenets of Catholic social teaching as his platform. (He resigned from the priesthood in 1888 to dedicate himself to politics.) But Georg Ratzinger was also a creature of his time and place, and his increasingly radical populism also led him to embrace anti-Semitic views that were fueled by resentment of the banking class, which he believed was controlled by Jews. In a series of ugly tracts, for example, Georg Ratzinger explained how he believed Jews were undermining the Christian faith and German values.[6]

His grand-nephew Joseph, now Pope Benedict XVI, has not commented in detail on Georg Ratzinger's record, saying only that "his achievements and political standing also made everyone proud of him."

As Georg Ratzinger moved his activism to the political sphere, liberal Catholics continued even after the reactionary First Vatican Council to push for greater openness. But their experiment took an almost mortal blow when Leo XIII, known otherwise for his liberal social positions, issued an 1879 encyclical, *Aeterni patris*, which named Aquinas as the model Christian philosopher, whose Scholastic teachings, albeit interpreted in a narrow way, would in effect be the official Catholic philosophy. Leo's successor, Pius X (1903–14) was a true revanchist who took Leo's Scholastic-friendly policy and enforced it with an iron fist, launching a campaign against liberal positions, under the vague title of Modernism—the "synthesis of all heresies," as Pius called it in 1907. Still, despite persecution and suppression, the liberal agitation against Scholasticism continued, especially in Germany. In this sense, Joseph Ratzinger was very much the beneficiary of earlier generations, who had suffered much from Rome to prepare the ground for future generations. Indeed, his own professor, the renowned biblical scholar Friedrich Wilhelm Maier, had been booted from his university chair during the anti-Modernist crusade for positing new theories about the textual sources of the Gospels. A few decades later, Maier's theories were considered mainstream ideas and he was back in the university teaching students like Joseph Ratzinger, though with a lasting bitterness toward Rome that Ratzinger found distasteful.

Ratzinger needed little encouragement to take up the baton of what was then known as progressivism. He liked the historical-critical method of Maier and others—as long as it was "restricted by dogma"—and he came to embrace the burgeoning movement for liturgical reform that he had once shunned. Ratzinger would later smile a bit when looking back at his youthful confidence, especially from the point of view of the curialists, whose "Roman pronouncements" he had once disdained: "Perhaps German arrogance also contributed a little to our belief that we knew what was what better than 'those down there.'"

Yet it would be a mistake to see Joseph Ratzinger, as many have done in retrospect, as a theological innovator who wanted to open up new avenues for belief. In fact, Ratzinger took the notion of being a "radical" literally, in the sense of going back to the roots, the Latin *radix*. In church terms, that meant studying patristics, going back to the early church fathers, specifically, Augustine of Hippo (354–430), the North African bishop and slayer of heresies.

Saint Augustine is one of the best known of the church fathers outside the church, though for reasons having less to do with his foundational Christian theology than with his famous autobiography, the *Confessions*, whose psychological insight and self-awareness have made it a central text of Western civilization and the modern era. This ageless memoir recounts Augustine's relatively privileged upbringing on the North African rim of the Mediterranean basin, beginning with his birth to a pagan father and a Christian mother—she would become better known as Saint Monica—and his classical education in philosophy and rhetoric. Like Ratzinger, Augustine was a brilliant young man who fell in love with wisdom and knowledge. But unlike Ratzinger, for many years Augustine did not find an outlet for his intellect in the church, and he fell in love with many other things, and women, along the way, which is what makes the *Confessions* such fascinating reading.

He took a concubine at eighteen, and she produced a son. He dismissed her some years later in order to take a proper wife in a marriage arranged by his mother, but took another mistress because he couldn't wait the necessary two years to bed his wife-to-be. "O Lord, help me to be pure, but not yet," as he put it in one of his many well-remembered phrases. In painfully honest, introspective detail, Augustine recounts his wastrel youth, his unfettered selfishness and insensibility to anything that did not provide him with pleasure. In Carthage, he and his good-for-nothing friends once stole fruit from a neighbor's orchard simply for the fun of it—shocking proof for him of the stubborn presence of original sin and his inability to overcome it on his own. "And this we enjoyed doing, merely because we knew it was wrong; and if the taste of the pears were at all sweet, it was only because they were stolen."

Naturally such decadence could only end in conversion, and Augustine's path to the true faith culminates with his baptism at Easter in 387, at the age of thirty-three and at the hands of Saint Ambrose in Milan. Augustine rejected his previous adherence to the heretical dualism of Manicheism (an esoteric gnosticism that saw the universe in terms of Dark and Light, Matter and the

Soul, Evil and Good, both contending on equal terms) and embraced a life of poverty and chastity dedicated to exploring the beauty of Christian orthodoxy with like-minded soul mates in a community he founded at his family's estate back in North Africa. Unfortunately, his plans went awry—as they would for Ratzinger—when he was acclaimed by the congregation during a visit to Hippo and forced, despite his tears and pleas, to accept ordination as a priest. He was later elevated to bishop of the city. There he would remain until his death in 430, while the Vandal hordes besieged the city, ministering to his flock and writing classic texts of the Christian canon.

If Augustine's *Confessions* showed him to be deeply humanistic, his theology showed him to be terribly severe—with himself, naturally, as well as the rest of humanity. Augustine was deeply pessimistic about the goodness of man and in everything stressed the *perditio,* or abject lostness, of mankind, and conversely the total dependence on God's grace to find salvation and everything else. Indeed, only God has being by himself, Augustine said, and his own *Confessions* were no more than an exploration, using God-given tools, of what God had given him, rather than a Cartesian declaration of his own identity. "To look at himself in his own memory without being grateful to God would be narcissism—what Augustine calls *praesumptio* which, together with *superbia,* constitutes man's greatest sin: egomania," writes Erik Erikson in his psychobiography of Martin Luther, who was also a devoted Augustinian. "Thus, whatever we are and become, whatever we can do and will do, is all a gift from God: *Ex Deo nobis est, non ex nobis.*"[1]

Augustine can be a paradoxical figure, which is not surprising given the extent of his writings, the transformations he experienced, and the varied roles he filled. At times he can sound like a Calvinist, or a Puritan like Jonathan Edwards, and his views on sex—the first fruit of original sin—are as negative as anything in Christianity or in the Manicheism he had rejected. In battling the heresy of Pelagianism (the view that man was born with the same freedom as Adam to choose good or evil, thus softening the concept of original sin), Augustine argued that, on the contrary, man is free only to sin. Man cannot achieve salvation by his own efforts. Augustine's twenty-two-volume opus, *City of God,* set the heavenly city far from that of the earthly City of Man, a society built on the prideful conviction that man can effect a better world—a delusion destined to fail, just as the Roman Empire had failed.

Yet Augustine was at heart optimistic about the possibility of grace even in the midst of enveloping iniquity. Augustine's church was a "hospital for incurables," an observation that sums up his views: No one is ever abandoned, but then no one is ever quite well. Little wonder that such a strong emphasis on man's fallen nature and a presumption for the primacy of grace appealed so strongly to the likes of Luther, and indeed Augustine has remained a touchstone for Protestant theology.

Augustine has been a dividing line for Catholics, however, one that stretches back to antiquity and forward to the present day. It is often said that the world is divided between Platonists and Aristotelians, and the same could be said about the Catholic Church. The Platonists had the first claim, as early Christian thinkers, intent on situating their new faith in the still-dominant culture of classical Greek thought, sought to reconcile the brilliance of philosophers like Plato (d. 347 BC) with the beliefs of Christianity. Plato's efforts to discover the truth of human existence led him to posit the existence of the Ideal, or the Form, of which the things in this world are merely an imperfect reflection. For Plato there was wide gulf between the pure Form of being and the imperfect, human world of becoming, which is what our imperfect human senses perceive.

By Augustine's day, seven centuries later, a school of Neoplatonism was the dominant mode of philosophy in the ancient world. The pagan thinker Plotinus was its chief expositor, and Augustine and other Christian leaders dedicated themselves to rehabilitating Neoplatonism for Christianity. In fact, Plotinus's focus on contemplation as the highest good and his concept of the material world as evil—he was ashamed that he even had a body—fit well with Augustine's natural belief in a truer and more intelligible spiritual world beyond this one, a world reachable only through a gift from God. "If you can grasp it, it isn't God. Let us rather make a devout confession of ignorance, instead of a brash profession of knowledge," as Augustine put it in a sermon.[8] In this context, Wisdom, rather than Knowledge, was the goal of the intellect. To know what we cannot know is as important as learning.

This view ruled Christian philosophy until the twelfth century, when one of the most remarkable and sudden developments in Western history took place with the recovery of the entire corpus of Aristotle, the Greek philosopher who was the successor to Plato but whose work was largely unknown to the Christian world. Over the course of a century (c. 1150–1250), all of Aristotle's works were translated into Latin from Arabic, the culture that had preserved them for centuries, along with commentaries by the Arabic and Jewish writers who had studied the Greek philosopher for so long. Aristotle wrote about everything, believing the world to be a knowable reality that was there to be categorized and comprehended. This view, however, was a serious challenge to the prevailing Christian philosophy dominated by Augustine, and it prompted a crisis in Western thought and a daunting effort by the church to harmonize these new vistas with the faith.

"Imagine, more than four centuries before Francis Bacon and René Descartes proclaimed the Scientific Revolution, a recognizably modern perspective—rationalist, this-wordly, humanistic, and empirical—ignited cultural warfare throughout Western Europe, challenging traditional religious and social beliefs at their core," Richard E. Rubenstein writes in *Aristotle's Children*. "The struggle between faith and reason did not begin, as is so often supposed, with Copernicus' challenge to earth-centered cosmology or Galileo's trial by the Inquisition but with the controversy over Aristotle's ideas during the twelfth and thirteenth centuries."[9]

But if one might say that Augustine "baptized" Plato, then Aquinas did the same with Aristotle, and thereby aided the medieval renaissance, as it is often called—the unprecedented flowering of intellectual creativity in the High Middle Ages. Building on Aristotle but making something wholly new and wholly Christian, Aquinas argued that God the Creator was perceptible in the *ordo divina* that he had created in the world, and that man's innate reason could help to make faith intelligible. Aquinas argued that part of that created world was man's reason and free will, and thus those gifts must be good and must be useful tools to achieve illumination. In other words, sanctity was a two-way street in which one could become good by habituation in order to fully cooperate with the divine gift of grace. "St. Thomas reserves a place for active and reasonable conjecture where before there was room for only faith and hope," Erikson says. "A greater synthesis between Antiquity and Christianity, Reason and Faith; its immediate results were a dignified piety, immaculate thought and an integrate cosmology well suited to the hierarchic and ceremonial style of the whole era."

This is a far more optimistic, world-centered view, which sees free will, and man himself, in far more positive terms than before. But it was also an alternative that presaged the bitter clash between Modernists and Integralists, progressives and traditionalists, liberals and conservatives, which would rage for much of the next millennium—indeed, up to the present day.

In this debate, Joseph Ratzinger came down firmly on the side of the bishop of Hippo. "I am a decided Augustinian," Ratzinger has said, adding that his two desert island books would be the Bible and the *Confessions*. He loved the

"human passion and depth" of the *Confessions* and by contrast "had difficulties in penetrating the thought of Thomas Aquinas, whose crystal-clear logic
seemed to me to be too closed in on itself, too impersonal and ready-made."

If this seems to contradict the portrait of Ratzinger as a searching intellectual, his true views on the value of the mind may clarify the apparent contradiction. "Seek not to understand that you may believe, but believe that you
may understand," Augustine once preached, in words that could have been
written by Joseph Ratzinger. Faith is a given for Ratzinger, a gift from God
(and one that he apparently has enjoyed since birth), and the dogmas and
doctrines of the church are not up for debate. Theology and the powers of the
intellect are not to create but to conserve—a task that requires just as much
energy, as he would discover—and to illuminate avenues to the *depositum fidei,* the deposit of faith, for the faithful. "This is *His* church and not a laboratory for theologians," as he put it.

While Ratzinger has been lauded as one of the great theological minds of
recent decades, this praise is more for the scope of his erudition than anything
his scholarship has added to theology—a demerit in the opinion of critics, an
attribute for him and his conservative supporters. "I have never tried to create
a system of my own, an individual theology. . . . The point of departure is first
of all the word. That we believe the word of God, that we try really to get to
know and understand it, and then, as I said, to think it together with the great
masters of the faith. This gives my theology a somewhat biblical character and
also bears the stamp of the Fathers, especially Augustine."[10]

In a sense, Ratzinger is more of a spiritual writer than a theologian. This fact
may help explain the paradox of Joseph Ratzinger as an intellectual who seems
to mistrust the human mind, a Catholic who prefers the pietistic formulations
of the Reformers to the insights of Catholicism's leading lights. Ratzinger said
in 1985 that if he were ever to return to academia, as was his lifelong desire,
he would dedicate his remaining years to writing on original sin. "In fact, if it
is no longer understood that man is in a state of alienation . . . one no longer
understands the necessity of Christ the Redeemer." It is a perilous and slippery
slope. "The whole structure of the faith is threatened by this."[11]

In starting out his theological training, Ratzinger saw Augustine as a counterweight to Aquinas and made him the focus of his studies. He wrote his dissertation on the ecclesiology of Augustine, that is, Augustine's interpretation
of what the "church" meant, and specifically the notion of the "People of God."
The image of the "People of God" that Ratzinger found in Augustine (though
Augustine never used that term; Ratzinger had to employ a highly inventive

exegesis of the sort he would later vilify) was not the bodily, priestly incarnation that the Second Vatican Council (1962–65) would later point to as a way of implementing a *congregatio,* a more horizontal church. Rather, Ratzinger found another ideal, one might say a Platonic form of the People of God as a spiritual *communio* based on the sacraments and handed down as a divine gift, protected by the hierarchy. "Providence has given to the French the empire of the land; to the English that of the sea; to the Germans that of—the air!" an eighteenth-century aphorism says. Indeed, Joseph Ratzinger's Catholic Church, as mediated by Augustine, was much like that German empire, existing most truly in its higher, unattainable ideal, and saved by its willingness to tolerate its many sinners until they saw the light of the Christian empyrean.

"Augustine can say: The Catholic Church is the true Church of the holy," Ratzinger wrote. "Sinners are not really in her, for their membership is only a seeming reality. . . . But on the other hand, he can stress that it is no part of the Church's business to discharge such sinners, just as it is not her affair to cast off this body of flesh. It is the Lord's task, who will awaken her (at the End) and give her the true form of her holiness."[12]

As the Dominican Aidan Nichols points out in his survey of Ratzinger's thought, the *ecclesia sancta,* the holy Church, is found within the *ecclesia catholica,* the Catholic Church, but they are not identical. Maintaining this distance between the material and the spiritually pure, as Augustine argued in the *City of God,* and recognizing our unremediated alienation from the eternal good this unending Holy Saturday of our existence would become, as Nichols noted, "perhaps the most insistent refrain in Ratzinger's criticism of the Catholic Church's modern self-reform."[13]

√ Reforming the church was very much the principal Catholic project of the postwar generation, and Joseph Ratzinger's embrace of a fourth-century North African theologian was actually a progressive decision in the 1950s. Not that Ratzinger was tacking his sails to the prevailing winds, or that Augustine was the final word on all matters. While Ratzinger is interpreted—too often, I think—principally through the lens of his intellect and through the words that he chooses to put into the public square, it is his character that always telegraphed his destiny. He has the academic nature of an intellectual, but an intellectual who uses his thought to make sense of the presuppositions he brings, whether they concern faith or his views of the world. His theology is fascinating and vital, and he hones in on great truths in expressive language.

Yet I agree with William James, who believed that "feeling is the deeper source of religion, and that philosophic and theological formulas are secondary products, like translations into another tongue."[14]

Basically, in Augustine, Joseph Ratzinger found the theologian and the theology that fit his personality and his experience of people's darkest pathways, and his goal was to adapt any rough edges to modern times. But Ratzinger's specialty was also very much in tune with the contemporary trend toward a recovery of original Christian wisdom, a return to the sources, a movement known by the French word *ressourcement*. With such expertise, combined with obvious intellectual power and an appealingly quiet style, Ratzinger was quickly singled out for advancement.

Ratzinger was ordained by Cardinal Faulhaber in the cathedral at Friesing along with his brother, Georg, on June 29, 1951, the Feast of Saints Peter and Paul, the founding apostles of Rome. There were forty new priests, the last wave of the midcentury surge in vocations, and a scene that is unknown anywhere in the world today. In the months leading up to the ordination, Ratzinger was beside himself with worry in the rush to finish his dissertation on Augustine, but everyone helped him out—his brother took over many of his preordination tasks, and his sister, Maria, who was helping to support the family as a legal secretary, typed his manuscript.

In the end, the ordination liturgy was yet another storybook episode in his life's journey—a radiant summer day, "which I remember as the high point of my life."

"We should not be superstitious; but, at the moment when the elderly archbishop laid his hands on me, a little bird—perhaps a lark—flew up from the high altar in the cathedral and trilled a little joyful song. And I could not but see in this a reassurance from on high, as if I heard the words, 'This is good, you are on the right way.'" The cadence of his memory is the same as the Gospel account of Christ's baptism, when the Holy Spirit descended like a dove and a voice from heaven said, "This is my beloved Son, with whom I am well pleased."

The right way for Joseph's brother Georg was through music. He always had the most talent in this very musical family, and he would eventually become conductor of the Regensburg Domspatzen, the cathedral choir at Regensburg in Bavaria, the oldest and one of the most famous boys' choirs in the world, dating from the tenth century. It was Father Georg's work with the popular choir that for a long time made him best-known of the brothers, at least locally, and the most feared. "He was a very strict director and people were scared of him," said Hans Zillner, vice-mayor of Traunstein and a former choirboy.[15]

Nobody was scared of Joseph Ratzinger, at least not yet. Indeed, the year he spent in the parish after ordination and before returning to the blessed seclusion of theological studies was something of a trial for Father Joseph. He never had any practical pastoral training or experience—in fact, this year would be the only parish experience of his life—and the duties that were piled on him, as well as the busyness of the rectory, were enormously unsettling.

His return to university was a relief but also a drama. He had to write another dissertation in order to qualify for a professor's chair, and this time he chose to write about Saint Bonaventure, a contemporary of Thomas Aquinas but a Franciscan who wrote about spirituality rather than theology. Bonaventure was the leader of the neo-Augustinian school that competed with the emerging Thomists. Ratzinger wrote on Bonaventure's "Theology of History," an exceedingly recondite topic that nonetheless is what Nichols calls "an eminently Augustinian project: to make the Church's present and future intelligible by relation to its past."

Ratzinger focused on Bonaventure's critique of Joachim of Fiore, a twelfth-century mystic who regarded Saint Francis of Assisi, founder of the Franciscans, as heralding a new age of earthly grace marked by the reign of the poor, a temporal fulfillment of the Sermon on the Mount. Nichols notes that Ratzinger also rejected Joachim's prophecy, just as he would other projects that sought to bring about God's justice in this world: "Before the name 'liberation theology' was ever heard of, Ratzinger had to arrive at some judgment about this uncanny thirteenth century anticipation of liberationist eschatology."

Yet even though Ratzinger's dissertation seemed like a sure thing, one reviewer stunned him by announcing that he would reject the thesis as too modernist—of all things—too reflective of a new French school of exploratory thought. In Catholic academics, the priest's motivating fear is not "publish or perish" but "publish or parish." So the prospect of a stillborn dissertation would be traumatic to someone with Ratzinger's talents and ambitions. "I was thunderstruck," he recalled. "A whole world was threatening to collapse around me." The life he hoped for looked about to end, and he dreaded being "branded as a failure." His parents were getting older and he fretted about them, and on top of it all he had problems with his typist, which forced him to hand in messy, badly typed, manuscripts that bothered the punctilious Ratzinger no end.

Fortunately, he was allowed to revise the paper, and in 1959 his dissertation was accepted. This would be the last hurdle before Ratzinger entered the ranks of the church's most promising theologians, and this at a time when theologians were like pop stars. Theologians were selling out auditoriums for their talks, and books of complex theology had the popularity of paperback thrillers and were featured on the cover of *Time.* After just a year teaching at Freising, Ratzinger moved to the University of Bonn, and in between he lectured at the university at Munster. Given the nature of academia, especially in such a competitive atmosphere, and Ratzinger's growing reputation, it was no surprise that his many job changes ruffled some feathers along the way. He did not have a warm relationship with Faulhaber's successor as archbishop of Munich, but he found an even more important patron when he came to the attention of the archbishop of Cologne, Cardinal Joseph Frings.

This relationship would become critical to Ratzinger's success, because in 1962 Frings chose the thirty-five-year-old wunderkind to accompany him to Rome as a *peritus,* or expert, for the Second Vatican Council, the churchwide gathering of the world's bishops that would chart Catholicism's course into the modern world—and become the wedge issue in the ensuing ecclesiastical civil war, in which Joseph Ratzinger would be a leading combatant.

Next to a conclave, a council is the most extraordinary event in the life of the church, a rare moment when the entire hierarchy comes together to act collegially rather than by fiat of the pope. Most councils are convened to define doctrine or to clarify and assert some aspect of the church's authority. The First Vatican Council (1868–70) set forth papal infallibility, for example, and the council before that, the Council of Trent (1545–63), was convened to battle the Protestant Reformation. Trent produced a raft of dogmatic decrees that highlighted the differences with Luther and his followers and cemented the Western schism. The Tridentine council also set a uniform template for the Latin Mass, regularized clerical training, and established the Index of Forbidden Books—many edicts that lasted until the Second Vatican Council (1962–65), or Vatican II, as it is usually called. Councils represent the greatest counterweight to papal authority, and so they have often been viewed with suspicion by papalists and with hope by church populists.

On July 25, 1959, when Pope John XXIII announced his intention to call a council, he surprised the church and the world and spurred the hopes of the populists, who felt their turn had come, given the way the authoritarian forces had carried the day at the First Vatican Council and for most of the intervening decades. The proponents of reform were encouraged by the presence of "Good Pope John," the amiable, avuncular pastor who had been a surprise choice a year earlier to succeed the aristocratic, ascetic Pius XII. The two men could not have been more different, and John's optimistic opening speeches cheered progressives, who thought that this would be a pastoral rather than a doctrinal council, one that would open the church to the modern world and, in turn, the world to the gifts of the church.

But those dreams were nearly stillborn. When the first of the council's four sessions opened on October 11, 1962, the world's 2,600 bishops were faced with an agenda predetermined by the Roman Curia, which was led by the arch-conservative Cardinal Alfredo Ottaviani, the imposing head of the Holy Office—the former Sacred Congregation of the Holy Inquisition that Ratzinger would later head. At this point in history, however, Ratzinger was on the other side of the table from the Curia, as were most of the German bishops and their *periti,* who were among the most accomplished and influential theologians in twentieth-century Catholicism. Indeed, this German contingent was so prominent that one of the principal accounts of Vatican II is titled *The Rhine Flows into the Tiber.* One of the best-known Germans was Father Joseph Ratzinger, personal assistant to Cardinal Frings. In the run-up to the council's opening session, Ratzinger, along with the renowned German Jesuit Karl Rahner, was indispensable in rewriting the preparatory documents, or schema. In bookstores and coffee shops and salons around Rome, he brainstormed with fellow theologians, and then briefed groups of European bishops to give them the intellectual rationales for the reforms they wanted to implement.

So much was at stake, as Ratzinger wrote a year later, in 1963, "There was a certain discomforting feeling that the whole enterprise might come to nothing more than a mere rubber-stamping of decisions already made, thus impeding rather than fostering the renewal needed in the Catholic church.... The council would have disappointed and discouraged all those who had placed their hopes in it; it would have paralyzed all their healthy dynamism and swept aside once again the many questions people of our era had put to the church."[16]

In a dramatic confrontation on October 13, at the first working session, Cardinal Frings was one of several leading cardinals who helped to thwart the plans of the curialists. As the session opened, Frings's chief ally, French cardinal Achille Liénart of Lille, rose before the assemblage to declare a firm *Non placet* (It does not please) to the Roman scheme to have immediate elections for the commissions that would take up the different topics. The curialists were counting on the fact that bishops from across the globe did not know each other well and so would rely on the deeply conservative documents the Romans had prepared. Despite a ban on outbursts, Liénart's declaration was met with cheering. When the war died down, Frings seconded the French cardinal's proposal. That effectively ended the curial machinations.

At the time of the council, Frings was one of the most respected men in the hierarchy, a bible scholar of moderate views and an impeccable reputation. But he was also seventy-six years old and going blind, so he relied on his *periti* to write the speeches that he then delivered with his forceful voice. And the *peritus* most responsible for the cardinal's addresses was Joseph Ratzinger. One such speech was the showdown with Ottaviani a year after the council's opening, when Frings denounced the Holy Office as "a source of scandal" to the world, a stunning public critique that one observer said had "blown the dome off of St. Peter's."[17] Ratzinger blasted the Curia's preparatory documents as reflecting the church's traditional "anti-Modern neurosis," and he welcomed the rejection of the original agenda as an "epochal" decision.

Frings, along with Liénart, succeeded in winning a delay so that the bishops from outside Rome could organize themselves to promote a council of reforms, which is what occurred. Yet if the forces for reform were in the majority, they were not a monolith. As church historians like Father Joseph A. Komonchak have noted, there were two principal streams of thought among the so-called progressives. Those advocating a *ressourcement,* including Ratzinger, were pushing for renewal through a return to the sources, while others, advocating an *aggiornamento,* were looking for an updating. Among the champions of *ressourcement* were great figures, such as Henri de Lubac and Jean Daniélou. Leaders of the *aggiornamento* were equally impressive figures, including Rahner, Marie-Dominique Chenu, Hans Küng, and Edward Schillebeeckx.

The tension between the *ressourcement* camp and the *aggiornamento* camp—between those wanting to go "backward into the future," as Ratzinger later put it, and those looking to engage modernity directly—mirrored the split between Augustinians and Thomists, Platonists and Aristotelians. As the council moved through its four sessions over three years, the divide grew wider, a split that can be documented by Ratzinger's own growing disillusionment with the council's work.

In the first session, Ratzinger delighted in the spirit of freedom won by the bishops—he was "filled with a joyful feeling, dominant everywhere, of an important new beginning." Ratzinger was everywhere, advising not only Frings but other leading cardinals and bishops, as well as writing papers and giving lectures around Rome to halls packed with audiences who knew they were witnessing history in the making and were eager to hear from one of the principal architects of the moment.

Ratzinger was enthusiastic about reforming the liturgy, especially de-emphasizing Latin, which he described as an "archeological" relic, "a picture so encrusted that the original image could hardly be seen," as Nichols puts it. Ratzinger declared that language was for men, not for angels, and he attacked the enforced use of Latin in Catholic higher education as a cause of the sterility of much of Catholic theology since the Enlightenment—a position that set him directly against a 1962 document from John XXIII praising the continued use of Latin in seminaries and universities. Ratzinger bordered on the sarcastic when he criticized the priority of popular devotions in the Catholic imagination, a view squarely contrary to that of his later patron, John Paul II. He said exaggerated Marian piety, for example, was undermining the ecumenical push for unity with other Christians, a movement he supported then, in contrast to his later actions.

Ratzinger also strongly backed a "horizontal Catholicity" of collegiality, a catchphrase for the view that the pope should consult local bishops and the wider church before making important decisions and take a more collaborative approach to church governance. He backed the organization of national bishops' conferences and the use of periodic synods, like mini-councils, to keep dialogue open between the convoking of major councils. He pushed for a reform of the Curia, and warned of the dangers of exalting tradition beyond the reach of rational criticism.

All of these criticisms of the status quo could, to a degree, be contained within the ambit of the notion of *ressourcement,* if only because *ressourcement* can mean so many things to so many people. Going back to the sources, to a supposedly purer, primeval state can be a slogan for both liberals, who believe everything in their agenda once existed but was suppressed by a close-minded patriarchy, and conservatives, who somehow reckon the second century after Christ to be a perfect echo of their own happy childhood, complete with the ice-cream confirmation suit. As much as the future is an open temptation for unrealistic projections, the past is a dimly lit room where our mind's eye fleshes out vague shapes according to our individual desires.

But as the council progressed, the *aggiornamento* camp gained the initiative to the extent that Ratzinger felt the church was clearly moving into the future by jettisoning the past. As *ressourcement* took a backseat, shadows of concern begin to fall across Ratzinger's opinions. For example, in the development of the church's formulations on revelation and preaching the message of salvation to the wider world, which would be woven into the council's dogmatic constitution *Dei Verbum,* he was disturbed that the Council Fathers did not make a greater mention of sin and the "mystery of the anger of God," and he worried that the bishops had been taken in by an "over-optimism."

√ The fourth and final session of the council (September–December 1965) proved to be the break. At this session, the alliance of French-speaking and German-speaking experts that had forced the revolution began to disintegrate, and Ratzinger's "mood of dis-engagement, and its cause, was unmistakable," says Nichols. The council's final document, *Gaudium et Spes,* dealt with the church's new attitude toward the modern world, and as indicated by its opening words—"The joys and hopes"—it struck a far more engaged and optimistic tone than ever before. The document represented the work of the French camp and its more progressive theologians; in fact, the document was distributed in French and later translated into Latin, the only council document to start in the vernacular.

Cardinal Frings did not like it at all, and neither did Father Ratzinger. He criticized *Gaudium et Spes* for "the fact that the strong stress, deriving from Luther, on the theme of sin, was alien to the mainly French authors of the schema, whose theological suppositions were quite different. Their thought probably sprang from a theological attitude which was Thomistic in tendency." He ripped the document's "downright Pelagian terminology" (Pelagius was the early Christian theologian condemned by Augustine for teaching that man's own efforts could aid his salvation) and said it left his own cherished Christology "in a conceptual deep-freeze."[18]

"In this case, what is salvation all about?" he asked. "What does its totality mean for man, if he can be described perfectly well without it, and have his portrait painted in an accurate and satisfying way as a result?"[19] In other words, if modernity works, of what use is the church to mankind? Ratzinger predicted that as a result of the council's later efforts, aided by the giddy enthusiasm of the bishops and the theological experts who he thought came to dominate them, the "renewal" sought by the council would lead to a "dilution and trivialization of the whole."

This dark tone of foreboding would be the hallmark of Ratzinger's views from that point on, but it was also consonant with his Augustinian views and his personality. What clouded his inherently pessimistic outlook was his bitter disappointment at the council's path away from his own opinions and his conviction that ill winds were blowing that would soon rattle the church to its foundations. Subsequent events would prove him right, he believed, and would set the course for the theological counterinsurgency that would carry him to the pinnacle of church power.

. . .

The first major work that Joseph Ratzinger produced after the council was also the one he considers his finest achievement. It is called simply *Introduction to Christianity,* and it is in fact just that—a survey of Christian beliefs using the Apostles' Creed as a template and exploring, in good trinitarian form, aspects of faith by their relation to God the Father, the Son, and the Holy Spirit. The *Introduction* was a huge success and continues to be so, apart from whatever coattails Ratzinger's later renown may have brought it. This was because the book is such a solid, and stolid (this is Ratzinger, after all), overview of the particulars of Christian belief and what they mean that the book could be, and was, used anywhere.

The *Introduction* has the feel of something written as a standard textbook, and that was the impression it left on me when the priest who was shepherding my conversion to Catholicism gave me Ratzinger's catechism as a baseline guide. I recall reading the book from cover to cover and finding it completely unobjectionable but also unmemorable. It was like encountering Ratzinger himself, which I did periodically in Rome in the 1980s, as our paths crossed in the middle of St. Peter's Square, he heading to his office at the Congregation for the Doctrine of the Faith, me to broadcast the news he was making on Vatican Radio. Ratzinger seemed unvarying—black overcoat, black beret, a small, pleasant smile, and perhaps a soft "*Buongiorno.*" The early editions of the book had a famously plain beige cover, like a company operating manual. Despite my slavish book-collecting habits, for some reason I cannot find my original copy, a loss that may indicate the lack of passion it stirred. I had no problem with the facts of the faith, which is what Ratzinger's "Sergeant Friday" presentation seemed to offer. It was the Catholic Church I needed to understand, and perhaps always will. Ratzinger was clearly fighting a battle I was not aware of, or interested in, since I had accepted the faith he was defending. In truth, I find it hard to believe the dense *Introduction* would be a terribly effective invitation to Christianity for a seeker. It is more of an *apologia* in a war of polemics that I was not aware of or interested in at the time, though it interests me and most Catholics quite keenly now.

On rereading the *Introduction* (the new edition has a lovely Florentine diptych adorning the snazzy cover; as Ratzinger would say, the form changes but not the substance) in light of all Ratzinger was doing in those years, I worry about how easily I glossed over his obvious purpose in writing the book and his attitude toward the developments that were already taking place. Ratzinger begins with a now-famous recounting of the Brothers Grimm's folktale of *Hans im Glück,* usually translated as "Lucky Jack." Hans, or Lucky Jack, is a young fellow who comes across a lump of gold but, finding it too heavy and troublesome to carry, exchanges it for a horse, then, finding the horse too much trouble, exchanges it for a cow, and so on, until he has gone through a pig and a goose and finally is left with a whetstone. He winds up tossing the stone into the water, believing himself to have gained complete freedom at no cost. Thus the insidiously imperceptible fate of the precious gold or, in Ratzinger's reading, the sacred deposit of faith entrusted to the church.

"Has our theology in the last few years not taken in many ways a similar path?" Ratzinger asks. "Has it not gradually watered down the demands of faith, which had been found all too demanding, always only so little that nothing important seemed to be lost, yet always so much that it was soon possible to venture on the next step?" It is, Ratzinger said, "undeniable that there is widespread support for a trend that does indeed lead from gold to whetstone." The *Introduction* was Ratzinger's *J'accuse,* his denunciation of the trend and his effort to provide an alternative with a re-presentation and argumentation of the foundations of the faith.

In the *Introduction*, and in its new preface written in 2000, the thrust of the postconciliar Ratzinger and the postconclave Benedict can be clearly seen: The modern world is more dangerous than we ever imagined, and, by flirting with the "spirit of the age" (Hegel's *zeitgeist,* that slippery dialectic of historical progression), the church was betraying itself. The only solution was a retreat to faith in Christ as expressed by the Roman Catholic Church. A church shepherded by a dedicated minority of orthodox believers would be required to see Catholicism through this crisis, which might or might not end. In his 2000 preface, Ratzinger noted two dates as marking a continuity of disappointment. One was 1989 and the fall of the Berlin Wall, which ended Soviet communism. But "Christianity failed at that historic moment," and the world was in just as bad shape after the fall as when Marxist-Leninism ruled half the globe. The other moment he cites is 1968, the year the *Introduction* was originally published and a period that would confirm all of Joseph Ratzinger's worst fears about unwarranted idealism left unregulated by an overaccommodating church and culture.

Midway through the council, the growing divide between the *ressourcement* and *aggiornamento* camps had left Ratzinger "deeply troubled by the change in the ecclesial climate," and he began to hit that refrain more insistently as the council closed. After a speech at the Bamberg Catholic Conference in 1966, Munich's Cardinal Julius Döpfner expressed surprise at Ratzinger's "conservative streak." Others were surprised, too. "Perhaps you were expecting a more optimistic, a brighter and more joyful picture," Father Ratzinger told the conference. "But it seems to me important that what at the Council made us joyful and grateful must now also be perceived in its two-fold historicity and thus make us understand the message that it contains. And it seems important to me to discern the dangerous new triumphalism, a tendency to which precisely the very critics of the old triumphalism often succumb. So long as the Church is in pilgrimage on the earth, she has no ground to boast of her own works. Such self-glorification could become more dangerous than the *sedia gestatoria* [the portable throne on which popes were once carried by footmen] and the tiara, which are more likely to elicit a smile than a feeling of pride."[20]

In other words, the church of the council risked looking foolish if it changed too much, just as the church before the council had risked looking foolish for not changing at all.

Ratzinger had moved to the University of Münster in 1963, as the council began, and in 1966, his reputation growing, he said he could no longer deny the "irresistible temptation" to take a Catholic chair in fundamental theology at the Protestant University of Tübingen, the country's flagship theology department. The university was in southern Germany, close to Ratzinger's Bavarian home and, he expected, a place where he could exchange ideas with scholars of Luther, who held such interest for him.

Hans Küng, the Swiss theologian and Ratzinger's fellow council *peritus,* was dean of Tübingen's Catholic theological faculty at the time, and he circumvented the normal selection procedures to make Ratzinger the sole candidate when the chair came open. Küng was one of many friends and colleagues with whom Ratzinger would fall out in the coming years. The rift would be theological, but it was also driven by personality; already in the 1960s Father Küng was zipping around Tübingen in a sporty Alfa Romeo, while Ratzinger rode his bicycle, wearing his black beret.[21] They were regular dinnermates, but their vastly divergent styles and beliefs soon ended that. In Küng's case, the estrangement would carry harsh consequences when Ratzinger helped in the effort a decade later to ban Küng from teaching at Catholic institutions. (Ratzinger refuted the rumor that the "Hans" of the "Lucky Jack" folktale in the preface to the *Introduction* referred to Küng.)

Ratzinger took up his post in 1966, feeling in frail health due to the demands of the council, but just as the impact of the council was revolutionizing the Catholic Church and the upheaval of the 1960s was threatening to descend into chaos. It is hard to recall at the distance of these years how unsettled the

world was, with the Vietnam War in full swing, civil rights protests and political assassinations seeming to alternate in the headlines, and the assault on
authority and institutions implacable. In Europe, especially, campuses were
aflame with left-wing agitation that often ended in violent clashes. The Cold
War was at its height, and a German Communist state lay just a short distance
to the east.

The tumult in the Catholic Church seemed no less acute, crystallized in the
furor sparked by Pope Paul VI's encyclical *Humanae Vitae,* which reinforced
the church's ban on artificial contraception, a teaching that, in the postconciliar era of the Pill, many expected to be relaxed. The encyclical was released in
July 1968 and only stoked the summer of fury. A thousand theologians around
the world announced their opposition to *Humanae Vitae,* and the German
and Austrian bishops published letters saying that Catholics could in good
conscience do what they liked regarding the teaching. But in September at a
national gathering of German Catholics, Cardinal Döpfner of Munich, a liberal who had chaired the papal birth control commission that had recommended changing the teaching, unexpectedly sided with Pope Paul's decision
to reject the commission's findings.

At Tübingen, Ratzinger saw firsthand the effects of these changes, which he
said grew out of a mistaken sense that the council had shown that everything
once believed eternal could be changed. "The faith no longer seemed exempt
from human decision-making but rather was now apparently determined by
it," he wrote in his memoir, *Milestones.* Theologians were usurping the authority of bishops, and laypeople, empowered by a newfangled use of the dangerously democratic-sounding phrase "People of God," thought teaching should
be determined by popular vote. Catholics wanted to make the faith "more
comfortable," a notion he detested, and worse, there was a sense that Catholics
could actually *do* something to make the church better or bigger. He saw that
as an egotistical fallacy that was vindicated by the unrest and subsequent decline in all indicators of religious observance, which he traced to "self-reform"
measures.

Ratzinger was also aghast at the student uprisings that reached their peak
in 1968. The Marxist wave kindled the whole university with its fervor, and in
fact theology, which was once a bulwark against communism, now became
its handservant, in Ratzinger's view. He was blistering in his judgment of the
"psychological terror" of the Marxists, their "atheistic piety," which overturned
every moral consideration as a "bourgeois residue." When the Protestant
Student Union passed out a flyer wondering if the Cross was nothing "but a

sado-masochistic glorification of pain," Ratzinger was scandalized. "There was an instrumentalization by ideologies that were tyrannical, brutal, and cruel. That experience made it clear to me that the abuse of the faith had to be resisted if one wanted to uphold the will of the council."[22]

In the local university parish, student worshippers were demanding decision-making authority on a range of issues, including the appointment of a chaplain, which was canonically the bishop's prerogative. Student protesters were regularly hijacking lecterns mid-lesson, and one report from the time says that Ratzinger had a microphone snatched away from him, an incident he says did not occur. Either way, the lecture hall was a battle zone, not Joseph Ratzinger's idea of academia. One of Ratzinger's students at the time, Benedictine father Kenneth Hein, says that he is "reluctant" to ascribe Ratzinger's eventual departure entirely to the student turmoil, but he noted that at Tübingen it was "particularly irksome." He paints a picture of self-identified Maoists staging nearly daily protests, which escalated into student strikes and classroom lockouts. "I was disappointed; but I can't blame him for finding that 'enough is enough.'"[23]

Küng agrees: "Even for a strong personality like me this was unpleasant. For someone timid like Ratzinger, it was horrifying."[24]

In 1969, wearied of the constant infighting and continually finding himself in the minority, Ratzinger left Tübingen—which would have been anyone's dream job—to become professor of dogma at a newly founded university at Regensburg, a small imperial town on the Danube just north of Munich. His parents had died by this time, and his brother Georg was since 1964 the choirmaster at the city's cathedral. Regensburg was a homecoming, a relative oasis for the exhausted Ratzinger. At the village of Pentling just outside the city, he built a small house with a garden, and he lived there with his older sister, Maria (she died in 1991). He kept the home after he became a cardinal and moved to Rome, and returned whenever he could, sitting on the balcony in the summers, walking in the garden, reading and relaxing and enjoying an early supper. At New Year's he and his brother would spend a quiet evening together.

For Professor Ratzinger, the Pentling locale was ideal. He did not drive, and the Regensburg university was within walking distance. There were many "very determined leftists" among the assistant professors, he recalled, but the "waves of Marxism" beat less violently there in the small-town campus. At Regensburg, he was able to pursue the "reform of the reform" that would become the chief project of his ecclesiastical career.

Ratzinger's conversion from progressive to neo-con—or perhaps "theo-con" would be the more appropriate term—in some respects follows the path trod by many former liberals. The old chestnut that a conservative is a liberal who has been mugged by reality would seem to apply. In the Ptolemaic psychology of so many converts, Ratzinger insists that the world shifted around him, not the other way around: "It is not I who have changed, but others."[25]

Yet there is a consistent thread to his thinking, which runs counter to the optimism of the Second Vatican Council and which grew more defined in later years. Indeed, the aftermath of the council only reinforced his suspicion of man's seemingly unending capacity to go wrong and to betray himself by believing he can accomplish things by himself. It also confirmed his view that returning to the sources, stripping away and simplifying and sanctifying rather than moving into uncharted territory with newfangled ideas, holds the true promise for the faith.

√ More than a "conversion," the postconciliar Ratzinger might be viewed as similar to the preconciliar Ratzinger, only more so. As the *aggiornamento* camp gained the upper hand, Ratzinger went more deeply into his *ressourcement*. But like many who repent of past associations, he also reacted by ratcheting up his criticisms of his opponents and their positions, as if to set off his wholly correct beliefs from their false views. Putting the necessary distance between himself and his erstwhile allies necessarily required some exaggeration, however. For example, like many conservatives, Ratzinger likes to interpret the social upheavals of the 1960s and the Catholic turmoil created by the Second Vatican Council as overlays of the same phenomena, which is a rather parsimonious explanation for an era of complex dynamics operating within society and within Catholicism. To be sure, there are interconnections between the two developments, and both events produced excesses, often regrettable, that needed to be corrected. But Ratzinger's cause-and-effect analysis is a classic *post hoc ergo propter hoc* argument: one development is necessarily the result of another simply because it followed chronologically.

Looking back at the theological tumult of the late 1960s, Ratzinger once remarked, "Anyone who wanted to remain a progressive in this context had to give up his integrity." But why? Ratzinger is someone who remains true to his ideals and prides himself on resisting the momentum of the crowd, so standing firm should not have been a problem. Moreover, if the principles of the progressive movement were valid at one time, their misuse by some adherents or outside forces should not automatically invalidate them. Ratzinger's explanation was typical of many disillusioned idealists: he did not change, but the church shifted away from him, leaving him to defend core truths from a stranded center.

Along with denigrating his foes, Ratzinger engages in some liberal retrofitting of his own record in an apparent effort to distance himself and his views from the council's decisions and aftermath. His rereading of history also makes his past and present appear more consistent than they actually are, thus portraying him as the unchanging protector of immutable orthodoxy that he says he always was.

For instance, in his 1997 memoir, Ratzinger writes that while he had some reservations about the documents prepared by the curialists ahead of the council, "I found no grounds for a radical rejection of what was being proposed, such as many demanded later on in the Council and actually managed to put through." He added that he thought the original documents "had a solid foundation and had been carefully elaborated." Neither statement squares at all either with his actions or his words at the time of the council, or with the recollections of others who were there.

Whatever his motivations, Ratzinger's reputation as a theologian and a conservative standard-bearer grew steadily during the Regensburg years. His critiques of the course of the church also grew in frequency and stridency. In 1970 he was invited to give a eulogy for Cardinal Frings before eight hundred priests at Cologne Cathedral, but he hardly mentioned Frings and instead spoke mostly about the dangers of marrying the Gospel to social reform, and faith to modern reason: "The intellect does not always grant vision, but provides the conditions for intellectual games, and artfully conjures syntheses into existence where there is really nothing but contradiction. This is not rejection of intellect and reflection, but a reference to their limits and dangerous corruptibility."[26]

Ratzinger also started downplaying or recasting his council-era views on such progressive matters as the role of synods, national bishops' conferences, liturgical reform, and, most famously, intellectual freedom for theologians. He saw the nineteenth century, whose theology he once set himself against, as a golden age for the church. He sharply denounced the changes Paul VI made in the liturgy. Doing away with the old Tridentine Latin rite was "tragic"— though he lodged his protests only long after Paul had made him a cardinal. Ratzinger cited the liturgical changes he once advocated (although he says he never meant the changes to go so far) as a principal source of the church's current crisis, and he charged that the Mass had become so idiosyncratic that one "could not ascertain the boundary between what was still Catholic and what was no longer Catholic." The "disintegration" of the Mass led to the impression, he said, that the community is celebrating itself, and that people themselves have an active role in "making" the liturgy, rather than simply receiving it as something given by God and tradition.

√ The church was awash in "confusing claptrap and pastoral infantilism," he said, and reform "seemed really to consist not in any radicalization of the faith, but in any kind of dilution of the faith."[27]

In 1972 Ratzinger left the board of a prestigious theological journal, *Concilium*, which he had helped found in 1964 to serve as the main platform for the council's progressive camp. Disillusioned with his former colleagues there, including Küng, Schillebeeckx, and Rahner, Ratzinger, along with several German-speaking colleagues, including von Balthasar, launched a rival journal called *Communio*. *Communio* served as Ratzinger's chief platform in the 1970s, and its founding signaled an increasing estrangement from friends and colleagues. In 1971 he agreed to help the German bishops investigate Küng's writings, and he was disturbed by the developing "political theology" of his friend and colleague Johann Baptist Metz. He also wrote that he and Rahner "lived on two theological planets," rejecting Rahner's work in terms that were unusually dismissive given the Jesuit's stature.

In adjusting his views, Ratzinger often argued that the council's documents themselves were actually fine, and it was only those who later hijacked the reforms by invoking the amorphous "spirit" of the council who were to blame for the excesses and problems that inevitably followed the revolutionary changes. If people would adhere to the letter of the texts, he argues, then they would see that he remains loyal to the "true" council, and that Vatican II represented perfect continuity with Trent and the First Vatican Council. In this sense, Ratzinger is something like a strict constructionist in American judicial terms, who sees his or her views as closer to the "original intent" because they add nothing that is not explicitly written down. Such a position, however, ignores the fact that an "originalist" approach can simply be a means to achieving the result you want by not taking action. As the traditional confession puts it, we are guilty for what we have done and what we have failed to do.

During the Regensburg years, Ratzinger's lectures were as brilliant and well attended as ever, and he developed a devoted following among his students, many of whom remain fiercely loyal. He continued to get together with many of them at annual retreats long after he left for Rome, and more than a few became influential churchmen in their own right. In fact one of his most faithful protegés was Christoph Schönborn, who became cardinal-archbishop of Vienna and reportedly one of the popemakers during the April 2005 conclave that elected Ratzinger.

Ratzinger's progress from avant-garde reformer to rearguard defender—or, if one prefers, the leftward shift in the church that left him marginalized where he had always stood—came at a fortuitous time. After the irrational exuberance of the immediate postconciliar years, an inevitable course correction was gaining momentum in Rome. No one foresaw the wholesale "restoration" that some believed Pope John Paul II would later pursue, but certainly many church leaders were alarmed at the amount of experimentation and polarization that the changes were provoking. In a famous address in June 1972, Pope Paul lamented that "the smoke of Satan has penetrated the Temple of God through some crack or other." He added that this "supernatural" evil was threatening to strangle the fruits of the council. Paul's mood grew darker as he grew older and more frail, and the writings of Ratzinger would have appealed to his desire for a reassessment of the forces the council had unleashed.

In July 1976, Munich's Cardinal Döpfner died, and rumors immediately had Ratzinger as one of the leading candidates. "I did not take them very seriously, because my limitations with regard to health were as well known as my inability in matters of governance and administration," he recalls with characteristic self-effacement. "I knew I was called to a scholar's life and never considered anything else." But like his hero Saint Augustine, Joseph Ratzinger's intellectual idyll was not to be. Pope Paul named him as Döpfner's successor; despite his hesitations and fears of what the "crushing burden" would do to him, he accepted and was installed in May 1977. A month later, he received a red cardinal's biretta from Paul. A year after that, Paul was dead, and Ratzinger took part in the first of the two conclaves of 1978. During the conclave that elected the short-lived John Paul I, Ratzinger became friendly with Karol Wojtyla, a little-known Polish cardinal and fellow intellectual whose German was impeccable. At the second conclave, following the death of John Paul I, Ratzinger had another chance to cast a vote, and he was by all accounts extremely pleased to see his new acquaintance elected John Paul II.

If he was not consciously ambitious, Ratzinger at least always had a knack for being the right person at the right time and knowing the right people—though the latter attribute is something he would deny. He contends he was shocked that Pope Paul named him archbishop and then cardinal, and said he met Paul VI for the first time in June 1977, when he went to Rome for his appointment as cardinal. But Ratzinger had actually known Cardinal Giovanni Battista Montini, the future Paul VI, for years. He worked with Montini during the council, and Montini believed that the two great figures to emerge from the council would be Ratzinger and Küng. In 1969, as Paul VI, Montini named Ratzinger to the prestigious International Papal Theological Commission, which was mandated by the council fathers in an effort to provide an independent counterweight to the dreaded Holy Office, recently renamed the Congregation for the Doctrine of the Faith, or CDF.

Throughout the 1970s, Ratzinger watched with satisfaction as foes such as Rahner left the commission in disgust at its rightward drift and were replaced with like-minded conservatives, who turned the commission into a rather innocuous body that would not bother the CDF either then or when Ratzinger took over a few years later.

By the time Joseph Ratzinger arrived in Munich as archbishop, German Catholics were referring to him as *ganz schwarz,* or "completely black," a phrase connoting strong conservatism but conveying so much more. He would remain there for less than four years, but during that time he honed his reputation as an unapologetic conservative and doughty infighter. His episcopal motto—which he would retain as pope—was "Co-workers in the truth," and defending the truth as he saw it became his principal task. He derided the "false good-naturedness" of those who tried to accommodate, and cited as role models men like Thomas More and Dietrich Bonhoeffer as Christians who died for matters of conscience. As always, his "great master" remained Augustine, who, apart from his theology and his autobiography, was known in his years as a bishop as a relentless battler against the many heresies that abounded in that rough-and-tumble era of the early church.

That is the kind of dedication to truth that Joseph Ratzinger took as his model when he became a bishop, and the one he would follow through the rest of his years as a cardinal and finally as pope: "The words of the Church Fathers rang in my ears, those sharp condemnations of shepherds who are like mute dogs; in order to avoid conflicts, they let the poison spread. Peace is not the first civic duty, and a bishop whose only concern is not to have any problems and to gloss over as many conflicts as possible is an image I find repulsive."[28]

Cardinal Ratzinger would not fall into that trap.

One of his first conflicts was with his former colleague, Hans Küng, the target of a long-standing inquiry. Küng's work had been under Vatican scrutiny since 1967, and his popular 1970 book questioning papal infallibility led to the first official condemnation of his views. Küng's most widely read book, *On Being a Christian,* was published in 1974 to much praise but serious reservations from conservatives. Among the harshest critics was his old friend Ratzinger, who blasted Küng's "undisguised arrogance" and said his interpretations left the faith as "an empty formula" that was "handed over to corruption at its very foundation." Küng said he felt stabbed in the back, and rejected the criticisms in a newspaper article as containing "numberless misrepresentations, insinuations, condemnations."[29]

Küng and Ratzinger were no longer on speaking terms, which apparently only exacerbated the tensions when Ratzinger became a cardinal. Küng was becoming the Döllinger of his day, a German enfant terrible whose criticisms grew sharper—later they would become almost outlandish—the more he himself was criticized. But in the liberalizing atmosphere of the day, and given the suspicion of Rome always latent in German Catholicism, Küng's case became a popular rallying point. The content of his views on infallibility and other matters was almost beside the point. In 1977, in the culmination of an investigation Ratzinger had worked on for years, the German bishops criticized Küng's work without a formal hearing. In 1979, with Cardinal Ratzinger's collaboration, that ruling became the basis of Rome's condemnation of Küng's work, also without a formal hearing. Germans were outraged, and it was widely noted that, in his 1963 broadside against the Holy Office, Cardinal Frings—Ratzinger's patron—had demanded that from then on "no one will any longer be the subject of complaint and condemnation, unless he and his local bishop are heard in advance, unless he knows the charges that have been brought against him, and unless he has been given the opportunity to answer what has been written and said against him."[30] Küng was afforded none of those rights, a precedent that would become the model for the CDF.

More poignant was Ratzinger's action against Johann Baptist Metz, a long-time friend and colleague whose views had grown more liberal as Ratzinger's grew more conservative. In the 1970s Metz was a top German theologian who was respected for his courteous, generous personality as well as his writings. He was a consultant to Germany's bishops and to a Vatican commission. When he came up for a post at the University of Munich in 1979, the university senate unanimously put him at the top of their list. But Ratzinger invoked a little-known veto and replaced Metz, whom he viewed as mixing the Gospel message and political ideas, with another candidate more amenable to his views. The power play outraged German Catholics.[31] The most powerful critic was Karl Rahner, also a onetime friend of Ratzinger's, who published an open letter to Ratzinger in the German daily *Süddeutsche Zeitung* saying the move against Metz violated a century-old tradition and "makes a farce out of your responsibility to protect academic freedom." He blasted the lack of detailed objections to Metz and noted that while Rahner himself did not agree with Metz on several points, Metz had never been accused of unorthodoxy.

In prophetic words that would resonate for decades to come, Rahner ripped the unaccountability of secretive church leaders in his critique, which became famous for its title, "I Protest!": "The average Christian often has the bitter impression that his faith-inspired loyalty to the church is abused. And yet, he knows that he is powerless before the law. In society in such a case one can legitimately revolt against such misused power. But not so for the believing Christian. We can truly say that sensitivity to basic human rights must still develop within the church."

The break between Rahner and Ratzinger was final, and Rahner died in 1984 without a reconciliation.

The controversies served to boost Ratzinger's reputation in Rome's eyes. From the start of his pontificate, John Paul II had been attempting to draw Ratzinger to Rome. In 1980 he offered Ratzinger a job as head of the Vatican department overseeing Catholic education around the world, but Ratzinger demurred. He said he had not been in Munich long enough. A year later the top post at the Congregation for the Doctrine of the Faith opened up, the second-most powerful job in the Roman Curia. This time, Ratzinger accepted. He understood that his brief in Rome would entail controversy, a prospect he seemed to relish.

"Not all news that comes from Rome will be pleasant," Cardinal Ratzinger, frank as ever, told his flock as he bid farewell to Munich.[32]

That's just what the Vatican was banking on.

Chapter Seven

DEFENDER
OF THE FAITH

T he church has been battling heresy as long as there has been a faith to defend, and it is hardly an exaggeration to say that heresy is as important to Christianity as orthodoxy. Without heterodoxy (alternate belief), orthodoxy (right belief) would be adrift in its own reflecting pool, with nothing to bump up against and therefore no way to take precise soundings on the truth. Orthopraxy—doing right—tends to be the distinguishing mark of other religions, mostly notably Christianity's "older brother in the faith" (Pope John Paul's phrase), Judaism, in which the Law is foundational and its observance determinant.

For Christians, on the other hand, it is what you believe that makes you Christian—or not. Whether you accept the divinity of Jesus, the Resurrection, the Trinity, and so on determines whether you are a true believer. There is, however, much potential for ambiguity in a religion in which the threshold is believing correctly. Right belief is more difficult to measure than right practice, so nonbelief or, more precisely, unorthodox belief is that much more useful in helping to separate the wheat from the chaff, in one of Pope Benedict's favorite Gospel citations.

Fortunately, Christianity is a religion of conversion, and entering the state of grace by definition presupposes a fallen condition that the believer left. Without the darkness there can be no light. "*O Felix Culpa!*" the great Easter hymn of the *Exultet* proclaims: "O happy fault, which gained for us so great a Redeemer." Without Adam's fall from grace there would be no journey to salvation. Without the Judas of Good Friday there would have been no Jesus of

Easter Sunday. Their misdeeds offered the possibility of restoration, and they also set the mysterious pattern by which sinfulness became the ally to sanctity. "There have to be factions among you in order that those who are approved among you may become known," the apostle Paul wrote to the fractious Corinthians (1 Cor 11:19).

As Joseph Ratzinger noted in his dissertation on Augustine back in 1954, every great theology grew out of "a polemic against error." In fact, he said a "movement of a living, spiritual kind is hardly thinkable" *without* error.[1] More than half a century later, as Pope Benedict XVI, he was still preaching the benefits of the counterpunch in keeping the church united around a single set of clear beliefs. At a June 29, 2005, Mass in St. Peter's Square for archbishops who had been appointed over the past year, Benedict quoted the original heresy hunter, St. Irenaeus (d. 202), the second-century bishop of Lyons and a tireless campaigner against deviations from orthodoxy.

"The Church spread across the world diligently safeguards this doctrine and this faith, forming as it were one family: the same faith, with one mind and one heart, the same preaching, teaching and tradition as if she had but one mouth," Benedict said, quoting *Adversus Haereses* (Against Heresies), Irenaeus's most famous work and a favorite of the pope. "Languages abound according to the region but the power of our tradition is one and the same. The Churches in Germany do not differ in faith or tradition, neither do those in Spain, Gaul, Egypt, Libya, the Orient, the centre of the earth; just as the sun, God's creature, is one alone and identical throughout the world, so the light of true preaching shines everywhere and illuminates all who desire to attain knowledge of the truth."

Pope Benedict loves those early days of the church for many reasons, not least of which is the clarity that the titanic theological battles brought to the nascent faith. In the first centuries of Christianity, the church was facing threats on two fronts—externally from the pagan empire and the barbarian hordes, and internally from heretical ideas and their exponents. Those were the years when the church, realizing that Judgment Day might be further off than they had once expected and finding the good news of salvation spreading fast around the known world, was trying to figure out how to formulate a creed that would provide a baseline measure for who was in and who was out. That required parsing the trickier questions raised by the faith but left somewhat vague by the Gospels and the apostles. What was Christ's nature: Was he human, or divine, or both? What was the nature of the Trinity—three gods in one, or one God in three? Was grace earned or an unmerited gift? There were practical issues as well. Could someone who apostasizes be returned to full communion? Was baptism a one-time sacrament that cleared the slate, so to speak, leaving a Christian open to perdition if he or she sinned again? (That belief prompted many pagans, such as the emperor Constantine, to gamble on the actuarial tables and delay baptism until old age, figuring infirmity would lower the odds of committing mortal sins and increase the chances of reaching paradise.)

At foundational church councils and in blistering tracts circulated around the Mediterranean basin, the church fathers—guided by the Holy Spirit and armed with devotion to truth—hashed out the tenets of the faith, finally defeating the array of Arians, Donatists, Gnostics, Nestorians, and Pelagians, some of which had dominated the church at certain points. Two centuries after Irenaeus (his chief legacy was the victory over Gnosticism), Augustine emerged to become one of the great foes of ancient heresies, especially the beliefs of the Donatists and Pelagians. "To reprimand and to rebuke" was part of his "service" to the church, and to unbelievers whose souls were in peril of eternal damnation if the church did not remonstrate with them. Augustine illustrated this in a sermon that Cardinal Ratzinger cited, adding italics for emphasis: "'*You* want to live badly; you want to perish. *I*, however, am not allowed to want this; I have to rebuke you, even though it displeases you.' He then uses the example of the father with sleeping sickness whose son keeps waking him up, because that is the only chance of his being cured. But the father says: Let me sleep, I'm dead tired. And the sons say: No, I'm not allowed to let you sleep. And that, he says, is precisely the function of a bishop. . . . And in this sense the Church must also raise her finger and become irksome."[2] And more than irksome, the cardinal noted, "She must be able to threaten the powerful; she must also be able to threaten those who neglect, squander, even destroy their lives, for the sake of the right and the good and their own well-being, their own happiness."[3]

✓Ratzinger knows, of course, that such threatening has too often descended into fearful abuses, which he condemns. Until the Middle Ages, such abuses were relatively contained because each bishop was responsible for combating heresy in his own territory. But with the rise of the monarchical papacy and the growing centralization of Christendom, Rome began to take charge of defending the faith. The spur to the creation of the Roman Inquisition, and the persistent archetype of inquisitorial abuse, was the crusade against the Albigensian heresy that flourished in the southern French region of Languedoc in the early thirteenth century.

Also known as the Cathars, the Albigensians preached a dualistic worldview in which all matter—the body, the world, and everything therein—was evil and had been created by the Devil, who was as powerful as God and was locked in a even-odds cosmic battle for domination of the universe. To demonstrate their worthiness to be included among the "Perfect," as they called those who had sloughed off the shackles of the material world, the Albigensians practiced a radical asceticism whereby they shunned sexual activity and avoided consumption of meat, eggs, and milk. Some even fasted unto death, believing that such mortification was the only way to salvation and out of the endless cycle of death and reincarnation. They rejected the idea of private property and all sacraments, including marriage, and they set up their own governing structures, in a direct challenge to both ecclesiastical and secular authorities.

Such rebelliousness could not stand, and in 1209 the pope sent a Cistercian monk, Arnold Amaury, to Languedoc to stamp it out by any means necessary. His knights laid siege to the town of Béziers, and on July 22, 1209, as the town was about to fall, the soldiers asked Amaury how they would determine who in the city was a Cathar and thus under sentence of death and who was a Catholic and therefore to be spared. "Kill them all; God will recognize his own," Amaury told them. The troops complied, slaughtering twenty thousand townspeople that day in order to extirpate the heresy. The monk's economical response was so chilling that it mattered little to history whether it was apocryphal; this collateral damage became the lasting emblem of the Inquisition. "The sack of Béziers was the Guernica of the Middle Ages," as Stephen O'Shea writes in *The Perfect Heresy*, his chronicle of the Cathars.[4]

The crusade against the Albigensians lasted twenty years, until 1229. But heresy remained a growing problem. This was a turbulent era in Christian history, with corruption rife and grassroots reform movements sprouting everywhere to purify the church. Oftentimes these movements produced laudable and lasting changes that the church was able to incorporate; many times they spun off into heresies that could not be reconciled with orthodoxy. After the Cathars, the popes were taking no chances, and in 1231 Pope Gregory IX established the Inquisition with the papal bull *Excommunicamus*. He dispatched Dominicans and Franciscans to parts of Germany, France, and Italy where other heresies were suspected of taking root. Accused heretics were given a month to recant without fear of penalty, but after that they were subjected to secret trials. If found guilty, they were handed over to secular authorities for burning at the stake—the church did not sully itself with such sins—but for the most part the horrors of Béziers were not repeated and the penalties were limited to penance, imprisonment, and the expropriation of property. This last penalty, and the opportunity for corruption it provided, led to so many difficulties that the medieval inquisition soon fell into disuse.

The most famous, and infamous, heresy fighter was the so-called Spanish Inquisition, which was actually a creation not of the Catholic Church but of the Spanish monarchs, Ferdinand and Isabella (better remembered, perhaps, as the patrons of Christopher Columbus), in 1479. At first the papacy considered the Spanish Inquisition a secular usurpation of the church prerogative to fight heresy, but the pope finally acceded to their project. The Spanish Inquisition (which was not abolished until 1834) turned out to be more ruthless than Rome would have imagined, tracking down any perceived heretics, especially converted Jews and Muslims who continued to practice their original religion in private. The Spanish Inquisition—centerpiece of what came to be known as the Black Legend—investigated future saints like Teresa of Ávila, and even censored books approved by the pope. Its first and most famous Grand Inquisitor was a Dominican friar, Tomás de Torquemada, the original "hammer of heretics," who was responsible for killing and torturing thousands and spreading a reign of terror across the Iberian peninsula.

The Reformation that erupted in the next century was the spur that got the papacy back in the inquisition business. In 1542, as Rome geared up for the Counter-Reformation, Pope Paul III established the Sacred Congregation of the Universal Inquisition to defend the church from heresy and to review the growing number of writings—made possible by the printing press—to determine which were dangerous to the faith and should be placed on the newly created Index of Forbidden Books. In 1588 the body's name was changed to the Sacred Congregation of the Holy Inquisition and the office was given pride of place in the Roman Curia and a headquarters next to St. Peter's Basilica. In 1908 its name was changed to the Sacred Congregation of the Holy Office, known generally—and still today by many—simply as the Holy Office. In 1965, when Pope Paul VI reorganized the Curia after the Second Vatican Council, he renamed it the Sacred Congregation for the Doctrine of the Faith, and in 1983 the "sacred" qualifier was dropped. (The Index of Forbidden Books was also eliminated in the 1960s.)

Today the Congregation for the Doctrine of the Faith is known by its initials, the CDF, but its mandate remains largely the same as it always was. According to *Pastor Bonus*, the 1988 papal constitution promulgated by John Paul II, the sweeping mission of the CDF is "to promote and safeguard the doctrine on faith and morals in the whole Catholic world; so it has competence in things that touch this matter in any way." The CDF is to be the church's vigilant guardian, "lest faith or morals suffer harm through errors that have been spread in any way whatever"; if it finds "dangerous doctrines" it is to offer an "apt rebuttal" and "bring suitable remedies to bear, if this be opportune."

Clearly, the CDF has a powerful but unenviable job, and the diligence of previous inquisitors hasn't helped the CDF's reputation. While the Roman Inquisition that Paul III established in the sixteenth century did not come close to rivaling the *Leyenda Negra* of its Spanish counterpart, its 1633 condemnation of the astronomer Galileo, who was made to recant (at least publicly) his hypothesis that the earth revolves around the sun and not vice versa as ancient belief had it, remained the episode that in the public mind defined the Holy Office, and indeed the entire Catholic Church's attitude toward rational inquiry.

The harsher penalties of the Holy Office were mitigated by the passage of time and the development of standards of human rights that even the church's heresy hunters respected. Yet its autocratic, secretive procedures toward theological inquiry remained a "source of scandal," in the words that Father Ratzinger wrote for Cardinal Frings at the Second Vatican Council in 1963. With his opening address to the council, Pope John XXIII was instrumental in setting the new tone that would lead to a historic reorientation of Rome toward differing opinions. Pope John told the bishops that while the church had always opposed errors, today "the Spouse of Christ prefers to make use of the medicine of mercy rather than that of severity. She considers that she meets the needs of the present day by demonstrating the validity of her teaching rather than by condemnations."

√ John died the next year, but Joseph Ratzinger and his allies continued to push for a wholesale reform of the Holy Office. In a 1965 commentary, Father Ratzinger criticized an "all too smoothly functioning central teaching office which prejudged every question almost before it had come up for discussion." At another point, in defending theological inquiry as grounded in the "essential content" of tradition, he argued that "theology must be left free to inquire afresh precisely what that essential content is." He said that "new groups and their questions are also legitimate forms of Catholic theological work." Beyond promoting theological exploration, he also suggested that the Holy Office adopt some of the legal protections that had been developed in preceding centuries by secular democracies.

Even as Ratzinger's pessimism about the council grew in the late 1960s, he was still a defender of the free practice of theology. Most notably, in 1968 he signed on to the Nijmegen Declaration (after the Dutch city where Ratzinger's progressive journal, *Concilium,* was located), which sought to warn the Vatican off any encroachment on academic freedom. The strongly worded statement was signed by more than 1,300 theologians from more than fifty countries—including Küng, Rahner, Metz, and others with whom Ratzinger would later clash. It declared that "the freedom of theologians, and theology in the service of the church, regained by Vatican II, must not be jeopardized again." The signers said that while they pledged loyalty to the pope, neither the pontiff nor the other bishops could "supersede, hamper and impede the teaching task of theologians as scholars." They concluded, "Any form of inquisition, however subtle, not only harms the development of sound theology, it also causes irreparable damage to the credibility of the church as a community in the modern world." The theologians made a series of requests, including that competent experts be appointed when proceedings were called against a theologian, and that a clear and public due process, including adequate notification and representation, be followed.[5]

A decade later, however, everything had changed, at least for Ratzinger, who was now a cardinal. The battle for the legacy of Vatican II was in full swing, and Cardinal Ratzinger was on the side of those who believed arrogant theologians were responsible for undermining the faith. "The Christian believer is a simple person: bishops should protect the faith of these little people against the power of intellectuals," Ratzinger preached in a sermon on New Year's Eve 1979. Something had to be done, he said, and within two years he was prefect of the CDF, the right man in the right place, and with the right pope above him.

Not surprisingly for a man so grounded in patristics, Joseph Ratzinger likes to view the situation of the church today as analogous to that of the church in the first centuries, when the faith was facing challenges from all sides. But the unique danger of the modern world that Cardinal Ratzinger faced when he became head of the CDF was the "democratization" of theology that led many Catholics to decide for themselves what is right or wrong, and thus to what he saw as a widespread "pathology of faith" that the CDF was compelled to combat.

For Ratzinger, it was not so much those outside the Catholic faith who worried him. That battle would come later. Real heresy is not apostasy, the abandoning of one's faith; heresy is far more dangerous because it is an internal challenge to orthodoxy. As canon law notes, only a baptized Christian can be a heretic. And if you don't bother challenging from the inside, Ratzinger says "Godspeed" to you.

A prime example of that approach was Benedict's September 2005 meeting with Hans Küng, his former friend and longtime foe, at Castelgandolfo. The meeting, which Küng requested shortly after Benedict was elected, surprised Catholics on both the left and right, with one camp seeing it as a welcome signal of openness and the other worried that Benedict was growing soft on the papal throne. In reality, the meeting was a personal reconciliation after their bitter falling-out. As a cardinal, Ratzinger had expressed respect for Küng for following his own path outside church circles—a path forced on him by the lifting of his license to teach Catholic theology. Even though Küng had "further distanced himself from the faith of the Church," Ratzinger said, he was no longer considered a Catholic theologian and was thus of little concern.

The September reconciliation was a warm four-hour encounter, including dinner, at which the two giants of German theology talked about the relationship between science and religion and Küng's efforts to articulate a *Weltethos,* a global ethic that believers and nonbelievers from all points of view can agree on. But the ground rules for the meeting were that they could not discuss the many "persistent doctrinal questions" that still divided them or the question of rehabilitating Küng as a Catholic theologian. "We should not have delusions," of what the meeting suggests about Benedict, Küng told *NCR.* "His stances on church policy are not my own."

In the modern world's romance with what Ratzinger called "the tyranny of caprice," heresy has become so popular that it is not so much a particular school of thought but the idea of relativism itself that is the problem—that truth cannot be known or, worse, that anyone can determine what is true. This is exemplified by theologians who routinely challenge the Vatican, claiming equal or even higher standing than Rome. "It is contended that it is not the Congregation but they, the 'heretics,' who represent the 'authentic' meaning of the transmitted faith," Ratzinger has said.[6] Widespread religious intermarriage, the popularity of religious reinvention through conversion, the large-scale movement of people and populations, as well as the decline in respect for traditions and institutions that once anchored religions across generations, have all led to an unprecedented level of religious pluralism and openness to different faiths. We are living in an era of choice, or overchoice, as social scientists call it. For some it can lead to an opting out, for others to a kind of religious freelancing. Either way it amounts to what sociologist of religion Peter Berger calls "the heretical imperative" in the title of his 1979 book.

Berger uses the term *heresy* in its primitive form, derived from the Greek word *haireisthai,* which means "to choose."

In that sense, we are all heretics now because we all choose what we want to be, and for the most part we do not condemn the choices that others make. When everyone claims to possess the truth, it makes battling error more like guerrilla warfare than the crusades of olden days. Orthodoxy is shaped not so much by a reaction against an alternate belief; rather, it is a battle over whether orthodoxy can really exist, and if so, who determines what is orthodox.

Moreover, modernity has shown once again that the church never really gets rid of anything, even when it tries to. Today, old heresies are trendy. Paganism, Wicca, Heathenism, and a host of "retro" religions that Christianity thought it had vanquished are now as hip as vintage clothing, even though their contemporary adherents have often had to invent their doctrines and traditions out of whole cloth or recast them in ways that play down some of their unattractive, patriarchal, or bellicose aspects. Any old religion will do, as long as it is not the same old religion you grew up in.

In a similar vein, today's Christian self-help movement echoes the do-it-yourself salvation of Pelagianism, and the never-ending search for the historical Jesus, on the one hand, and the "Jesus is my best friend" theology of the bumper sticker, on the other, can smack of a kind of neo-Arianism that maximizes Christ's humanity at the expense of his divinity. Alternatively, Gnosticism, with its alluringly evanescent spirituality, has proved especially resilient, thanks to the startling recovery of a slew of ancient Gnostic scrolls in the Egyptian desert in 1945, plus the modern desire for an individualistic faith that features exclusive knowledge but easy access. Even the Cathars have made a comeback, their own grievous excesses having been erased from the collective memory by the whitewash of victimhood. Nothing is more malleable or marketable than the mystery of a lost secret—just ask the publisher of *The Da Vinci Code*—and nothing proves a faith's bona fides better than having been crushed by the Inquisition. The Albigensians went two-for-two, and their appeal flourished even as the Cathars themselves died. Thus in the 1930s an SS officer could resurrect the Cathar doctrine as an Aryan religious legacy, while the counterculture of the 1960s found in Catharism an esoterica so tantalizingly recondite that converts invaded Languedoc in search of an alternative Holy Land. Suicide cults of the 1990s also thought the Cathars were the real deal, and Marshall Applewhite used references to the ascetic Cathar teaching of a "level beyond human" to inspire his Heaven's Gate cult members to lace up their purple sneakers and join him on a postmortem trip to the Hale-Bopp Comet.

This presumption for personal choice in the culture at-large was also at work within the Catholic Church, and that was where Cardinal Ratzinger, as prefect of the Congregation for the Doctrine of the Faith, first focused his attention.

As he often did, Ratzinger saw an alleged misuse of the Second Vatican Council as the starting point for the spreading corruption, and again, theologians were at the root of the problem. The difficulty began with the council itself, which rehabilitated theologians who only a few years earlier had been marginalized or silenced by Rome for teaching in error. "The names of John Courtney Murray, Pierre Teilhard de Chardin, Henri de Lubac, and Yves Congar, all under a cloud of suspicion in the 1950s, suddenly became surrounded with a bright halo of enthusiasm," wrote Father Avery Dulles, a leading American theologian and a Jesuit whom John Paul made a cardinal in 2001 in recognition of his distinguished career. "By its actual practice of revision, the council implicitly taught the legitimacy and even the value of dissent. In effect the council said that the ordinary magisterium [teaching] of the Roman Pontiff had fallen into error and had unjustly harmed the careers of loyal and able scholars."[7]

Moreover, the rehabilitation of once banished theologians occurred just as the council was projecting the image of a church that seemingly could change anything. The council recast so many long-standing Catholic prohibitions that Catholics were intoxicated by the possibilities. The council fathers embraced the principle of religious liberty that popes and councils had once condemned and reversed the papal adage "Error has no rights." They endorsed dialogues with other religions and even suggested that the seeds of grace could be found in non-Christian faiths. They overturned centuries of condemnatory teachings on Judaism and became champions of ecumenical dialogue with other Christians who a few years earlier had been still under ancient anathemas. The modern world, which had been condemned so vociferously for centuries as inimical to the Catholic faith, was now welcomed as a partner in building up the Kingdom of God.

The old Roman Catholic motto *Semper idem* (Always the same) seemed patently untrue, and that was an ominous sign to Joseph Ratzinger.

"The impression grew steadily that nothing was now stable in the Church, that everything was open to revision," he wrote in *Milestones*. "More and more the Council appeared to be like a great Church parliament that could change everything and reshape everything according to its own desires.... In any event the faith could be changed—or so it now appeared, in contrast to everything we had previously thought. The faith no longer seemed exempt from human decision-making but rather was now apparently determined by it."

Still worse were the deeper implications for authority growing out of that "political" model of ecclesiology. "If the bishops in Rome could change the faith (as it appeared they could), why only the bishops?" Ratzinger asked. Not only were once errant theologians being exalted, but their cachet in the Catholic ferment of the 1960s was such that they were—in Ratzinger's eyes— displacing bishops who would normally and canonically be the supreme authority in matters of faith. Catholics knew that "the bishops had learned from theologians the new things they were now proposing. For believers, it was a remarkable phenomenon that their bishops seemed to show a different face in Rome from the one they wore at home. Shepherds who had been considered strict conservatives suddenly appeared to be spokesmen for progressivism."

And not merely spokesmen, Ratzinger suspected, but perhaps dupes. "The role that theologians had assumed at the Council was creating ever more clearly a new confidence among scholars, who now understood themselves to be the truly knowledgeable experts in the faith and therefore no longer subordinate to the shepherds. For, how could the bishops in their exercise of their teaching office preside over theologians when they, the bishops, received their insights only from specialists and thus were dependent on the guidance of scholars?"

And if scholars were teaching the bishops, could they not also teach ordinary lay folk, who might then feel as authoritative as the hierarchy?

"Behind this tendency to dominance by specialists one could already detect something else: the idea of an ecclesial sovereignty of the people in which the people itself determines what it wants to understand by Church, since 'Church' already seemed very clearly defined as 'People of God.' The idea of the 'Church from below,' the 'Church of the People,' which then became the goal of reform particularly in the context of liberation theology, was thus heralded."

Liberation theology was the unrivaled bogeyman of church conservatives in the 1970s; by the 1980s, with a Polish pope confronting the Soviet communism that had for so long subjugated his homeland, and a doctrinal prefect in Ratzinger who was still aghast at 1968 leftist rebellions that had upended his academic life, the Marxist theories of liberation theologians were a prime target.

It would not be easy to dislodge liberation theology, however. Led by church intellectuals, liberation theology inspired a mass movement fueled by the groaning poverty that was crushing the populace of the Latin American continent, where four in ten Catholics lived and where the Catholic Church was a preeminent force in society and politics. But the hierarchy's sympathies and influence had too often been exerted on behalf of the entrenched oligarchies or dictatorships that ruled Latin America and maintained the ironclad order and stability that provided such a congenial environment for a tradition-bound church. The seeds of change in the church were planted with the emergence in the 1960s of theologies that sought to take Catholic social justice teaching to an unprecedented level of political activism.

Again, the Second Vatican Council's opening to modernity and the social upheavals of the 1960s, combined with resentment in the developing world at an American economic and political hegemony that was considered as threatening as Soviet domination, prepared the ground for liberation theology to spread in Latin America. In 1968, at a historic meeting in Medellín in Colombia, the bishops of Latin America, citing the council as their inspiration, used the theories of liberation theology in endorsing a "preferential option for the poor" and proposing an economic, social, and political engagement that would revolutionize the church's traditional role on the continent. Entire national hierarchies were swept up in the liberation movement, and priests and lay activists began setting up base communities and other forms of grassroots Catholicism that had been unknown in the rigidly hierarchical church of years past.

Though liberation theology has come to mean many things to many different people, from women to racial and ethnic minorities or any oppressed group, its original intent remains its most prevalent and compelling: to use the Gospel message to undo the "structural" or "social sin" of economic injustice visited on the poor. The movement took its name from the 1971 work, *A Theology of Liberation,* by Gustavo Gutiérrez, a Peruvian theologian who was an adviser to the bishops at Medellín. The heavy reliance on social analysis naturally led many of its proponents to use Marxist models, and it is widely agreed that some liberation theologians and their progeny went too far in marrying scripture to risky political causes or to movements promoting violence as the principal means of reform. A few priests even joined rebel or terrorist groups, like Peru's Maoist Shining Path army. When they died, they were hailed as saints.

Three priests took jobs with the Sandinista government in Nicaragua after the 1979 overthrow of the U.S.-backed Somoza regime. The best known, Ernesto Cardenal, was a poet and liberation theologian who became the minister of culture. Under canon law no priest is allowed to hold political office, no matter what the politics or the office. But Cardenal's association with a Communist government was especially galling to John Paul, who was engaged in his own struggle against communism in Eastern Europe. Cardenal refused the pope's order to resign from his post. When John Paul visited Nicaragua in 1983, Cardenal was in the line of government officials greeting the pontiff at the airport. But when Cardenal knelt to kiss the Holy Father's ring, as tradition required, John Paul instead wagged his finger at him and scolded Cardenal before a global television audience in one of the most enduring images of the Cold War era. Later that day, as he read his homily before 700,000 people in Managua's vast central plaza, John Paul was interrupted by shouts of "We want peace!" Some heard Marxist slogans yelled out as well, and many believed the demonstrators were Sandinista provocateurs. Shocked by such a reaction—the pope always faced adoring crowds—an angry John Paul shouted, "*Silencio!*" three times at the crowd. "The Church is the first to want peace!" he thundered.

When John Paul returned to Rome, whatever sympathy he may have harbored for liberation theology was gone, and he gave Joseph Ratzinger the job of stamping out this movement. Ratzinger did not have to be convinced. In Rome there has always been a whispered debate as to whether John Paul was the brake on a more conservative Cardinal Ratzinger or vice versa, that Ratzinger actually softened John Paul's more tempestuous inclinations and then himself took the heat for the Vatican's harsher edicts. In the case of liberation theology, most would agree that Ratzinger was certainly more willing than his boss to cut the movement down root and branch. John Paul had always keenly promoted social justice as an integral part of the church's message and a Catholic's life. He dedicated many of his most famous encyclicals to social justice themes, invoking the ire of political conservatives with his critiques of both capitalism and communism in *Laborem Exercens* (On Human Work) in 1981 and with *Sollicitudo Rei Socialis* (On the Social Concern of the Church) in 1988.

√   Ratzinger has made it clear that he had little input or interest in those texts, which were born out of John Paul's personal experience. It is easy to forget, even a short remove from the fall of the Berlin Wall, that Soviet bloc countries were repressed economically as well as politically, and that Poland was as much a Third World nation as many Southern Hemisphere nations in Africa or Latin America. In a sense, just as Bill Clinton was said to be the first African American president, so too John Paul could be said to be the first pope from the Third World. While Ratzinger saw communism and Nazism as equal evils, John Paul made distinctions between them as movements even as he unequivocally condemned Stalin and Hitler. "From the moral point of view, both are reprehensible. If Stalin has been better judged, it is simply because

Communism had a more profoundly sustained program than National Socialism. National Socialism and Fascism, which were very closely related, were inhumane ideologies, as well as simplistic and superficial. Communism was and will always be recognized as a system that promotes a greater social justice," John Paul II said in a 1988 interview. The interview, with a Polish journalist, was not published at the pope's request, and it only emerged in an Italian newspaper six months after his death.[8]

"John Paul II was always a man with a divided heart," said Brazil's Cardinal Paulo Evaristo Arns. "We in Latin America saw the poor as evangelizers, but he did not see it in exactly the same way." In fact, in a 1986 letter to the Brazilian bishops that was never released by the Vatican, John Paul said that liberation theology was "not only opportune but necessary to the theological evolution of the church." He was careful to stipulate that such a liberation theology must not dilute the faith. The Brazilians and other supporters of the movement had no fears of that happening, and *Alleluias* were sung as the letter was read.

Cardinal Ratzinger's experience in West Germany, however, left him with no desire to even dialogue with anything that smacked of Marxism, which he still resented for its excesses in the 1960s. "I learned that it is impossible to discuss with terror and on terror, as there are no premises for a discussion—and such a discussion becomes collaboration with terror," Ratzinger said in a 1985 profile in the *New York Times Magazine*. "I think that in those years, I learned where discussion must stop because it is turning into a lie, and resistance must begin in order to maintain freedom." Liberation theology's dalliance with Marxist remedies also deeply offended Ratzinger's iron principle against using eternal faith to advance temporal aims. "What is theologically unacceptable here, and socially dangerous, is this mixture of Bible, christology, politics, sociology and economics," he said in 1984.[9] "Holy Scripture and theology cannot be misused to absolutize and sacralize a theory concerning the socio-political order." In his 2000 preface to a new edition of *Introduction to Christianity,* he wrote that what liberation theologians were trying to do for Karl Marx in the twentieth century—reconciling his thought to Christian belief—was comparable to Aquinas's baptism of Aristotle's pagan philosophy in the thirteenth century.

When Ratzinger was promoted to his CDF post, the Stasi—the East German spy network that had been keeping a file on him since 1974 and had predicted that Ratzinger would get the CDF job two years before John Paul gave it to him—expressed concern about the effects of his long-standing antipathy to communism. They feared that he would "increasingly have influence over the anti-communist bias of the Roman Catholic Church, particularly in Latin America." Excerpts were released in a German newspaper in October 2005, with Benedict's permission.[10]

Ratzinger did praise the idea of a "true theology of liberation," one that focuses on freeing men from sin, and thereby, ideally, contributes to a more just society that would alleviate the undeniable social injustices that exist. And with typical frankness he was certainly tough on the "hellish" culture of Western capitalism, seeing "a sign of the Satanic" in today's widespread market exploitation. "There is something diabolical in the coldblooded perversity with which man is corrupted for the sake of money and profit is drawn from his weakness," he said in 1984.[11] In the West, he said, the free market has imposed its "implacable laws" on everything, with a direct moral consequence: "Economic *liberalism* creates its exact counterpart, *permissivism*, on the moral plane" (his italics).

But as bad as capitalism can be, Ratzinger says Marxism is worse, "a more insidious temptation" because it is intellectually ambitious, but also because it cloaks itself in Christian garb. Unfettered capitalism is something that the church opposes; liberation theology actually co-opts the faith, turning the Gospel in a "godless prophetic movement" directed to a "merely earthly hope." He continues, "This perversion of the biblical tradition deludes many believers who are convinced in good faith that the cause of Christ is the same as that proclaimed by the heralds of political revolution." Liberation theology, according to Ratzinger, fed into the dangerous view that "all religions are basically just instruments for advocating freedom, peace, and the conservation of creation, so they would have to justify their existence through political success and political goals."

As he often does with ideas he opposes, Ratzinger painted liberation theology in stark tones that distorted the movement's tenets beyond all recognition. Whatever the undeniable excesses of some proponents of liberation theology, Ratzinger was in reality criticizing a movement that did not exist. But that tactic also made liberation theology—and other deviations Ratzinger perceived—much easier to condemn since they were made to seem so patently corrupt. This is in keeping with Ratzinger's grim, purist theological outlook, which sees even the slightest deviation from his view of tradition as tantamount to despoiling an entire theory or movement or person, a seduction so subtle we may not even realize it is happening. The Protestant Reformation, as he noted, "occurred almost imperceptibly," so that, like today, "one frequently could not ascertain the boundary between what was still Catholic and what was no longer Catholic." Faith is lived on a slippery slope for Joseph Ratzinger, and the smallest misstep will inevitably lead to disaster. In a 1996 interview, for example, Ratzinger said liberation theology had contributed to the rise of Islamic terrorism and had inspired a militant feminism that he sees as an insidious means to try to free men and women from their biologically determined —that is, God-given—roles.[12] What this all points toward, Ratzinger said, is that "man is to be his own creator—a modern, new edition of the immemorial attempt to be God, to be like God."

From suicide bombings to radical feminism to the divine ambition that damned Lucifer, Ratzinger extrapolated a dark lineage from the black arts that he saw in liberation theology.

Despite early opposition to Ratzinger's campaign from Latin American bishops and the international theological community, the outcome of the Vatican's struggle against liberation theology was never in doubt.

Ratzinger led the way by targeting the movement's leading voices, such as Gutiérrez and Leonardo Boff, a Franciscan priest and theologian from Brazil who was one of the more charismatic exponents of liberation theology. He also challenged the movement as a whole, attacking its theological and intellectual underpinnings, first with an August 1984 document, the *Instruction on Certain Aspects of the "Theology of Liberation,"* which denounced liberation theology as "a perversion of the Christian message as God entrusted it to His church."

The *Instruction* was published by the CDF and approved by the pope, but it was unusual in that it included an accompanying exegesis by Ratzinger himself, once again conflating, for many commentators, his personal and official roles. Ratzinger expanded in more personal terms on his opposition to liberation theology, but also spoke revealingly of the uniquely modern danger he saw—namely, that given the terrible conditions of the world's poor and the undeniably prophetic words of Jesus on behalf of the oppressed, a movement like liberation theology "has an almost irresistible logic." The movement seemed to integrate religious belief and social action perfectly, so that to reject it would seem to be "a flight from reality as well as a denial of reason and morality." It was this aspect—the reasonableness of liberation theology to the contemporary believer—that made it so novel, so dangerous, and so thoroughly modern: "The very radicality of liberation theology means that its seriousness is often underestimated, since it does not fit into any of the accepted categories of heresy; its fundamental concern cannot be detected by the existing range of standard questions."[13]

A new vigilance was required, which Ratzinger recognized might seem counterintuitive and unpopular to many. But he believed the threat to the faith was grave enough to merit tough actions. In March 1985 Ratzinger issued a "notification" on Boff's book, *Church: Charisma and Power*. The CDF said the book was "dangerous" and silenced Boff for a year, prohibiting him from writing or speaking publicly. In March 1986 the CDF issued a second major document against liberation theology, titled *Instruction on Christian Freedom and Liberation,* which focused on trying to out-maneuver liberation theology by providing an orthodox theory of liberation based on personal conversion rather than reforming sinful structures.

While many liberation theologians thought Ratzinger had so misconstrued their ideas that his proscriptions would not apply to them, others were more clear-eyed in their assessment of what was happening. As they feared, the investigations and penalties continued, and by the 1990s, liberation theology had been effectively defeated. Gutiérrez was reined in; other theologians were silenced and their books banned; and in 1992, following another six years of investigation by the CDF and an order barring him from teaching, Boff left the priesthood. "Ecclesiastical power is cruel and merciless," he said. "It forgets nothing. It forgives nothing. It demands everything." (Boff had a long memory as well. On the eve of the 2005 conclave, Boff wrote in a Brazilian daily that "Ratzinger is one of the church's most odious cardinals because of his rigidity, and because he humiliated the bishops' conferences and fellow cardinals in an authoritarian manner on questions of faith." He also predicted that Ratzinger "will never be pope, because it would be excessive, something the intelligence of the cardinals would not permit.")

Ratzinger was also aided in his campaign by the Vatican's inexorable promotion of Latin American bishops who were openly hostile to liberation theology. For years, until those John Paul bishops became a majority, the bishops throughout Latin America were deeply divided between the old guard prelates, who wanted to make social justice an imperative, and the new traditionalists, whose priority was piety. Until Ratzinger could be sure he had enough loyalists in place in the Latin American hierarchies, he frequently went behind the bishops' backs, taking action against priests in their own dioceses without letting them know, a patent breach of policy and Ratzinger's own promises to the bishops to keep them apprised of any actions.

At the same time as the Vatican was cracking down, other forces were also working against liberation theology, or almost any Catholic social justice voice that could be stuck with the Marxist tag associated with liberation theology.

The deadliest opponents were the right-wing regimes, whose death squads and paramilitaries acted with impunity. By 1980 more than eight hundred priests and nuns had been killed in Latin America for trying to relieve the plight of the poor, among them three American nuns and an American church worker who were abducted, raped, and killed in El Salvador in December 1980.[14]

The most famous victim was Archbishop Oscar Romero of San Salvador, who was gunned down while saying Mass on March 24, 1980. Romero was an erstwhile conservative whose experience with the crushing poverty and injustice of his native land converted him into one of the most outspoken champions of the underclasses. One of Romero's friends, a priest who worked with the poor, was machine-gunned in 1976 on his way to Mass. That was a turning point for Romero. Romero was not a formal adherent of the liberation theology movement, but his vocal denunciations of the regime caused him trouble at home and in Rome all the same. The Vatican's representative in El Salvador wrote that Romero was a dupe of Jesuits and Marxists (they amounted to much the same thing for church conservatives). When Romero came to the Vatican to meet John Paul, he was humiliated by papal aides, forced to wait a week to gain an audience. Such treatment was unheard-of for a man of Romero's standing.

Romero's meeting with John Paul apparently had little effect. In March 1980 senior Vatican officials decided to remove Romero—a shocking move under almost any circumstances—but a few days later a gunman shot the archbishop once through the chest just after he had finished a homily on Jesus's parable about the grain of wheat that bears fruit when it falls to the ground, also a favorite image of Joseph Ratzinger's. The Vatican offered perfunctory condolences for Romero's death. But despite the huge number of beatifications and canonizations that John Paul presided over, Romero's cause for official sainthood remained stuck in bureaucratic limbo, the result of objections by Ratzinger's CDF. In fact, in 1988, Ratzinger silenced Brazilian bishop Pedro Casaldaliga for his support of liberation theology and for publicly referring to Romero as a martyr—a label the Vatican has refused to give him. Romero remains a saint in the eyes of Latin Americans.[15]

The violence against church personnel continued throughout the 1980s as Central America became a hot front in Ronald Reagan's Cold War strategy. In 1980 Reagan advisers adopted recommendations in the so-called Santa Fe document that called for combating liberation theology because it fomented church criticism of a "productive capitalism." The document also counseled aiding Protestant groups in Latin America in order to undermine progressive Catholicism. In 1989 six Jesuits at the University of Central America, along with their housekeeper and her fourteen-year-old daughter, were dragged into the courtyard of their residence by U.S.-trained Salvadoran army troops and assassinated. Among them were some of the greatest intellectual architects of liberation theology.

Ratzinger's Congregation for the Doctrine of the Faith was active on many other fronts during this time, as John Paul sought to rein in the penchant for theological experimentation in the progressive heyday of the postconciliar era.

In 1985 Ratzinger completed an investigation that had begun in 1979, before his tenure, with the suspension of Father Charles Curran, a moral theologian at Catholic University of America, for his views on certain issues of sexual morality that departed from church teaching. Curran argued that he was dissenting from noninfallible teachings, which should be allowed. In 1986 Dominican father Edward Schillebeeckx, a leading voice in European theology since Vatican II, was notified that his work was "in disagreement with the teaching of the church," particularly regarding ordination and the possibility of laypeople presiding at the Eucharist. No action was taken against him since he was already retired. A Dominican priest, Father Matthew Fox, was dismissed from his order in 1992 following a lengthy battle with the CDF over his theories of "creation spirituality." Religious pluralism was also a bugbear for Ratzinger; many theologians, especially in Asia, where Christianity is a small minority, were considered too accommodating in their efforts to reconcile the exclusive message of salvation through Jesus with other religious traditions. A Sri Lankan priest, Father Tissa Balasuriya, was excommunicated in 1997 for showing how Christianity can be expressed through Eastern concepts; a year later the excommunication was lifted when he signed a loyalty oath. Even death was no escape. In 1998, ten years after his death, the CDF declared that the writings of an Indian Jesuit, Father Anthony De Mello, were "incompatible with the Catholic faith and can cause grave harm."

In 2001 the highly respected Belgian Jesuit Father Jacques Dupuis was rebuked for his writings on religious pluralism. Dupuis died in 2004, anguished over the cloud that had shadowed the end of a career devoted to the church. In 2004 an American Jesuit, Roger Haight, was forbidden to teach as a Catholic theologian because his writings on Christology were deemed to contain "serious doctrinal errors against the Catholic and divine faith of the church." Anticipating a negative judgment, Haight had already left the prestigious Weston Jesuit School of Theology, where he was a highly regarded professor attracting students from around the world, to take a post at a Protestant seminary in New York. Thus the CDF's ruling had little practical effect, except to further narrow the range of views available to Catholic theology students.

Scores of other theologians, of varying degrees of renown, were silenced, disciplined, or otherwise punished—as many as one hundred all told during Ratzinger's tenure, though the number is uncertain because the CDF keeps all proceedings secret. Those who were not under formal investigation were left looking over their shoulder.

In 1989 close to four hundred theologians from Europe signed the so-called Cologne Declaration, blasting the Vatican's increasing efforts to deny university posts in Europe to theologians as "a serious and dangerous interference in the free exercise of scholarly research and teaching. . . . The power to withhold official permission to teach is being abused; it has become an instrument to discipline theologians." The theologians' letter was prompted by the appointment of Joachim Meisner as archbishop of Cologne against the express wishes of local Catholic leaders. Meisner would later become a cardinal and was instrumental in campaigning on behalf of Ratzinger's election as pope. In 1989, a group of theologians from France wrote to Ratzinger with similar complaints, and other petitions followed.

The protests had little effect and may have hardened Ratzinger's resolve. For example, in response to the 1989 Cologne Declaration, signed by hundreds of theologians—which was very similar to the 1968 Nijmegen protest that Ratzinger had signed—Ratzinger opened investigations on the signatories. He also suggested that some of the theology positions at German universities should be eliminated. "It was insulting," Ratzinger said of the theologians' letter. "It was in a bad manner, bad style, not respectful of the persons."

In 1989 the CDF mandated that all newly appointed presidents, rectors, and professors of theology and philosophy at Catholic universities and seminaries sign a loyalty oath and make a profession of faith. The move was shocking for several reasons, not least because it was done with virtually no consultation and came as a surprise even to other curial departments that would be affected by the new policy. The oath also smacked of the McCarthyist paranoia of the anti-Modernist purge of the early twentieth century, when all priests and seminary teachers were required to take an oath against Modernism. That oath had been dropped in 1967 as an embarrassing anachronism. The new oath was not much better, and in fact it had so many imprecise wordings and irregularities in its promulgation that it was widely ignored. Less than a year later, in May 1990, the CDF issued another document, an *Instruction on the Ecclesial Vocation of the Theologian,* in another effort to rein in theologians by calling on them not to use the media to publicize their views or pressure for change in the church. The central portion of the *Instruction* was titled "The Problem of Dissent" and critiqued the so called parallel magisterium of theologians. The document called on theologians who are reprimanded to suffer "in silence and prayer," keeping faith that if they are right, the truth will prevail eventually. In 1992 the CDF reaffirmed a little-noticed church law requiring prepublication theological review of manuscripts dealing with church teaching.

Many on the liberal side of the Catholic spectrum have naturally viewed the litany of actions by Ratzinger's CDF as wrong in and of themselves, as well as maddening because they inhibit the advancement of the progressive views they would espouse. But the reality is that it was not so much the content of the arguments as the means Ratzinger used and the manner with which he prosecuted the investigations that troubled the Catholic intelligentsia, and many others. Some of the disciplined theologians were considered marginal figures, or their work was viewed as debatable even by the mainstream theological community. And theologians generally recognize the right of the Vatican to condemn ideas and writings that cross the line. As Pope Paul VI said, the best way to fight bad books is by writing good books. But the peremptory silencings, dismissals, and above all the use of secret proceedings by Vatican officials of marginal expertise to make these judgments were considered authoritarian abuses that were inconsistent both with the reforms of Vatican II and with the views once held by Cardinal Ratzinger.

This is the crux of the controversy over Joseph Ratzinger: Was he a principled defender of truth or a captious puritan? Or some admixture of both?

Complaints against the CDF generally start with the way the congregation begins investigations and then how they are carried out. Immune to the reforms that a younger Ratzinger had advocated at Vatican II, Cardinal Ratzinger's CDF still operated in complete secrecy, to the extent that those who came under scrutiny often did not know they were being investigated until they were informed of the judgments against them. They also never knew who their accusers were, since investigations could be started by delations, complaints submitted under a guarantee of confidentiality.

Ratzinger did acknowledge that most of the delations to the CDF come from the United States, but he defended the letter writers as nonpartisans "who are preoccupied with the thought that the Catholic church would remain the Catholic church."[16] In reality, such people are invariably conservatives who share Ratzinger's outlook and know their concerns will be heard, and probably acted on. Liberals would not say that they do not want the Catholic Church to remain Catholic, but Ratzinger's prejudgment of their views did not exactly encourage them to delate, or report on, others, even if they would prefer such an uncharitable course. Such a skewed correspondence from the Catholic world may have contributed to Ratzinger's glum view of the state of the church or perhaps affirmed his pre-existing disposition to that pessimism. Like a police officer or a firefighter dealing with crime and tragedy day in and day out, Ratzinger's daily experience with deviations from the faith could lead to a distorted view of human nature. Live too long on a steady diet of wrongdoing and tragedy and before long you think everyone is suspect, or every house—including your own—is about to burn down.

It does not appear that the system of anonymous denunciations will end anytime soon. When Charles Curran met with Ratzinger in Rome in 1986, before he was stripped of his teaching post, he demanded to face his accusers. Ratzinger said, "Your own works have been your 'accusers,' and they alone." Curran told the cardinal, "You are a respected German theologian, and are on a first-name basis with six German moralists whom I could name, and you know as well as I do that they are saying the same things as I am saying." Ratzinger replied, "Well, if you would want to delate these people, we will open a dossier on them." Curran responded: "I'm not here to do your dirty work."[17]

Other participants in meetings with Ratzinger and the CDF report similar uncomfortable moments, part of which can be chalked up to Ratzinger's innate unease with social interactions. Boff said that Ratzinger commended the Brazilian on the cassock he wore to the interview, and suggested that he should wear it more often as a sign of witness. Boff responded that it could also be seen as a symbol of power. The conversation did not get any better after that. The Redemptorist priest Father Bernard Häring said his encounter with Ratzinger and the CDF offended him more than the four times he was brought into court by the Nazis. Lavinia Byrne, an English writer who left her religious order in 2000 after a lengthy investigation by the CDF, which demanded that she publicly recant her writings on the ordination of women, called it an "infantilizing" process. The late Cardinal Basil Hume, a Benedictine monk with a sharp intellect and a keen sense of justice, didn't like Byrne's treatment either. He wrote to the CDF, "strongly" advising that its investigation cease. "She [Byrne] is a much respected person in this country, and not only in the Catholic Church. She has done much good and will continue to do so. I am sure the Congregation will act wisely and with prudence, and now leave the matter to rest. Any other policy will be harmful for the Church in this country," Hume wrote. Paul Collins, an Australian priest and theologian whose book, *Papal Power,* came under scrutiny (among other things, the CDF objected to the word "power" in the title), said, "The CDF lives in a time warp: despite attempts to tart it up in modern dress, it is essentially a creature of the sixteenth century whose methods have survived to the present day."[18]

"The relationship between theologians and the papacy is worse today than at any time since the Reformation," Father Thomas Reese wrote in *Inside the Vatican*. "The number of theologians investigated, silenced, or removed from office is at an all-time high, even exceeding the numbers during the Modernist crisis. . . . The rhetoric used by theologians in response to Vatican actions has been bitter and biting. The chasm between the two appears to be getting wider, not narrower. A breach between the intellectual and administrative leaders of an organization is, of course, a recipe for disaster. If this breach continues into the next century"—Reese was writing in 1996—"the church will be incapable of creatively responding to new needs and new opportunities, instead repeating old formulas that do not address new questions and ideas. If the papacy continues to lose credibility in the intellectual community, schism could be the disastrous consequence."[19]

The CDF has about forty staffers covering four sections; three of them deal with issues such as the authenticity of religious visions. It is the fourth, the doctrinal section, that receives the greatest volume of work and, by the nature of that work, the greatest attention, though it operates with less than a dozen staff people. "And so a bit less than we would need in order to organize the theological *putsch* which some suspect us of planning!" Ratzinger once remarked.[20] Yet their power far outweighs their numbers.

Investigations proceed through several stages, from an initial inquiry to a decision, taken at the doctrinal section's weekly Saturday morning meeting, to pursue formal action. If that step is taken, then two staffers are named to examine the theologian's works for deficiencies, while an "outside" expert— almost always someone working in Rome who is amenable to the Vatican—is named as a kind of public defender to examine the person's works to find what may be valuable in them. The investigators and the defender give their reports, then the advocate for the accused theologian leaves the room while the investigators and the CDF staff make the final ruling. At this point, the target's bishop or religious superior may or may not have been alerted to the investigation, but the person in question is generally still unaware that he or she is being scrutinized. If no action is deemed necessary, the case is put on hold in case further concerns arise. The defendant may never know any of this transpired.

If a decision is made to proceed with disciplinary action, the pope must sign off, and then the theologian is invited to respond to the verdict by defending his or her work or by making public amends and conforming writings to the CDF's demands. There is no presumption of innocence, no right of appeal, and no separation between prosecutor, defender, and judge. And when theologians are silenced, they cannot defend themselves publicly. Curran and others have tried for years to gain access to their case files, but the Vatican has no Freedom of Information Act, and their requests have been denied. When accused theologians come to Rome, they may be allowed to have one person accompany them to the hearing, though that is up to the CDF.

The back-and-forth correspondence can drag on for years, and may or may not include a face-to-face meeting in Rome. Accused theologians are not told who was the "expert" called to represent their own writings, and when they try to respond on their own behalf they often run into a brick wall. When Father Jacques Dupuis met with Ratzinger and his staff to address the CDF's long-running charges regarding his work on the role of non-Christian religions in salvation, Dupuis brought along a copy of the two-hundred-page defense he had sent the CDF for the earlier stages of the investigation. When Ratzinger raised a question at their face-to-face meeting, Dupuis noted that he had already addressed that issue in the dossier he had sent. Ratzinger chuckled and said, "You don't expect us to read that."

It is a frequent complaint of targeted theologians and others that the CDF staff is not large enough to do justice to these inquiries, nor expert enough without calling in a range of outside scholars, a reform suggested during Vatican II but never implemented. Ratzinger frequently conceded that his staff could not keep track of all theologians and readily admitted that the CDF was overburdened given the scope of their task. But he denied that the workload affected the quality of their work, and rejected charges of secretiveness. The CDF was simply operating with "maximum discretion," he said.

Few outside the CDF agreed. When Ratzinger launched an inquiry into Dupuis's writings on religious pluralism, he prompted an unusually sharp and public exchange with Cardinal Franz König of Vienna, then ninety-three and considered the grandest of old men in the European hierarchy. Writing in the *Tablet,* the leading English Catholic weekly, König said the CDF's move was "a sign, an indication, that mistrust, suspicion and disapproval are being prematurely spread about an author who has the highest intentions, and has earned himself great merits in the service of the Catholic Church." He said that given the Holy Office's centuries of experience, "one should surely be able to rely on the doctrinal congregation to find better ways of doing its job to serve the Church effectively." Dupuis's book, *Toward a Christian Theology of Religious Pluralism,* drew on his decades of experience in India in an effort to place Christ in a religiously diverse Asian context. König said that the congregation's Western mind-set contributed to its suspicion of Dupuis's work and Eastern religions, and it was "reminiscent of colonialism, and smacks of arrogance." With uncharacteristic force, König concluded, "I cannot keep silent, for my heart bleeds when I see such obvious harm being done to the common good of God's Church."[21]

Ratzinger responded with even greater force, expressing "astonishment and some sadness" at König's letter and wondering if the Cardinal seriously believed what he was saying. He said he found König's charges incomprehensible, depicting the investigation as merely a private conversation and omitting any reference to the CDF's penal powers. "Is dialogue with authors to be forbidden to us? Is the attempt to reach confidential clarification on difficult questions something evil? Is it not rather a way of striving to serve in a positive way the further development of faith and theology? You will understand from these questions that I find it unjust and damaging when you state that you cannot keep silent when you see such obvious harm being done to the common good of God's Church, which is to say, by our attempt at dialogue." Ratzinger said the issue at hand—the uniqueness of salvation through Christ—was crucial, and he added that contrary to König's suspicions, the CDF did not question Dupuis's orthodoxy in that regard.

In fact, contrary to Ratzinger's assertion, two years later, in January 2001, the CDF did criticize Dupuis's work for its "ambiguities," though the intervention of König and others was credited with softening a much harsher verdict that the CDF first drafted. Dupuis had many allies, in the Curia and elsewhere, who were upset at the treatment of him and of a work almost universally recognized as a classic treatment of the controversial topic. The Dupuis case demonstrates that the CDF did not need to impose juridical penalties to achieve its goals. "No theologian will be wanting to write his thoughts, if this is the approach," worried Archbishop Henry D'Souza of Calcutta, president of the Indian bishops' conference and a defender of Dupuis's orthodoxy. Two years later, as John Allen recounted in the *National Catholic Reporter,* Dupuis's scheduled presence on a panel at the Gregorian University in Rome, the flagship school of his own Jesuit order, was enough to force the event off campus for fear of upsetting the Vatican.[22]

A year later, in 2003, Dupuis gave a poignant talk in which he recalled being asked—apparently by a CDF interrogator—"If, at the end of time, Christ were to ask you to give an account of the work you have done, what would you say to him?" Dupuis said he answered, "I cannot imagine myself giving to the Lord, on the other side of this life, an account of the work I have done. Nor do I think such an account would be necessary. The Lord will know my work, even better than I know it myself. I can only hope that his evaluation of it will be more positive than has been that of some censors and, alas, of the church's central doctrinal authority."

In December 2004 Jacques Dupuis died at age eighty-one, haunted by what one of his eulogizers called the "unspeakable sadness" of having been accused by the church he had loved and served so dearly for his entire life.

The accumulation of cases provoked growing criticism from around the church. "The procedures of the Congregation for the Doctrine of the Faith used in investigations of theologians' views fail to honor fundamental human rights and the safeguards regarded in our countries as absolutely necessary to protect these human rights," the Catholic Theological Society of America said in a statement.[23] In 2001 *America* magazine, the prestigious national Jesuit weekly then edited by Thomas J. Reese, wrote a blistering editorial ripping the CDF for secretive and destructive practices worthy only of a "totalitarian state." The editors wrote, "The congregation's inquisitional procedures are indefensible. The church should of course safeguard its faith, but not by means unworthy of that faith." The editorial would come back to haunt the magazine after Ratzinger was elected pope.

√ Ratzinger naturally rejected the "bad cop" view of his job, voicing frustration at being considered someone "who has practically sold his soul as a researcher and theologian in order to have power."[24] Such interpretations reflect a "Marxist framework," he said, and not a church in which people like himself, at the pinnacle of the hierarchy, are in fact the lowliest servants, whose lack of influence and repeated public excoriation actually confirm the rightness of their positions. Taking a cue from Saint Augustine, Ratzinger declared himself no more than "a good, sturdy ox to pull God's cart in this world." He was only protecting the truth of the church and the faith of the "simple people of God" from the flights of theologians who are "stamped by the typical mentality of the opulent bourgeoisie of the West," as he put it once, in rather classist phrasing for someone who abhors everything Marxist.[25]

But how can he be so sure he is right and others are wrong? Ratzinger has said that he can be certain of the rightness of his and the CDF's judgments because the congregation takes a bare-bones approach to theology—working "within the great ideas of faith" rather than "inventing" anything, which is for him the great sin. "What is important is that we don't go beyond what is already present in the faith . . . and that we then see that a reasonable consensus emerges." Ratzinger has acknowledged that "in a personal controversy I occasionally react too harshly." But he claimed that any of his private feelings were erased in the consensual nature of the congregation's decision-making;

the CDF's rulings over the quarter-century of his tenure were not the result of his personal desires, he said, but of a collaboration that guaranteed that individual personalities would not sway judgments, and that the only bias was on behalf of the truth.[26]

That view, however, would seem to idealize beyond reality the actual dynamics of most any office, and especially one like the CDF, in which the prefect, in this case Ratzinger, has absolute control over his choice of staff members, who are likely to both reflect the boss's views and know that their future in a hierarchical church will be dependent on their prefect's opinion of them. Moreover, the positions and even the wording of the CDF's documents so closely mirror Ratzinger's personal views and writings that the legacy of the past twenty-four years there is clearly his. "The feeling that I am someone powerful has hardly ever occurred to me," he said, asserting that the power of the CDF "is in reality very little."[27] Given his record, such an assertion seems disingenuous, to put it charitably, but it is a posture of self-effacement from which he never wavers, even when all the evidence tilts to the contrary.

"All we can do actually is appeal to the bishops, who in turn must appeal to the theologians or to the religious superiors. Or else we can attempt dialogue. There are, of course, also disciplinary measures, which we try to apply as sparingly as possible. After all, we don't have executive power. . . . Ultimately, we have no weapons besides argument and appeal to our faith."

Ratzinger also tended to offer an irenic version of his disciplinary measures, using anodyne language with unsettling echoes of prison wardens who express satisfaction at having "convinced" recalcitrant inmates to see the error of their ways—neglecting to mention the fact that the warden wielded both power and penalties in rectifying their "failure to communicate." What the public sees as crackdowns, Ratzinger sees as fraternal dialogues in which he and the CDF are always "careful and respectful" in their efforts to free wayward theologians from their "illusory myths," and he laments that his efforts are so often rejected out of hand. "Anyone who really has to deal with us also sees that we're not inhuman but always try to find a reasonable solution," he said. Ratzinger has cited the case of Gustavo Gutiérrez as an "outstanding example of the positive impulses that our instructions gave." The CDF "entered into dialogue with him," as Ratzinger described the investigation. "That helped us to understand him, and he, on the other hand, saw the one-sidedness of his work." That Gutiérrez did not exactly see things that way, and that Ratzinger's power to penalize Gutiérrez may have swayed him and others more than the power of Ratzinger's arguments, did not figure into the cardinal's recollection.[28]

. . .

The CDF under Ratzinger sought to blunt critics by drawing a clear line be-tween the ideas being condemned and the people who were behind those ideas. But this is perhaps the most problematic aspect of his record and his personality.

In the CDF's 1990 document on the role of the theologian, the congrega-tion said that a penalty "does not concern the person of the theologian but the intellectual positions which he has publicly espoused. The fact that these pro-cedures can be improved does not mean that they are contrary to justice and right. To speak in this instance of a violation of human rights is out of place for it indicates a failure to recognize the proper hierarchy of these rights as well as the nature of the ecclesial community and her common good." But an edito-rial in the *Tablet* after Ratzinger's election as pope called on him to reform the congregation, pointedly noting, "The CDF's mistake has been to understand itself as dealing only with a theologian's opinions and hence not with the theo-logian as a person with rights. But for opinions read convictions, and to put someone's convictions on trial comes very close to putting the individual on trial. That is certainly how it feels to the accused."

When it comes to matters of doctrine and discipline, Ratzinger can display a similar personal detachment even regarding those he has known and admires. For example, in writing about his old seminary professor, the biblical scholar Friedrich Wilhelm Maier, Ratzinger warmly recalled how much he had learned from him and how Maier's scholarship, which led to Maier's condemnation and exile from the university for many years, was now fully accepted and "re-mains fundamental to me." Although he acknowledged that Maier's treatment was unjust, Ratzinger did not raise a finger to protest his shabby treatment. Instead he coolly criticizes Maier for not getting past the "trauma" of his dis-missal and for harboring "a certain bitterness against Rome." More to Ratzing-er's liking was the example of another professor of his, Gottlieb Söhngen, who in 1949 argued strongly against the burgeoning movement to have the teach-ing on the bodily assumption of Mary into heaven proclaimed a dogma. Asked what he would do if the pope did proclaim the Assumption a dogma—as Pius XII subsequently did in 1954—Ratzinger notes with satisfaction that Söhngen replied, "If the dogma comes, then I will remember that the Church is wiser than I and that I must trust her more than my own erudition."

Certainly some of Ratzinger's seeming disconnect can be attributed to his intentional cultivation of an aura of serenity, which contributes to his own well-being, both spiritual and emotional. "One of the things which is evident from working with him, that will now become evident to the whole world, is that he's a person of tremendous inner tranquillity," said Dominican father Augustine DiNoia, an American who worked with Ratzinger for years as undersecretary for the Congregation of the Doctrine of Faith. "You sense immediately in his presence, a person who, as the old spiritual writers used to say is 'recollected.' That is to say, he's not thrown into a kind of panic by anything, I mean, he's just a calm (and therefore one supposes), deeply spiritual person. Usually that's a sign of an inner life and a person who is in communion with God."[29] Yet as Father Richard John Neuhaus, a leading intellectual of the Catholic Right and an ally of Ratzinger, said, "It would be a serious mistake to think gentleness and serenity mean weakness or lack of firm resolve."[30] Or, as Ratzinger's brother Georg put it, "He is not aggressive at all, but when it's necessary to fight, he does his part, as a matter of conscience."[31]

So how could such a nice guy be such a hard-liner? The odd detachment between Joseph Ratzinger the man and his actions as prefect of the CDF can perhaps be best explained by understanding his temperament. Ratzinger is by all accounts a shy and congenial man who intensely dislikes personal confrontation, and yet he found himself in a job whose chief mission is to challenge and reprimand. That may not be entirely accidental. The paradox of the ivory tower is that scholarly academics are among the most combative people, fiercely promoting their ideas and principles, but their dirty work is usually (at least before the advent of today's celebrity eggheads) done at a bloodless distance, in journals or from the parapet of the conference lectern.

Moreover, not only was Ratzinger an academic, but his field of inquiry is faith, where the stakes are higher and the arguments more personal than even the high-end parlor game of, say, literary theory. The infamous *odium theologicum* has historically been of an entirely different order of intellectual disputation. "The most savage controversies are those about matters as to which there is no good evidence either way," the famously militant atheist, Bertrand Russell, once wrote, happily falling into the same trap himself.

Beyond a lack of proof, however, the bitterness of theological battles can be traced to the fact that convinced partisans are defending a truth given from on high, and thus see themselves not as flawed beings espousing personal views that may be wrong and thus susceptible to argumentation, but as defenders of an indisputable reality. Historically, heresies have often suffered from the vice of too much virtue—from the disembodied spiritual excesses of the Gnostics to the harsh asceticism of the Cathars, from the Catholic puritanism of the Jansenists (an overdose of Saint Augustine was their problem) to today's liberation theologians bringing down the rich to raise up the poor. Heresy hunters can fall prey to the same tendency to self-righteousness. Fights over belief are not matters of the police catching the criminal, the standard Good versus Evil story line. Rather, they are conflicts of My Good versus Your Good.

Change and compromise are not allowed under those parameters, and personal traits and desires are dismissed as irrelevant, even if they obviously are central to the conflictual dynamic. Likewise, with characteristic self-effacement, Ratzinger sees himself as a servant of the truth, a person of little consequence who is only acting on behalf of something far greater than himself. "He is a man completely unconcerned with the trappings of power—in fact, it is precisely his humility that enables him to speak with such courage in defense of the truth," says David Schindler, editor of *Communio,* the journal Ratzinger founded in 1972. "His assertions, although clear and trenchant, are not made on his own behalf but rather always at the service of something much greater than himself, the integrity of which he desires to safeguard."[32]

That, of course, is the rationale of many great religious martyrs. But the comfortable distance that such a remove puts between a religious figure who holds power and his actions on behalf of the faith can also allow an introverted personality to channel the passion they cannot otherwise express into official condemnations that take on the harsh tone of the zealot or the clinical chill of the technocrat. In that case, the contrast between the quiet private person and the noisy public persona can be confusing, or can feed into the type of dichotomy that characterizes opinions on Joseph Ratzinger. Those who know Ratzinger, or who support his positions, see him as a sweet soul whose critics must be uncharitable louts for bashing such a kind person or imputing underhanded motives to him. "As everyone who knows him has experienced, his demeanor is self-effacing and gentle, and there is a childlike wonder about him, an intense interest in the topic at hand," says Schindler.

But those who run afoul of Ratzinger see a far different person—very calm, yes, but also very harsh, someone who stresses "the primacy of truth over goodness" because "under the pretext of goodness people neglect conscience. They place acceptance, the avoidance of problems, the comfortable pursuit of their existence, the good opinion of others, and good-naturedness above truth in the scale of values."[33] To those with whom he agrees, Ratzinger is indeed the soul of courtesy and kindness. But the vast majority of Catholics do not know Ratzinger personally, nor, until his election as pope, had they even seen him in a public setting. Given his reserved nature, Ratzinger's social circle is especially small, and because he does not have the personality or position that fosters a warm image, he can seem even more remote. For the public, then, Ratzinger is the sum of his public record, a legacy of sharp denunciations, thwarted careers, and embittered souls that seems to belie any claims he might make to promoting the love of Christ.

This divergence was of interest largely to the church insiders and journalists who were the principal audience and interlocutors for Joseph Ratzinger for the twenty-four years of his tenure as prefect of the CDF. But now that Ratzinger is pope, the split-screen version must be harmonized in order to make an intelligible image. Catholics recognize that the papacy is about a person as much as it is about the office, and during the first year of Benedict's papacy there was an intense focus on how well this low-key man was playing on the world stage. When he donned a firefighter's helmet at one public audience, for example, or spoke to an ill woman on a cell phone handed to him by a well-wisher, reports hailed his adaptability and the natural display of the human touches that are indisputably part of his make up. These events, it was claimed, showed that Benedict would be different as pope than he had been as prefect. Yet it is hard to understand the magic by which wearing a firefighter's helmet signals a profound change in one's character, or why those who loved Cardinal Ratzinger for his toughness would be so eager to see him morph into a papal pussycat. The qualities that so many Catholics admired in Cardinal Ratzinger were presumably the same qualities they would want to see in Pope Benedict. If Benedict is now a soft-hearted pastor, how does that square with the harshness of the past twenty-four years or his similar decisions as pope? Are they to be forgotten, or forgiven without the effort at reconciliation that the Gospels require? Or is it enough to say that holding one church job gives a man license to behave in a certain way, while another job—the papacy, in this case—allows him to live by some alternate Christian ethic?

In his perceptive biography of Otto von Bismarck, the English historian of Germany A. J. P. Taylor sought to understand the contrast between the Iron Chancellor's heavy-handed policies and the searching intellect that he tried all his life to hide from public view. Taylor's explanation was that Bismarck went through his life as his "clever, sophisticated" mother masquerading as his "heavy, earthy" father. Conversely, it might be said that Joseph Ratzinger has gone through his life as his father, the village policeman, disguised as his mother, the devout *hausfrau*. Such an internal dichotomy makes a man a genius or a neurotic, Taylor said, arguing that Bismarck was both.[34] Pope Benedict may be neither genius nor neurotic, but his two faces are part of a disconcerting whole—the quiet priest with a kindly manner and an aversion to personal conflict, and the powerful church official with strong personal views that he delivers with bureaucratic detachment.

Bismarck suppressed his internal contradictions—"Faust complains of having two souls in his breast. I have a whole squabbling crowd," he remarked—through an application of self-control, which he said "has always been the greatest task of my life," and also through a conversion to rigorous Pietism. "Doubt was not fought and conquered; it was silenced by heroic will," said a friend. However he achieved it, Pope Benedict seems at peace with the two aspects of his personality. But to many Catholics, or to those who might look to the Catholic Church as a prospective spiritual home, his internal equanimity can seem like a false truce. Reviewing Ratzinger's record at the CDF shows that too often he too easily ignored the fact that he was dealing with fellow human beings, with other Christians, and not just with ideas. Abstracting people into their positions can make personal confrontations more palatable, especially for someone with Ratzinger's mix of zeal and timidity. But defending tenets while wounding people—and demoralizing the church—compromises the very Gospel truths that Ratzinger is supposed to safeguard. It also echoes the past sins of the church. Life in the Christian community is always a tug-of-war between love and belief, between offering the limitless clemency of Christ and upholding the moral law that makes a community truly Christian. It is never easy; in fact, it is usually impossible. But that is the inherent tension of the Christian life, or any fully lived religious life. It is an ambiguity that the credible believer acknowledges in himself, and one that he allows for in others.

If Cardinal Ratzinger's record had been limited to his brief as prefect of the Congregation for the Doctrine of the Faith and his battles with theologians, his tenure would still have been historic in terms of his assertiveness and the results he achieved. But almost from the beginning, Ratzinger extended his influence well beyond the walls of the Holy Office, expanding the CDF's authority over the rest of the Roman Curia and raising his profile outside the Vatican by writing dozens of books, giving extensive interviews, and engaging in high-powered debates about a host of topics that showcased his views in the public square to an unprecedented degree for someone in his position.

In fact, Ratzinger made his acceptance of the CDF job in 1981 contingent on being allowed to continue to write and speak on his own behalf, a highly unusual personal privilege for someone in such a sensitive church post. John Paul agreed, and, in a rare exception to the golden Roman rule that no Vatican official should outshine the Holy Father, the pope seemed perfectly content to have Ratzinger as his front man on the most contested issues of the day. Not everyone was as enthusiastic about this development.

"The attempt to combine the role of Prefect and theologian arouses considerable criticism," Nichols writes in his generally laudatory examination of Ratzinger's career.[35] "To more traditionally minded members of the Roman Curia it was innovatory and imprudent. No previous Prefect, since the foundation of the Congregation by the reforming Farnese pope Paul III in 1542, had behaved in this manner. The arousing of the debate about the state of the church in general, and of its theological schools in particular, by way of interviews, articles and books was regarded as encouraging error by airing it. Criticism of tendencies in the episcopate, though possible shared in private, was thought to be, if it went public, a tasteless offence against the respect that was the bishops' rightful due."

To anyone to the left of Ratzinger's hard-right fan club, Nichols said, "the co-existence within Ratzinger of the two roles of Prefect and personal theologian provided a stick with which to beat him. What was this but the palming-off, as the common faith of the Church, of an essentially private theology?" Ratzinger argued that his personal opinions and those he expressed as the Vatican's doctrinal guardian were completely distinct. But few saw the difference, either outside Rome or inside the Vatican. Over the years, Ratzinger made the CDF the de facto editor for documents coming out of almost every other Vatican congregation, often forcing changes in the work of other departments or issuing documents on matters normally handled by other curial offices. The CDF's mission creep did not make him popular with his fellow curialists, whom Ratzinger was never eager to please anyway.

For example, the CDF's 2000 document *Dominus Iesus,* on the Catholic Church's relationship to other Christians and non-Christian believers, sparked a public row between Ratzinger and other Vatican prelates. Among other things, *Dominus Iesus* asserted that "there exists a single Church of Christ, which subsists in the Catholic Church," adding that Protestant churches are not "churches in the proper sense." The declaration also claimed that followers of religions other than Christianity are "in a gravely deficient situation" in regard to the salvation of their souls. Australian cardinal Edward Cassidy, Rome's chief ecumenical official at the time, tried to downplay the document's importance, pointing out that it was issued under Ratzinger's signature, not that of Pope John Paul. Cassidy's second-in-command at the ecumenical office and his eventual successor, Cardinal Walter Kasper, was more pointed in critiquing the document's claim of the inferior status of Protestant churches. "That affirmation offended other people," Kasper told reporters, "and if my friends are offended, then so am I. It's an unfortunate affirmation—clumsy and ambiguous." He disliked the CDF's "abstract, doctrinaire language" and added, "The tone is not appropriate."

Two years earlier, Ratzinger offended Anglicans with a commentary he published along with a papal document on infallibility that seemed to indicate that Rome was declaring priestly ordinations in the Anglican Communion—a sensitive topic of long-standing dispute—to be definitively invalid from a Catholic point of view. Vatican ecumenists were once again left to clean up the mess. Similarly, in 1998, Cardinal Cassidy announced with much fanfare a joint declaration with Lutherans, a milestone in repairing the breach of the Reformation, that listed more than forty areas of common understanding, including the contentious issues of the role of grace and good works. But Lutherans felt ambushed—as did many in the Curia—when the Vatican issued a simultaneous "response" to its own document pointing out several reservations about the agreement with Lutherans. It was a bizarre moment—the Vatican releasing a document and a counterdocument at the same time—and the dialogue was only rescued a year later, when Ratzinger, who was widely believed to be behind the response to Cassidy's document, personally negotiated a follow-up agreement that calmed the waters.

Ratzinger also caused difficulties in the church's interfaith dialogue through his periodic comments about other religions. He was always especially suspicious of the influence of Eastern spirituality on Roman Catholicism. In a 1997 interview, Ratzinger said that Buddhism was nothing more than "an auto-erotic spirituality," and he said this religious masturbation would be "the undoing" of the Catholic Church. A U.S. bishop actually had to apologize to Buddhists for Ratzinger's words. Ratzinger saw Hinduism as equivalent to relativism, and as constituting "several religions" rather than a single religion. He caused consternation among Vatican diplomats when he came out against Turkey's application for membership in the European Union, saying that as an Islamic nation Turkey has been "in permanent contrast to Europe." And while admiring Islamic piety, he was sharply critical of Islam as a "thin covering" of religious belief, and he blamed Islam for much of the slave trade, among other things. Ratzinger also sparked a fury by stating that the World Council of Churches, based in Geneva, supported Marxist revolutionaries.

Veteran Vatican hand Sandro Magister said that Ratzinger's power in Rome was unprecedented for a prefect of the CDF: "Before him, the heads of the Holy Office responded to inquiries on individual doctrinal cases, and questioned unorthodox theologians. Ratzinger does this, and much more. He releases doctrinal documents that customarily are produced by the pope. He writes encyclicals, circular letters to the bishops of the whole world, another typical papal prerogative."[36]

On the record, most Vatican officials speak about how helpful the CDF has been, and there have in fact been documents that Ratzinger's interventions have clarified. But, in private conversation, Ratzinger's fellow curialists are often withering in their dislike of the CDF's sovereignty. In a rare public acknowledgment of Ratzinger's influence, Canadian cardinal Edouard Gagnon, a longtime curial official who once headed the Vatican's Council for the Family, a major curial department, said he left his post because of Ratzinger's machinations against him. "I have been a teacher of moral theology more years than he has," Gagnon said in an interview for Thomas Reese's 1996 book, *Inside the Vatican.* "But I am an ignorant person for him. It is annoying. . . . He is a very nice man, but there is a profound conviction that they [Ratzinger and the CDF staff] are the only ones who know."[37]

However, Ratzinger always had the confidence of the one man whose opinion counted—Pope John Paul II. In 1986 John Paul appointed Cardinal Ratzinger as head of a twelve-member commission charged with drafting a new edition of the *Catechism of the Catholic Church,* the compendium of church teachings governing every aspect of religious and moral behavior. It was the first such revision since the Council of Trent in the sixteenth century, and it gave Ratzinger even greater standing.

The catechism would eventually reflect many of Ratzinger's ideas, such as his repeated condemnations of homosexual orientation as "objectively disordered." That view built on a 1986 document from Ratzinger's office that referred to homosexual orientation as an "intrinsic moral evil." Later CDF documents criticized civil antidiscrimination protections for gays and lesbians, and in 1998 the CDF had the U.S. bishops rewrite portions of their pastoral letter to parents of homosexuals, titled "Always Our Children." Ratzinger ordered that the bishops refer to homosexuality as a "deep-seated" rather than "fundamental" dimension of personality, and deleted a passage that encouraged the use of terms such as *homosexual, gay,* and *lesbian* from the pulpit in order to "give people permission" to discuss homosexuality. In 2003, at the height of the clergy sexual abuse scandal in the United States, and with Catholic outrage at bishops for covering up for child abusers for decades without any penalty for the prelates, Ratzinger's office issued a statement against civil unions for homosexuals that described adoption by gay couples as a form of "violence" against children and "gravely immoral." Catholics were stunned. Targeting gay couples with such language at the same time as the public was learning that so many in the hierarchy had covered up actual violence against children by some priests looked like an offensive moral equivocation that no one with any connection to the real world or any pastoral sense would presume to make.

But such statements were the staple of Ratzinger's office. The CDF under Ratzinger issued a steady stream of pronouncements aimed at reinforcing or clarifying church stands on a range of issues. In 1989 the CDF reaffirmed that contraception is an "intrinsically disordered act" that is prohibited without exception. In 1994 Ratzinger's office reminded bishops and priests not to give communion to divorced and civilly remarried Catholics, and in 1995 the CDF responded to a debate over John Paul's apostolic letter *Ordinatio Sacerdotalis,* which reasserted the long-standing ban on women priests, declaring that the church's teaching belongs "to the deposit of faith" and has been taught "infallibly." In 1991 Ratzinger had intervened as the U.S. bishops were seeking to put the finishing touches on a landmark pastoral letter on women in the church that had been a decade in the writing and was based on extensive consultations with American Catholic women. Ratzinger objected to some of the gender-neutral language and to the phrasing of the ban on women priests, which he felt was too vague. The bishops could not overcome the problems, and the next year, for the first time in the history of the conference, the bishops spiked the entire project.

√ Ratzinger also led the pope's project to rein in national bishops' conferences, which were seen as stealing Rome's thunder. Ratzinger was an unusual choice for the job, since he had once been a stout defender of the role of national conferences, writing in 1964 that conservative claims that such bodies lack a "theological basis" are "one-sided and unhistorical." Twenty years later, Ratzinger had switched sides. "We must not forget that the episcopal conferences have no theological basis," Ratzinger said. The Catholic Church, he said, "is based on an episcopal structure and not on a kind of federation of national churches. The national level is not an ecclesial dimension." In 1998 Ratzinger helped codify that sentiment in the apostolic letter *Apostolos Suos,* which stated that conference documents on church teachings (a broad and vague category) must be approved unanimously. If they receive anything less, the documents must be submitted to Rome for a final okay. Thus one negative vote out of nearly three hundred American prelates could botch an initiative.

Ratzinger interventions seemed to range over every hot-button issue in the church, whether they were within the CDF's jurisdiction or not. Joseph Ratzinger also used his time at the Vatican to air the pessimistic views on the failings of the modern world and the uncertain future of Catholicism that would become his trademark, making his sober realism a counterweight to John Paul's dogged optimism. He decried the "false zeal" of the aftermath of the Second Vatican Council, and in books and interviews he began repeating several mantras, a principal one being that the church should probably grow smaller and more zealous in order to remain faithful: "Perhaps the time has come to say farewell to the idea of traditionally Catholic cultures," he said in

1997. "Maybe we are facing a new and different epoch in the Church's history, where Christianity will be characterized more by the mustard seed, where it will exist in small, seemingly insignificant groups that nonetheless live an intensive struggle against evil and bring good into the world—that let God in."[38] At another point he said that "we must speak ... of a crisis of faith and of the Church. We can overcome it only if we face up to it forthrightly."[39]

Ratzinger painted a future that resembled the Christian past in the catacombs, in which believers would be nonconformists whose credibility would be honed by suffering for their faith at the hands of an oppressive culture. He continued to sound that theme of persecution as an avenue for purifying the church, which he saw as having grown rife with internal corruption. But he also played that off against a modern world that had become so enamored of the dogmas of rationalism and relativism—the diktat of the Enlightenment, as he put it, using Hitler's loaded term for the Versailles treaty that burdened Germany after the First World War—that contemporary society was in his view *more* vulnerable to totalitarianism than Nazi Germany: "I would say that, at the moment that a similar regime would return, the resistance against such things (euthanizing the sick or mentally handicapped) among the people would be far less than it was when I was young."[40]

From the sensitive boy in wartime Germany in the 1930s to the Bishop of Rome at the dawn of the third millennium, Joseph Ratzinger had traveled an enormous distance only to find himself back where he started.

Given the length and tone of his tenure as the church's doctrinal guardian, lumping Ratzinger together with the "Grand Inquisitor" of Fyodor Dostoyevsky's novel *The Brothers Karamazov* was an inevitable and facile commonplace. Dostoyevsky's heartless creature, confined to a single chapter often read to the exclusion of the rest of the work, offers what appears to be the stereotype of the sadistic true believer. He is a Torquemada-like character, a fearsome old cardinal and monk who commands more respect from the masses than does Christ himself, who has mysteriously appeared one day in fifteenth-century Seville at the height of the Inquisition. The Grand Inquisitor just the day before burned more than a hundred heretics in an auto-da-fé, and he quickly slaps Christ in prison with a promise to burn him at the stake the next day.

The frequent linkage between the perpetrator of such maniacal crimes and the real-life Ratzinger was meant to be an unfair jibe and should be seen as such. But moving past the obvious association, there is an important parallel to be drawn from this episode. During Christ's imprisonment, the Grand

Inquisitor cannot help but address the Savior, fiercely, on questions of man's freedom and the positives or negatives—all negatives, from the cardinal's point of view—of human liberty and happiness. Yet throughout this "dialogue" Jesus never says a word, which is in fact just what the cardinal wants.

"Don't answer, be silent," he commands the wordless Christ. "What canst Thou say, indeed? I know too well what Thou wouldst say. And Thou hast no right to add anything to what Thou hast said of old." Christ only listens and looks gently into his face. "The old man longed for Him to say something, however bitter and terrible," Dostoyevsky writes. "But He suddenly approached the old man in silence and softly kissed him on his bloodless aged lips. That was all his answer." Shaken, the cardinal shudders and opens the door to the cell, commanding Jesus to leave and never return. The Inquisitor watches Christ disappear into the dark town. "The kiss glows in his heart, but the old man adheres to his idea."

The idea to which Cardinal Ratzinger adhered, and which he shared with the Grand Inquisitor, is that the essence of the faith must remain not only as the foundation of belief but also as its highest expression. Simplicity and minimalism are the great virtues and disciplines, especially in a heretical age like ours. Ratzinger's project was not to expand the interpretations of truth but to ensure that nothing was added to what existed at the beginning, to present the faith as it was, as it is, and as it always shall be. No filigree or self-indulgent imaginings should obscure the pure ideal.

"My basic impulse," as he put it, "was always to free up the authentic kernel of the faith from encrustations and to give this kernel strength and dynamism. This impulse is the constant of my life." What is important, he says, "is that I have never deviated from this constant, which from my childhood has molded my life, and that I have remained true to it as the basic direction of my life."

Less is more, and Joseph Ratzinger has been religiously faithful to that principle, even as he served a pope who took a quite different approach to evangelization. If John Paul II was a medievalist who saw the organic beauty of the Middle Ages as a bully inspiration for today's fragmented modernity, Joseph Ratzinger—now Pope Benedict XVI—might be considered a primevalist who believes the stripped-down verities of early Christianity are the tiny mustard seed that is the only hope for a renewed springtime of faith after today's endless ecclesial winter.

These are two vastly different visions of the faith, the church, and the papacy, and it is this great divide—surprising to those who assume Benedict to be little more than John Paul's literary executor—that will mark the future of Catholicism.

Chapter Eight

PONTIFEX MAXIMUS, PONTIFEX MINIMUS

O n April 24, five days after his stunning election as pope, on the Sunday morning when Joseph Ratzinger was supposed to be introducing himself to the world as Benedict XVI, the new pontiff was instead confounding everyone around him by doing everything possible to disappear into the background. First off, he wanted to hold his installation Mass inside St. Peter's Basilica, a sacred arena but one that could accommodate at best several thousand worshippers. That would leave up to half a million outside to watch the papal inauguration on video feeds, and they would likely be as happy about it as concert-goers stuck in an overflow room. The idea would have been laughable, except that one didn't laugh at a pope, especially when his motives were so serious. "Because there the architecture better directs the attention toward Christ, instead of the pope," Benedict said in explaining to the masters of ceremonies who were organizing the grand liturgy why he felt the basilica was a better location than the piazza out front.[1]

John Paul, of course, would never hold an event inside that he could possibly do alfresco, and his flock was so used to the walk-up informality of papal events that anything less would have been seen as an insult. In the end, the enormous turnout anticipated for Benedict's installation convinced the new pontiff to celebrate the Mass outside. But he did prevail on several other points aimed at directing the spotlight away from himself and onto the transcendence of the Mass and the papal office, rather than onto the person of the pope. Unlike previous installations, Benedict began the procession at the tomb of Saint Peter, tucked away underneath the main altar, the spot where the first pope was buried after Emperor Nero had him executed nearby, crucified upside-down at the apostle's request. "I leave from where the apostle arrived," Benedict said. Waiting for him were the two symbols of papal authority, the stole of white lamb's wool known as the pallium, and the Ring of the Fisherman, size 24. "I like 24, it's the double of 12," he quipped to the goldsmith who measured his finger, referring to the dozen original apostles.

From the crypt, Benedict and a line of more than 150 cardinals and patriarchs began processing slowly up the nave while the crowd outside waited for the drama to become visible to them. The choir of the Sistine Chapel accompanied the procession with the *Laudes Regiae,* a Gregorian chant from the time of Charlemagne—classic polyphony, all in Latin, and used at the specific request of Pope Benedict, whose knowledge and taste in music could not be gainsaid. With metronomic rhythm, the choir recited the litany, invoking dozens of saints in a mesmerizing petition that seemed to reach back through the centuries. "*Sancte Petre,*" it began, ending fifteen minutes later with "*Sancte Benedicte*" for the pope's new namesake. "*Tu illum adiuva*" was the response every time: "Sustain him."

Symbol and meaning dominated in the back-to-the-future time warp that has gradually been transforming the papacy since Pope Paul VI (1963–78) began simplifying the papal rites in order to bring the monarchical papacy that arose in the Middle Ages into line with the exigencies of preaching the Gospel in the modern era. Pope Paul VI was the last pope to be crowned with the standard three-tiered beehive tiara of gems and precious metals, which he later decided to sell, donating the proceeds to the poor. Paul also did away with the traditional six-hour coronation Mass in which the grandly bedecked new pope was carried by footmen on the *sedia gestatoria,* a sedan chair, while being fanned by ostrich plumes. John Paul I also shunned a coronation—though only after a "long and tedious argument" with the Curia—and instead celebrated a briefer liturgy for the "inauguration of his ministry," a custom John Paul II maintained.

All those changes were largely ad hoc, however, and Benedict's installation was the first systematic revamping of the papal inauguration since Vatican II. But Benedict did not adopt changes to update—*aggiornare*—the ceremony to please a modern sensibility. Rather, he made it another advertisement for *ressourcement* by returning to traditions from more than a millennium ago. For example, he adopted a type of pallium that had not been used since 1000 AD, and the fisherman's gold ring was engraved with an ancient design. Like his two predecessors, Benedict did without the tiara, but he scandalized many in his conservative base by going a step further and dropping the crown from his coat of arms, a departure from eight centuries of tradition and a return to the premonarchical customs of the church's early days. Conservative Catholics didn't buy that, and their biting critiques revealed them as papal royalists more than as the gospel purists they claimed to be.

As much as Benedict tried to put the focus on the meaning of the Mass and the historic tradition of the papacy, however, the memory and style of his predecessor were everywhere. Benedict began the installation Mass by speaking of the "days of great intensity" around John Paul's passing, a reference that prompted the first great round of applause. As he had in his funeral oration, Benedict virtually canonized John Paul: "He crossed the threshold of the next life, entering into the mystery of God," Benedict said. "We knew that his arrival was awaited. Now we know that he is among his own and is truly at home." Benedict wore the shimmering gold vestments that John Paul had often used, to great visual effect, and there were the many multicultural touches that John Paul had encouraged.

But this was also the moment for Benedict to define himself, an opportunity for the ivory tower theologian to become the pastor to a global flock.

In Bavarian-accented Italian, he began with an affecting plea for spiritual aid, a humble recognition of his anxieties at assuming a burden "which truly exceeds all human capacity," especially following such a great pontiff as John Paul. "How can I do this? How will I be able to do it?" Benedict asked, then provided the answer, which drew shouts of encouragement: "I am not alone. I do not have to carry alone what in truth I could never carry alone. All the Saints of God are there to protect me, to sustain me and to carry me. And your prayers, my dear friends, your indulgence, your love, your faith and your hope accompany me." He buoyed the pilgrims with his declaration that even during the "sad days of the pope's illness and death, it became wonderfully evident to us that the church is alive." And, he added to applause, "the church is young! She holds within herself the future of the world and therefore shows each of us the way toward the future."

Yet undercurrents of the old cardinal could not help but emerge in the homily of the new pope. Benedict acknowledged that his strict ways might bring him rebukes from the world, but he said he was willing to suffer for the truth. "Pray for me, that I may not flee for fear of the wolves," he said. He painted a vivid, desperate image of modern man as a sheep lost in a barren, arid desert of "abandonment, of loneliness, of destroyed love. . . . The external deserts in the world are growing, because the internal deserts have become so vast." Then, returning to the idea of the fisherman, he said that souls today are like fish "living in alienation, in the salt waters of suffering and death; in a sea of darkness without light."

With his audience anticipating much more of the doctrinaire *Panzerkardinal,* the new pope drew laughs and handclaps when he said that he was not going to present a *programma di governo* (a program of governance), the Italian phrase for a campaign platform. That would come later, he added, also drawing laughs. Instead, he said, "my real program of governance is not to do my own will, not to pursue my own ideas, but to listen, together with the whole Church, to the word and the will of the Lord, to be guided by Him, so that He himself will lead the Church at this hour of our history." Again, this was not Benedict onstage, but Christ, the Truth; Benedict was merely the facilitator. Indeed, ever the theologian, even in this most pastoral of moments, Benedict spent much of his lengthy homily presenting an extended catechesis on the two principal symbols of the day: the pallium, which the bishops of Rome have worn since the fourth century, since the age of Augustine, and the Fisherman's Ring, a sign of the evangelizing commission to be "fishers of men" rescuing souls otherwise doomed for eternity.

The first emblem signifies the pope's duty to preserve the flock, while the other signifies the mandate to cast out the nets and draw others in. Benedict's career before becoming pope showed he could clearly fulfill the former task. But could he also be the fisher of men who attracts others to Christ? How would a man whose entire pastoral experience consisted of a single year as an assistant at a Bavarian parish more than a half-century earlier fare in a world in which religious leaders are seen as counselors as much as rule-keepers?

Even at this moment, Benedict seemed more comfortable with John Paul's rhetorical flourishes than with anything he himself might coin. He finished his homily, surprisingly, by returning to John Paul's own inaugural sermon from 1978, in which John Paul urged the world to "be not afraid!"—which became John Paul's unofficial catchphrase, to the extent that it was often forgotten that it was Jesus's catchphrase first. Benedict rode it as well, as best he could. For a full half-hour Benedict plowed through the homily, reading from behind large glasses, his voice almost uninflected, like a standard-issue university lecture. Beautiful words, powerful sentiments, but a workmanlike presentation given in a sometimes wavering voice. His listeners were rooting for him to succeed, and many were simply relieved to have a pope who, if he was not theatrical, could at least read his homily, which John Paul had been unable to do intelligibly for years.

Yet John Paul in his last, mute moments could be more dramatic than Benedict at his most expansive. Unlike the compulsively polylingual John Paul, Benedict spoke only in Italian and tossed no bones to his cosmopolitan audience—much to the chagrin of many who had trekked from other countries, even other continents. Benedict would not court popularity, because it would inevitably draw attention away from the reason for the Mass, which is Christ's sacrifice and atonement. Through much of the Mass, Benedict sat and observed, almost blankly, at the kind of moment when John Paul would draw himself up into a prayerfulness so quiet that it would drown out all else, and every eye would marvel at his mystical intensity, envying it to no small degree. Everything else faded into the background at those moments.

I had the sense, standing there for nearly three hours on the mild April morning, that this installation Mass for Benedict was really the final farewell to John Paul, the true passage from one era to another. Then, as the Mass finished and Benedict began the recessional in an open-topped white popemobile Jeep, the loudspeakers set around the piazza interrupted my distracted mourning with the ominous opening chords of Bach's Toccata and Fugue in D minor for organ—the classic horror movie soundtrack, which unfortunately most people would associate with the arrival of Vincent Price or Bela Lugosi rather than the Roman pontiff (that Bach was a decided Lutheran is another nice point). With this *Tales from the Crypt* send-off, the funereal effect of a moment earlier suddenly became almost comical, except that once again Pope Benedict wasn't joking. Cardinal Ratzinger had never played to the crowds, and Pope Benedict wasn't going to start. This was pure Joseph Ratzinger, asserting his personal taste as the ideal of Catholic practice. From Gregorian chant to a Bach fugue, in every nuance of liturgy and in the carefully contained presence he showed on the altar, Pope Benedict was announcing to the world that things would be different.

Despite his efforts to get out of the way, however, Benedict, like any pope, cannot help but impose his personal stamp on the papacy, and thereby on the church. This is the nature of such a vertiginous hierarchy; with so much focus on the man at the top, his character becomes identified with the dynamic of the institution. Pope Benedict is exceedingly humble, but his self-effacement has not created a vacuum at the Vatican, any more than it did at the Congregation for the Doctrine of the Faith.

The pressing question after Benedict's installation, then, was how his vision for the church would manifest itself, and whether his new vista from the papal apartment would alter the outlook that he had become famous for. In other words, how much of Ratzinger would we see in Benedict, and how much would Benedict be something altogether different?

Whether a new pope can maintain his old self, and to what degree he becomes a new creation, is a central drama of any papacy. Becoming a pope is a profound, even traumatic, personal transformation because it is the extremes at once of self-denial and self-fulfillment, repression and liberation. Nothing else compares to this spiritual and psychological gauntlet, except perhaps the comic book agonies of a fledgling superhero, which is probably why everyone, believers and agnostics, lay folk and cardinals, remains so entranced by the process.

"The fascinating thing is that in the course of a few moments, history changes," Washington's Cardinal Theodore McCarrick said, recalling the moments of Joseph Ratzinger's changeover. "There are 115 cardinals gathered together, and then, at a certain point, there are only 114. One of them is already the pope." McCarrick recalled that in the conclave on Tuesday, just after lunch and shortly before Benedict was elected on the first ballot of the afternoon, he and Cardinal Ratzinger were conversing casually, as two colleagues. "I forget what it was about, but we chatted just for a moment, standing in the back of the room. By suppertime, he was in white, sitting at another table, and he was the Holy Father—an extraordinary moment in our lives, because we who are Catholic, we who are people of faith, believe that once the man becomes elected pope, he is no longer thus the normal, ordinary brother in the College of Cardinals, but he is the vicar of Christ, the successor of Peter."[2]

While much of the world sees a cardinal's election to the papacy in secular political terms, like a successful campaign capping a long career that could have no other aim than this summit, the reality is far more ambiguous. The process of becoming a pope can be dehumanizing, a moment of losing oneself as much as a gaining a powerful office. To be sure, the man who receives two-thirds of the votes of his fellow cardinals in the conclave is immediately confirmed as the spiritual leader of more than a billion Catholics and automatically inducted into the select club of the world's most powerful statesmen. And over the colorful history of the papacy, there have been more than a few princes of the church who sought the throne through every means possible, including bribery, simony, nepotism, and, not infrequently, assassination. At certain points, being pope was just a kick, particularly in the high-living days of the Renaissance papacy, when the Medici pontiff Leo X could remark at his election, "Now that we have attained the papacy, let us enjoy it."

More telling, however, are examples of popes fleeing the conclave in fear of the prospect of being chosen. The monk who would become Saint Gregory the Great was terrified at his election and, according to one story, fled into the forest and hid for three days, until his hiding place was revealed by a "supernatural light." Some 1,500 years later, the humble Albino Luciani's death after just thirty-four days as John Paul I was chalked up to the pressures that he saw coming from the moment of his election. "May God forgive you for what you have done to me," Luciani said in his first official words as pope. His personal secretary, Monsignor Pasquale Macchi, said years later that Luciani had vowed he would turn the job down if elected, but when that moment came, Luciani realized he would have created a "farce" if he rejected the cardinals' choice. "I served John Paul I for 33 days, and he was an anguished pope, every day more so, about the problems that confronted him," Macchi said.[3]

A few weeks later, Luciani was dead, yet the scene repeated itself as even the indomitable Karol Wojtyla, at the instant of his election, in the brief seconds before he became Pope John Paul II, plunged his face in his hands at the gravity of what had befallen him, raising his head a minute later to pronounce his submission to the vote. With an eerie foretaste of his own senescence decades later, John Paul told a biographer that at that moment his first thought was of his long-ago pastoral work with bedridden patients, "those incurable invalids condemned to the wheelchair or chained to their sick bed; people who are often young and conscious of the implacable advance of their illness, prisoners in their sufferings for weeks, months or years." John Paul found in the "terrible irreversibility" of their condition a parallel to his own new circumstances as pope.[4]

To a great extent, world leaders' lives are not their own. But the papacy takes that sacrifice to an unparalleled level. At the moment a cardinal becomes pope, everything in his life is so transformed that mundane routines become a disorienting gauntlet. In a sense, it is the institutionalization of a person, body and psyche. "Here you are a prisoner de luxe; you cannot do all you would like to do," John XXIII's brother warned him after his election. A new pope immediately dons a full-length white simar, the last cassock he will ever wear, and he adopts a new name. It was poignant to watch Ratzinger, shortly after his election, in a photo-op practicing his new signature, "Benedictus," like a seventy-eight-year-old first-grader. The tradition of taking a new name began in the sixth century when a pope named Mercurius deemed it unwise for a pontiff to be called after a pagan god. Mercurius took the name John II, and only two popes in the past millennium have kept their original names, the most recent being Marcellus II in 1555. (He died after only three weeks in office but is memorialized in Palestrina's *Missa Papae Marcelli*.) The new pope will serve until he is dead—at least if the tradition of the past seven centuries is a guide—and the name by which his parents christened him will be used again only to ascertain his death.

A new pope bears the power of infallibility and the honorific of Holy Father. He does not return home to collect his belongings or put his affairs in order, or bid farewell to friends and family. He receives a new passport and acquires a new nation, which he also rules, and, most likely, now that Italian popes are passé, in a language not his own. Centuries of tradition and ritual suddenly govern his every movement as he is immediately ushered into a new life, the principal landlord of a vast labyrinth of ancient apartments that he may know less than a casual tourist. John Paul I returned from the balcony after his introduction to the world and wondered where he could find something to eat; there wasn't a crumb to be found anywhere and of course no way to order take-out for the papal apartment.

From the beginning of his transformation, a pontiff struggles to hold on to the old life, the old self. As votes in the second 1978 conclave tilted toward Karol Wojtyla, he at first tried to deny the reality of what was happening. But when Cardinal Franz König, the late archbishop of Vienna who helped engineer his victory, impressed on him that he must accept the vote as God's will, Wojtyla then suggested that he might take the name Pope Stanislaus, after the patron saint of Poland. "You will be called John Paul II," König firmly informed him. Wojtyla was to park his nationalism at the Vatican gate. More than ever, a pope must be a pastor for all peoples, which requires—or is supposed to—that he be a man without a country.

It is not easy. In 1981, in one of the least noted but most remarkable episodes of the Cold War, John Paul II retained such loyalty to his innate Polishness as to threaten, in a note to the Soviet authorities, to resign his office should Moscow invade Poland to crush the nascent Solidarity trade union movement. "The Holy Father in those days was very troubled and worried about the fate of his country," Warsaw's Cardinal Josef Glemp told reporters in confirming the story in 1998. "He was ready to do anything, even leaving the leadership of the church in order to be able to defend the freedom of his country." If John Paul had followed through on the threat, he would have been the first pope in seven hundred years to resign, and he would have sparked a crisis in the church that could have led to schism. The years in the Vatican "prison," as John Paul called his new home, have a way of loosening the bonds of national identity, however. By the time he died, Papa Wojtyla had rejected the idea, which he apparently had once considered, of being buried in Poland, or even of placing a pouch of earth from his homeland in the casket, as many believed he would do.

Today, the papal identity crisis is more acute than at any time in church history because of the demand for a humanized, personal pontiff to whom we can relate and, on the other hand, the countervailing—and contradictory—push for the monasticizing of the papacy. The latter phenomenon, which can turn popes into holy ciphers, grew especially pronounced after the nineteenth century, as the loss of the church's temporal realm bore spiritual fruits that were not necessarily native to the papal office. Priests and brothers from religious orders were elevated to the papal throne, often during periods of spiritual reform, when it was thought that a monastic touch was needed to counter the worldliness of the Holy See.

By and large, however, the College of Cardinals tried to elect popes who could govern the church firmly and defend her temporal realm across central Italy with guts and guile, a job for which the pastoral naïveté of, say, a Franciscan, was not exactly a résumé-builder. In the ranks of the hierarchy, the cardinals found plenty of other candidates—lordly bishops and cardinal-statesmen rather than friars—willing to get their hands, and souls, dirty on behalf of the church's kingdom on earth. But that changed decisively in 1870, when a rout of the papal forces by the new Italian government reduced the Holy See's holdings to the 108 acres of its walled city-state and turned the pope at the time, Pius IX, from the all-powerful *Papa Rex* into a "prisoner of the Vatican." This development did two things: it largely freed popes from the messy duties of political power-brokering (though it took a while to wean some of them away from secular machinations), and it turned the pope, in this case Pius IX, into a household name. Before this time, most Catholics probably did not know who the pope was at any given time. Early catechisms never even mentioned the papacy. Not anymore. Pius was loathed in anticlerical Italy, yes. But they loved Pius everywhere else, seeing in him a victim of persecution who was suffering for the church like an ancient martyr.

√ With the papacy stripped of much of its temporal influence, personal piety rather than political savvy became the hallmark of a pope, and subsequent pontiffs exalted that priority by turning dead popes into saints, which was also something new for the church. When Pius X (1903–14) was canonized in

1954, he became the first pontiff since the sixteenth century to be so honored, and just one of five papal saints in the past thousand years. Moreover, Pius XII, who canonized Pius X, is on the way to sainthood, as are John XXIII and John Paul II, whose canonization was given a jump start less than a month after his death, when Pope Benedict waived the mandatory five-year waiting period for the process to start. The emphasis on papal holiness is expected now, but it was initially a shock, especially to the Italians, who knew the foibles of their popes like one knows the faults of a difficult uncle. "Madam, this Pope was a real Christian. How could that be?" a Roman chambermaid said to Hannah Arendt when the author visited Rome during the final illness of John XXIII. "And how could it happen that a true Christian would sit on St. Peter's chair? Didn't he first have to be appointed Bishop, and Archbishop, and Cardinal, until he was finally elected to be Pope?"[5]

Today the cardinals still don't elect monks, but they don't need to. Regardless of their previous position, all popes now take on the persona of a public hermit, or they exalt that monastic part of themselves that was under wraps before. Joseph Ratzinger always admired the cloistered life, especially the rule of the Benedictines, and his choice of St. Benedict, the father of Western monasticism, as his namesake both revealed his own priorities and was in keeping with the current trend.

The problem is that the pressure to be a living saint, especially in the 24/7 spotlight of the modern media, can camouflage the natural impulses of a pope's personality, as well as leaving the pope isolated from the human contact that is essential to any successful pastoral ministry. John XXIII was beloved in large part because of he retained his pastoral, peasant ways, so different from the aristocratic rigidity of his predecessor, Pius XII. Yet John was a rarity. Once, when Paul VI was struggling with a difficult decision, a longtime friend asked him what Montini would do—Pope Paul was born Giovanni Battista Montini. The Holy Father answered, "*Montini non esiste più*" (Montini does not exist anymore).

John Paul II liked to say, "They try to understand me from the outside, but I can only be understood from the inside." Yet, for all his love of people and travel, the inner Wojtyla was so remote and so heavily fortified that he left many, even those closest to him, trying to figure out who he really was. "You know, one cannot be friends of a pope," one of John Paul's closest acquaintances once confided to a colleague. Eamon Duffy, the Cambridge historian of Catholicism, recalled a visit that a friend of his, a young theologian, made to the Vatican in the 1980s, at a time when John Paul enjoyed inviting a dozen or more people to debate various topics of the day over supper. Duffy's friend was seated next to the pope, which naturally made him especially anxious to have something intelligent to say, to make a connection with the Holy Father. So at one point he turned to the pope and said, "Holy Father, I love poetry, and I've read all your verse. Have you written much poetry since you became Pope?" John Paul responded quickly, "I've written no poetry since I became pope." Anxious to try to keep the conversation going, the theologian inquired, "Well, why is that Holy Father?" The pope immediately froze, changed the subject, and then turned to the person on his other side. About twenty minutes later, John Paul turned back to the embarrassed theologian, leaned over, and said two words by way of an answer: "No context."[6]

Yet popes remain the person they were, even beneath the crushing disguise of the papal cloaks. When Benedict's voluble brother, Georg Ratzinger, was asked if his younger sibling's election as pope would change their relationship, he quoted Aquinas's dictum that "grace does not destroy nature."[7] Indeed, grace is said to build on nature.

This can work to the benefit of the church or to its detriment. John XXIII, the "prisoner de luxe," was an elderly, little-known Vatican diplomat who was elected in 1958 as a transitional pope who was expected to keep the throne warm for a few years until the College of Cardinals figured out what they really wanted to do. But "transitional" is a term of art when one is the supreme pontiff. Sure enough, shortly after his elevation, Pope John indulged in what he called "a little holy madness" in convening the Second Vatican Council, directly counter to the wishes of the Roman Curia and to the great benefit of the modern church. Then there was the archconservative Pius IX, convener of the First Vatican Council, who responded to one bishop's critique of his effort to dogmatize papal infallibility by calling the poor man on the carpet and shouting, "*Tradizione! La tradizione son'io!*" (Tradition! I am tradition!).

Again, character drives plot in contemporary Catholicism, and the self-evident power of the papacy makes it a dangerous if soothing myth that the person of the pope does not matter, that he is only a clear lens magnifying the verities of the faith rather than a flawed pane, like all of us, refracting a vision of Catholicism through his unique character. For a pope to say that he is only representing truth, rather than interpreting those truths for application to today's world, can be in fact the height of egotism. It can lead to an unconscious identification of one's own aims with those of Holy Writ. So it is crucial that a pope recognize that he remains himself even as he becomes something wholly new. And it is vital that Catholics recognize this as well, however much they may wish their pope to be either their best friend or a plaster saint.

In that sense, John Paul II was the perfect pope for the modern age, a "celebrity of self-abandonment," as the writer John Garvey once said of the best-selling Cistercian monk, Thomas Merton. Like Merton, John Paul fulfilled the dual demands for popular fame and profound interiority. He carried an inner cloister within him across the globe, fully realizing that this only added to his appeal without—though some would disagree—cheapening his message. Distance creates mystique. For the movie star, that means fame; for the religious leader, it connotes holiness. Moreover, John Paul had no dark secrets for a scandal-hungry media to expose, and yet he was a heroic figure who played well in the spotlight and enjoyed himself doing so.

Yes, John Paul was an active and activist pope. But Benedict has shown that he is no less forceful, though in his own particular way.

The stark differences between the two popes start with their roots, one in Poland, the other in Germany.

When Karol Wojtyla was elected, he was hailed as a king by his countrymen, most all of whom were fellow Roman Catholics who thus saw "their" pope as a modern-day messiah, not only the first Slavic pontiff but also the fulfillment of a nineteenth-century prophecy that Poles would one day have one of their own on the Throne of St. Peter. Polish Catholicism was always indistinguishable from Polish nationalism, since the faith had, across the centuries, been the one insurmountable defense for a country with no natural boundaries. Poland was repeatedly conquered, suppressed, pillaged, and partitioned, and yet the Polish church was so faithful that it was known admiringly in Rome as the *antemurale christianitatis,* the rampart of Christendom.

As Poles tried to survive under the heel of their second totalitarian regime of the twentieth century—the Soviet communism that followed German Nazism—Poland found in John Paul their Moses. "My cry will be the cry of the entire fatherland!" John Paul said during his second visit to Poland, in 1983, at the height of the showdown with Moscow. "I will continue to consider as my own every true good of my homeland, as though I were still living in this land, and perhaps even more, because of the distance."[8] True to his word, he led them out of slavery, even if he found the Promised Land something less than what he had hoped.

Joseph Ratzinger, on the other hand, came from a nation that had brought Christianity to Poland a millennium earlier, in the year 966, but then proved a bane not only to Poland but also to Rome for centuries thereafter. Yet

Ratzinger's negative image was so strong at home that after his election Pope Benedict was actually more popular in Poland, which Germany had so recently conquered, than he was in his native Germany. Even before the conclave, a poll for *Der Spiegel* magazine showed that 36 percent of Germans were opposed to Ratzinger becoming pope, with just 29 percent saying they would back his candidacy. When Ratzinger did emerge as Benedict, the reaction in Germany was fairly muted, not only because of his controversial image but also because of the postwar German burden of guilt that casts a public modesty on any national triumph. Moreover, the joy that Germans did show was more a point of national expiation rather than religious pride, seeing in Ratzinger's elevation another step toward Germany's rehabilitation instead of a sign of divine approbation for the nation. "Even as a Protestant I can say that we are very much moved by the fact that a German, one of us, has become Pope," German president Horst Koehler said in welcoming Benedict to the church's World Youth Day festivities in Cologne four months after his elevation.

The German church also has a far different domestic profile than the Polish church. While 90 percent of Poles are Catholic and about half of them attend Mass each week, Germany today is largely a secular country that retains the scars of the Reformation; in terms of religious affiliation, the nation is divided into roughly three equal parts among Protestants, Catholics, and Neither-of-the-Aboves, and among German Catholics the weekly churchgoing rate is less than 15 percent. Indeed, Germany could be the poster church for all the ills of European Christendom that Benedict so acutely diagnosed. Furthermore, there are sharp divisions among those German Catholics who are involved in religious life, and many of them put the blame for the controversies squarely on the shoulders of the man who even before his election as pope was the most influential German in Catholicism. "I have a certain image in Germany. I'll have to live with that," Ratzinger once told another German prelate.

Clearly, Ratzinger's nationality does not give Benedict the same platform that Wojtyla's nationality provided John Paul, nor have historical circumstances offered him a chance to play the hero's role. There is no Soviet empire to slay, and in fact his toughest criticisms are aimed directly at his coreligionists, which is not exactly a way to score points with the hometown crowd. Moreover, the quarter-century Ratzinger spent at the Vatican before his election led many to view him as more Roman than German. "My idea of him is not of a German pope," Monsignor Charles Scicluna, an official at the CDF who had worked with Cardinal Ratzinger for years, told Catholic News Service.[9] "He is a pope for the universal church, and he has lived that in his ministry in the

Roman Curia for 23 years." One German writer called Benedict a "pope without a country."[10] No one could imagine saying such a thing about John Paul.

Another key difference between the two men, and perceptions of them, is that Joseph Ratzinger was a fully known quantity when he was elected, and not necessarily to his advantage. Not only was he renowned for controversy, but his every opinion had been spelled out in frank, often brutally frank, book-length interviews and television and radio segments. Karol Wojtyla was a stranger even to many of his fellow cardinals. "*Chi é Bottiglia?*" an Italian cardinal asked during the second conclave of 1978, when he heard his fellow electors whispering about Karol Wojtyla, whose last name did not even ring a bell. (The cardinal was soon enlightened. "Now you know who 'Bottiglia' is," John Paul teased him a short time later, when the cardinal came to pay respects to the newly elected pontiff.)

The cardinal from Krakow was better-traveled than many of his fellow bishops behind the Iron Curtain, but still, his entire clerical career had unfolded in a country with no free press, no mass media, under a government that tried to muzzle church leaders, and in the pre-Google days before databases could instantly spit out a paper and video trail cataloging a person's every public utterance. If Cardinal Wojtyla had been giving television interviews and press conferences every week and publishing dozens of books in the Western marketplace, who knows what controversies he would have stirred?

When he did become pope, Wojtyla's relative anonymity worked to his advantage in the public eye; from the very start he was able to define himself the way he wanted, to the church and the world. Ratzinger's project, conversely, has been to redefine himself, to change deep-seated impressions, and that is a far tougher task.

As much as their different environments, it is their distinct temperaments and worldviews that distinguish these two popes, with the baseline divergence being that John Paul was a Philosopher and Benedict is a Theologian. The distance between these two intellectual pursuits may not seem far, but when viewed from the perspective of two millennia of Christianity, the gulf is profound, and the enduring split is personified in Karol Wojtyla and Joseph Ratzinger.

From the very beginning, the church looked on philosophy with profound suspicion, associating it with the dominant Greek culture of the region that was enamored of the kind of intellectual exploration and debate that Christians felt could only undermine the revealed faith of Jesus. Philosophical speculation seemed like an endless string of questions leading nowhere, while Christian believers were preaching a message promising answers. "See to it that no one captivate you with an empty, seductive philosophy according to human tradition, according to the elemental powers of the world and not according to Christ," Saint Paul wrote to the Colossians. Paul was disillusioned especially with Greek thought by that time, having failed in his missionary efforts at the Areopagus in Athens, the public square of the ancient world, to convince all those layabout sophists who "used their time for nothing else but telling or hearing something new." Paul could not win souls to Christ by fighting the Stoics and Epicureans on their terms, so he decided not to try. Many years later, church leaders agreed with him. "What has Athens to do with Jerusalem?" Tertullian (155–230 AD) sneered in his tract, the *Prescription Against Heretics*. In other words, what do the word games of the philosophers have to do with the revealed faith of the church?

It was an attitude that heralded the never-ending tug-of-war in the Christian heart between revelation and reason, the heart and the head, which has pockmarked Christianity's reputation up to the present day. And while church fathers after Tertullian succeeded in harnessing Greek thought to the cause of evangelization, it was not until the arrival of—once again—Thomas Aquinas that philosophical speculation received a full-immersion baptism. Whereas Joseph Ratzinger disdained Thomism, Karol Wojtyla was enamored of the vistas that Aquinas opened up. He was trained by Dominicans at Rome's Angelicum theology school (now called the Pontifical University of St. Thomas), which was dedicated to the neo-Scholastic revival that Leo XIII had demanded (and Ratzinger dismissed), and, as pope, John Paul remained a champion of Aquinas every bit as much as Ratzinger embraced Augustine. "Saint Thomas celebrates all the richness and complexity of each created being, and especially of the human being," John Paul wrote in his 1994 *Crossing the Threshold of Hope*. "It is not good that his thought has been set aside in the post-conciliar period; he continues, in fact, to be the *master of philosophical and theological universalism*." The italics were John Paul's; the intent was straight from Pope Leo.

It was this exercising of the mind that Wojtyla enjoyed. After theological studies on Aquinas, he returned to Poland and in his doctoral studies explored phenomenology, a philosophical school developed in Germany (where else?) that focused on describing the nature of experience and human consciousness without recourse to presuppositions from science or other disciplines. "This off-putting term translates into a relatively simple idea: it is that one can come to understand the truth of something not simply by reference to the authority of science, or revelation, or dogma, but by 'moving around' it, experiencing it from different perspectives and letting the reflections of each perspective communicate the truth of the object," says Father Kevin Wildes, a Jesuit philosopher.[11]

Phenomenology makes no judgments, which is what makes it potentially risky for a Christian like Wojtyla. Phenomenology leads wherever the evidence goes. It is perhaps the most philosophical of all philosophies, reveling in knowledge for the sake of knowledge, in exploration, and in the objective experience of people. But phenomenology could also, at least for Wojtyla, help to provide rational grounding for the religious truths that people apprehend by faith or instinct, and contribute to the cultivation of the virtuous life by showing us the correct moral choices. Phenomenology has been described as making you aware of what you already know, and that suited Wojtyla's aims, since he saw moral truth as something innate in man and waiting to be discovered.

Unfortunately, the necessarily roundabout method of phenomenology also played into his penchant for impenetrable prose and arcane terminology. Poles used to quip that they needed to translate Wojtyla's writings into Polish to read him, and local priests joked that their first assignment in Purgatory would be to read Wojtyla's books. Wojtyla's obscure style, however, was due in part to the fact that he was grounded in two very different schools of thought, Thomism and phenomenology, and was trying to discern the links between them, which is a bit like trying to get two incompatible pieces of software to communicate.

Wojtyla never ceased in this quest, though whether he was successful in reconciling a philosophy of perennial observation with a school that used observation to affirm religious certainty is debatable. Reading John Paul's writings has been compared to walking around in a phenomenological fog and smacking into a brick wall of Thomism, an allusion to the way he reveled in the search for truth while always knowing where he must end up, which was in Christian revelation. This alternation between questing and certainty was a principal source of the ambivalence that surrounded John Paul in life and ultimately in death. Because of his philosopher's love of inquiry, John Paul was always curious about the human experience. He was genuinely open to how people lived and wanted to engage them in a free-ranging discussion about the problems of life and faith. He was so pastoral, so passionate, and so *understanding* that people assumed he would *change* things. But then when it came to matters of faith or doctrinal issues, such as the ordination of women, for example, they would find John Paul falling back on the authority of tradition for justification and rejecting all appeals to the knowledge and experience that he relied on for so much else. Many felt misled by his charm, while still feeling charmed.

In contrast, no one would ever be misled by Ratzinger, now Pope Benedict, or accuse him of the foggy imprecisions that Wojtyla routinely committed. "He's a much better writer than John Paul," George Weigel, John Paul's most diligent biographer, told me a few days after Benedict's election. Yet John Paul the Philosopher was also engaged in the difficult (and very Thomistic) project of trying to make faith intelligible to man and the world, and vice versa. This was a different endeavor than that of Ratzinger the Theologian, peeling away the accretions of philosophy to find the bright, hard truths of faith glimmering beneath. To Ratzinger, as to Karl Barth, the Swiss Protestant theologian he so admired, theology needed no philosophical justification. "Belief cannot argue with unbelief, it can only preach to it," Barth said. Ratzinger underscored the primacy of Christology, the study of the divine truths about the Son of God, over Wojtyla's love of anthropology, the study of man and the world.

John Paul was a Christian humanist, befitting his outgoing nature, and he amplified his phenomenological approach, the first pillar of his intellectual framework, with Christian personalism, the second pillar. Personalism is an orientation that emphasizes the dignity and value of each person, the importance of dialogue—between man and God, and among men—and the centrality of human solidarity.[12] This personalist approach allowed Wojtyla to focus intently on the messy drama of the human person, limning arguments to bolster the church's belief in the unrepeatable, inherent dignity of each individual, created by God and deserving every support from womb to tomb, and every protection from oppressive ideological systems, be it Marxism or capitalism, or from immoral laws, like those legalizing abortion or euthanasia. "In every phase and stage of my university life and pastoral ministry, one of the essential points of reference for me was attention to the human person, who is at the center of any philosophical or theological investigation," John Paul said. His first encyclical as pope, *Redemptor Hominis,* or Redeemer of Man, emphasized that the path of the church's mission runs through the daily lives of human beings. He was fascinated by people. Pythagoras declared that "man is the measure of all things," and John Paul, following Aquinas, fused that Greek philosophy to the Hebrew Bible's understanding of man as created in God's image.

These two schools of thought—a "philosophy of consciousness" from phenomenology and a "philosophy of being" from personalism—are the keys to understanding John Paul's pontificate and his differences from Benedict's.

√ John Paul's personalist philosophy is also directly connected to his popular status as a people's pope. Contrary to his doctrinal statements (and those of his theologian-in-chief, Cardinal Ratzinger), John Paul's love of engagement and his innate optimism made him something of a soft touch, in the view of many, on everything from his ban on the death penalty to the futility of war to the question of whether anyone was in fact condemned to hell. In his 2004 memoir, *Rise, Let Us Be on Our Way,* John Paul offered a rare glimpse of his internal debate about his approach: "Admonition certainly belongs to the role of the pastor," he writes. "I think that, under this aspect, perhaps I've done too little. There is always a problem of equilibrium between authority and service. Maybe I have to criticize myself for not having tried hard enough to command. To some extent, this derives from my temperament. In a way, however, this could also be traced to the will of Christ, who asked his apostles not so much to command as to serve. Naturally, the bishop has authority, but much depends on the way in which it is exercised. If the bishop puts excessive emphasis on it, the people will think all he knows how to do is command. On the other hand, if he puts himself in an attitude of service, the faithful naturally will feel compelled to listen to him and to submit voluntarily to his authority."

Of course, John Paul had Cardinal Ratzinger to be the official disciplinarian, which both shielded the pope from criticism and freed him to be the pastor he preferred to be. As Cardinal Dulles said in an October 2003 lecture on John Paul's philosophical approach, "Personalism undoubtedly favors the use of persuasion rather than force. It makes for a reluctance to admit that negotiation can at a certain point become futile." Pope John Paul II, Dulles said, "shies away from threatening words. Fear, in his view, diminishes the scope of freedom and makes only a poor Christian. He holds up the more perfect motives of hope, trust and love as grounds for joyful adherence to the Lord. Amid all the anger and turmoil of our times, John Paul II stands as a beacon of hope."[13]

In Wojtyla's words to his friend, Henri de Lubac, a decade before his election, "We have firmly hoped, we will always hope, and we are and will be happy."[14]

When an interviewer asked in 1997 if Joseph Ratzinger was a happy man, his response was indirect and almost anodyne, saying only that he accepted his lot in life, "because to live against oneself and one's life would make no sense. And I think that I have been able to do something meaningful after all, in another way than I had foreseen and expected."[15]

When Karol Wojtyla became Pope John Paul, he embraced his destiny with a gusto that was infectious and as expansive as the very office he now held. No person was unimportant, no project too grand. Providence had placed him in this place at this point in history, and the phenomenologist in him was determined to take his own measure of the world and the church by traveling constantly, "part of his attempt to circle human experience," as Father Kevin Wildes put it. "Many people say that the pope travels too much, and at too close intervals," John Paul said in a 1980 interview, responding to criticism inside the Vatican that he was neglecting the governance of the church. "I think that, humanly speaking, they are right. But it is Providence that guides us and sometimes prompts us to do something *per excessum*."[16]

Doing things "to excess" was the hallmark of John Paul's personality and the ethos of his papacy. Though he faced hurdles with members of his administration, John Paul never ever doubted his own authority and central role as the Roman pontiff. "*È papa, e lo sa,*" shell-shocked curialists said when Wojtyla took over—"He's pope, and he knows it."

Such supreme confidence also enabled John Paul to make all manner of innovations when he felt it would make his message more intelligible to the modern world. After John Paul's death, one of his aides, Archbishop Celestino Migliore, dubbed him "*pontifex massmediaticus,*" saying that "never before him did a pope use the media as effectively." The pope would meet regularly with journalists when he traveled, and he put himself in the spotlight whenever he possibly could. "If it doesn't happen on television, it doesn't happen," the pope liked to say, and he made sure that both he and his events were as telegenic as possible. He did that not only through his impressive talents as an actor, but also in the unprecedented liturgical novelties he allowed and in the choice of locales for his public Masses—backdrops ran from Tierra del Fuego to Central Park to the African savannah and even Havana's Plaza de la Revolución, where he appeared opposite a mural of Che Guevara.

In fact, for all his traditionalism, John Paul's flexibility in adapting tradition was almost revolutionary, earning him the abiding enmity of orthodox Catholics, who, out of earshot of the mainstream media, blasted John Paul's innovative leanings. At a 1984 Mass in Papua New Guinea, for example, a young woman, nude from the waist up, read the Epistle from a lectern next to John Paul, while similarly clad aborigines in face paint and native costume danced in the aisle and John Paul looked on approvingly. At a 1998 Mass in St. Peter's Basilica to celebrate Catholicism in Oceania, the procession with the Gospel was announced by the blowing of conch shells and prayers in Samoan, while bare-chested men in native dress flanked the Holy Father in his Roman vestments, all of them standing under Bernini's ornate baldacchino—surely a scene even that master craftsman of the Baroque would never have envisioned. If it better communicated his message to his audience, John Paul was willing to adapt the Mass, taking the post–Vatican II shift from Latin to the vernacular to extremes no one would have predicted in 1965.

The architect of John Paul's liturgical *coup d'église* was Archbishop Piero Marini, longtime papal master of ceremonies and chief liturgist whose altar-boy good looks masked a firm intention to set the Mass, the heartbeat of Catholic religious life, to the varied rhythms of the new millennium century. "In the old liturgy used before the Second Vatican Council the role of the celebrant consisted of applying a series of rigid norms, that could not be changed," once said Marini. "Today one cannot organize a celebration without first thinking: who is celebrating, what is being celebrated, where is the celebration taking place. We find ourselves acting in some way upon a stage. The liturgy is also theater."[17]

While conservatives savaged Marini for the papal masses he arranged, it was John Paul, not Marini, who set the tone. When preparations were under way for a major celebration to open the 1994 Synod for Africa, a landmark month-long Vatican meeting on Catholicism on the continent, the African church-men involved in planning the opening Mass for St. Peter's Basilica tried to incorporate what is called the Zaire Rite, a special African adaptation of the liturgy that allows sacred dance, hands raised in prayer, and much swaying and other elements alien to Roman rituals. "You cannot have drums and dancing at St. Peter's!" Marini told the African bishops. He instructed them to use Latin and the colonial languages of French, Portuguese, and English, which every-one would understand. At a lunch some time later, however, John Paul asked the African prelates how the synod preparations were coming, and when they told him of the problems he did not even let them finish before taking their side: "The more African, the better," he said.[18] And that's how the Mass went. Even cardinals were dancing.

Cardinal Joseph Ratzinger was not one of them.

If Pope John Paul II was a "showman of God," as one of his aides called him admiringly, Pope Benedict most certainly is not, and he has gone out of his way to criticize in the bluntest terms the trend to clerical showmanship. "The priest is, in fact, not a showmaster who invents something new and skillfully com-municates it," Ratzinger said in 1996. "On the contrary, he can entirely lack any talents of a showmaster, because he represents something completely different, and it doesn't depend on him."[19] So strong was his aversion to this personal-izing of the Mass that he claimed the trend had helped foment the agitation on behalf of ordaining women: "Importance is attributed to the *person* of the priest; he must be able to handle things skillfully and to be able to present everything well. He is the real center of the celebration. In consequence, one has to say: Why only this sort of person? When, on the contrary, he withdraws completely and simply presents things through his believing action, then the action no longer circles around him. Rather, he steps aside, and something greater comes into view."

Though Ratzinger acknowledged the spiritual hunger that John Paul's large-scale outdoor masses reflected, he also warned that "we ought not to read too much into certain events and mass demonstrations of Catholicism"—a dig at his boss's preferred means of communicating the faith.[20] And in contrast with Marini's analogy of the liturgy as theater, Ratzinger was dismissive: "This is not liturgy, this is entertainment."

"The liturgy is not a show, a spectacle, requiring brilliant producers and talented actors. The life of the liturgy does not consist in 'pleasant' surprises and attractive 'ideas' but in solemn repetitions," Ratzinger said.[21] Any attempt to enhance the liturgical experience in modern terms, he said, gives man a sense of "agency" in creating something that only happens through divine ac-tion. In that vein, he called the post–Vatican II rite "a fabricated liturgy"[22] and the new vernacular missal "tragic." In his memoirs he called the push for "in-culturation," that is, adapting the Mass to local cultures and customs, which John Paul forcefully supported, a "false" movement that too often lowers the sacred Mass to the level of the modern world—"adapting it to our medioc-rity"—and thereby diminishes an ageless tradition that could save the world.

For John Paul, modern culture was not so much an enemy to be sneered at as a untamed spirit to be harnessed—an unruly spirit, yes, but one whose heart was in the right place. Modern culture was also the portal to the audience he wanted to reach. To that end he beefed up the Vatican's television service, embraced the Internet, marketed CDs of himself praying and singing, and bowing to the rock-concert reality of his public masses, eventually allowed the hosts of his trips to license papal merchandise rather than letting freebooters take all the profits—and sell tasteless souvenirs.

Rock music was a favorite gateway to the world. John Paul met often with Bono, the lead singer for U2 and a prominent poverty fighter, who dubbed him "history's first funky pontiff" and eulogized him at his death as "the best frontman the Roman Catholic Church ever had." John Paul liked the rocker's wraparound shades so much that he once tried them on, to the chagrin of Don Stanislau. Boyz II Men served as John Paul's warm-up band at a 1995 Mass in Baltimore's Camden Yards, and in 1997 he hosted a rock concert in Bologna for 200,000 young people, called "Jesus Live Superstar." The concert came after a beatification Mass and in the midst of the country's Eucharistic Congress, normally a solemn liturgical celebration. The concert's headliner—after the pope—was Bob Dylan, who serenaded John Paul with "Knocking on Heaven's Door," perhaps intending the classic make-out song as a single-entendre tune for that evening. Dylan also performed his famous ballad "Blowin' in the Wind," and afterward John Paul offered his own riff, asking, "How many roads must a man walk down? One! There is only one way for man, and that is Christ, who said, 'I am the way.' It is he who is the way to truth, the way to life." In 2000 John Paul hosted another concert, this time in Rome to promote debt reduction for poor countries. The pontiff joined the Eurythmics, Alanis Morissette, and Lou Reed—not exactly your standard choirboys and -girls.

Pope Benedict detests rock and roll. In a 1986 speech, Cardinal Ratzinger called rock music the "vehicle of anti-religion," and said that rock "is the complete antithesis of the Christian faith in the redemption." Rock and roll, he said, "is the expression of elemental passions, and at rock festivals it assumes a cultic character, a form of worship, in fact, in opposition to Christian worship. . . . The music of the Holy Spirit's sober inebriation seems to have little chance when self has become a prison, the mind is a shackle, and breaking out from both appears as a true promise of redemption that can be tasted at least for a few moments." The musical sense of the younger generation, he said elsewhere, "has been stunted since the beginning of the sixties by rock music and related forms."[23] Such related forms would principally be pop music, which he said is a "phenomenon of the masses, is industrially produced, and ultimately has to be described as a cult of the banal."

This cult would include "easy melodies, catchy tunes," or what he sums up as "utility music." The appeal to "active participation" by churchgoers, a main thrust of Vatican II's liturgical reform, is behind this "surrender of the beautiful," which Ratzinger sees as the beginning of the end. "A Church which only makes use of 'utility music' has fallen for what is, in fact, useless and becomes useless herself." Opposed to this "unholy spirit," Ratzinger said, is the Gregorian chant and polyphony that Pius X mandated a century ago as the only forms suitable for the sanctuary. Outside the liturgical setting, classical music, principally the Germanic geniuses of Bach, Beethoven, and Mozart, represents the cultural standard proper to a Christian sensibility.

Playing piano in his free time, often to relax in the evenings, Benedict tends toward Mozart, since he feels he does not have the time to practice the more challenging Bach pieces he would like to try. After his election, Benedict had the sixteenth-century papal apartments renovated—they certainly needed it after John Paul's long reign—but also doubled in size, in part to accommodate a new piano. While the renovations went on—through the summer and early fall, during which time Benedict lived mostly at Castelgandolfo, the papal villa in the Alban hills outside Rome—other provisions were made so that the new pope could continue to enjoy the music that is so vital to his spirit. One morning, during a September academic conference at Castelgandolfo on cosmology and natural evil—the villa is also home to the Vatican observatory (yes, the same church that harried Galileo has historically been a leader in astronomy)—the participants were surprised to hear piano music drifting through an open window. "We were listening to a description of hyenas ripping apart other animals in the wild," said Mark Dowd, a television producer who was making a documentary on God and the South Asian tsunami that had struck earlier in the year. "Suddenly we heard the sound of a piano wafting in from the courtyard. The proceedings stopped briefly while we listened, but it was only later that we were told that we had been listening to the pope playing the piano."[24]

As a cardinal, Ratzinger had lived across the street from the Vatican, under the windows of the papal apartment, so the move was much less drastic for him than it is for out-of-town cardinals who suddenly find themselves pope. Still, Benedict found it hard to surrender the orderly domestic setting he had so carefully arranged over the years. He surprised his aides, and the public passing outside the Vatican gates, by returning to his old apartment for several days after his election. One reason was to look after the transfer of his massive book collection, which he had diligently gathered for years, and which required further renovations to the papal apartments so they could accommodate the volumes. "His library is his little empire, and he wanted to move it all himself," Benedict's friend and neighbor Paul Badde, Vatican correspondent for the German newspaper *Die Welt,* told *Newsweek.* "Often I would be sitting at my computer, and through the window I could see him walking outside. He looked a very lonely person, without any bodyguards, dressed in black. He'd cross the street and look in the window of a bookshop at new titles, because he's really a very passionate reader, and a passionate writer."

Benedict and John Paul—everything about the energy the two men exuded was different.

Wojtyla was a physically dynamic presence, an avid outdoorsman who relished adventure like an Eagle Scout. In *Rise, Let Us Be on Our Way,* John Paul recalled how as a priest he was on a canoe trip in the mountains in July 1958 with friends when he received an urgent summons to see Cardinal Stefan Wyszynski in Warsaw. He paddled as far as he could, then hitched a ride on a truck full of flour sacks, and slept overnight in the train station waiting for a connection. Wyszynski informed him that he had been nominated as an auxiliary bishop in Krakow. Wojtyla protested that at thirty-eight, he was too young to be a bishop. "It is a weakness of which you will soon be freed," Wyszynski told him. All Wojtyla wanted to do was return to his canoeing trip. He was told that wouldn't be appropriate, but he persisted and was allowed to return to the lake region of Masuria. He boarded an overnight train, reading *The Old Man and the Sea* by Ernest Hemingway, a writer of similarly rugged sensibilities.

Wojtyla conveyed an infectious sense that all things were possible, and that there was little time to waste. An English bishop recalled being charmed by Wojtyla from the first time they met, at a Vatican meeting of bishops in the 1970s. The weather was dreadful, and Cardinal Wojtyla would arrive at the meeting with the other prelates on foot, his cassock soaked with rain. He would promptly remove his dripping shoes and socks and put them on the radiator, getting the group down to business without further ado. "And they were just so entranced by a bishop with balls," said the historian Eamon Duffy.[25]

Wojtyla loved the very rough-and-tumble of sports and human interaction that Ratzinger had avoided as a child. As pope, John Paul always hosted meals with many guests, whereas Benedict prefers to dine alone, or at most with a trusted friend or two. He tends to eat quickly, often a bowl of pasta or German specialties, and as a cardinal used to frequent a Swiss restaurant in the Borgo, his neighborhood next to the Vatican walls. Whatever he ate, Ratzinger always took dessert, indulging a sweet tooth he had all his life. This preference extends to beverages, too. Benedict rarely touches wine, may indulge in the occasional beer, but his drink of choice is orange juice or Fanta, the orange-flavored soda pop, which he likes to consume at dinner. "In my rhythm of work, and the necessity always to be very lucid, I do not even allow myself a glass of wine," he told a dinner companion, Alessandra Borghese, an Italian noblewoman.[26]

The new pope spends much of his time by himself, alone in his office studying papers, reading books or writing. He writes in a cramped, miniscule script that only his longtime secretaries can decipher, though, like his musical hero,

Mozart, Ratzinger is able to dictate books and lectures while pacing about his office, tearing off twenty pages of densely argued text with nary an error and complete with verbal footnotes. That is why his book-length interviews can read like carefully researched dissertations. Benedict speaks Latin so fluently that he is perhaps one of the twenty or so best Latin speakers in the world, at least according to the Vatican's official Latinist, Father Reginald Foster, who dismissed John Paul's fluency in the church's mother tongue as "spaghetti Latin." The morning after his election, after an evening dinner with the College of Cardinals, Benedict delivered a lengthy homily to the cardinals that he himself had written in perfect Latin. A project that would take a scholar or a preacher a month he did overnight.

So prodigious is his memory that Ratzinger's favored style is to write his talks or books, complete with references to lengthy quotations from years ago, only later returning to his large private library to track down the details of the citations for the footnotes. As impressive as this talent is, it would still not be up to the demands of the papal grind, which can require dozens of communiqués, speeches, and administrative missives, not to mention homilies, each day. Yet Benedict tried to carry his more academic and personal style across the street to the papal apartments, writing his own talks and chewing over matters that needed immediate action. Sources close to the pontiff said that delegating such duties, especially the task of writing, as John Paul had, was one of the ongoing adjustments of Benedict's first year in office, and one that he may never fully make. Benedict only trusts himself to express his ideas.

√Compared to John Paul, Benedict is paying much closer attention to the management of the Curia, whose faults he knows all too well. John Paul was famously indifferent to administration, which helped create much of the dysfunction that Benedict must fix. Wojtyla was always far more interested in pressing the flesh than keeping the trains running on time, which most bishops have to do. "It's enough if the motor spins," he used to say. In the early 1980s, when the Vatican bank scandal was threatening the Holy See with bankruptcy, John Paul smiled to his friends and said, "I'm really curious to see how they'll get out of this," the "they" referring to the Curia, to whom he delegated the mundane tasks he disliked.[27]

One of Benedict's more curious passions is his love of all things feline. Actually, as Los Angeles cardinal Roger Mahony, himself an owner of two tabbies, put it, "The street talk that the pope loves cats is incorrect. The pope adores cats."[28] When first elected, it was rumored that Benedict harbored a menagerie of cats in his apartment. That turned out not to be the case; Benedict has only a collection of cat porcelains made for him by Benedictine nuns who learned of his passion. But for years Ratzinger was known around Rome for feeding the strays that inhabit the city and the Vatican gardens. He was especially popular among the felines in the cemetery behind the Teutonic College, right next to the Congregation for the Doctrine of the Faith, where Ratzinger used to wander among the gravestones. "It was full of cats, and when he went out, they all ran to him," Konrad Baumgartner, the head of the theology department at Regensburg University, said in recalling a visit with the future pope. "They knew him and loved him. He stood there, petting some and talking to them, for quite a long time. He visited the cats whenever he visited the church."[29] Italian cardinal Tarcisio Bertone of Genoa, who worked under Ratzinger at the CDF, said Ratzinger had his own language with the cats. "I thought maybe it was a Bavarian dialect, but I don't know," Bertone told Vatican Radio.

Cardinal Ratzinger included his affection for animals in his theology, telling biographer Peter Seewald that animals must be respected as "companions in creation" and condemning industrial farming, saying, "This degrading of living creatures to a commodity seems to me in fact to contradict the relationship of mutuality that comes across in the Bible." Both the Humane Society of the United States and People for the Ethical Treatment of Animals, known as PETA, were among Benedict's biggest fans when he was announced as pope.

When Baltimore's Cardinal William Keeler was interviewed on CNN after Benedict's installation, he was asked what the new pope was like, the first question everyone wants answered. "You know," Keeler said thoughtfully, "I was telling a friend the other day that he reminds me of my mother—very sweet, but very clear in what she said."

It is a long way from a bishop with balls to a stern old matron.

The impact of the shift in personality was evident early on in Benedict's papacy. The day after his election, he pointedly told the College of Cardinals that his task was to show "not his own light, but that of Christ," and from his installation as pope in St. Peter's Square to his installation as Bishop of Rome at St. John Lateran a few days later, Benedict signaled that his would be a lower-profile reign. "The pope must not proclaim his own ideas, but rather constantly bind himself and the Church to obedience to God's word, in the face of every attempt to adapt it or water it down, and every form of opportunism," he said in his homily at the Lateran.

Benedict was and is a *vir ecclesiasticus,* a "man of the church," said Cardinal

Georges Cottier, the theologian of the papal household.[30] According to Benedict's former CDF collaborator, Father DiNoia, the new pope held that "once the tradition is exhibited like a great painting or work of art, it doesn't need explanation. Once it's presented, people see it and love it."

In other words, Christ needed no papal salesman, however appealing the pitchman. In an important but little-noted change, just three weeks after John Paul's death Benedict's decided to end John Paul's practice of presiding personally at beatification ceremonies. Beatification is the second step on the three-tiered ladder ending with canonization, and it has historically been the result of grassroots devotion recognized by holding the beatification in the country where the prospective saint was popularized. During his time, John Paul became the chief presider at such services, believing that would highlight the importance of sainthood. But it wound up with Rome once again effectively co-opting a local custom. Benedict believed that was wrong, and so he devolved beatifications back to the local churches. He also indicated he would scale back what was derisively known as John Paul's "saint-making factory" at the Vatican. Fewer saints and fewer papal spectacles.

Similarly, Benedict shortened the Synod of Bishops in October 2005 from a month to three weeks. The move was met with hosannas in the hierarchy, where bishops had fumed at having to leave their dioceses for such a long time and for what had become a fairly perfunctory confab of little value. He also held far fewer audiences, and he did not open his daily private morning Mass to small groups of visitors, as John Paul had.

The change in tenor was clear from Benedict's meeting with journalists four days after his election. The encounter is part of the postconclave ritual, but in 1978 John Paul II had taken the perfunctory meeting and turned it into a sign that his would indeed be a pontificate of a different sort. Meeting in the crowded Sala Clementina, John Paul gave a brief speech and greeting and then did the unthinkable — he opened the floor to questions. For forty minutes he and the press corps batted questions and answers and bon mots back and forth, and in several languages.

When Benedict was elected, the Vatican initially billed his postconclave meeting with the media as a "press conference." But it was quickly changed to the more passive "audience," and that was largely what it turned out to be. Several hundred journalists were dwarfed in the capacious, modern Paul VI audience hall, and the atmosphere was clearly different. The secular media were kept several rows back behind a low barricade, while Vatican employees and other personnel and dignitaries were put up front, putting distance between the pope and the press corps. Precisely at 11:00 AM Pope Benedict walked in, nodding almost shyly and quickly taking his place on a throne on stage. He read a two-paragraph note of thanks to the journalists in English, French, German, and Italian, leaving out Spanish, the mother tongue of nearly half the world's Catholics.

Benedict took no questions, shook no hands, and made not the slightest gesture toward the Fourth Estate, which would be his microphone to the world. One Vatican aide told me the pope knew exactly what he was doing and was sending a signal of his own. An American churchman in attendance chalked it up to Benedict's temperament. "He is not a very dynamic personality. That's who he is." Either way, after less than twenty minutes, most of it taken up with formalities, Benedict turned and left, his small, quick steps accentuated by the fact that his cassock was still several inches too short, exposing slim ankles in white socks set off by an eye-catching pair of bright red shoes with buckles. "The pope is king, and the king can wear whatever shoes he likes," one of the haberdashers at Gammarelli's said when asked about the footwear, which harked back to a more princely era of the papacy.[31]

Benedict's fashion sense continued to depart sharply from that of his predecessor, in an unusual combination of sartorial *aggiornamento* and royal *ressourcement*. On the avant-garde side, Benedict went for the best: his red shoes were rumored to be a Prada design, though the Vatican later let it be known that they were crafted by the pope's personal cobbler. And the sunglasses he sported during open-air events were a pricey Serengeti model from Bushnell Performance Optics. Still, while Benedict does have refined tastes, he would not normally be considered a fashion plate. The likely source of his makeover is his personal secretary, Georg Gänswein, a canon lawyer and monsignor with rugged movie star looks that draw comparisons to George Clooney and Hugh Grant. Gänswein, known in Germany as the "Black Forest Adonis," became such a heartthrob—to men and women alike—that he wound up attracting as much comment as his boss at public events. (Certainly, no one ever mistook John Paul's personal aide, Don Stanislao, for clerical eye candy.) Gänswein is tall, athletic, Bavarian, and deeply conservative—and knows high fashion. So it was likely no coincidence that during Benedict's July vacation in the mountains of northern Italy he decked the pope out in a white Nike hat, designer shades, and a Cartier wristwatch.

On the traditional side, Benedict surprised many by donning a *mozzetta,* an ermine-trimmed red cape, in addition to the elaborately embroidered stoles that from the start of his pontificate he had made a part of his regular dress. Then, just before Christmas 2005, Benedict appeared in a *camauro,* the fur-trimmed cap that was a fixture of medieval and Renaissance papal headgear—think of Raphael's portraits of the fierce warrior–pope Julius II, or the monarchical Medici pope Leo X. It is attire reserved only to the pope and, with the exception of a brief restoration by John XXIII forty years earlier, had not been seen in centuries. The animal rights folks who welcomed Benedict's concern for animal welfare gave him the benefit of the doubt on the source of the ermine, saying that it was probably from the Vatican's vintage collection. But across the Catholic spectrum the reaction to Benedict's retro fashion ranged from disbelief or embarassed amusement at his Santa Claus effect to serious concern over what his move signaled. "Return to your roots," read the front-page coverage in *Il Tempo*, a Rome daily. On his personal Web site, Father Guy Selvester, a New Jersey priest who specializes in ecclesiastical heraldry, noted that many would see Benedict as "purposely dressing in a way that evokes images of a papacy of bygone days. The pope is reviving the image of the Renaissance papacy. He is clearly utilizing perogatives that set him apart, and above, other bishops rather than underscore his equality with them. He may still see himself as a first among equals, but the emphasis is to be placed on *first,* not equals."

Apart from fashion, however, nothing illustrated the shift in style and priority more clearly than Benedict's travels. As a seventy-eight-year-old with a somewhat fragile constitution, Benedict was never going to resemble the Polish mountaineer who became pope at age fifty-eight and was a global whirlwind for the next two decades. Indeed, unlike most curial officials, who jockeyed for position in John Paul's cortege, Cardinal Ratzinger rarely accompanied the pope on his many trips. As John Paul's "trusted friend" in the Curia, Ratzinger did not have to travel with him. As pope, he could now set his own pace and style.

The difference was immediately visible in Benedict's first trip outside Rome, on May 29 to the city of Bari on the Adriatic coast of Italy, for the closing of the Italian church's annual Eucharistic Congress. The visit, like most public events of the first few months of Benedict's papacy, was scheduled while John Paul was alive. At a Eucharistic Congress in Bologna in 1997, John Paul had hosted a rock concert and spent all day presiding at events and liturgies. For the liturgy in Bari, Benedict left Rome on a helicopter at 7:30 AM, arrived at 9:30 AM, celebrated an outdoor Mass and was in the air again by 12:30 PM and back at the Vatican by 2:30 PM. Four hours in the air, three on the ground. He did not attend the gathering the evening before of fifty thousand Catholic young people who camped out and watched a light-show concert of contemporary Christian pop, and instead focused in his homily on his priority of moving toward unity with Orthodox Christianity. Benedict maintained his professorial style throughout, peering over his large reading glasses to hit another theme, that of today's Christians as a persecuted minority, just as they were under the Roman emperors. "Even without imperial vetoes," he said, "it's not easy for us either to live as Christians." He also took up the theme, from his installation Mass, of the bleakness of modernity. "From a spiritual point of view, the world in which we live, so often marked by runaway consumerism, religious indifference and by a secularism closed to transcendence, can seem like a desert."

About 400,000 people were expected for the closing Mass presided over by Benedict; organizers claimed 200,000 showed up, and security officials put the final tally at 100,000.[32]

When Benedict traveled to Germany in mid-August for World Youth Day, he was also walking in John Paul's footprints. John Paul began the event, a weeklong international jamboree for Catholic youth, in 1984, and it soon developed into a biennial event taking place on different continents. The audiences of young adults, ranging from a few hundred thousand to four million, gave John Paul an opportunity to be his crowd-pleasing best; to watch him at these events, more than perhaps any other venue, was to marvel at the intimate rapport one man could have with a throng of millions. John Paul was at turns funny and serious, profound and entertaining, and always riveting. No one should have to follow such an act. Benedict was blessed in that the 2005 event had been scheduled long in advance for Cologne, in his homeland, surely a neat bit of providence for a pope who would need a lot of help.

Yet Benedict made it apparent that he not only *could* not be like John Paul, but that he *would* not do so. Benedict did not hold an in-flight press conference with the Vatican press corps, as John Paul had enjoyed doing, and most noticeably he did not kiss the ground on his arrival. He scheduled fewer events and gave twelve addresses or homilies. During a 1980 visit to Germany, Pope John Paul II had given twenty-nine major talks over a similar period.

Benedict included on his schedule high-profile meetings with leaders of other Christian denominations to talk about ecumenism and with Islamic leaders to talk about terrorism, as well as a visit to a synagogue, just the second such papal visit in history (John Paul, of course, was the first), to meet with Jewish leaders in the country that engineered the Holocaust. As important as those encounters were, they took time and coverage away from the culmination of this biennial event, a huge outdoor Mass with an expected one million Catholic young people from nearly two hundred countries. In the days leading up to the pope's arrival, cardinals and bishops from around the world led catechism classes that reflected the tenor of most World Youth Days. Cardinal Angelo Scola of Venice, for example, read from Jack Kerouac's *On the Road* for ten minutes before launching into a discussion about faith.

Not Pope Benedict. At a vigil on the starry night before the closing Mass, the pontiff ignored a jongleur tossing hats in front of the altar—one of the John Paul pop touches that survived—and launched into a lengthy meditation, inviting his listeners "to that inner pilgrimage which is called adoration." He then slipped into the shadows without a trace of applause to mark his departure. The next morning on the huge meadow at Marienfeld, he presented a lengthy catechesis on the Eucharist, including a lesson on "the different nuances" of the words for adoration in Greek and in Latin. "The Greek word is *proskynesis*," he said, referring to "the gesture of submission, the recognition of God as our true measure, supplying the norm that we choose to follow." In Latin, he explained, the word "for adoration is *ad-oratio*—mouth to mouth contact, a kiss, an embrace, and hence, ultimately love. Submission becomes union, because he to whom we submit is Love." The subtleties were proper to a classroom but not so much to a public address system, and the pope's careful exegesis was largely lost on the multilingual crowd.

The biggest applause came at the mention of John Paul's name, and Benedict shushed attempts by the young people to chant his own name. In his meeting with seminarians Benedict never spoke of his own calling, in his meeting with Jews he never referred to his own background, and when a teenager at an encounter with young people asked him if he had any dreams as a child, he said he probably did not analyze his feelings much at that age. Some of the participants wanted to hug him, which John Paul would do in a heartbeat. But not Benedict. As Lubica Javonovic, a nineteen-year-old from Australia, said, "We had to be respectful."

The young people at the encounter did not dislike Benedict; in fact, they were rooting for him. But the change was obvious. "John Paul concentrated more on the relationship with the people. Benedict puts more weight on the message," Reinfried Rimmel, a German youth, told Catholic News Service. A staffer at the Vatican newspaper, *L'Osservatore Romano*, told a reporter, "Young people don't want to hear theology. They want to hear someone be a witness to the faith." Publicly, Vatican officials sought to put the best spin on Benedict's debut. "There were twelve apostles and each of them had his characteristics," said Cardinal Angelo Sodano, the Vatican's secretary of state. He noted that each of the 264 previous popes was different. "Some were more extroverted," he said, "some more reflective." Papal spokesman Joaquin Navarro-Valls was more explicit after Benedict's first day: "John Paul expressed himself in gestures; this pope gives great space to words. This will be a pontificate of concepts and of words."

And many of those words would be John Paul's. "My personal mission is not to issue many new documents, but to ensure that his [John Paul's] documents are assimilated," Benedict told Vatican Radio in October. "The Pope is always close to me through his writings: I hear him and I see him speaking, so I can keep up a continuous dialogue with him. He is always speaking to me through his writings."

The low-profile, high-concept papacy of Benedict was evident as his travel schedule emerged from John Paul's imprint and took on its own shape.

A return trip to Germany, this time to his native Bavaria, was planned for fall 2006, along with a May visit to Poland. One trip would capitalize on the guarantee of a warm welcome for Benedict from his fellow Bavarian Catholics, while the other would once again feed off the enduring popularity of the late John Paul II. A trip to Spain was a possibility, and perhaps to the Holy Land. A brief visit to Latin America and the United States in 2007 was also likely.

Benedict wanted to make a visit in November 2005 to Istanbul, the seat of the patriarch of Constantinople (the pre-Islamic name of Istanbul) and the "first among equals" in Eastern Orthodox Christianity. Healing the eleventh-century rift between Eastern and Western Christianity is a passion for Benedict, and a more realistic possibility than many other ecumenical dreams. There is little that separates these two communions theologically. The primacy of the pope in the authority structure of Latin-rite Christianity is the main stumbling block for the Eastern churches.

Ecumenical Orthodox patriarch Bartholomew of Constantinople had invited Benedict to the Turkish city shortly after his election. Benedict wanted to go for the November 30 celebration of the feast of St. Andrew, patron of the ecumenical patriarchate. Up until mid-September 2005, Vatican officials were confidently predicting that Benedict would make the trip. But the pope also needed an invitation from Turkey, a Muslim country. Here, Benedict's aura as pope could not blot out his track record as cardinal. Over the years, Ratzinger had delivered many harsh critiques of Islam. In 1997 he said of Islam, "One has to have a clear understanding that it is not simply a denomination that can be included in the free realm of a pluralistic society." And in two widely noted 2004 speeches, the cardinal said Turkey should be barred from membership in the European Union because it represented a Muslim rather than a Christian culture and because its history was one of constant conflict with Europe.

That angered Turkish leaders, and those comments alone would likely have thwarted an invitation. But during an August meeting with Islamic leaders in Cologne, Benedict was surprisingly blunt in focusing on the scourge of terrorism and their responsibility to help end it. In August he also held a secret meeting at Castelgandolfo, his summer villa outside Rome, with the Italian writer Oriana Fallaci, who was facing charges in Italy for insulting the Islamic faith. After 9/11, Fallaci, a renowned atheist, became a fierce critic of Islam and said Arab immigration to Europe—which she calls "Eurabia"—amounts to an "Islamic invasion" that Europeans are welcoming with "servility." She preferred Cardinal Ratzinger's hard-line approach: "I feel less alone when I read the books of Ratzinger," she told the *Wall Street Journal*.

News of Benedict's meeting with Fallaci leaked out in late August, however, and in mid September the Turkish government said Benedict was welcome to come, but in 2006, not 2005 as the pope wanted. In diplomatic terms that was a snub.

Such short-hop journeys are Benedict's style—low-key and infrequent, with a conceptual framework rather than a pastoral visit to the flock. Yet they are also forced on him by his age and health. Vatican insiders said the pontiff's doctors do not want him traveling much more than a few hours by plane because of circulatory problems that were a concern in the past.

In September 1991, Benedict spent ten days in the hospital after he suffered a hemorrhagic stroke that temporarily affected his vision. In August 1992, during a vacation in the Italian Alps, he was knocked unconscious when he fell against a radiator and bled profusely, also apparently the result of a small stroke. In the months after his election, Benedict looked tired on occasion, prompting some worry among Vatican officials and observers. A small group of Vatican officials wrote to the pope's personal secretary, Monsignor Georg Gänswein, to advise Benedict to slow down and perhaps consider bringing back the "gestatorial chair," or portable throne, which had not been used by popes in decades. But the new pope has also been careful not to overtax his health in travel and public appearances. That is part of his approach to the papacy, but he is also following the advice of his doctors. Where Benedict expends himself—and where his aides have difficulty reining him in—is in his exhausting predilection for writing and studying and overseeing the river of paper that streams forth from the Vatican. It is an impossible task, which may lighten as Benedict begins to place trusted collaborators in key positions, people to whom he can confidently delegate some tasks. Still, preserving his energies is a challenge for Benedict.

The Vatican already announced that the next World Youth Day, traditionally a biennial event, would be pushed to 2008, a three-year interval, and would be held in Australia. The Vatican, and Benedict himself, were careful not to promise his appearance at the event, and it is possible he might not make such a trip, which would make WYD 2008, a signature papal event for John Paul, the first ever without a pope in attendance. "I'm not sure it's absolutely essential [that the pope be present], but it helps make it an enormously important event," Sydney's Cardinal George Pell conceded, as he and other church leaders began laying the groundwork for what they anticipated would be a popeless World Youth Day.

In effect, much like the early apostles he hopes to emulate, Pope Benedict is restricted largely to the Mediterranean confines of what was once the Roman Empire but trying to reach a global audience that values presence over text. True, the world still comes to Rome. And this professor-pope could use his pulpit like a university podium. But when American Catholics were asked during the conclave what characteristics they would like to see in the next pope, more than 93 percent said he should be an expert communicator and almost 80 percent said he should be charismatic. But some things cannot be routinized, however powerful the traditions and mystique of the papacy.

Was John Paul II one of a kind? Was he an anomaly in the history of the papacy, never to be repeated? Is Benedict a return to normalcy, the set point for all future popes? And is that sufficient for the demands of preaching the Gospel today?

In our celebrity-saturated culture it would be easy to see the contrast between John Paul and Benedict as so lopsided as to be unfair, a comparison that obviously favors Wojtyla over Ratzinger. John Paul had such a winning personality that he would run away with any "Favorite Pope" sweepstakes. Yet popularity is no guarantor of success beyond the lifetime of the celebrity, or even during his lifetime, as many downward trend lines in Catholicism during John Paul's tenure show.

It is said that God has no grandchildren, that belief cannot be inherited like DNA. Surely every person must make a decision of faith for himself or herself, if that decision is to mean anything consequential. Within the Christian cosmos, however, Catholicism was able to shade that truism for longer than most churches. To be Catholic was to be so much more than "just" a believer. Catholicism was bound up in ethnicity and identity, it was being part of national heritage and an international community. In North America, especially, Catholicism was an immigrant faith and thus a bulwark against an often hostile host society. Long after members of other denominations loosened the ties that reflexively bound them to the faith of their fathers, Catholics were born, raised, and buried Catholic, and they still are to a greater degree than most other Christians.

But the world continues to change, irrevocably. George Weigel has called this the "post-Constantinian" era of Catholicism; in other words, for the first time since the fourth century, when Emperor Constantine granted state privileges to the Catholic Church, the papacy is without the temporal supports that assured it a permanent place in state and society, and made it the only religious option for many people. That has thrown the Catholic Church, and the pope, back on their spiritual resources to survive and flourish, a development that Weigel and most everyone else rightly welcome.

With the Barque of St. Peter adrift as never before, however, and in an everchanging culture, the great question pressing in on the church, and on Pope Benedict, is how to attract believers and reinvigorate the baptized. With his intellectual approach, Benedict is making a noble gambit by tossing out the anchor of truth and refusing to tack his sails to the prevailing winds. Under this pope, the world must come to Rome, not vice versa. It is tempting to argue that if the truth of a thing cannot convert hearts and minds, then so be it; those who reject the right path must face the consequences of their decision.

But from the beginning the apostles were not afraid to go out into the prevailing culture, engaging as well as challenging, being in the world though not of the world.

Yes, a new pope can surprise people. The day after Benedict was elected, his brother Georg, still amazed at the turn of events, shrugged when asked how his younger sibling might fare: "Maybe the sight of rejoicing people loosens one up," he told the AP. Perhaps, but even a looser Benedict would still be Joseph Ratzinger, certainly no Karol Wojtyla. That is obvious by now. The ambivalence that greeted Benedict when he emerged from the grayish smoke to greet the crowd at St. Peter's has dissipated. The surprise is that Benedict has shown less continuity with John Paul than expected. It is no surprise, however, that he has also shown far more continuity with his old self than many predicted. Ratzinger had a shorter distance to travel from cardinal to pontiff, literally and figuratively, than many earlier popes. He was practically a Roman already and had been John Paul's alter ego for decades. He is also a man convinced of his own consistency, whatever evolution others may read into his turbulent biography, and he is convinced of the rightness of the ideas he says he has always held.

Central to those ideas is the view that the modern world is a dark and dangerous place where believers venture at their peril, a throwback to the fortress Catholicism that prevailed before the opening of the Second Vatican Council. How very different that is from the intrepid spirit that Czeslaw Milosz saluted in his ode to John Paul on his countryman's eightieth birthday, a generous confidence that refused to shy away from the turbulent uncertainties of the age:

> You are with us and will be with us henceforth.
> When the forces of chaos raise their voice
> And the owners of truth lock themselves in churches
> And only the doubters remain faithful,
> Your portrait in our homes every day reminds us
> How much one man can accomplish and how sainthood works.[33]

Is one model superior to the other? In the immediate aftermath of Ratzinger's election as pope, it was said that John Paul filled the squares but Benedict will fill the churches—the *pontifex massmediaticus* giving way to the *vir ecclesiasticus*. One leading the faithful doubters, the other, the owners of truth. Yet the survival of Catholicism as it is traditionally understood, as a universal community of sinning saints on a pilgrim journey through history, means that the church cannot be limited to one arena or the other. A church that lives too much in one camp, in the world or in the sanctuary, is destined to dissipate into the social ether or shrivel into a hard husk of piety. For both realms to flourish, the border between the two must allow for safe and constant passage, so that Catholicism can help a modern world hungry for the church's wisdom and salvation, and that modernity, for all its perils, can bring its undeniable gifts to bear on a church that so desperately needs them.

But that frontier is also the battle line in a war in which Pope Benedict XVI has already taken sides, and with his election the faint hopes for a truce with the modern world, much less a collaboration, dimmed considerably.

Chapter Nine

JOYS AND HOPES,
GRIEFS AND ANXIETIES

By the 1960s, the Catholic Church's campaign against modernity had gone on for so long and with such tenacity that any hint of a truce, or any suggestion that contemporary developments might assist, rather than undermine, the mission of the faith, would have been regarded as a tectonic shift in Rome's antagonism to the postmedieval world. The rise of nation-states and the Protestant Reformation, the triumph of Reason in the Enlightenment and the apotheosis of Reason in the French Revolution, runaway democratization, and repeated military and political humiliations all took a heavy toll on the psyche and patrimony of the Vatican, especially the papacy. By the end of the nineteenth century, the popes were confined to a small patch of land on the far side of the Tiber, while Darwin and Freud were the toast of the Western world. In the next century, two brutal world wars emanating from Europe shredded Christendom's claims to moral supremacy and paved the way for a new god, Marxism, to ascend the throne. Capitalism, led by the United States, responded with entrepreneurial vigor, harnessing fantastical breakthroughs in science to construct a nuclear balance of terror that kept the peace only by threatening to annihilate creation in a single conflagration.

Never had the world seemed so dangerous, or so inimical to the Gospel preached by Roman Catholicism. Never had Roman Catholicism been so fearful of the world, so angry, and so inclined to lash out. Over the previous two centuries, popes seemed to condemn every innovation, from religious freedom to gas streetlamps (they would provide light for seditionists to gather and conspire). From the Syllabus of Errors promulgated by Pius IX in the nineteenth century to the multiheaded heresy of Modernism condemned by Pius X in the twentieth, Rome was coiled in a defensive crouch, a paranoid with real enemies.

In this context, any olive branch would have been noteworthy, but the revolution in Catholicism's stance toward modernity augured by Vatican II was nothing short of a marvel. The council was the most important event in the life of the church since the Counter-Reformation and the Council of Trent in the sixteenth century, and it remains so largely because it was the first council with a specifically *pastoral* focus, called not to combat a heresy or to define or enforce beliefs, but rather to reach out to the world in order to promote a more just society, as well as bringing the church's thinking in line with intellectual and theological trends.

The overarching mood of Vatican II was one of optimism, and that tone was set from the start by the historic address by Pope John XXIII at the opening of the council, in front of 2,600 bishops arrayed around the sanctuary of St. Peter's, before television cameras and a mass audience that had not existed the last time the Catholic Church held a council. Pope John confidently declared that the council would produce "new sources of energy" that would enable the church "to face the future without fear," and he dismissed the "prophets of gloom" who would say otherwise.

Such words from a Roman pontiff were in and of themselves momentous, and the faith-filled optimism of John's address electrified the imagination of the entire church and most of the bishops in attendance, who proceeded to put John's vision into action. The council produced sixteen major documents—four constitutions, which are the most authoritative, nine decrees, and three declarations. But the final constitution approved by the council was the one that anchored John's opening vision and remains the most memorable of the Vatican II statements, the manifesto officially titled "The Pastoral Constitution on the Church in the Modern World," but universally known as *Gaudium et Spes* for the original Latin of its inspiring opening words: "The joys and hopes, the griefs and anxieties of the men of this age, especially those who are poor or in any way afflicted, these are the joys and hopes, the griefs and anxieties of the followers of Christ. Indeed, nothing genuinely human fails to raise an echo in their hearts. For theirs is a community composed of men. United in Christ, they are led by the Holy Spirit in their journey to the Kingdom of their Father and they have welcomed the news of salvation which is meant for every man. That is why this community realizes that it is truly linked with mankind and its history by the deepest of bonds."

Gaudium et Spes takes up nearly one-quarter of the entire printed output of Vatican II—some 23,335 Latin words out of 103,000 all told—and no other document better embodies the spirit of the council, or the ongoing and increasingly divisive arguments over what Vatican II meant then and what it means for the uncertain future of the church.[1] *Gaudium et Spes* can be seen as the battle line along which the opposing forces in the church lined up then, and today, with one side promoting engagement with the world, particularly on issues of social justice, and the other anxious to keep modernity at arm's length. The struggle was prefigured at the document's birth, when some council fathers reportedly wanted to reverse the opening words so that the text would begin by referring to the *luctor et angor* (griefs and anxieties) rather than the *gaudium et spes* (joys and hopes).

The optimists won out, but it has been a struggle ever since, with one of the main antagonists to *Gaudium et Spes* then, as now, being Joseph Ratzinger.

While Ratzinger initially aligned himself with the progressive forces at Vatican II, the drafting of *Gaudium et Spes* was a primary wedge that began splitting the reform forces between those seeking renewal through *ressourcement* (recourse to the past) and those looking to *aggiornamento* (an updating) to refresh the faith. Ratzinger was firmly in the first camp. In the *aggiornamento* camp were the main authors of *Gaudium et Spes,* many of them friends and colleagues of Ratzinger's with whom he would later part company. Ratzinger's German rival, the Jesuit Karl Rahner, was a force behind the document. But the final text was very much a product of the leading French *periti,* such as Yves Congar, Jean Daniélou, and above all the Dominican Marie-Dominique Chenu. As Father Joseph A. Komonchak explained, Chenu was inspired by Pope John's exhortation to the church to discern "the signs of the times" in order to better present the church's timeless message. He called such modern developments *pierres d'attente,* toothing stones that jut out from a wall to provide a firmer grip for an addition. "It was an extension of the basic Thomist understanding of the relation between nature and grace to the realm of the social and historical," Komonchak wrote in an essay after Benedict's election.[2]

But Ratzinger was no Thomist, and as the British theologian Aidan Nichols points out, *Gaudium et Spes* was the low point of the council for Ratzinger and, in Ratzinger's mind, the cause of many of the troubles the church has since suffered as a result of its dalliance with modernity. In a 1965 commentary near the end of the council, Ratzinger scored *Gaudium et Spes* for leaving his beloved theology in a "conceptual deep-freeze" because the document—in his view—jettisoned Catholic beliefs in order to find "spiritual-ethical" common ground with other believers and nonbelievers and work for social betterment. With this generic do-goodism he felt the document blurred the lines between the church and the world. The text indulged "the fiction that it is possible to construct a rational philosophical picture of man intelligible to all and on which all men of goodwill can agree, the actual Christian doctrines being added to this as a sort of crowning conclusion." He preferred that it start with the Creed in order to set out the ground rules of belief that he thinks must precede any and every interaction with secular society. Otherwise, if the church and the world overlap so well, then why believe?

After the council, Ratzinger continued to point out what he saw as the document's fatal flaws. In subsequent commentaries, he lamented the fact that "the strong stress, deriving from Luther, on the theme of sin, was alien to the mainly French authors of the schema, whose theological presuppositions were quite different." (That a Catholic theologian was citing the Reformation's firestarter to criticize a Vatican council that sought to redress some of the complaints of Protestantism illustrates the many paradoxes of the day and within Joseph Ratzinger.) Ratzinger said *Gaudium et Spes* "is not at all prepared to make sin the center of the theological edifice."[3]

Postconciliar developments would only confirm Joseph Ratzinger's worst fears about the church's opening to modernity, as the modern world itself seemed to spin out of control, taking much of the church's once stable foundation down with it.

"Today it is regarded an act of pride, incompatible with tolerance, to think that we have really received the truth of the Lord," Ratzinger said in a 2004 interview. "However, it seems that, to be tolerant, all religions and cultures must be considered equal. In this context, to believe is an act that becomes increasingly difficult. In this way we witness the silent loss of faith, without great protests, in a large part of Christianity. This is the greatest concern."[4] The explosion of New Age faiths and sects, and the West's romance with the occult and alien traditions, especially Eastern religions, confirmed for him the dominance of a religious relativism that diluted Christianity. "In the 1950s someone said that the undoing of the Catholic Church in the twentieth century wouldn't come from Marxism but from Buddhism. They were right," Ratzinger said in the same 1997 interview in which he labeled Buddhism "an auto-erotic spirituality."

Compounding Ratzinger's distress was the fact that, at the same time as the church was suffering the ill effects of the council's *aggiornamento,* the world that the church was accommodating was itself growing darker and more inimical to truth and beauty and any remnants of decent behavior. A "contraceptive mentality" was leading to unbridled promiscuity, while divorce and abortion became not just legal but rampant. The drug culture, the social rebellions that had sent Ratzinger fleeing his university post, and a reflexive suspicion of authority that overnight replaced a reflexive respect for tradition undermined the stable world within which the church had flourished—and to which it preached—from generation to generation. "We have moved from a Christian culture to an aggressive and sometimes intolerant secularism," Ratzinger said in a November 2004 interview with the Italian daily *La Repubblica*. "A society from which God is completely absent self-destructs. We saw that in the major totalitarian regimes of last century."

The supplanting of religion by psychology was further evidence of modern man's narcissism, which led not to fulfillment but to despair, he often said. That was the fate of the hero of Hermann Hesse's novel *Steppenwolf,* a work Ratzinger appreciated for its keen diagnosis of the dangers of too much introspection, a German penchant that he assiduously avoids: "The novel . . . is actually about one person, but one who analyzes himself into so many personalities that the analysis finally leads to self-disintegration. . . . In other words, there aren't just two souls in one breast; man disintegrates altogether. I didn't read this to identify with it but as a key that with visionary power pierces through and exposes the problem of modernity's isolated and self-isolating man."[5]

Every aspect of modern, postconciliar culture, from pornography to rock music, was, for Ratzinger, a symptom of the crisis. It was no surprise, though bad timing for Benedict, that shortly after his election—and just as the sixth of the blockbuster Harry Potter young adult novels was being released—letters emerged from 2003 showing that then cardinal Ratzinger had praised a German author's attack on J. K. Rowling's books about the young wizard. "It is good that you enlighten people about Harry Potter, because those are subtle seductions, which act unnoticed and by this deeply distort Christianity in the soul, before it can grow properly," Ratzinger wrote to the author, Gabriele Kuby. That Ratzinger would so easily accept Kuby's negative assessment—he apparently never read the novels himself—contrary to the opinion of the vast majority of Catholics and church leaders and the culture at large, is indicative of his instinctive prejudice against contemporary developments.

If the cultural and ethical and intellectual developments of the contemporary world led Benedict to raise the church's gates against the oncoming barbarians, he was just as distraught about Catholicism's apparent willingness to harness its mission of social justice—the central thrust of *Gaudium et Spes*—to what he saw as inappropriate secular aims, a misalliance that could only undermine the faith without saving mankind.

For Benedict, the greatest sin of the modern world was its overly confident belief in progress, in the ability to improve conditions on earth, which represented a hubristic faith in man's power. Liberalism and Marxism, Ratzinger once said, are the two salient manifestations of this illusion, and the most dangerous because they posit a utopianism that foresees a secular paradise of perfected human beings in some soft-focus future. Not only does this vision deny the reality of sin, he argued, but it also attempts to usurp the power of God, who alone can create such a paradise. Moreover, it obviates the need for religion, if religion is seen as little more than a vehicle for social improvement.

Certainly, the Catholic Church always put its faith in Christ, not man, and in God's omnipotence in history. If Karl Marx and his fellow travelers thought they were constructing a world free of suffering, Catholics never believed they were replacing the work of Christ on the cross by eliminating the tragic condition of humanity. The poor will be with us always, Jesus said, but that doesn't free Christians from God's mandate to work for justice. As Nicholas Boyle, a Cambridge professor of German intellectual history, wrote in an essay published in 2005, on the fortieth anniversary of *Gaudium et Spes,* "The work to which the Christian can see the human race is called is not that of the gradual construction of a perfect world, but that of the permanent reconstruction of a world threatened and damaged by sin."[6]

Yet Cardinal Ratzinger did not read *Gaudium et Spes* that way, and his deep suspicion of social action by the church, represented by his antagonism to *Gaudium et Spes,* ran directly counter to the church's extensive teachings and traditions on social justice, which have for centuries provided perhaps the most distinctive and effective witness for the Catholic faith and the chief arena for the church's interaction with the secular world. Those teachings were given a powerful new impetus by Vatican II. "The influence of *Gaudium et Spes* extended beyond any single issue," said Father Bryan Hehir, an American priest who is one of the leading exponents of the church's social justice teachings. "It is impossible to understand the highly active and effective social engagement of the Catholic Church in the postconciliar era apart from this document."[7]

But the election of Ratzinger as Pope Benedict XVI, particularly after the energetic social apostolate of John Paul II, means that the church may be in for a sea change in its profile in the global culture—a shift that could have an enormous fallout given the evangelizing power of social action among the vast numbers of the world's poor, hundreds of millions of whom are Catholic.

Christianity's social justice teachings, if not always designated by that modern term, are a foundation stone of the church itself, and like the Christian faith, they draw on Jewish traditions that stressed the religious duty to pursue justice beyond acts of charity. The Old Testament is full of exhortations to reform society and to treat others as you would have them treat you. For advocates of social justice, however, the reigning motif is the Exodus story, the fulfillment of God's promise to deliver his people from slavery in Egypt to a land flowing with milk and honey.

While Jesus came to offer a new kind of liberation, one that looked to deliverance from sin and hope in life everlasting, he was also steeped in the wisdom of his Jewish forebears, and he preached about justice for the poor and oppressed forcefully, and more frequently than about any other topic in the Gospels. Poverty was bred in his bones. Jesus was born into a hardscrabble existence and raised in a backwater village under the boot of the Roman Empire. He took his message first to the poor, called his first apostles from the poor, and made "Blessed are the poor" his first words in the Sermon on the Mount. This was revolutionary in itself because at the time poverty was seen as a kind of a curse. Later in the Beatitudes he promises, "Blessed are they who hunger and thirst for righteousness, for they will be satisfied."

Jesus lived poor and with the poor, and he died poor and naked, unable to afford even a burial place. "The poor are accepted as constituting the primary recipients of the Good News and, therefore, as having an inherent capacity to understand it 'better' than anyone else," Father Jon Sobrino, a Jesuit who teaches at the University of Central America in El Salvador, has written.[8] (Sobrino was investigated by Ratzinger and the CDF in the early 1980s. In 1989 he happened to be out of town when six of his confrères were dragged into the courtyard of their residence by soldiers and murdered.)

Jesus said that responding to the cry of the poor and outcast, as much as belief in the one true God, was a condition of salvation. He told the rich man to sell all he had and give it to the poor if he wanted to get into heaven, because it would be harder for the rich to get into heaven than for a camel to pass through the eye of a needle. (The young man went away saddened, because he did not want to give up what he had.) In the Gospel of Matthew, Jesus foretells the Messiah's final judgment and astonishes his listeners by telling them that their fate will be reckoned by how they treated the poor, whom Jesus, the Messiah, identifies with himself.

Jesus's immediate followers took those words to heart, and in the early years of the church Christians were recognized as much for their care of the marginalized as for their new beliefs. That social commitment, inspired by the Old Testament prophets but given a broader scope by Christianity, helped fuel the astounding growth of the faith in the first centuries after Christ. When the Roman Empire collapsed in the Dark Ages, and with it the social and economic structures that kept its citizens fed, the Catholic Church took over many of the functions of food distribution and other services. Pope Gregory the Great (590–604 AD) kept a detailed list of every poor person in Rome and allocated weekly rations of food and wine and oil to each. To wealthy families fallen on hard times, he sent food from his own table (as a way to soften the embarrassment of their reduced state), and he had twelve poor people—the number of the apostles—dine at his table each day. Gregory had been a monk before his election, and very happily so (he was a great admirer and popularizer of Saint Benedict, Ratzinger's role model). But he was not about to "flee the world" when concrete needs beckoned.

In the Middle Ages, the church, assisted by Thomas Aquinas, the great codifier of natural law, further developed the notions of legal and social justice that would characterize its communitarian ethos, and the mendicant orders, like the Franciscans, put those principles into practice. "Always preach the Gospel," St. Francis of Assisi said. "Use words if you have to." The story is likely apocryphal, but it sums up the incarnational spirit of Catholic social teaching, which provides a sharp contrast to the more individualistic and capitalistic ethic embraced centuries later by Protestantism and its various offshoots. Still later, in the nineteenth century, the same abuses of unrestrained capitalism that inspired Karl Marx to write his *Communist Manifesto* prompted Rome to address the misery of its largely working-class flock (as well as spawning various Protestant social justice movements and the storied Social Gospel tradition).

The foundational document of the church's modern tradition of social justice teaching is Pope Leo XIII's 1891 encyclical *Rerum Novarum* (Of New Things), also called "On the Condition of Labor" and familiarly known as the Worker's Charter by masses of grateful Catholic laborers. Growing class divisions and a concern that the church was not addressing the needs of its people inspired Leo to put Catholic tradition behind the right of laborers to decent working conditions, to organize in unions, and to earn a just wage. Leo's encyclical inspired subsequent popes, whose social justice statements grew increasingly prophetic about the need to view economic justice and structural reform as Gospel imperatives. Pius XI in the 1931 *Quadragesimo Anno* (Forty Years After, meaning after *Rerum Novarum*), Paul VI in the 1971 *Octogesimo Adveniens* (The Eightieth Anniversary), and John Paul II in the 1991 *Centesimus Annus* (The Hundredth Year) all took Leo's encyclical as their starting point. Throughout the twentieth century, the popes pushed the realm of social justice from the national to the international plane with encyclicals like the two from John XXIII, *Mater et Magistra* (Mother and Teacher), issued on the seventieth anniversary of *Rerum Novarum*, and *Pacem in Terris* (Peace on Earth) in 1963.

John XXIII seemed to bring together in himself the two strands of Christian activism that the Catholic social justice tradition sought to combine— the hands-on pastoral work of countless religious and laypeople, and the clear principles setting out the mandate to change oppressive systems that deprive people of food, shelter, and work. A pontiff who never forgot his working-class roots, John left aides nonplussed when he insisted on visiting prisoners in jail. (He called them "sons and brothers.") But his pastoral sense also informed his passion for justice. When strolling through the Vatican gardens one day (he ordered that the gardens not be shut to others when he took a walk, as was done for previous pontiffs), he inquired of a laborer how he was making out. When the workman confessed that the Vatican didn't pay enough to feed his family, John vowed to do something about it. On hearing news of the pope's plans to boost the Vatican payroll, his aides protested, saying it would cut into the Holy See's charitable donations. "Justice comes before charity," he told them.[9] John elevated that principal to the global plane in *Pacem in Terris* when he wrote that peace is bound up with economic justice.

Paul VI took that still further in his great social encyclical, *Populorum Progressio* (On The Development of Peoples) from 1967, when he argued that "peace is not simply the absence of warfare." Therefore, he wrote, "development is the new name for peace" and, he said, part of God's plan. Delivering one of the most direct Catholic critiques of capitalism, Paul advocated fair and equitable trade, international cooperation to reduce the growing gap between rich countries and poor, and direct aid by rich countries to poor nations. And consistent with the example of *Gaudium et Spes,* Paul addressed his pleas not just to Catholics but to the entire world—to other Christians, other believers, and "all people of good will." The Catholic Church was declaring itself a partner in the global enterprise of justice.

John Paul II raised the church's social justice profile further still in his extensive writings (three of his fourteen encyclicals were dedicated to the topic) and above all in his powerful presence on the most important stages of world history. His rallying cries in Poland on behalf of the Solidarity trade union were world-shaking events, placing him, and his church, squarely on the path of political reform. During a visit to Assisi a month after his election, a voice from the crowd called out, "Long live the Church of silence!"—a reference to Catholics oppressed under communist rule. John Paul shot back, "There is no longer a Church of silence, because she speaks through the Pope!"[10] At his appearances at the United Nations and other venues of international governance, with his white cassock and papal bearing, John Paul magnified Pope Paul's cries against war and on behalf of human rights, placing the church's highest authority behind social change. Although such unprecedented involvement disturbed many church leaders, especially in Rome, John Paul did not care. At crucial junctures in Nicaragua, the Philippines, and around the world he was a fearless voice for change. "It is necessary to change something here!" he cried in Haiti, directly challenging the Duvalier regime, which was not long for this world.[11]

John Paul's campaign for social justice was based on the church's longstanding regard—observed in the breach on too many occasions, and solely in the catechism on too many others—for the innate dignity of each human being as created by God. For Catholics, that means protecting and fostering life, especially the lives of the poor, the marginalized, and the defenseless, from womb to tomb, and by working to change the conditions that undermine life as well as by performing acts of charity. The selfless life of Mother Teresa of Calcutta is probably the best-known example of Catholic social action, but her ministry to the poor and homeless is just one side of the equation. The other is rectifying the conditions that create poverty and other miseries. Such an all-encompassing "consistent ethic of life," or "seamless garment," as the late Cardinal Joseph Bernardin called it (referring to the unhemmed garment Jesus wore), helps to explain why Catholics are difficult to classify according to traditional political categories. Conservative on so many issues of personal morality, Catholics (or at least recent popes) would be considered radically liberal on many matters—much like the Gospels—because of the church's social justice teachings. John Paul II was the same mix of conservative and liberal, which helps to explain the wide range of feelings about him. However, undergirding everything he did was his emphasis on the God-given value and uniqueness of the human person, a tent that John Paul made the centerpiece of his pontificate, from his first trip and his first encyclical.

But John Paul's focus was also informed, as was so much of his teaching, by his life experience, especially his manual work during World War II. "I was a laborer for four years, and for me those four years of work are worth more than two doctorate degrees," he once said.[12] Despite his crusade against liberation theology, John Paul easily invoked such loaded terms as the "struggle" of the "oppressed" and "exploited" who suffer at the hands of the "powerful," and he expressed regret that the church did not speak out enough in support of the poor. He backed agrarian reforms, equitable property and wealth distribution, and a host of specific social welfare policies. He called for a radical correction in both communism and capitalism, and his campaign to reduce the debt of Third World countries was one of his signal achievements. He vowed "to leave nothing untried in serving the cause of justice and solidarity."

Of course, John Paul showed great blind spots, such as the lengths he would go to for justice in Eastern Europe as opposed to his much more equivocal approach in other regions, particularly his scorched earth approach, fueled by Cardinal Ratzinger, to liberation theology. Yet on balance John Paul "reshaped Catholic teaching on issues such as human rights, war and peace, and international economic justice," as Father Bryan Hehir said. "By reshaping, he did not contradict earlier teaching there, but he pushed it further."[13] In fact, at the behest of Latin American bishops, whose stake in social justice is enormous given the great needs of their region, John Paul commissioned a first-ever compendium of the social doctrine of the church, which was published in 2004. It includes more references to John Paul's writings and speeches than to all other popes combined, to all conciliar documents and church fathers, or even to biblical references. That was in part the result of the natural deference due a sitting pope. But the ratio also reflected John Paul's dedication to the issues.[14]

Benedict XVI took a sharply different view of the proper role of the church's social teaching before he became pope, and he maintained a much more hands-off approach after his election.

Benedict's more passive attitude stems both from his theology and from his conservative nature. He believes social justice movements, as opposed to acts of Christian charity, are risky because they can lead to an improper comingling of the spiritual and the secular, which can only corrupt the religious mission of the church and will probably lead to no discernible benefit to society anyway.

Benedict also believes that there is a danger in stressing social progress because it can induce sinful man to believe that he can accomplish God's work on his own. This can lead to pride, to a forgetting of God, and to a utopianism that replaces a biblical eschatology stressing Christ's irreplaceable role in determining the true end of history.

As Cardinal Ratzinger said in a 1985 interview, "It is . . . painful to be confronted with the illusion, so essentially un-Christian, which is present among priests and theologians, that a new man and a new world can be created, not by calling each individual to conversion, but only by changing the social and economic structures. For it is precisely personal sin that is in reality at the root of unjust social structures. Those who really desire a more human society need to begin with the root, not with the trunk and branches, of the tree of injustice."[15]

No passage better encapsulates Benedict's approach: an Augustinian emphasis on individual sinfulness as the source of the world's woes, and the absolute priority of right belief as an indispensable prerequisite to any effort to alleviate those woes. And even then such action should be limited in scope, avoiding grand schemes for societal change. "Ratzinger's Augustinian spirituality downplays man's earthly accomplishments and highlights instead the 'City of God,' the kingdom wrought by God's grace that is not of this world," wrote Father Thomas D. Williams, a leader of the strongly conservative Legionaries of Christ movement, in reviewing *Salt of the Earth,* a 1996 book-length interview given by then cardinal Ratzinger. "Borrowing John Courtney Murray's useful distinction between two valid Christian orientations, an incarnational humanism (which emphasizes Christianity's immanence and the close link between grace and the nature it perfects), and an eschatological humanism (which focuses on Christianity's otherworldliness and man's pilgrim condition), Ratzinger clearly leans toward the latter—whereas John Paul II tends toward the former."[16] Indeed, Ratzinger rightly noted in *Salt of the Earth* that John Paul saw *Gaudium et Spes* "as a maxim for his life."[17]

This distinction between two types of Christian humanism—engaged or detached—is a primary fissure running through the church since the council, particularly between the last pontificate and the present one. Benedict's clear affinity for a more "cloistered" Catholicism was apparent decades before his election. In 1984, for example, he criticized the "active" nuns, priests, and brothers, who led the church's efforts to promote social justice, for replacing "love of neighbor" with what Ratzinger called a worldly concept of "social welfare."[18] (He also critiqued the new "feminist mentality" of women religious, the popularity of Asian meditative techniques such as yoga and Zen Buddhism, and the acceptance of the psychoanalytic teachings of "profane professors," all of which, he said, undermine the faith.) The religious orders would strongly dispute the assertion that they are separating the two concepts, arguing that their social ministry is simply fulfilling the commandment of Jesus through the application of Catholic tradition and the teachings of Vatican II. Yet Benedict much prefers piety to activism, promoting the holy detachment exemplified by the contemplative religious who remains in the cloister. These monastics have "withstood very well because they are more sheltered from the *Zeitgeist*, and because they are characterized by a clear and unalterable aim: praise of God, prayer, virginity and separation from the world as an eschatological sign." That sentiment foreshadowed by two decades Ratzinger's adoption of St. Benedict, the father of Western monasticism, as his namesake. The monastic model is his preferred stance toward the culture and the world.

A sharp dispute more than a decade later between the Vatican and the German bishops over abortion counseling illustrated how Ratzinger's view played out in practice. The disagreement arose out of the reunification of Germany in the 1990s, which required the government to reconcile the former East Germany's liberal abortion laws with the former West Germany's more restrictive statutes. A compromise was reached by which abortion would be legal in the first twelve weeks of a pregnancy, but only after the woman had received counseling on her decision. If the woman decided to go ahead with the abortion, she was required to present a certificate at the clinic proving that she had been counseled. The Catholic bishops in Germany responded by setting up a counseling network funded in part by government money. Some twenty thousand women a year were visiting the church centers, and about five thousand of them every year opted not to have an abortion after their session. The rest were given a document certifying that they had been counseled and therefore could procure an abortion if they chose.

In 1997, Pope John Paul instructed the German bishops to end the counseling system because he saw it as effectively allowing the Catholic Church to sign off on legalized abortions. The German bishops, and an angry German laity, saw the system as a practical prolife policy that prevented five thousand abortions a year. A long-running struggle between Rome and the German hierarchy ensued, with Cardinal Ratzinger taking the lead for John Paul—an unusual task for the doctrinal chief, and one that would normally be given to the secretary of state, Cardinal Angelo Sodano. But Sodano was seen as too conciliatory to the German position. Ratzinger led the negotiations with the

German bishops, at one point curtly instructing them to end their association with the state in abortion counseling. In 1999 the bishops unanimously
rejected the Vatican's demand. But in 2000, after more Vatican pressure, the
hierarchy acquiesced, although they continued to explore ways to continue the
counseling. The episode further darkened Ratzinger's image in his homeland,
but the logic was inescapable to Ratzinger: even if the church counselors were
preventing five thousand abortions a year, they were participating in a sinful
system and thus cooperating in an objective evil.[19]

The sum of all Ratzinger's fears about everything that could go wrong with
the church's opening to modernity remained, as always, the scourge of liberation theology: "Since the phenomenon of liberation theology indicates a
lack of conversion in the Church, a lack of radical faith, only an increase in
conversion and faith can arouse and elicit those theological insights and those
decisions on the part of the shepherds [that is, the bishops] which will give an
answer to the magnitude of the question," Cardinal Ratzinger wrote in a 1984
statement that laid the groundwork for a full-scale assault on liberation theology. The individual, not the community, is the priority, he wrote, and "people,"
"experience," and "history" are concepts that should not be privileged in seeking Christian solutions to temporal problems such as poverty, disease, and
economic exploitation. For Joseph Ratzinger it was always the Cross of Christ,
rather than the Exodus of the Israelites, that should guide the Christian's social
action. As Ratzinger's theological soul mate, Hans Urs von Balthasar, once put
it, "Societal situations can be unjust, but in themselves they cannot be sinful.
Only those persons can be sinful who are responsible for the existence of such
situations and who continue to tolerate them even though they could abolish
or ameliorate them."[20]

This represented a significant departure from centuries of Catholic teaching on social justice. Yes, the church has always held that personal conversion
is the starting point and the indispensable motivation for correcting social injustices. The Catholic Church is a divinely mandated vehicle for the salvation
of souls, not just a social service agency. But baptized Catholics are enjoined to
manifest their conversion with corporal works of mercy; both the Old and the
New Testament make it clear that this is not an either/or proposition. "O man,
what is good, and what does the Lord require of you but to do justice, and to
love kindness, and to walk humbly with your God?" said the prophet Micah.
Jesus said that man does not live by bread alone. But man needs bread, too,
and wherever he went Jesus made sure everyone had enough to eat. For popes
and councils, implementing Christ's example in the world has meant work-

ing to correct "structural sin," especially in societies that purport to be largely Christian. Ratzinger's rereading, through the dark lens of liberation theology, distances the Catholic community from social policy more than ever, seeming to prefigure the "compassionate conservatism" that President George W. Bush, an evangelical Protestant, would promote nearly two decades later—a free-market model of individual initiative aimed at "unleashing armies of compassion" rather than promoting common policy goals.

True to his record as cardinal, Benedict as pope has continued to stress, with an emphasis that overshadows all else, the primacy of individual sanctity over communal action, warning of accepting the illusion of progress over the reality of suffering.

"It is not power but love that redeems us!" Benedict declared in his installation homily. "This is God's sign: he himself is love. How often we wish that God would show himself stronger, that he would strike decisively, defeating evil and creating a better world. All ideologies of power justify themselves in exactly this way; they justify the destruction of whatever would stand in the way of progress and the liberation of humanity. We suffer on account of God's patience. And yet, we need his patience. God, who became a lamb, tells us that the world is saved by the Crucified One, not by those who crucified him. The world is redeemed by the patience of God. It is destroyed by the impatience of man."

Promoting faith over action continued to be the pontiff's motif in the first months of his pontificate.

In July, for example, Benedict met with the bishops of Zimbabwe, the southern African nation ravaged by the unchecked abuses of President Robert Mugabe, who has been singled out by the world community and many in the nation's hierarchy as one of the most egregious violators of basic human rights. Zimbabwean archbishop Pius Ncube, in particular, was scathing in his criticism of Mugabe's policies, calling for peaceful opposition and facing regular harassment and death threats for his stands. In March, Mugabe won parliamentary elections widely viewed as fraudulent and subsequently denounced by the bishops' human rights office, though others in the divided episcopate continued to support Mugabe. Then, starting in May, Mugabe launched "Operation Drive Out Trash," one of his most appalling moves, in which riot police demolished homes and markets in shantytowns around major cities, leaving hundreds of thousands of poor people without food and shelter and subject to near-freezing temperatures at night. On June 20 the bishops released a sharply worded pastoral letter denouncing Mugabe's campaign as a "gross injustice done to the poor."

Yet when Benedict addressed the bishops in Rome, on July 4, he offered only anodyne support for their efforts, backing their pastoral letter, *The Cry of the Poor,* but offering no critique of his own on the issue. Most surprisingly, he seemed to endorse the fraudulent March vote, saying, "The recent elections have laid the basis for what I trust will be a new beginning in the process of national reconciliation." He spent most of the talk on internal church concerns, such as encouraging the bishops to improve their catechetics programs. Vatican observers were apparently not the only ones nonplussed by Benedict's remarks. Archbishop Ncube later revealed that he personally complained to Benedict about the pope's address and his implicit endorsement of the Mugabe government. "Seeing that you were so optimistic in your speech, it may be that you don't know what's happening: when I left, they were smashing houses," Ncube bluntly told Benedict. In a subsequent interview with the *Tablet* in early 2006, Ncube said he himself had given Benedict a sheet detailing the dire situation and abuses before the pope gave his talk. "For me, every tacit approval is driving one more nail into the coffin of many Zimbabweans," he said.[21]

Contrast Benedict's approach with the steady pressure Pope John Paul kept on the apartheid issue in South Africa through the 1980s, appealing for the release of Nelson Mandela and clearly giving his support to the country's activist hierarchy. In recalling John Paul after the pope's death, Cardinal Wilfrid Napier of Durban said that "it was quite clear that the church here had to take a 'political stand' on the situation of apartheid," and he said that during the bishops' visits to John Paul at that time "he stated quite clearly to us that when it came to questions of justice, the Church had to take a stand. We felt affirmed in the positions that we had been taking then."

Benedict's approach seems quite different. Later in July, Filipinos were shocked to learn that the Vatican, through Benedict's emissary, had admonished the hierarchy of the Philippines for joining in widespread calls for the resignation of President Gloria Macapagal Arroyo, who was facing impeachment on election fraud charges. The Vatican's reprimand reportedly cut short an effort by the bishops to press Arroyo to resign. The church in the largest Catholic country in Asia had been instrumental in helping to topple two previous corrupt presidents, most notably Ferdinand Marcos in 1986. John Paul's 1981 visit to the Philippines was credited with helping to launch the "People Power" movement that ousted Marcos, and John Paul remained enormously popular, drawing a crowd of four million when he returned in 1995. In 2005, after the bishops issued a neutral statement on Arroyo at Benedict's behest, she praised them as a "collective voice of moderation and temperance at this time of national soul searching."

In a similar vein, speaking to a group of bishops from some of the poorest regions of Mexico, Benedict said that societal woes represented "a profound crisis due to the loss of the sense of God and the absence of the moral principles that must govern the life of every man," and urged them to preach the Gospel more effectively as an antidote to "social sins." "The separation between the faith professed and daily life of many is one of the most serious errors of our times," Benedict said. In a private encounter with a Mexican prelate whose Gulf Coast diocese includes subsistence fishermen who struggle to survive, Benedict suggested that "we promote businessmen more so that they will generate sources of employment." In an address to the new ambassador to the Vatican from Paraguay, one of South America's poorest countries, Pope Benedict pledged that the Catholic Church in Paraguay would carry out its mission "without seeking to meddle in the nation's politics in any way."

Even Benedict's August address to Islamic leaders in Germany focused on the problems of terrorism and religious intolerance suffered by Christians in many Muslim countries and pointed to personal failings, rather than social conditions, as the cause. While John Paul frequently condemned terrorism, he did not link it directly to a religion. In meeting with Islamic groups, John Paul emphasized areas of cooperation and commonality. As he put it once to Muslim leaders, it should "never be forgotten that situations of oppression and exclusion are often at the source of violence and terrorism." That was very *Gaudium et Spes*.

Perhaps the most unusual aspect of Benedict's focus on the priority of right belief, on orthodoxy, is the fact that he has often prioritized holiness not only over traditional social welfare concerns but also above many of the hot-button issues of personal morality from which John Paul never shied away.

A month after Benedict's election, for example, Italy held a referendum on whether to overturn certain aspects of its restrictive fertility laws. The Italian bishops led a campaign of abstention, rather than a "no" vote, because if fewer than half of eligible voters cast ballots, as frequently happens in national referendums, the results would be discounted. As the vote approached, Benedict only obliquely referred to the issue, telling the Italian bishops in a speech that they are "committed to illuminate the choice of Catholics and of all citizens in the imminent referendum on assisted procreation." The referendum in fact did not garner the necessary 50 percent, which was no surprise but which was mistakenly hailed as a victory for Benedict and an augury of further church efforts to restrict the country's abortion laws. Italian church leaders knew better, discounting somewhat the role of the church in the politically apathetic country—this was the fourth referendum in a row since 1999 that failed for lack of voter turnout—and dampening speculation about an anti-abortion campaign. "We are certainly opposed to abortion, but we don't want to change the law," said Cardinal Camillo Ruini, president of the Italian bishops' conference. That hardly sounded like the proxy of the moral crusader most expected Pope Benedict to be.

An autumn 2005 campaign against Italian moves to legalize a form of civil marriage for cohabitating adults or homosexuals ran a similar course. Benedict issued his standard defense of traditional heterosexual sacramental marriage and his condemnations of homosexual unions designed to look like marriage. But Vatican leaders also let it be known that they would be amenable to domestic partnership laws that would give rights to same-sex partners and cohabiting couples. In fact, Benedict's most controversial action as the new primate of Italy was his August call to keep crucifixes in public buildings and sites in the Roman Catholic country—a reminder of the "splendor of God in one's face" that he said was integral to finding common ground in the public square. Benedict was similarly low-key regarding the first test of his papacy's profile in the public square, a move by the Spanish parliament to legalize gay marriage. While Benedict made it crystal clear, as he had as Cardinal Ratzinger, that he found same-sex unions unacceptable—an expression of "anarchic freedom" that threatens the future of the family, as Benedict said—he left it up to the Spanish bishops and lower-ranking officials to oppose the law, which passed in July.

This strategy partly reflects the fact that protocol requires that a pope must be more circumspect in his language than a cardinal. And Benedict's approach also reflects his desire to lower the personal profile of the pope, to deploy his version of collegiality and decentralization—namely, letting a nation's bishops, not the Roman pontiff, figure out how to defend church teachings. But it also demonstrates his priorities.

The most notable illustration of Pope Benedict's new emphasis was his four-day trip to Germany for World Youth Day in August. In a dozen speeches to a variety of audiences, Benedict said nothing about social justice. He never mentioned abortion or birth control, or sex at all, even avoiding the issue of celibacy in his talk to seminarians. Nothing on gay marriage or euthanasia or biotechnology. This represented a signal departure from the style of Pope John Paul, whose speeches and homilies during his trips abroad were like those old roadside Burma Shave ads—a reference to family life here, social welfare there, abortion in the next talk, human rights later, and so on, until it all added up to a comprehensive survey of Catholic teachings on how to be good and how to get the rest of the world to follow along. Benedict, on the other hand, is going back to fundamentals, back to the "why" of being good, which is, or should be, based on a belief in God. If orthodoxy comes first, society will follow of its own accord. "I think he will speak less about sexual morality to avoid the impression that the church is always focused on these issues," said Heinz-Joachim Fischer, a German journalist in Rome and longtime friend of Benedict who authored a book after his election, *Pope Benedict XVI: A Personal Portrait.*[22]

Long before his election, Benedict said that relativism—the idea that one man's truth is as good as another's—was the central crisis of modern culture, and as pope he aims to halt that trend by reinvigorating the faith and reconstituting the very idea of holding a firm belief in a divine, unchanging, and uncompromising truth. But that starting point is also where Benedict's agenda ends, and it is a powerful indication that the great era of Catholic social activism may be drawing to a close. "The saints," Benedict told young people gathered in Cologne for an evening eucharistic adoration, "are the true reformers. Now I want to express this in an even more radical way: only from the saints, only from God does true revolution come, the definitive way to change the world.

"In the last century we experienced revolutions with a common programme —expecting nothing more from God, they assumed total responsibility for the cause of the world in order to change it. And this, as we saw, meant that a human and partial point of view was always taken as an absolute guiding principle. Absolutizing what is not absolute but relative is called totalitarianism. It does not liberate man, but takes away his dignity and enslaves him.

"It is not ideologies that save the world, but only a return to the living God, our Creator, the guarantor of our freedom, the guarantor of what is really good and true. True revolution consists in simply turning to God who is the measure of what is right and who at the same time is everlasting love."

From his installation in April to World Youth Day in August to the Synod on the Eucharist in October, Benedict kept the focus on holiness in the opening year of his pontificate. Even the Vatican's annual World Peace Day in January 2006, traditionally a stage for a church campaign on some aspect of social justice, such as Third World debt or the arms trade, reflected Benedict's pietist approach: "In Truth—Peace" was the theme the new pope chose, because "truth enlightens, it allows one to discern the path of genuine human relationships, to correct errors, to be reconciled with oneself and with others, and to be transparent in negotiations and faithful to one's word."

At his installation as pope in April, Benedict drew laughs by declaring that he was not there to present a program of governance. But on reflection that deeply Christological homily was his agenda. In presenting a volume of Benedict's collected addresses from World Youth Day, a book titled *God's Revolution*, aides to Benedict stated that those addresses formed the "pastoral program" of Benedict's pontificate, which was summarized with three key verbs: "seek, find and adore Christ, the Redeemer of mankind." The book had been published, the Vatican said, because there was so much focus on the Youth Day events themselves that Benedict wanted his words collected so that they could be "read, reread and reread again patiently." Again, it was content that must lead to an experience of Christ, more than the other way around. Or, as George Weigel put it, "This is a man who knows you have to re-convert Europe from the head down."

In some ways, Benedict is as much the product of a trend as its agent, because in the years leading up to his election bishops around the world, and particularly in the United States, were already beginning to move the focus of the church away from engaging the culture at large and toward an internal focus on shoring up the faith inside the church. In the 1980s, the American bishops produced a series of prophetic and profound explorations of challenges facing the contemporary world, most notably a 1983 pastoral letter on war and peace and a 1986 pastoral letter on Catholic social teaching and the U.S. economy titled, "Economic Justice for All." Both letters were truly countercultural, but they also offered inspiring alternatives to the prevailing culture that were grounded in Catholic tradition and energized by hope and a call to activism.

However, the political and social conservatives who increasingly came to dominate the Catholic forum had an open line to Rome, and especially to the CDF's Cardinal Ratzinger, who was instrumental in hobbling the bishops' conference juridically and in the political maneuvers that led to the appointment of bishops more amenable to Rome's preference for doctrinal issues at the expense of social activism. Over the 1990s, while the bishops continued to release statements on various social issues, their once unified voice was muted by internal differences and their focus shifted to the easier targets of sexual immorality, doctrinal dissent, and remonstrating with the lower clergy and the laity for not following the rubrics of the Mass and the catechism. When the clergy sexual abuse crisis erupted in 2002, revealing many bishops to have been enablers who allowed predator priests to roam through parishes unsupervised, the American hierarchy responded not by cleaning its own house but by cracking down on priests and insisting that the root cause of the scandal was a lack of fidelity among American Catholics. They had a powerful ally for their cause in Rome. "I think the essential point is a weakness of faith," Cardinal Ratzinger said in a 2003 interview about the cause of the scandal. "So, two things are essential: Conversion to a profound and deep faith, with a life of prayer and sacraments, and clear moral teaching and awareness of the teaching that the Church has the Holy Spirit and can give us the way."[23]

Likewise, the American bishops explored ideas such as calling a plenary council that would find ways to better instruct Catholics in the faith, and issuing documents encouraging Catholics to avoid artificial contraception. Burdened by bankruptcies due to huge payouts in sexual abuse cases and by the hemorrhaging of their own credibility, the bishops today "increasingly ask whether it is now necessary to *rebuild* the Church in America, through reform and renewal," Milwaukee archbishop Timothy Dolan, an up-and-comer in the hierarchy, said in an October 2004 lecture. "They wonder if we need to start internally, concentrating first on pastoral issues such as widespread catechetical illiteracy, the collapse of marriage and family life, the restoration of a 'culture of life,' genuine liturgical reform, a return to the sacrament of penance, a national commitment to obey the third commandment, and the promotion of authentic renewal in the lives of our priests and religious.... Bishops today seem to prefer to do this prayerfully, patiently, and away from the blinding light of the media."[24]

In a 2005 interview with the *National Catholic Reporter* after Benedict's election, Archbishop Joseph Fiorenza, a former president of the United States Conference of Catholic Bishops, acknowledged that many American bishops had been accused of placing too much emphasis on *Gaudium et Spes* and its call to work for justice, and not enough on Vatican II documents that dealt with purely religious topics, such as ecclesiology. "I think that's unfair, because I think we've done both. I think we'd make a mistake if we didn't do both," Fiorenza said. "We cannot forget *Gaudium et Spes*. It would be a tragedy if we don't involve ourselves in issues coming to the fore, such as immigration. If we don't show Hispanics that the church is committed to them we're going to lose them, and this too is part of evangelization.... Today, however, there are probably more bishops in the conference who would tend to accent *Dei Verbum* [the council document on divine revelation] rather than *Gaudium et Spes*. I think that's a fair statement."[25]

That trend seems likely to continue, since the younger generation of priests and seminarians, who are the talent pool for future bishops, tend to be more conservative than the socially conscious prelates of the Vatican II era. The Vatican also seems to be ensuring they stay that way.

With the eruption of the clergy sexual abuse scandal in America, Rome authorized a Vatican-supervised inspection, called an apostolic visitation, of all 229 seminaries and houses of priestly formation in the United States, to determine what, if anything, had gone wrong in the education of priests. With Benedict's blessing, the visitation got under way in autumn 2005. Apart from issues of sex and chastity (with a special focus on gay seminarians, whom the Vatican seemed to believe, contrary to all evidence, incapable of chastity), the visitation was also aimed at gauging the overall formation of seminarians, and the guidelines for the inspectors, contained in a document called *Instrumentum Laboris,* were remarkable in their almost total focus on issues of doctrine, devotion, and orthodoxy, with hardly a word about pastoral practices and not a whisper about social justice.

The nearly one hundred questions posed to all seminarians and faculty dealt with their fidelity to the church's magisterium (teaching), their understanding of moral theology, and whether anyone—teacher or student—seemed prone to dissent. The seminarians were asked about their sex lives and those of their fellow students and faculty, about the frequency with which they attended Mass and confession, and whether they prayed the Liturgy of the Hours. They were asked about their devotion to Mary and the saints, whether they recited the Rosary, and how often they practiced eucharistic adoration and other "exercises of piety." With this exclusive focus, the Vatican seemed to signal that it was more interested in forming a generation of priests who could recite the catechism than one that understood the pastoral realities of *Rerum Novarum.*[26]

If Benedict's election appears to mark another blow to the fortunes of those pushing for a more socially engaged church, the battle is not quite over.

From a historical perspective, an era of contention is not unusual after an event as important as a churchwide council. It takes years, even decades, for Catholicism to assimilate the teachings of a general council, and the process can be fraught with conflicts, even schisms. Hence, the period after Vatican II has proved to be very polarizing, and council documents and debates continue to be the framework in which conservatives and liberals work out their respective gripes and agendas. This is not surprising given that Vatican II was a pastoral rather than a dogmatic council, one born of Pope John's "sudden flash of inspiration" and concluded with its capstone document, *Gaudium et Spes,* which focuses on a discernment of the spirit of the age. *Gaudium et Spes,* much like the council itself, is a template for the church's ongoing approach to modernity more than a final word, an attitude more than a doctrine. That orientation leaves much room for interpretation, and thus argumentation, which the church has provided in abundance. All sides invoke the council, and all use the same terms—collegiality, communion, People of God, deposit of faith, and the like. But as always happens in religious exegesis, they mean vastly different things by the same terms. And today the battle is sharper than ever.

The argument for the continuity rather than the creativity of the council is in keeping with Benedict's long effort to deflate the optimism of John XXIII and *Gaudium et Spes*, as well as the hopes of the champions of *aggiornamento* who take Vatican II as a touchstone for progressivism. Yet the faith-filled energy and missionary impulse of the council inspired a generation of Catholics to reach out to the world in dialogue, not necessarily to be co-opted but to sanctify the world and to learn from it in return. Yes, Catholicism likes to define itself as countercultural, and given the state of modern culture, especially since the 1960s, that is often an undeniable virtue. But in identifying the joys and hopes and griefs and anxieties of mankind with those of Jesus—language never before proclaimed by Rome—the church declared that there is also much in contemporary society that is good and even sacred, especially the people of the contemporary world whom the church exists to serve. A dour Christianity led by "prophets of gloom" who cannot engage the good in humanity and in the world is not likely to spark the enthusiasm needed to fulfill the great commission to spread the Gospel.

As he opened the October 2005 Synod on the Eucharist, a gathering of 250 bishops from around the world to discuss the sacrament that is the "source and summit" of the church's life, Pope Benedict's sermon—like his homily before the conclave in April—seemed a shadowed counterpoint to Pope John's luminous words more than four decades earlier. Benedict chastised modern man for wanting "to possess the world and our own life in an unlimited manner," and asked, "Is not our life often, perhaps, more vinegar than wine? Self-pity, conflict, indifference?"

Once again, Benedict drew an exclusive bead on "the Church in Europe, the Church of the West in general," saying Western Christians are under "the threat of judgment" unless they repent. "We would do well to allow this warning in all its seriousness to resonate in our souls," Benedict said.

Benedict has protested that he is not a pessimist but rather a "realist" who is describing circumstances as they are—he can do no other. Optimism, Benedict warned the Austrian bishops in a November 2005 address, "is always a lure for us . . . an obstacle to calling things by their names with complete objectivity and without embellishment." As Australian cardinal George Pell, one of Benedict's allies in reasserting orthodoxy, puts it, Pope Benedict XVI "does not seem to share those surges of optimism which touched Pope John Paul II once in a while"—as if an upbeat outlook were a bit of lunacy that passes with the application of a cold compress to the forehead.[27] Benedict himself simply dismisses labels like "pessimistic" and "optimistic" as "emotional categories not worthy of mention." As he once put it, "If someone is analyzing a community situation he should not ask if he is 'pessimistic' or 'optimistic' but rather he should look for certain parameters which throw light on developing tendencies in the community and thus on its state of health."[28] An expert diagnostician, always rigorously clinical, Benedict can say he is not a pessimist, but in his undifferentiated critiques of modernity, which lump together everything from human cloning to Harry Potter, and in his diffident attitude toward the church's social mission, he comes off as not just countercultural, but anticultural, and even fatalistic.

"Today more than ever the Christian must be aware that he belongs to a minority and that he is in opposition to everything that appears good, obvious, logical to the 'spirit of the world,' as the New Testament calls it," he has said. "Among the most urgent tasks facing Christians is that of regaining the capacity of nonconformism, i.e., the capacity to oppose many developments of the surrounding culture. In other words, we must revise this euphoric view of the early post-conciliar era." For Benedict, the *fuga mundi,* or flight from the world, practiced by ancient hermits and monastics like Saint Benedict, is the best option for believers who want to remain true to the faith.[29]

In 1975, a decade after the close of Vatican II, Pope Paul VI wrote, "The split between the Gospel and culture is without a doubt the drama of our time, just as it was of other times." Pope Benedict would certainly agree. But Pope Paul, and John Paul after him, did not respond to that drama by closing the church up in a fortress. As Paul wrote in that 1975 exhortation, "The kingdom which the Gospel proclaims is lived by men who are profoundly linked to a culture, and the building up of the kingdom cannot avoid borrowing the elements of human culture or cultures. Though independent of cultures, the Gospel and evangelization are not necessarily incompatible with them; rather they are capable of permeating them all without becoming subject to any one of them. Therefore every effort must be made to ensure a full evangelization of culture, or more correctly of cultures." If culture is the main arena of the church's mission, then the church must be prepared to engage and convince, rather than just presenting a take-it-or-leave-it package of dogmas.

Cardinal Ratzinger liked to quote Goethe's observation that "the one and only real and profound theme of the world and of human history—a theme to which all others are subordinate—remains the conflict between belief and unbelief," and as Pope Benedict he has followed his compatriot's maxim, stressing the priority of a firm belief to the exclusion of many of the other riches of the Catholic tradition. Yet Benedict does not seem to understand that Goethe's battle is one that a great many modern men and women find either tiresome or tragic or simply beside the point. The din of intolerant moralists with feet of clay and the bloody wars carried out in the name of God lead much of the world to turn a deaf ear to the pieties of true believers. Moreover, most people today do have a belief of one sort or another—they just want to find a home worthy of their faith. In that context, a church racked by scandal, especially across the English-speaking world, should see its social justice mission as a more powerful witness than ever, the witness of concrete action over words.

Since their founding in the thirteenth century, the Dominicans have earned a reputation for creating comprehensive, if abstract, systems of moral theology that they would then preach—their initials, O.P., stand for *Ordo Praedicatorum*, or Order of Preachers—with great vigor to audiences who were impressed with their zeal even if they did not always understand the content.

Today the Dominicans, God bless them, are the first to poke fun at their reputation for moral abstraction, with jokes like the one about the man who was flying about the countryside in his hot-air balloon until his gondola got stuck in a tree, leaving him stranded and unsure of his whereabouts. The balloonist soon spotted a monk walking along the road below him and called out, "Excuse me, sir, but can you tell me where I am?" The fellow looked up and replied, "You're in a tree." "Ah, you must be a Dominican," said the balloonist. "How did you know?" asked the perplexed friar. "Because," said the frustrated balloonist, "what you say is perfectly true, and perfectly useless."

Whether Benedict likes it or not, the reality is that today more than ever, men and women consider that the truth of beliefs is proven not by words alone but by the practical application of beliefs to the realm of justice. Sermons, however beautiful and well-crafted, are just more hot air for many people and are too often seen to be platitudes preached by so-called paladins of orthodoxy. Yes, the high-end theology of the sort practiced and preached by Pope Benedict is of great importance to the faith and will be immensely attractive to many people—most of them, unfortunately, already in the choir of believers convinced of the rightness of Benedict's ideas.

Since the earliest days of Roman Catholicism, people have found a home in the church through different doors, drawn by Catholic art, tradition, liturgy, philosophy, community, and, yes, Catholicism's unshakable and unchanging core of beliefs. But the church's tradition of social justice has a legacy of evangelization that is just as powerful and just as storied.

In the industrialized world where Benedict wants to focus his crusade for orthodoxy, social justice, if too often overlooked, is part of the Catholic DNA, and it continues to attract people to the church who might otherwise never have darkened the door of the sanctuary, or bothered to listen to one of Pope Benedict's extended sermons on the undeniable transcendence of the Christian message. Catholic hospitals, orphanages, refugee services, soup kitchens, AIDS clinics, human rights offices, antiwar and antipoverty campaigns, and innumerable other ministries constitute rare points of contact across the social and economic divides in our fragmented world. They join those who need to help others together with those who need help, all under the umbrella of a service that exists for the greater glory of God, offering the opportunity of sanctification for all, those who serve and those who are served.

In the developing world, the Catholic social justice apostolate is more than just a missionary tool or a means of engagement. It can be a life-or-death imperative—for people living on the brink and for the church itself. Scholars like Philip Jenkins, author of *The Next Christendom: The Coming of Global Christianity,* note that Catholicism, and Christianity as a whole, is growing so fast in the southern hemisphere that by 2050 some eight in ten Catholics will live in Asia, Africa, and Latin America. If Catholicism really is dying in Europe and the industrial North, as Benedict believes, then it is all the more important that the church not delay in addressing the needs of those continents, both spiritual and material. The disappointment that so many in the Third World expressed at Benedict's election was a sign of the hopes that had been raised that the church's leadership would for the first time in history recognize their enormous presence in the community of faith and put a stronger focus on issues of economic and social justice. Those expectations were not assuaged by the revelation that an Argentine cardinal finished second in the conclave voting. All of this would seem to militate for a vigorous approach toward social justice—especially since Benedict is a nearly eighty-year-old pope who will likely spend little time in the Southern Hemisphere.

Such a reorientation does not seem to be in the offing, however.

As head of the CDF, Joseph Ratzinger expressed deep satisfaction that his campaign against liberation theology had protected the faith in Latin America and strengthened the church by reasserting the primacy of an orthodoxy un-sullied by ideological entanglements. Yet the reality is that millions of Latino Catholics have fled the Catholic Church since the Vatican's "victory" over lib-eration theology, disillusioned by the church's sudden quiescence on social justice and often drawn to the various Protestant denominations and sects that hold out the fool's gold of the Gospel of Wealth and the emotional payoff of entertaining worship services. At the October 2005 Vatican Synod on the Eucharist, Brazilian cardinal Claudio Hummes, who was considered a leading Latin American candidate at the conclave a few months earlier, noted that the Catholic share of Brazil's population had fallen steadily from about 90 percent in the 1960s to 83 percent in 1991 and 67 percent today. "We ask ourselves with anxiety: how much longer will Brazil be a Catholic country?" Hummes told the assembly, with Benedict looking on. "Many indications say the same is true for all of Latin America, and also here we ask ourselves: How long will Latin America be a Catholic continent?"

Benedict himself has lamented these "sects," his term for free-range Protes-tantism; once in his homily at the start of the conclave that elected him pope, and later that summer in a speech to priests in northern Italy, he spoke of the challenge to Catholicism in Africa, where Protestants often "present themselves as the best, the simplest and the most accommodating form of Christianity."

Yet it is often those same conservative Protestants with whom Benedict and his allies make common cause in the industrialized North—on issues such as banning abortion, gay marriage, condom distribution, and the like—who in the developing world continue to aggressively proselytize the very Catho-lics that Benedict is supposed to shepherd. Pope Benedict has vowed that the church under his direction will not "meddle" in politics, yet his willingness to try to influence political decisions on matters relating to sexuality and bio-technology, for example, also leaves many wondering why he would not bring some of that activism to social welfare issues.

It is important to recall that in his powerful jeremiad at the Mass before the cardinals went into conclave, when Cardinal Ratzinger diagnosed the ills of the modern world and the challenges to the church from the "dictatorship of relativism," he reserved not a single word for the masses of the poor and mar-ginalized groaning under the weight of economic and social injustice across the globe.

These souls—billions of people in underdeveloped nations, making up the bulk of the world's population and more than two-thirds of the Catholic flock—are desperate for the powerful voice of the church to ease their suffering.

Given the push for Cardinal Jorge Mario Bergoglio in the conclave that elected Benedict, it seems probable that the next pontiff will be a Latin American with a more engaged attitude toward social justice. But the cry of the psalmist—"How long must we wait, O Lord!"—is also the cry of the world's poor today. The carefully measured statements of an octogenarian German theologian delivered from faraway European pulpits, counseling patience and suffering as pathways to right belief, with hardly a nod to the structural sins that oppress so many, does not sound like the answer they are looking for or deserve. As theologian Christopher Ruddy put it, "The church and the world seem to need a St. Francis as much as a St. Benedict."[30]

Though the church's outreach to the world can be a source of inspiration for Catholicism, Benedict is right when he says that the church's future is grim unless it undergoes an internal renewal. For Benedict, however, that reconversion seems to be a strictly spiritual phenomenon achieved through prayer rather than one aided by the reforms that so many Catholics, especially in the postmodern West that Benedict views as his arena of principal concern, say are necessary for the institution to restore the trust of its flock and regain a positive vision for the future of faith.

This internal church focus, as opposed to the church's role in the wider culture, is the other side of the dilemma of modernity for Benedict—the demands of most contemporary Catholics, especially in places like the United States, for a church that will open itself to debate and to changes that are consonant with the spirit of the age but not inimical to the faith. And it is here, in the push for justice within the church, that Benedict seems most resistant to change.

Chapter Ten

AMERICA AND THE BATTLE FOR CATHOLICISM

I n Pope Benedict's quest to replenish the Catholic faith amid the desert of modernity, the American church presents him with the best opportunity for success and the biggest challenge to his firm views on how that faith should be practiced and, indeed, what it means to be Catholic. That is because the nearly 70 million Catholics in the United States, like their fellow citizens across the American landscape of faith, are the most observant believers in the secular world but also the most deeply imbued with the liberal civil religion of their homeland. The sociologist of religion Peter Berger has observed that if India is the most religious country in the world and Sweden the most secularized, then the United States must be a nation of Indians ruled by Swedes.

This paradox has fed the strange dynamic by which the Vatican is constantly remonstrating with its most loyal and influential flock, always on guard in case American Catholics should become, in Rome's view, more American than Catholic. The confrontation has alternately simmered and flared since Catholics arrived in North America in colonial times, and a prime example of how those tensions have persisted is the long-running dispute that Cardinal Joseph Ratzinger had with the flagship Jesuit journal in the United States, *America*—a conflict that culminated when he became Pope Benedict XVI but which is destined to have unsettling ramifications for the church's future in contemporary society.

America is dedicated to the proposition—controversial as much for the Vatican as for many non-Catholic Americans—that one could be both a good Catholic and a good American. That *America* has survived so long, nearly a century, is a testimony to the intellectual and political savvy of the Jesuits and, ironically, to the election of the last Pope Benedict. *America* was founded in April 1909 at the height of Pius X's anti-Modernist purge, a witch hunt that nearly gutted the Catholic intelligentsia and left the survivors looking over their shoulder. "Hysterical paranoia ran rampant, and Catholic intellectuals and writers were one after another accused of heresy by anonymous sources in Rome," wrote James T. Keane, a Jesuit seminarian. In 1908, a year before *America*'s founding, the *New York Review*, a well-regarded Catholic journal that opened in 1905 with the aim of educating clergy in both faith and the latest trends in modern thought, was shuttered following Pius's condemnation of Modernism.

With characteristic confidence, the Jesuits—that name was originally an epithet for the Society of Jesus, but they now wear it proudly—plowed ahead despite the ill omens and started their magazine, basing it in New York and giving it the decidedly un-Roman title of *America* rather than the other options under consideration, such as the *Witness* or *Truth*. The founder, John J. Wynne, S.J., and his fellow editors announced that *America* would boldly engage American culture, neither running from contemporary trends nor failing to promote the values of Catholic thought, culture, and faith in American society. "True to its name and to its character as a Catholic review," they said, "*America* will be cosmopolitan not only in contents but also in spirit."[1]

Such words were a red flag to Pius X's bounty hunters, and Wynne's bid was nearly ended before it could get going. But the magazine was saved by the sudden death of Pius in 1914 and the election of Benedict XV, who put an end to the anti-Modernist persecution. *America* thrived as an indispensable forum for presenting the Catholic case to a skeptical American public. Just as important, the magazine was also a vehicle for Catholics to show Rome that a tradition-minded, hierarchical religion could, without compromising the faith, embrace some of the modern developments that the United States embodied, such as freedom of expression, freedom of religion, and the free development of the intellect. This mission was part of the historical effort of American Catholics to overcome a dilemma that the dean of U.S. church historians, Jay Dolan, likened to the "twoness" felt by the American Negro as portrayed by W. E. B. DuBois—"two souls, two thoughts, two unreconciled strivings."[2] Resolving this internal division between the ideals of the faith and the values of the nation was a goal of American Catholics from the beginning. The nation's first bishop, John Carroll (his cousin, Charles Carroll, was the lone Catholic signatory of the Declaration of Independence), was elected by the local clergy (a procedure that would be impossible today), and Carroll was forceful in representing his flock to Rome. Defending the autonomy of America's Catholics, he told the Vatican that the faithful in the United States required "that Ecclesiastical liberty, which the temper of the age and our people requires." (It is perhaps no coincidence that Bishop Carroll had been a Jesuit before the Vatican suppressed the order for several decades at the end of the eighteenth century.)

Still, the Vatican was not impressed by what were seen as congregational tendencies emerging in American Catholicism—an inevitable conformity with the dominant individualistic ethos of the Protestant culture, in Rome's view—and in the nineteenth century the popes began tightening the reins on the U.S. church. Fired by their desire to prove their fidelity to Rome, American Catholics reacted by building a Catholic infrastructure that remains a wonder of the Catholic world. The Catholic parish, educational, and hospital systems in the United States—constructed by lay Catholics with lay funding and without the state privileges enjoyed by the church in Europe—are unparalleled, as is the church's social services network. The American laity is also deeply observant and devotional. While weekly Mass attendance fell sharply after the 1960s, American Catholics remained more faithful churchgoers than most other U.S. denominations and most Catholics elsewhere. After Vatican II, American Catholics become pioneers in developing lay ministries and becoming deacons, both innovations of the council, and they formed parish finance and pastoral councils to a degree unheard of in the rest of world. They also supported Rome with their growing economic might, and in 2004 they became the single largest contributor to the Vatican (German Catholics rank second), providing one-quarter of the Holy See's approximately $260 million annual budget.

Whatever they did, it never seemed to be enough to assuage Rome's fears of American Catholic aims. From the second half of the nineteenth century, when Pope Leo XIII condemned the vague trend of "Americanism"—the name said everything the Holy See needed to know about the movement, whatever it was—through the reign of Pope John Paul II, the Vatican grew increasingly concerned about the American church.

Given the historical mission of the Jesuits to spread the Gospel in whatever culture they found themselves, it was natural that Jesuit thinkers, often published in the pages of *America,* led the way in trying to help Rome see the advantages of the American way while pushing for Catholic values in the public square. The Jesuit John LaFarge (1880–1963) led the American church's crusade for interracial justice from the pages of *America,* which also provided a forum for emerging Catholic voices like John F. Kennedy, then a junior sena-tor from Massachusetts. *America* was a prominent stage for the writers behind Catholicism's midcentury cultural resurgence, giving space to such talents as Flannery O'Connor, Dorothy Day, and Thomas Merton. Recipients of the magazine's prestigious Campion Award included Catholic luminaries like Walker Percy, Shusaku Endo, and Muriel Spark, and non-Catholics like T. S. Eliot, John Updike, and Lutheran church historian Martin E. Marty.

One of the magazine's nationally known thinkers was Father John Court-ney Murray, who became the chief American Catholic architect of the propo-sition that the principles of the separation of church and state and religious liberty were compatible with Catholic teaching. Yet in 1954, while an editor at *America,* Murray was silenced on that topic by Cardinal Alfredo Ottaviani, a predecessor of Cardinal Joseph Ratzinger at the Holy Office. But silenc-ing was no more effective then than it is today, and the presidential vic-tory of John F. Kennedy, the first Catholic nominee since Al Smith in 1928, thrust Murray and his writings once again into the headlines. Muzzled by his church, Murray was given a global secular platform when his face appeared on the cover of *Time* in December 1960. Two years later, when Vatican II con-vened, New York cardinal Francis Spellman wielded his considerable influence to have Murray brought along with him as a *peritus,* or council expert. Many conservatives did not appreciate that move, or the efforts of the council fathers to produce a document reflecting Murray's views. But Spellman and his allies prevailed, and Murray's ideas were enshrined in the council's Declaration of Religious Freedom, a milestone in the development of Catholic doctrine.

After the council, Murray began to apply his ideas on religious liberty in society to the equally contentious realm of internal church polity, but his death in 1967 cut short that exploration. While many other journals, most of them edited by lay Catholics operating beyond the reach of church authorities, focused on the internal life of the church, *America* was the most prominent journal operated by a religious order to press the cause of dialogue within Catholicism.

That profile was elevated still further when Father Thomas Reese, S.J, took over as editor in 1998. Reese, a wiry, youthful fifty-three-year-old with a keen sense of humor and a knack for pithy phrases, quickly became a favorite of journalists covering the church (including myself), who needed a middle-of-the-road pundit, with clerical credentials, to lucidly explain the impenetrable politics of the church, and especially the hierarchy. To a degree, Reese didn't have much competition. With Rome cracking down on anything that hinted at disagreement, there were fewer church leaders who would comment candidly on the state of the church or analyze the stresses and strains at work in Rome. Moreover, the increasing polarization in the church made the once-popular phrase "common ground" a synonym for heresy and fostered the rise of Catholic special interest groups. Many of them were liberal, but a growing number emerged on the right, funded by wealthy conservatives, aided by the explicit or implicit approval of Rome, and led by fulminating ideologues who brashly pressed their agendas while drowning out more sober commentary.

Reese was perfect for the pundit role. He had a doctorate in political science from the University of California at Berkeley as well as a masters in divinity, and he had spent time lobbying on Capitol Hill for a tax reform group. He wrote several widely read and highly respected studies of the power structure and inner workings of the hierarchy, including *Inside the Vatican: The Politics and Organization of the Catholic Church*. Reese became well known to newspaper readers and television viewers by offering balanced, reliable commentary that educated the public about the pressing questions of the day in the Catholic Church. And he helped inform Catholics themselves—also an important task—by printing essays that expressed varying viewpoints on a wide range of often controversial issues facing the church. *America* had a subscriber base of just 45,000, but like many opinion journals, its readers were an influential cohort, including Catholic bishops, theologians, writers, and academics. Even the Web site of the United States Conference of Catholic Bishops maintained links to articles that *America* ran on the clergy abuse scandal and its fallout.

But it was that prominence, combined with the magazine's role as a forum for airing debate, thus feeding the sense that the church was in flux, that led to trouble.

America under Reese ran articles debating whether homosexuals should be ordained, with views both pro and con, including a con essay by a Vatican official that would prefigure one of Pope Benedict's most controversial policy crackdowns. There were articles on stem cell research and the evolving church teaching on end-of-life issues, including debates over the proper course of treatment for Terri Schiavo, the Florida woman whose feeding tube was removed in 2005, creating a national uproar. And it published pieces on popular culture and national politics, as well as profiles, essays on spirituality, poetry, and a range of other writings aimed at engaging mind and spirit.

On internal church issues, the magazine's editorials tended to center-left, even though the church's huge "center" had become "new liberals" under the rightward tack of John Paul's Vatican. The editorials could be sharp, most notably an April 2001 editorial that chided Ratzinger's Congregation for the Doctrine of the Faith after the CDF's verdict on a fellow Jesuit, theologian Jacques Dupuis. The editorial blasted the CDF for acting like a "totalitarian state" with its "indefensible procedures" conducted in secret. In the interval between John Paul's death and the conclave, *America* published an editorial calling for the next pope, whoever he might be, to discuss a range of topics long considered off-limits for debate, including optional celibacy for priests and women's ordination, along with birth control, the selection process for bishops, inclusive language in the liturgy, and the role of the laity in church governance.

Whatever the magazine wrote, Reese and the editors always encouraged responses and regularly printed essays from leading bishops and cardinals, including one from Cardinal Joseph Ratzinger responding to a critical essay by his German compatriot, Cardinal Walter Kasper, over the issue of Rome's exercise of power and authority over local churches. Yet even as *America* was publishing Ratzinger and like-minded conservatives, Ratzinger's office was quietly carrying out an investigation of the magazine aimed at reining in its penchant for running articles that did not sit well with Rome.

According to news reports, confirmed and expanded through my interviews with Jesuit leaders and churchmen outside the order, the CDF's scrutiny began in 2000, although the magazine initially heard only vague rumors of Roman concerns. Only in 2002 did Reese and the editors learn that the CDF was officially scrutinizing the magazine, basing its probe on several articles that the CDF did not like. One was a review, by the Jesuit historian John W. O'Malley, of the best-selling book by Garry Wills, *Papal Sin,* which the CDF said was too kind; another was an editorial against the abortifacient pill RU–486, which the CDF deemed not harsh enough. Other problematic articles included an essay on condoms for AIDS prevention, which was parsing a Vatican document that appeared to offer leeway on their use; an essay that expressed support for ordaining celibate homosexuals; plus a number of critical pieces on the CDF document *Dominus Iesus,* whose language about the deficiencies of other "ecclesial communities" (they weren't called churches) and religions prompted public criticism from other prominent Vatican officials, including Ratzinger's fellow cardinals.

At that point, the editors were told that they faced the prospect of a Vatican-imposed board of censors, composed of three bishops named by the CDF. The implicit alternative was the dismissal of Reese, or perhaps even action against the magazine itself. Reese reportedly approached three unidentified American archbishops in an effort to get them to intercede on the magazine's behalf, but though they said they were sympathetic, they also said that it would not do any good for them to write Rome because they were not trusted. When Cardinal Avery Dulles, the distinguished and very orthodox Jesuit theologian at Fordham, heard that *America* was under threat of censorship, he reportedly wrote Cardinal Ratzinger telling him it was a terrible idea. Reese and the editors redoubled their efforts to include articles by bishops and Catholic conservatives. Whatever the effect of those actions, the following year, 2003, the editors heard that the CDF was no longer considering a board of censors but that the Vatican would be watching closely for *America*'s take on an upcoming document from Rome, which turned out to be a statement, written by Ratzinger's CDF, declaring same-sex marriage to be "against the natural moral law" and warning Catholic politicians that it would be "gravely immoral" to support such a measure. The document, published in July 2003, said adoption by gay couples "would actually mean doing violence to these children."

The document was a test for *America,* and magazine avoided problems by not commissioning articles about it. For almost a year, the magazine apparently did nothing the CDF considered offensive.

Then came the presidential race of 2004, with the candidacy of John Kerry, the first Catholic nominee in forty-four years, and all the attendant hot-button issues his campaign raised, especially on communion for abortion rights politicians and the emerging matter of same-sex marriage. In June 2004, *America* finally addressed the Vatican document against same-sex marriage by publishing an essay by Monsignor Robert Sokolowski, a professor of philosophy at the Catholic University of America, forcefully supporting the Vatican's position. In December, the magazine ran an essay by Boston College theologian Stephen J. Pope critiquing Sokolowski's article and calling for more consideration of the moral reasoning on behalf of same-sex unions. In the same issue, the editors gave Sokolowski space to respond in detail to Pope's critique. The magazine also ran more than a dozen articles exploring the deeply divisive matter of giving communion to abortion rights politicians, including a June 2004 article by St. Louis archbishop Raymond L. Burke, who took a hard line against such Catholic political leaders. In August, David R. Obey, a leading Democratic congressman from Wisconsin, wrote an essay in response to Burke explaining his stance as a practicing Catholic and abortion rights politician.

Though the articles drew great public interest, for Ratzinger and the CDF it was too much. The CDF flagged the Pope article on same-sex unions and the Obey article on communion as unacceptable. In December 2004 the magazine heard that they were under the gun again, and in mid-March 2005, Ratzinger sent an ultimatum to Father Peter-Hans Kolvenbach, head of the Society: Reese had to go.

One reason Ratzinger went after *America* is because he could. The Jesuits are unique among religious orders in that professed members take a special fourth vow of obedience to the pope, beyond the usual three-fold vow of those in religious orders to live a life of poverty, chastity, and obedience in community. Often misconstrued as blind loyalty, the vow of obedience to the pope actually regards obedience in "mission"—that is, in the specific work that Jesuits do. When Ignatius Loyola founded the Society of Jesus in 1540, he envisioned it as a tool to spread the Catholic faith. Ignatius, later proclaimed a saint, wanted to put his priests and brothers (it is an all-male order) at the disposition of the pope to send wherever needed because it was believed the pope would know best the greatest needs of the universal church. Thus Jesuit missionaries became famous for promoting the faith in the royal courts of Europe and in the dangerous jungles of South America and beyond, bringing zeal and intellect in equal measure. And everywhere they went, the Jesuits founded universities and engaged the culture, becoming famous for their top-flight scholars and scientists, and "finding God in all things," as Saint Ignatius recommended.

The Society's very success also created problems. The Jesuits became the largest order in the church (with nearly twenty thousand members, it remains so) and famous as much for their political machinations and casuistical reasoning (both rather overblown) as their record of conversions. The order was so influential that it often ran afoul of both secular and Vatican authorities, who resented their power. In fact, the overall head of the order, the superior general, is known as the Black Pope (Jesuits wear a distinctive black robe), as opposed to the pope in white who resides across St. Peter's Square in the Vatican. In 1774, thanks to byzantine maneuvers by several European royal houses, Pope Clement XIV suppressed the Society of Jesus, virtually eliminating it as a functioning entity. (Interestingly, the society survived in Russia—always a problematic theater for Rome—because Catherine the Great refused to promulgate the pope's decree of suppression, thus keeping the Ignatian flame alive.) When the society was officially restored to good graces in 1814, the Jesuits picked up where they had left off and became a thrumming engine of the church's intellectual and missionary endeavors.

In fact, the Society became known as a staunch defender of the Vatican and the Roman establishment, and Jesuits were close advisers to Pius XII during World War II. After the war, figures such as Karl Rahner, Walter Burghardt, Joseph Fuchs, Richard McCormick, Augustin Bea, and Joseph Jungmann, among others, pioneered openings in ecumenism and religious liberty, as well as studies in liturgy, patristics, scripture, and moral theology that helped prepare the way for Vatican II. The order's commitment to social justice, however, was the trigger for renewed scrutiny from the Vatican. The Jesuits saw themselves as responding to the council's call for religious orders to return to their roots, a kind of *ressourcement*. One of Ignatius's founding principles, set out in his famous *Spiritual Exercises,* was for Jesuits to "choose poverty with Christ's poor," so that is what his spiritual descendants did, especially in Latin America. But the Roman Curia had a different view and focused on what was seen as the order's improper involvement in politics.

The crackdown began after the election of John Paul and reached its nadir in 1981, when the pope pushed aside the Superior General at the time, Father Pedro Arrupe, a Basque priest like Saint Ignatius. Arrupe was renowned for his understanding of Ignatian spirituality and his deep commitment to the Jesuit mission for justice, and he was revered by the Society and highly respected by other religious communities. But the order's growing involvement in political issues was in Rome's view an involvement in politics, and politics of a left-wing strain. Arrupe had been trying for more than a year to talk directly with the pope to reassure him that the order was acting appropriately, and in the spring of 1981 he seemed to be making some progress. Then came the attempt on the pope's life on May 13 and John Paul's long convalescence. In August 1981, Arrupe suffered a paralyzing stroke and lay incapacitated in Gemelli Hospital. Those unforeseen developments put an end to the incipient dialogue between John Paul and the Society. But the fact that the Vatican then exploited Arrupe's doleful condition to unilaterally impose its will on the Jesuits remains one of the most shocking aspects of the entire affair.

After the stroke, Arrupe knew that his illness would require a change in leadership, so he appointed his top assistant, New York Jesuit father Vincent O'Keefe, a former president of Fordham University, to take over as vicar general until the next general meeting of the entire order could choose a permanent successor. That arrangement lasted just two months. In October, with Arrupe still immobile and effectively unable to speak, John Paul stepped in with a takeover plan reportedly engineered by Cardinal Eduardo Martinez Somalo, a Spanish curial official who would later serve as the powerful camerlengo during the transition after John Paul's death. The plan called for Paolo Dezza, an eighty-year-old, nearly blind Italian Jesuit who had been confessor to Paul VI, to take over as the "papal delegate"—an office invented for the occasion—to run the order, with another Italian Jesuit, Giuseppe Pittau, to serve as coadjutor with the right of succession to the top post when Arrupe did formally resign. The news dropped on the Society like a bombshell. No pope had ever intervened in the Society's internal governance, and no Jesuit official had been consulted or advised of the maneuver before the order was presented with the fait accompli. The pope barred Arrupe from calling a general congregation to address the matter; nor was he allowed to resign. As Arrupe lay incapacitated, Dezza and Pittau ran the order, in his name, but the way the Vatican wanted.

The Vatican takeover was a terrible grief to Arrupe, who lingered on for a decade, paralyzed, in the Jesuit infirmary in Rome. It was also a humiliation for the Jesuits, and a warning shot to other religious orders because it is so extraordinary for a pontiff to interfere in the internal governance of an order. So great was the consternation that in 1983 John Paul finally relented and allowed the Jesuits to convene a general congregation to elect their own superior. They chose not Pittau but Father Peter-Hans Kolvenbach, a Dutch Jesuit and a linguist by expertise. (A decade later, John Paul made Dezza a cardinal; he lived to be ninety-eight years old.) Kolvenbach is highly regarded for his savvy and spirituality, but one of his chief tasks has been reassuring the Vatican that they have nothing to fear from the order, no easy job.

Thus, given their recent history and their vow of obedience to the pope, the Jesuits and Reese were not in a strong position vis-à-vis Ratzinger, who also knew that he had the backing of the Roman Curia in taking action against the Jesuits, and probably the pope's support, though in his last years whether John Paul was even aware of the confrontation over *America* is highly doubtful.

Still, even after five years of increasing pressure, Reese and *America* almost escaped Ratzinger's 2005 edict.

The prefect's letter hit Kolvenbach's desk in mid-March, about two weeks before Pope John Paul II died. (There was understandable speculation as to the timing of Ratzinger's ultimatum, arriving after so many years of jousting and just weeks before the pope's death—an event that would have prevented Ratzinger from pursuing the case against *America,* since he had to resign as CDF head on John Paul's passing.) Kolvenbach eventually sent it on to the president of the Jesuit Conference for the United States, Father Bradley M. Schaeffer, to implement. By the time the letter arrived, however, Reese was already in Rome to serve as a commentator for John Paul's funeral and the conclave to follow. In those circumstances, everything apart from the succession was forgotten. Under the terms of the interregnum, Ratzinger formally resigned his office, and the Jesuits knew that whoever was elected pope, Ratzinger was unlikely to return for long, if at all. Reese and the Jesuits were also understandably hoping for a new pope who would take a more expansive view toward public debate within the church and *America*'s mission. The day before Benedict's election, Reese met with Kolvenbach at the Jesuit headquarters, a long, imposing palazzo in Borgo Santo Spirito next to St. Peter's Square. During the meeting Kolvenbach alerted Reese that the CDF had raised new concerns about the Stephen Pope and David Obey articles, but he said nothing about the Ratzinger letter.

The next day Ratzinger was elected pope. Reese was in Rome watching along with the rest of the journalist corps, and in the hours and days after the announcement he looked ashen. Most of us chalked it up to surprise over the conclave's outcome and the foreboding many of us felt for the church. We didn't know then that for Reese the conclave's outcome hit home in a more personal way.

When Reese returned to New York, he was uncharacteristically downcast, and his friends were worried for him, as well as anxious about the magazine's future. At an editorial meeting the following week, Reese told the staff he thought it would be best if he resigned for the good of the magazine. But they all strongly disagreed. Buoyed by their support, Reese decided to take a few months off and return to the magazine with his batteries recharged. But when Reese told Schaeffer, the head of the U.S. Jesuit conference, of his plan to stay on as editor, he was informed for the first time about the Ratzinger letter and told that remaining was no longer an option. With Benedict as pope, Ratzinger's letter was non-negotiable.

Obedient to his vows, and wanting to spare the magazine and the Society any turmoil, Father Thomas Reese resigned. During the five-year investigation, the editors were never contacted directly by Ratzinger or his office, and were never told what in the articles was problematic. They were never allowed to present a defense to Rome and could never take their case to the public. Moreover, the editor of the leading church-run journal in the United States was forced out by the Vatican without any formal consultation with the bishops of the United States, most of whom were as surprised as everyone else. The editor of a magazine whose motto is *Veritatem facientes in caritate* (To practice the truth in charity) was treated as uncharitably as possible for practicing the truth.

On May 6, a Friday, Reese announced in a press release that he was leaving the magazine that he had dedicated seven years to improving, and would return to his native California for a sabbatical. He gave no explanation; he decided not to speak publicly for fear of making the pope look bad and bringing further sanctions to the Society and *America*. The magazine was reeling but quickly righted by announcing the promotion of Father Drew Christiansen, an associate editor and well-respected Jesuit commentator, to replace Reese. Still, such an abrupt, unexplained departure in the scandal-hyped circumstances of the day could easily have led people to conclude that he had come under suspicion of sexual impropriety. Fortunately, others spoke out, on and off the record, to let the public know that Reese was both the last victim of Cardinal Ratzinger and the first victim of Pope Benedict.

The news of Reese's dismissal hit like a thunderbolt. In the Catholic world, theologians, academics, writers, and journalists—and readers of the publications they wrote for—were aghast at the action. But they were also embarrassed for the church. The story made the front page of the *New York Times* and other newspapers. Reese, so familiar to the general public as a genial commentator, especially after the blanket coverage of the papal funeral and conclave, was suddenly seen as a martyr at the hands of an overweening Vatican hierarchy. American Catholics had been striving for centuries to overcome the stereotype that Catholics could not think for themselves, and Benedict's strong-arm tactics to enforce unanimity in thought were seen as a shameful confirmation that the worst aspects of the premodern church lived on. During the sexual abuse scandals, American Catholics grew tired of having to explain again and again how they could remain in an institution whose leadership allowed such horrors to occur without penalty to themselves. Now they had to figure out how to explain yet again why they stayed, if they stayed.

"It is hard to judge what is more appalling, the flimsy case made by the Congregation for the Doctrine of the Faith . . . against Reese's orthodoxy and stewardship of *America*, or the senselessness of silencing perhaps the most visible, and certainly one of the most knowledgeable, fair-minded, and intelligent public voices the church has in this country," *Commonweal*, a lay-run biweekly, wrote in an editorial. *Commonweal* is considered to be left-of-center, but it gave voice to a wide range of Catholic opinion. "Those calling for the strict regulation of Catholic discourse argue that public dissent from church doctrine creates scandal, confusing or misleading the 'simple faithful.' What really gives scandal to people in the pews, however, is the arbitrary and self-serving exercise of ecclesiastical authority. What the CDF has done to Thomas Reese and *America* is the scandal."

The *National Catholic Reporter*, a popular, liberal, independent Catholic weekly, called Reese's removal "tragic" and said Catholicism was "perilously close to becoming a fundamentalist sect" where thoughtful debate is off limits. "If Reese is the kind of Catholic leader the Vatican feels it must remove from a position of responsibility," *NCR* wrote, "then this church is in far worse shape than many of us imagined."

In London, the *Tablet,* a leading Catholic weekly in the English-speaking world and a model for *America,* denounced the move and said it would have a "chilling effect" on the church. "This is a risk-averse philosophy which is of no benefit to the faith and intelligence of the Catholic laity in particular, and betrays a certain lack of confidence in the Holy Spirit."

The Catholic Press Association (CPA) held its annual convention the week after Reese left, and most delegates were angry and disturbed by Reese's treatment. "Silence and not dissent is the greater disservice to the church," said Maryknoll father Joseph Veneroso, director of social communications for his order. But the association voted down a sharp statement of protest. They instead called for "open, honest, respectful, responsible, and charitable dialogue among the faithful," and published a three-page appendix quoting papal documents on press freedom and responsibility.[3] There was concern among the Catholic journalists that they did not have the full story on Reese's departure, but they were also honest about their fears: "It would be hard for any Catholic editor not to say, 'Well, if this happened to *America* magazine, perhaps it could happen to others,'" said Father Pat McCloskey, the editor of *St. Anthony Messenger,* a Franciscan monthly based in Cincinnati with a circulation of 311,000.[4] Also, while critics of Reese pointed to the CPA's rejection of a formal protest as evidence that Reese was in the wrong, Reese had actually written privately to the CPA board saying that since many of their papers are published by diocesan bishops who have the power to hire and fire the staff, he did not want anyone to risk his or her job by voting for the resolution.

The shock waves went well beyond the Catholic press. A Jesuit priest who went to celebrate Mass in a cloistered convent the Sunday after Reese's departure was surprised to find himself peppered with questions from the nuns about how such a thing could happen. Fay Vincent, the former baseball commissioner, resigned from the board of trustees at the Jesuit-run Fairfield University in Connecticut and refused to accept an honorary degree from Sacred Heart University in protest. "I'm really worried that some Catholic organizations, especially universities, are at some risk," Vincent said.[5] Father Kenneth R. Himes, chairman of theology at Boston College, a Jesuit school, said members of his faculty were concerned. "The chilling signal sent by this action is that church-related publications will have questions raised about their legitimate autonomy, and therefore the integrity of Catholic journalists and scholarly editors will be impugned."[6]

Even some conservatives who disagreed with the direction of *America* under Reese were startled. Philip F. Lawler, then the editor of *Catholic World News,* a vigorously conservative news outlet, told the *New York Times* that he thought Reese "reasonably politic. I watched him during the [papal] transition, and I cannot think of a single thing I heard that would have put him in jeopardy." Father Richard John Neuhaus, a trenchant conservative who edits *First Things,* a New York-based interfaith journal with a strongly conservative tilt, said Reese was always "fair-minded."

In Rome the day after the Reese story broke, the pope traveled across the city to take formal possession of his cathedral, the Basilica of St. John Lateran, and gave a homily in which he firmly asserted his authority, deriving from Christ, to protect the faithful against "attempts to adapt and water down" the church's teaching. Benedict was not reacting to the Reese departure, but his comments reflected the unease that the episode raised: "This teaching authority frightens many men within and outside the Church," Benedict said. "They wonder if it is not a threat to freedom of conscience, if it is not a presumption that is opposed to freedom of thought. It is not so."

Many now had good reason to disagree with the pope. And they were not exactly encouraged when, after the Mass, Benedict's motorcade traveled a short distance to another of Rome's major churches, the Basilica of St. Mary Major, where he was met by Cardinal Bernard Law. Law was the former archbishop of Boston who had been forced to step down from that post after unceasing public anger at his actions in failing to discipline predator priests and in covering up numerous cases of sexual abuse of children. Those crimes were dug up by the Boston media, mainly the *Boston Globe,* but were largely dismissed as overreactions by many in the Vatican, including then cardinal Ratzinger. "In the Church, priests also are sinners. But I am personally convinced that the constant presence in the press of the sins of Catholic priests, especially in the United States, is a planned campaign, as the percentage of these offenses among priests is not higher than in other categories, and perhaps it is even lower," Ratzinger told Zenit news service in December 2002. Ten days later, Law stepped down and went to live at a Maryland monastery of cloistered nuns.

A year after his resignation, Law was plucked from his semi-exile (he traveled widely and well, often to Rome, during his sojourn at the monastery) and given his new plum job, and a large stipend, in grand surroundings at St. Mary Major, further outraging American Catholics. The day after Benedict's visit to Cardinal Law was the Catholic Church's World Day of Social Communications, and at his Sunday Angelus prayer Pope Benedict cautioned the media that if they did not act responsibly they could "fuel prejudice and contempt among individuals and peoples." He urged journalists to "ensure objectivity, respect for human dignity and attention to the common good."

Concerned that the fallout from Reese's defenestration could hurt Benedict's papacy before it got started, the Catholic Right in the United States moved immediately to insulate the pope. In columns and interviews, they criticized Reese—who could not defend himself—and they often did so with inventive flair.

Deal Hudson, a conservative Catholic editor with close ties to the Bush White House, claimed in a June 3 newsletter that *l'affaire Reese* was all part of a Jesuit plot and that in dumping the *America* editor, Father Kolvenbach had "created the perfect opportunity for the media, both Catholic and secular, to generate negative buzz over the selection of Benedict XVI." Hudson, who was one of the fiercest critics of Bill Clinton's sexual escapades, also repeated his regular criticisms of the Jesuits for what he claimed was their attitude of dissent. Hudson did not mention that in 2004 he had to leave the editor's job at *Crisis*, a journal of neo-con Catholicism, after it was revealed that he had resigned his faculty post at the Jesuit Fordham University a decade earlier due to charges that he had sex with an eighteen-year-old student in his office after getting her drunk at a New York bar—a Mardi Gras party at the start of Lent. Hudson was kept on by the magazine's publishing house and continued to publish a newsletter skewering the supposed moral failures of liberal Catholics.

Father Neuhaus, the *First Things* editor who initially expressed surprise at Reese's departure, subsequently argued in a May 16 op-ed in the *Boston Globe* that Reese was removed by his Jesuit superiors rather than by "an allegedly oppressive Pope Benedict XVI." He said that the reason for Reese's removal was the magazine's dissent from church teaching and its commitment to providing a forum for debate among church leaders and other Catholics. Neuhaus wrote that Reese "seriously misunderstood the meaning of fair and balanced. The Society of Jesus decided it would be better for the magazine and for him if he moved into a different ministry. End of story. Unless, of course, one is interested in generating suspicion and hostility against the pope. Needless to say, no faithful Catholic would want to do that." In other words, anyone who told the truth—that Benedict was involved in Reese's termination—was being unfaithful. (Several months later, in the August/

September issue of *First Things*, Neuhaus acknowledged being told by a source close to *America* of the CDF letter calling for Reese's dismissal. But he said his source had not seen the letter, and added that it was "not pertinent" even if it did exist.)

All of these arguments were either disingenuous in the extreme or patently misleading. For one thing, Neuhaus's critique of Reese was striking, given that Neuhaus himself is one of the sharpest critics of the hierarchy, or at least those segments he disagrees with, and he often takes issue with the Vatican on matters that go against his politically conservative grain. Yet as a priest of the New York archdiocese, and one who enjoys the backing of influential conservatives, Neuhaus is not accountable the way a Jesuit like Reese must be. Thus he can do the same things he criticized Reese for doing, but without the risk.

More important, conservative claims that Benedict had nothing to do with Reese's ouster ignored the many news reports of Ratzinger's direct involvement in Reese's departure and the public statements to that effect. Catholic News Service, the *National Catholic Reporter*, and most secular news outlets cited Vatican sources regarding the CDF's direct intervention against *America*, and Father Jose de Vera, the chief press officer for the Jesuits in Rome, was open about the sequence of events. Reese "knew the situation. He didn't want to embarrass the society, and he didn't want to fight the pope, so he resigned," de Vera told Catholic News Service on May 9. In the May 14 edition of the *Tablet*, de Vera added, "It is clear that the person who was not satisfied with Tom Reese was Cardinal Ratzinger." He said that Reese would likely have been "substituted" had he not stepped down. "By inviting articles that covered different sides of disputed issues, Father Reese helped make *America* a forum for intelligent discussion of questions facing the church and the country today," de Vera said. "But that approach did not sit well with Vatican authorities." De Vera said Ratzinger had repeatedly expressed his displeasure with *America* to Kolvenbach.

It doesn't get much clearer than that.

Still, in a May 13 column in the *Wall Street Journal*, Russell Shaw, a conservative-minded commentator and a former spokesman for the U.S. hierarchy, piled it on by blasting the Jesuits for becoming too liberal and saying that Reese did not understand that as a cleric he had to promote church teaching, not offer space for debate. The oddity of Shaw's critique was that he was a regular contributor to *America*. In fact, in the edition following Reese's ouster, three days after Shaw had criticized Reese in the *Journal*, *America* published an article by Shaw titled "Is This Transparency?" In that article Shaw chided the hierarchy for being secretive and not allowing public debate. "More and more," Shaw wrote, "the attitude appears to be that the church's business is the bishops' business and no one else's; openness and a desire to involve others in church affairs seem to have become *passé*."

Just a month later, *America* published yet another article by Shaw, in which he used Pope John Paul's final official document, an apostolic letter on the media, to press for an even greater degree of "honest, open communication in the church." Shaw lauded the papal letter, *Rapid Development,* for stating that "there is still room among Catholics for an exchange of opinions in a dialogue which is respectful of justice and prudence." But he expressed hope that the church would go further still, and he cited earlier documents that made his point more forcefully, such as the "Pastoral Instruction on Social Communications," published by the Vatican in 1971. That document stated, "Clergy and laity will encourage a free expression of opinion and a wide variety of publications and points of view. They should do this because it will satisfy the different interests and concerns of readers and because it contributes to the formation of public opinion in the Church and the world." It encouraged "an unrestricted liberty of expression" for official Catholic publications, and hoped the church "will be a forum, a meeting place for the exchange of views." Shaw noted that in a follow-up document twenty years later, the Vatican articulated a "fundamental right of dialogue and information within the church." As that document stated, "Partly this is a matter of maintaining and enhancing the church's credibility and effectiveness. But more fundamentally, it is one of the ways of realizing in a concrete manner the church's character as communion."

Such was the looking-glass logic of the self-styled champions of orthodoxy: they could castigate a deposed editor for airing debate in a magazine that continued to publish their own articles chastising the Vatican for not allowing more debate on topics they wanted discussed.

Knitting all of these thin defenses together was a single thread: the argument that Reese and *America* were dissenting from church teaching, and therefore Benedict was rightly defending orthodoxy by forcing him out. "*America* is not Salon.com or *The New Republic* or Fox News," said Mark Brumley, chief executive officer for Ignatius Press, Benedict's official publisher for the English-speaking world. "It's published by the Jesuits, a religious order of the Catholic Church. It should not be publishing articles contrary to the teaching of the Catholic Church. Period."[7]

The reality, however, is that the sins of Reese and *America* were not against the magisterium of the church. Their sin, if it could be called such a thing, was airing and engaging in existing debates in the church and encouraging dialogue.

America under Reese published articles that examined issues being openly discussed within the church, by official church leaders and others, on open questions. The magazine published an exchange between Cardinal Ratzinger and Cardinal Kasper, for example, on the proper balance of power between Rome and the local churches. Both men were cardinals, both men were ranking Vatican officials, and they held differing opinions on a debatable topic. (One also wonders what Reese was supposed to do with submissions from bishops or from the august likes of Cardinals Ratzinger and Kasper—reject them?) On using condoms to prevent AIDS—also a topic on which the Vatican has taken no official position—and denying communion to Catholic politicians who support abortion rights, *America*'s articles reflected the debate going on within the hierarchy. Their articles on ordaining celibate gay priests were models of clarity and comity compared to the ugly, contradictory, and sometimes inane comments that preceded the late 2005 publication of a Vatican document on gay seminarians.

On a raft of other controversial topics, *America* provided a forum for church leaders as well as lay Catholics across the spectrum, so that Catholics could hash out ideas, contest developing positions, and educate themselves and each other.

But that was the problem. Ratzinger did not want such discussion within the church. Part of it was a matter of signaling who was in charge. It was no secret that Rome and many bishops did not like Reese's profile as an authoritative voice on church affairs. In addition, sources in Rome said Ratzinger felt the magazine's tone was "anti-hierarchical," even though between 2001 and 2002 the magazine published nearly thirty pieces by bishops and cardinals. Yet those complaints are matters of personal pique, not dissent. Moreover, Catholics could wonder how it was that a younger Joseph Ratzinger, as an expert at the Second Vatican Council, could skewer the Curia, and specifically the Holy Office, as "a source of scandal," and yet years later, when he headed that same office, nearly identical criticisms merited suppression by the Holy Office. One could say it smacks of relativism. Yes, *America* and Reese and the Jesuits themselves are certainly "progressive" in many of their opinions and some of the positions they espouse on church policies and teachings, just as Joseph Ratzinger once was. But so, too, are many cardinals, bishops, priests, and lay people. And many popes across the ages.

The central conflict that the Thomas Reese saga brings into such sharp relief concerns the very *idea* of change in the church—what changes are needed, how they are to be brought about, and, more fundamentally, whether anything in the church needs to be changed at all or can be changed.

Catholicism in the United States has historically contained within itself, albeit uneasily at times, the dual impulses of a great devotion to the faith and a desire to adapt the church to the needs of an ever-changing world. The same thing could be said of the Catholic Church, throughout its tumultuous history. Yet in the wake of the sexual abuse scandals, in the white-hot anger over the dishonesty bred by secrecy, and in an era when Catholics on the left and right feel freer than ever to opt out of the institutional church, the demands for true reform, or at least honest discussions and debates that recognize the need to engage and answer those demands, cannot be postponed. This is the great challenge for Catholicism in the modern world—and the church's response will determine what sort of Catholicism it will be.

Yet Benedict XVI has shown throughout his life, and now as pope, that reform as envisioned by many American Catholics is largely irrelevant, and probably inimical, to his vision of the church. For all of his differences with John Paul in temperament and theology, this is one area on which the thinking of the two men was perfectly synchronous. That means that those praying that the church would now broach the idea of reform, even tentatively, after waiting through the twenty-six years of John Paul's papacy, now face the prospect of further years of frustration.

Chapter Eleven

THE COUNTER-
REFORMATION

For Catholics pushing for change, there are essentially two main arenas for reform in the church. One concerns church teachings and practices, which vary widely in their prospects for adaptation and the amount of agita they induce—from the ordination of women (no way, no how) to the ban on contraception (not likely) to the church law on mandatory priestly celibacy (maybe we can talk). The other arena is the push to reform church structures to promote greater collaboration, dialogue, transparency, and accountability. Benedict XVI has made it clear that he is not likely to be flexible in either area and would instead focus on a third option, the cultivation of personal holiness, as the preeminent means to renew, rather than change, the church. As he wrote in the *Introduction to Christianity*, "The Church is most present not where organizing, reforming and governing are going on but in those who simply believe and receive from her the gift of faith that is life to them."[1]

Benedict's opposition to structural reform draws together several aspects of his personality and theology. One is his innate conservatism, which translates into a preference for keeping bureaucracy to a minimum. It is an ingrained personality trait, but one that finds a perfect rationale in his theological minimalism. Individual responsibility and unadulterated belief are theological priorities, so structures just get in the way. As Benedict has argued, churches, especially in the West, are "suffocating on account of their own over-institutionalization," and the flame of faith "can't, you might say, burn through because of the excess of ash covering it."[2] His words could have been those of Luther or Calvin in the sixteenth century, or any one of the other great Protestant reformers.

Benedict's distaste for structural investments also stems from his reading of the German church's principal failure during the Nazi era, which was to make too many compromises in order to protect the cherished Catholic network of schools and universities and hospitals. Referring to the pastoral letters from the German bishops that he heard read from the pulpit when he was a young boy, Benedict recalled, "Already then it dawned on me that, with their insistence on preserving institutions, these letters in part misread the reality. I mean that merely to guarantee institutions is useless if there are no people to support those institutions from inner convictions."[3] Later, as a cardinal, Joseph Ratzinger held the same view: "It's precisely the fact that the Church clings to the institutional structure when nothing really stands behind it any longer that brings the Church into disrepute." The church, he says, has not shown any capacity to shed possessions voluntarily, so they have been taken away by force, which he says "turned out to be her salvation."[4]

Benedict has tried to buck the historical trend by either discarding what he considers to be extraneous or bloated structures or trying to reinforce the "Catholic identity" of the church institutions that do remain, such as Catholic colleges and universities. One of those oversized structures, he has said, are the national bishops' conferences, which he worked to rein in while he was prefect of the CDF. To Benedict, the collective action of a national hierarchy undermines individual responsibility (of the bishop, in this case), as well as posing a potential alternate source of authority to Rome. In the *Ratzinger Report* of 1984, Benedict rejected the idea that national hierarchies could "vote on truth," and worried that "the group spirit and perhaps even the wish for a quiet, peaceful life or conformism" allowed "active minorities"—by this he meant liberals—to hijack the agenda. "I know bishops who privately confess that they would have decided differently than they did at a conference if they had had to decide by themselves," Ratzinger continued. "Accepting the group spirit, they shied away from the odium of being viewed as a 'spoilsport,' as 'backward,' as 'not open.' It seems very nice to always decide *together*" (his italics). But Ratzinger claimed such an attitude only aggravated the crisis of the church.[5]

The constant pleas for "decentralization," to Benedict's thinking, would not be addressed by creating collaborative or consultative bodies, or by Rome granting "local control." Rather, decentralization was about the bishops making decisions the way Rome wanted so that Rome did not have to do so for them. "If the bishops have the courage to judge and to decide with authority about this battle for the Gospel, the so hoped for decentralization is automatically achieved," then cardinal Ratzinger said at a 2001 synod of bishops on the role of the bishop in the third millennium.

Synods themselves are a relatively new structure for which Benedict has no great love. Synods are regular meetings of bishops in Rome (they usually convene every three years) created by Paul VI after the Second Vatican Council to create an avenue for greater collegiality among the bishops. Instead they turned into rubber stamps controlled by the Roman Curia that effectively tie up an entire month of a bishop's valuable time away from his home diocese. The October 2005 Synod on the Eucharist, which was Benedict's first chance to show how he would govern, was highlighted by his decision to reduce the meeting from a month to three weeks. A few small changes were made to allow more give-and-take among the 250 bishop-delegates, but there was so little confidence that the results would be anything but foreordained that the reaction to the shortened synod was one of relief.

Even before the synod convened, the road map to the bishops' discussion, known as an *Instrumentum Laboris,* or working paper, was being privately criticized as inadequate at best. One bishop who spoke out publicly voiced the concerns of many when he said the *Instrumentum* was "an echo of the chronic complainers who have an impoverished understanding of liturgy and Vatican II." The author of the critique, Bishop Donald W. Trautman of Erie, Pennsylvania, was writing in—yes—*America,* even post-Reese, and he was no marginal voice but chairman of the American hierarchy's committee on liturgy.[6] Trautman wrote that the synod's working paper reflected "a narrow, preconciliar view unworthy of a world meeting of bishops," and that it "spends more time looking in the rearview mirror than looking ahead and steering the church into the future." (Perhaps the stale familiarity of the *Instrumentum* may be partly attributed to the subsequent revelation that its principal author, an Italian priest named Nicola Bux, had been dismissed from a pontifical university for plagiarism.)

Unfortunately, by the end of the synod it seemed that too many of Trautman's fears would be realized.

Similarly, one of Benedict's early priorities was a reform of the Roman Curia, which bishops around the world hoped would mean a curtailing of the Curia's tendency to involve themselves in local affairs. Instead, Benedict saw the reform as downsizing the bureaucracy, trimming unnecessary departments, though not vital organs such as the Congregation for the Doctrine of the Faith. Benedict's approach recalls the story of a French priest a century earlier who suggested that the Roman Curia should consist of just two offices, one a congregation for the defense of the faith and another to defend Catholics against the actions of the first congregation. The priest wound up sanctioned by Rome as a Modernist.[7]

In short, Benedict's preferred model for the institutional church would be analogous to Judaism after the destruction of the Second Temple in 70 AD by the Romans, who crushed the Jewish rebellion and scattered the tribes of Israel to the ends of the earth. Judaism then was held together by religious feasts and "the shared life of the rites," as Benedict once put it with admiration, rather than being focused on a physical structure and a national identity.[8]

For Benedict, "reform" of the church (he puts the word in quotation marks, an indication of his attitude toward the topic) parallels his view of the church's role in the world: if it is to have any meaning, it is in a passive sense, without active agency by believers apart from individual, internal spiritual labor. As the theologian Christopher Ruddy has noted, Benedict invokes traditional sexual typologies that cast the church in feminine, and therefore passive, terms—the Bride of Christ or, more specifically, his mother Mary: "Receptive before active, contemplative and not bureaucratic, seeking only to let God's will be done."[9]

True church reform, Benedict has said, "does not mean to take great pains to erect new façades (contrary to what certain ecclesiologies think). Real 're-form' is to strive to let what is ours disappear as much as possible so what belongs to Christ may become more visible. It is a truth well known to the saints. Saints, in fact, reformed the Church in depth, not by working up plans for new structures, but by reforming themselves. What the Church needs in order to respond to the needs of man in every age is holiness, not management."[10] He cites his namesake, Saint Benedict, as a model for reform, retreating to his monastery and living a life of poverty and simplicity, which later fostered a mass movement. "Reform will come from convincing personalities whom we may call saints."[11]

That view in fact idealizes saints out of their historical context, where holy men and women like Gregory the Great and Catherine of Siena were hands-on reformers and gadflies who nagged popes and bishops until they made real efforts to change the church and make it better reflect the beliefs that the church itself preaches.

But to Benedict, the church—like absolute truth and the liturgy—is a "given" from God, not something that can be constructed or in any way reformed by man. As Cardinal Ratzinger once put it, "The fundamental structures [of the church] are willed by God himself, and therefore they are inviolable. Behind the *human* exterior stands the mystery of a *more than human* reality, in which reformers, sociologists, organizers have no authority whatsoever. If the church, instead, is viewed as a human construction, the product of our own efforts, even the contents of the faith end up assuming an arbitrary character: the faith, in fact, no longer has an authentic, guaranteed instrument through which to express itself."[12] In other words, tinkering with the visible structures in any way leads to the slippery slope of heresy in belief.

More challenging for proponents of reform is Benedict's extension of the church's divine structure to include not just the hierarchy but the hierarchs themselves.

The bishops are the main target of reformers' hopes and, more frequently, their frustrations, because in traditional Catholic ecclesiology, which was reinforced as recently as the Second Vatican Council, the bishop's threefold mandate is to teach, to sanctify, and to govern. It is that last leg of the tripod that causes so much difficulty, for two reasons: first, lay Catholics do not necessarily want to vote on the nature of the Trinity but they certainly want a say in how the diocese is spending their money or who their pastor might be; and, second, though they respect the traditions of the faith and the sacred role of their bishops and priests, lay Catholics find it hard to understand what is so sacred about the bishop's role as CEO of the diocese. This is a matter not of subjecting all decisions to a kind of shareholder vote but rather of collaborating on matters that do not directly affect the faith, thereby engaging and involving lay Catholics in a way that may actually lead to a greater practice of the faith.

Yet Benedict has shown himself to be deeply suspicious of even those types of reforms, arguing that by their nature they undermine the obedience that he says is due the church, which in his view is equated with the hierarchy. The "deep and permanent structure [of the church] is not *democratic* but *sacramental,* and consequently *hierarchical,*" he says (his italics). The hierarchy "is the indispensable condition to arrive at the strength, the reality of the sacrament. Here authority is not based on the majority of votes; it is based on the authority of Christ himself, which he willed to pass on to men who were to be his representatives until his definitive return. Only if this perspective is acquired anew will it be possible to rediscover the necessity and fruitfulness of obedience to the legitimate ecclesiastical hierarchies."[13]

By divinizing the structures of authority in the church so completely, however, Benedict effectively inoculates the bearers of that authority—the bishops—from personal accountability, except of course to God. The problem is that when that exalted ecclesiology runs smack into the horrific reality of something like the sexual abuse revelations that burst forth in 2002, the inevitable result is to cause the very scandal that the culpable bishops were commanded to avoid by the Catholic Catechism: "Scandal takes on a particular gravity by reason of the authority of those who cause it or the weakness of those who are scandalized. . . . Scandal is grave when given by those who by nature or office are obliged to teach and educate others" (Catechism of the Catholic Church, 2285).

On that point of the catechism, lay Catholics were in agreement. Polls consistently showed that although Catholics were horrified by the abuses committed by some priests, they felt the bishops were the real culprits for perpetuating the scandal by reassigning abusers for years. A fall 2003 survey by sociologists James D. Davidson and Dean R. Hoge found that 72 percent of Catholics agreed that "the failure of bishops to stop the abuse is a bigger problem than the abuse itself." Two-thirds believed "the cases that have been reported to date are only the tip of the iceberg." More than 60 percent said the bishops "are covering up the facts," and only 20 percent said they thought the hierarchy was "being open and honest." A Pew survey during the contentious 2004 campaign showed that just 29 percent of Catholics said they looked to their faith for guidance on political matters, a lower level than any other denomination.

During the last year of John Paul's life and the first year of Benedict's pontificate, things did not get much better for the bishops.

In February 2004, the National Review Board, a blue-ribbon panel of lay Catholics set up by the U.S. bishops to help implement and oversee the hierarchy's response to the sexual abuse crisis, published a research study showing that over the previous half-century nearly 4,400 priests had abused more than 10,600 minors. That represented 4 percent of all priests who had worked in the United States over the previous five decades. Though the numbers were no higher than the rate suspected for similar professions, like teachers and athletic coaches (so little research on child abuse is available that exact comparisons are hard to make), and though the figures were cumulative totals from across fifty years, the sudden impact of the huge numbers made it appear that the priesthood was awash in abusers. But the National Review Board tried to put the acts of abuse in context by placing the blame for much of the scandal squarely on the systematic actions of bishops who practiced "secrecy and concealment" to protect their own interests rather than those of vulnerable children. "Sexual abuse of minors is an evil and, as one priest told the board, knowingly allowing evil conduct to continue is 'cooperation with evil,'" the board wrote.

For the rest of 2004 and through 2005, the price tag for the hierarchy's actions continued to mount. Dioceses around the country continued to make huge payouts, often topping $100 million each, until the total bill for the U.S. church soared past $1 billion—a figure that critics had predicted for years but which was always dismissed by church officials. Lawsuits forced several dioceses to declare bankruptcy, which was an unprecedented and troubling development for Rome because it meant bishops were effectively taking orders from secular authorities in the management of their churches. In November 2004 the bishops of the United States elected Bishop William S. Skylstad of Spokane president of the conference; a month later his diocese filed for Chapter 11 protection, arguing it could not meet the $80 million in outstanding abuse claims. As part of the plan, the diocese was to sell its headquarters and Skylstad's house, certainly an unprecedented circumstance for the leader of the U.S. hierarchy.

The payouts and bankruptcies led to enormous confusion and further anger among the faithful, as bishops were forced to close parishes or, in the case of bankruptcy proceedings, to argue that the diocese did not in fact own or control the parishes and thus they should not be included in assets subject to forfeiture. This was a sharp historical turnabout that many other bishops did not accept. Over the history of American Catholicism, bishops in most parts of the country had set themselves up as the "corporation sole" of the diocese, a legal status that allowed a bishop to control all aspects of diocesan life and to prevent laypeople from running parishes or attempting to hire or fire pastors, for example. But now that episcopal monopoly was turned against the hierarchy. In July 2004, the Portland archdiocese became the first in American history to file for bankruptcy. In an effort to limit its exposure, the archdiocese claimed that it did not control its 124 parishes and 3 high schools, worth some $500 million, and thus those should not be considered assets. A year later the judge rejected those arguments. As a result, all Catholic parishioners in western Oregon—more than 389,000 people—became subjects in a class-action suit. Potentially, that could mean that the churches built by the laity would be sold off to pay for abuse perpetrated by a few priests and allowed to spread by a series of bishops.

To make matters worse, one of those Portland bishops was William J. Levada, who headed the archdiocese from 1986 to 1995 before becoming archbishop in San Francisco. Levada had a record of keeping abusers in ministry and of taking a hard line with abuse victims who sought justice through the courts.

In responding to a 1994 lawsuit, for instance, Levada's lawyers argued that a woman who had been impregnated by a seminarian and was suing for $200,000 was negligent because she engaged "in unprotected intercourse . . . when [she] should have known that could result in pregnancy." The seminarian, Arturo Uribe, was later ordained a priest and the woman was given just $215 a month in child support from the church. News of Levada's tactics emerged in July 2005, and a month later the archbishop left to take up a post in Rome as the new head of the Congregation for the Doctrine of the Faith—Benedict's personal choice as his successor at the CDF. The following March, Benedict made Levada a cardinal, along with fourteen other churchmen, giving him a vote in the conclave.

Thus the church's new chief doctrinal overseer left behind not only an archdiocese in bankruptcy but a legal record in which he had argued that a woman should have violated the very church teachings that he has a sacred duty to defend. While it is probable that Levada never saw the motion before it was filed, it was characteristic of his willingness to use hard-line tactics, and it was also troubling to Catholics, left and right, that he did not repudiate the maneuver. Moreover, at his farewell Mass at a San Francisco cathedral on August 7, Levada was served in the sacristy with a subpoena to testify about his handling of clergy sexual abuse in Portland. (Things didn't get much better for Levada when his cousin, a priest across the bay in Oakland, published a letter to Levada pleading with him to change the CDF, which he said had become "heavy-handed and unilateral." Father Richard Mangini cited Reese's dismissal as a prime example of what he was talking about.)

So it was that, at the start of Benedict's papacy, the most powerful American ever to serve at the Vatican remained embroiled in court battles in the United States over his role in the scandals, while the leader of the American hierarchy headed a bankrupt diocese that was about to sell his house out from under him.

Then in Philadelphia, in September 2005, a grand jury released a scathing 418-page report, three years in the making, that recounted in horrifying detail how previous two archbishops, the late Cardinal John Krol and Cardinal Anthony Bevilacqua, then retired, engaged in a systematic cover-up over four decades to shield dozens of priests who sexually abused hundreds of children. "We mean rape," the grand jury report said. "Boys who were raped orally, boys who were raped anally, girls who were raped vaginally." It concluded, "What makes these allegations all the worse, the grand jurors believe, is that the abuses that Cardinal Bevilacqua and his aides allowed children to suffer—the molestations, the rapes, the lifelong shame and despair—did not result from failures or lapses, except of the moral variety. They were made possible by purposeful decisions, carefully implemented policies, and calculated indifference."

In Los Angeles, the nation's largest diocese, and across Ireland, Christendom's most faithful land, and elsewhere, new revelations continued to shake the church to its foundations.

It was Boston all over again, and Boston was not even over.

Cardinal Bernard Law, the only prelate to step down because of public pressure from the scandal, continued to make headlines, none of them welcome to American Catholics. Despite his resignation as archbishop, he retained his post in numerous influential Vatican offices, including the Congregation for Bishops, the powerful body that vets candidates for promotion to bishop, thus giving him a major voice in shaping the U.S. hierarchy he left behind. In fact, Law was a member of more Vatican departments than any other American bishop not resident in Rome. For Americans, the topper was Law's promotion in May 2004 to the head of the Basilica of St. Mary Major in Rome. That move shocked American Catholics, not least because it came just two days after his successor, Archbishop Sean O'Malley, announced that he would have to close sixty-five parishes in large part to help cover the financial wreckage that Law left in his wake.

That was salt in the wounded psyche of the American church; to American Catholics, the bishops seemed immune from any penalties and inured to the cries for dialogue and openness that continued to ring forth from lay Catholics, especially grassroots movements like Voice of the Faithful (VOTF). This lay-led organization sprang up from the outrage over the Boston scandals, and it quickly mushroomed to more than thirty thousand members across the country. VOTF maintained a laserlike focus on pressing for structural reforms that would make the church more transparent and accountable to avoid such scandals and restore trust in the hierarchy. Yet many bishops continued to bar VOTF from church property, with some going so far as to describe them as "anti-Catholic." If that was discouraging to laypeople, the fact that a few bishops allowed or even welcomed VOTF was downright confusing. How could an organization be anti-Catholic in one diocese and in the neighboring diocese be perfectly acceptable? And why, when canon law explicitly acknowledged the right of the laity to "cooperate in the exercise" of governance with the pastors, were laypeople so persistently excluded from participation?

In the wake of the scandals it also became clear that structures that were available were underutilized, or worse. Parish finance councils, for example, are the only parish-level body mandated by canon law, yet it was estimated that at best only two-thirds of the nation's nineteen thousand parishes had such councils, and there were serious doubts about how well many of those that existed worked. (In fact, the bishops' conference keeps no such figures, so even the bishops are in the dark about much of this information.) Similarly, diocesan pastoral and finance councils were poorly or too rarely implemented, and one church official estimated that in recent years as few as twenty of the nearly two hundred U.S. dioceses released annual financial statements to the people who put $6 billion a year into the collection plate.

Rather than focusing on improving transparency and lay participation, however, or adopting measures to sanction wrongdoers in their own ranks, either past or future, the thrust of the American bishops' response was aimed largely at abusive priests and toward ensuring that the parish of the future would be a safe environment for any boy or girl. Many of the bishops' programs were laudable efforts and put the Catholic Church—albeit later than necessary—ahead of other U.S. denominations in terms of child protection. Indeed, almost unnoticed amid the wave of reports was the fact that the number of abusers in the priesthood had declined sharply in the previous decade as many seminaries—there were terrible exceptions—began more rigorous screening of priest candidates, and many bishops, motivated either by lessons from lawsuits or outrage at the abuses, instituted stricter policies on their own. But many leading bishops continued to try to rein in the National Review Board, expressing concern that as laypeople, they were overstepping church bounds by being perceived as wielding authority over bishops, a canonical no-no.

Moreover, the exclusive focus on the sins of individual priests struck many as diverting the focus from the responsibility of the bishops as supervisors. Many also felt that the vaunted zero-tolerance policy, which put priests out of ministry permanently after one credible accusation, was Draconian and a denial of the core Christian belief in the ever-present opportunity of atonement and redemption. The defrocking, or laicization, of priests was also seen as an unacceptable nullification of the sacrament of holy orders. Others simply did not trust the bishops to implement the policies, which they felt were barely tough enough on priests.

For his part, Benedict, then cardinal Ratzinger, initially downplayed the reports of the abuse, calling them exaggerated and driven by an American media industry that he viewed as inherently biased against the church. Ratzinger's own experience with the American media made his views somewhat understandable. Father Neuhaus recalled inviting Cardinal Ratzinger to give a lecture in midtown Manhattan in 1988. The talk was interrupted by gay activists "who waved their pink triangles while screaming pleasantries such as 'Sieg

Heil!' 'Nazi Ratzy!' and 'Inquisitor Go Home!'" Neuhaus said. He called the police to clear the protesters but said Ratzinger remained "the very picture of tranquility" and later spoke spontaneously about his experience with the 1968 student rebellions and the indispensability of civility in human relations. Neuhaus said the tabloid headlines the next day read, "Gays Protest Vatican Biggy." He said Ratzinger chuckled at the "Biggy" moniker, but his close friends and his brother, Georg, have said that the unceasing stream of bad press over the years did gnaw at Ratzinger.[14]

The ongoing revelations of abuse, however, began to raise suspicions among some in the Vatican that all was not as they had hoped. Cardinal Ratzinger was especially disturbed by the prospect of what he would later decry, in his Augustinian manner, as the "filth in the church . . . even among those who, in the priesthood, ought to belong entirely to [Christ]." When members of the National Review Board requested meetings with Vatican officials to brief them on the crisis, Ratzinger was one of several curial cardinals who met with the lay leaders, spending two and a half hours with them and his top aides in January 2004. "Cardinal Ratzinger was far more open to meeting with members of the national review board than our own bishops and cardinals," said Judge Anne Burke, who led the board at the time. Burke said Ratzinger was very engaged in the topic, beyond his department's responsibility for dealing with most cases to determine whether a priest should be laicized. "He took in everything we had to say and answered our questions. And we pulled no punches: We told him what was going on in terms of the extent of the actual abuse by the priests and about our dismay with the U.S. church hierarchy." It was also characteristic of Cardinal Ratzinger's personal pastoral solicitude that he wrote Burke a warm letter after her thirty-year-old son was killed in a snowmobile accident the following month. "He had heard of the sad news of my son and he expressed his sorrow and condolences, and reminded us to have consolation in our faith," Burke said. "It was a very, very beautiful note. I still have it."[15]

Still, Ratzinger always had qualms about the American bishops' one-strike policy, as did many in the church, because it seemed to slight the chance of redemption and rehabilitation, and because it viewed all violations with equal gravity. Under the policy, a single advance to a seventeen-year-old three decades ago carried the same penalty as that faced by an unrepentant serial pedophile. Perhaps if the flock had had more faith in the bishops, there would have been greater leeway for a more flexible policy.

The steady stream of terrible stories finally overcame Ratzinger's reservations about the one-strike policy, however, and as prefect of the CDF he took steps to accelerate the process for laicizing offending clerics. In fact, there was such a glut of cases and appeals by accused priests as a result of the tough new policy that at one point the CDF, which became the chief arbiter of the cases, reportedly had a backlog of some seven hundred cases. Benedict appointed Levada as prefect of the CDF, less for his theological expertise—Benedict will remain the church's top theologian—than for his experience in dealing with sexual abuse cases. Yet Levada did not endear himself to victims with his legal-istic, careful, close-to-the-vest manner of dealing with cases. Even a member of his own lay review board resigned in protest at Levada's decisions. But Levada had served on a commission of U.S. bishops and Vatican officials charged with translating the bishops' zero-tolerance policy into church law. That is the kind of juridical experience the CDF needed.

Benedict's approach bore fruit in May 2006 when, after a long and fitful investigation, the CDF finally disciplined Father Marcial Maciel Degollado, the charismatic founder of a powerful worldwide order of archconservative Catholics known as the Legionaries of Christ. Maciel, a Mexican cleric, had for years been the subject of complaints that he sexually abused boys and young seminarians under his tutelage; in fact, he had faced charges in the 1950s but was eventually cleared. Over the ensuing decades the Legionaries under Maciel grew in numbers and influence as hyper-orthodoxy came into vogue in Rome. The allegations against him continued, but were not particularly welcome at the Vatican, where Maciel enjoyed the special protection of John Paul. In 1999 Ratzinger effectively halted an inquiry into Maciel's case, and the Legionaries' founder seemed in the clear.

But to their enormous credit, Maciel's accusers continued to come forward, despite the official opposition. Harvard law professor Mary Ann Glendon, for example, a favorite conservative of the Vatican, publicly praised Maciel's "radi-ant holiness" and blamed anti-Catholicism and "irresponsible journalists" for the supposed calumnies against Maciel. Many of the victims were also spurred in their pursuit of justice by John Paul's continued public praise for the "in-tense, generous and fruitful priestly ministry" of Father Maciel, who the pope once called "an efficacious guide to youth." A 2004 book, *Vows of Silence,* by investigative journalists Jason Berry and Gerald Renner, was a powerful and al-most irrefutable indictment of Maciel that lent further momentum to the case against him. By 2004, so many accusers had lodged complaints—several dozen according to reports—that Ratzinger and the CDF pushed forward with the investigation, which was led by a dogged Maltese priest, Monsignor Charles Scicluna.

In May 2006 the Vatican announced that it "invited" Maciel, now eighty-six years old, to halt his public ministry, such as celebrating mass and giving lectures, and to lead a "reserved life of prayer and penitence." The Vatican said it would pursue no canonical penalties against Maciel because of his age and health, and the CDF made no declaration on the merit of the allegations, although it seemed obvious that Rome considered at least some of them to be legitimate. The Vatican also stressed that the Legionaries were considered a valued organization in good standing.

These careful hedgings allowed the many conservatives who had strongly defended Maciel (usually by harshly attacking his critics) to save face by continuing to raise doubts about the case against him, or to assert that anything that did happen took place fifty years ago or more. And it allowed Maciel to maintain his innocence while accepting the invitation to retire (he had already retired in 2005) with "complete serenity and tranquility of conscience." In his parting shot Maciel compared himself to Jesus, saying that, like Christ, he decided not to defend himself, and that his suffering, like Christ's, was a Cross that would bring glory to the Legionaries. Still, Benedict's action was commendable. It left many conservatives flummoxed or looking foolish, and it underscored Benedict's impatience with personal sexual misconduct.

Similarly, as cardinal, and then as pope, Benedict backed the inspection of U.S. seminaries in late 2005 aimed at weeding out "dissenters" and some homosexual seminarians. Characteristically, Benedict saw the crisis in terms of a personal failing on the part of the priests who directly perpetrated the abuse rather than blaming the system that protected them or the bishops who ran that system. The scandal was, as he noted, "a weakness of human beings, even of priests. Temptations are present also for the priests. I think the essential point is a weakness of faith."[16] But the epitome of this approach, and a nadir of Benedict's first year as pope, came with the publication of a long-awaited document that sought to bar gay men from the priesthood. The document, which was released just after Thanksgiving and just before Advent, presented a heavy-handed policy that seemed to contradict every claim Benedict's supporters made about his being a papacy of intellectual prowess and managerial aplomb.

The issue of homosexuality has always been of great interest to Benedict, who wrote far more about the topic while at the CDF than any other churchman ever had. Characteristically, however, Ratzinger also seems to have formed his judgments with little, if any, real-life interaction with homosexual men and women to inform his views. In a telling exchange, Sister Jeannine

Gramick, the American nun whom Ratzinger would eventually banish from her ministry to gays and lesbians, ran into Ratzinger by chance on an airplane ride from Rome to Bavaria in July 1998. (The cardinal was going to see his brother; the nun was going to pray for aid at the Munich shrine of her order's foundress.) Gramick struck up a pleasant conversation with Ratzinger, at first not recognizing him and believing him to be a simple priest. When he revealed his identity, they began talking about the issues on which Ratzinger was investigating her. When Gramick asked whether the cardinal had ever met any gay people, Ratzinger replied: "Yes, in Berlin. They were demonstrating against the pope."[17] That Ratzinger's only interaction with homosexuals was at such a remove and under such circumstances does not inspire confidence in his conclusions, nor does it square with the reality that there are many gay priests and bishops, not only in the worldwide church, but most certainly in the Roman Curia itself. That this would be unknown to Ratzinger is either remarkably ingenuous, willfully blind, or simply evidence of the don't ask, don't tell policy that permeates much of clerical life, and in fact can foster sexual dysfunctions of all kinds.

It was in 1996, two years before Gramick's meeting with Ratzinger, that the cardinal began exploring a policy statement to bar homosexuals from the priesthood. This was well before the sexual abuse scandal erupted in 2002, a scandal that many conservatives would try to pin on homosexual priests, despite a lack of evidence to back up such charges. Estimates are that anywhere from 20 to 40 percent of priests—and bishops—may be gay, but there is no indication that they are any more likely to break their promise of celibacy than straight priests. (Nor was there a recognition of the culpability of bishops who either ignored or covered up for abusers.) The abuse scandal, however, gave Ratzinger's project new life, and became a useful pretext for taking action against gay men in the priesthood. Still, so great was the resistance among bishops around the world, and especially in America, where chaste and celibate homosexuals were serving as priests of great distinction, that the document was stuck in a kind of bureaucratic limbo. Ratzinger's election as pope finally cleared the way for it to be published, on November 29, 2005—without the customary press conference to elaborate on its contents.

This document would actually need more explanation than most, however, because after years of research and debate, the paper, called an "instruction," was in the end just six pages and raised more questions than it answered. The instruction boiled down to a three-fold policy: it said that the church cannot ordain men who are active homosexuals, who have "deep-seated homosexual tendencies," or who support the "gay culture." The first and third proscriptions, against ordaining those who are sexually active and those who work as gay activists, were hardly surprising; they would apply equally to heterosexuals. It was the second proscription, against men with "deep-seated homosexual tendencies," that caused the most consternation. Because the instruction did not use the English equivalent of homosexual "orientation," there was initial debate as to what the Vatican phrase meant. The definition soon came from two sources, neither of whom burnished the Vatican's image.

First, Cardinal Zenon Grocholewski, head of the Congregation for Catholic Education that officially produced the document (because it deals with the formation of seminarians), tried to explain the phrase in an interview with Vatican Radio on November 29 by contrasting "deep-seated tendencies" with those of a "transitory" nature. Transitory homosexual inclinations he defined as "some curiosity during adolescence; or accidental circumstances in a state of drunkenness; or particular circumstances, like someone who was in prison for many years." As long as someone has sobered up, or matured beyond adolescent experimentation, or been released from prison and refrained from homosexual acts for at least three years, he can be ordained, he said. Those who identify as homosexual, even if they have shown themselves capable of chastity, cannot.

An article that same day in the official Vatican newspaper, *L'Osservatore Romano,* went further still. Penned by a French priest and psychoanalyst, Monsignor Tony Anatrella, the article said that "deep-seated homosexual tendencies" means those with "an exclusive attraction to persons of the same sex—independently of whether or not they have had erotic experiences." In other words, chastity does not count for gay men. In a series of questionable and inflammatory statements, Anatrella said homosexuality does not have a biological basis but rather is "a problem in the psychic organization" of a person's sexuality. "Unfortunately, for many years in some countries a permissive attitude has allowed people to think that candidates (for the priesthood) who have this tendency could be ordained as long as they assumed perfect continence," he wrote. He said the scandals were due to "typical behaviors and expressions on the part of these personalities." Anatrella wrote that gay men tend to have few friends, to close themselves off from others in "a clan of persons of the same type," to resent the claims on their time made by parishioners, to encourage other gay men to enter the priesthood, and to deal with authority predominantly as a matter of "seduction and rejection."

"One must free oneself from the idea that leads one to believe that, insofar as a homosexual person respects his commitment to continence lived in chastity, there will not be problems and he can therefore be ordained a priest," Anatrella wrote. A seminarian must attain "a sufficient affective and sexual maturity coherent with his masculine sexual identity. . . . He must, in principle, be suitable for marriage and able to exercise fatherhood over his children. And it is under those mature conditions that he renounces exercising them in order to give himself to God in the priesthood," the monsignor wrote. He said a priest must be heterosexual in order to be seen as a "bridegroom of the church" and as a "spiritual father" to those to whom he is ministering.

"A homosexual person would have difficulty incarnating this symbolic reality of the spousal bond and spiritual paternity," he continued. Because the priest acts in the "person of Christ," Monsignor Anatrella said, the church calls only "men mature in their masculine identity" to the diaconate and priesthood.[18]

Few theologians could cite any basis for Anatrella's analysis, nor was there any legitimate scientific or sociological underpinning for his other assertions. Indeed, the document was clinical in its language, yet showed a lack of any understanding of the latest research on homosexuality. The instruction declared, for example, that homosexuals "find themselves in a situation that gravely hinders them from relating correctly to men and women"—a blanket statement with no apparent justification. Nor, on a pastoral level, was there the slightest nod toward the remarkable sacrifice and great ministry of countless homosexual priests, nor any hint of a Gospel orientation beyond a standard disclaimer that homosexuals should not be discriminated against. Yet by painting homosexuals in such a distorted light, and by appearing to pin on them the canards of sexual deviance and an inability to function as chaste, psychologically healthy priests, Benedict's action opened the door to a wave of homophobic commentary and nasty attacks on gay men and homosexual priests in particular.

Moreover, the publicly released version of the instruction declared that the new policy did not apply to men already ordained. Yet within days it was revealed that an unpublished letter accompanying the Vatican document was sent to all bishops and ordered them to remove any priest who is gay from positions of responsibility at seminaries or in teaching seminarians. There were many other ramifications of the instruction, nearly all negative. For one thing, the Vatican policy seems likely to drive gay priests even further into the clerical closet—a dark corner that sad experience shows is often crowded with the very conservatives who are loudest in their denunciations of homosexuals, and also likely to act out in unhealthy and often criminal ways. There was no explanation as to exactly how seminaries were to determine whether someone was gay, if in fact that could be done without the kind of honest and mature exploration that the policy in fact inhibits. (In his *L'Osservatore Romano* article, Monsignor Anatrella suggested that red flags included seminarians who had trouble relating to their fathers; have difficulty in discussing sexual questions; view pornography on the Internet; demonstrate a deep sense of guilt; or often see themselves as victims.)

The document also demonstrates, albeit through a warped lens, the kind of utilitarianism of the modern world that Pope Benedict himself decries—the idea that because gay men may cause trouble for the church, their vocation should be rendered invalid. If that is the motivation, then sexually active or sexually abusive heterosexual priests, who are an enormous problem in many parts of the world, should also be the subject of Vatican action. Instead, for the meanest of rationales, and one that does not hold up to scrutiny, the Vatican is essentially thwarting what God has desired.

The problems with Vatican instruction were manifold and the reaction was enormous and varied and usually harsh, both for and against Rome's instruction. Having failed in their efforts to convince the pope to alter the document's wording, most United States bishops, even many prominent conservatives, as well as the leaders of religious orders, opted to ignore the Vatican's edict. They said the document affirmed what they had been doing all along, which was to ordain psychologically mature men regardless of their sexual orientation, which is what they would continue to do. Behind the American reaction was the assumption that the document on gay priests was so flawed that it would be quietly shelved. But in late February 2006, Cardinal-designate Levada, Benedict's chosen successor at the CDF and the church's top doctrinal officer, put an end to that hope. Levada was preaching at a mass for the installation of the new rector of the North American College, the Roman seminary that is considered a training ground for the elite among future priests, when he began a disquisition on gay priests that several observers called bizarre. In his homily, Levada repeated the theological formula that because the Bible describes God's love for his people as the love of a husband for a wife, and because Jesus is described as the bridegroom of the church, and because homosexuals desire men and not women, and because men cannot marry men, then gay men cannot be priests because priests are supposed to represent Christ who marries the female-gendered church. Never mind that Levada completely literalizes (and sexualizes) a tender nuptial metaphor, or that God's love of his people is more often described as that of a parent for a child, a metaphor that might cause trouble for the church's celibacy laws were it also taken so literally. Moreover, among the many metaphors for the church (including the church as mother), an equally sacred one is that of the church as the Body of Christ himself—a gender-bender that ought to give Levada pause. In general, using poetic images to make church policy is bad ecclesiology and bad policy.

The kicker, however, was when Levada referred to a few gay priests who, upset at the Vatican instruction on homosexual seminarians, decided to announce that they were gay—and celibate. "I think we must ask, 'Does such a priest recognize how this act places an obstacle to his ability to represent Christ the bridegroom to his bride, the people of God? Does he not see how his declaration places him at odds with the spousal character of love as revealed by God and imaged in humanity?'" Levada said to the 170 seminarians. "Sadly," he said, "this provides a good example of the wisdom of the new Vatican instruction." Sad indeed as it was also a warning to gay priests (and would-be priests) to stay in the closet, hardly a healthy or honest—or Christian—response.

Also sad was Levada's order two weeks later to his successor in San Francisco, Archbishop Niederauer, to stop Catholic Charities from placing children for adoption with gay couples. That action came shortly after Levada intervened to halt gay adoptions by the Catholic Charities in Boston, which led church officials there to suspend their entire adoption program—a pillar of the church's campaign to reduce abortions. Equally disconcerting was that Levada himself, while he headed the San Francisco archdiocese, allowed gay couples to adopt through his Catholic Charities agency. Now, in shutting down that option, Levada argued that the placements he approved were "prudential judgments" for "difficult to place" children, but that even those would no longer be allowed—a move he based on a 2003 document from Ratzinger's CDF, which he now headed. "The reasons given in the document, as well as the potential scandal for the faithful should an archdiocesan agency act contrary to the clear teaching of the church's magisterium, require that a Catholic bishop follow this clear guidance from the Holy See in his oversight of Catholic diocesan agencies," Levada wrote, without explaining or apologizing for the fact that he had ignored that very same "clear guidance."[19]

What effect Benedict's clampdown will have on the priesthood and the vocations shortage will play out in coming years. What is certain is that Benedict's action sowed deep pain and confusion in a priesthood that had already taken more than its fair share of lumps in the sexual abuse scandal. It also did nothing to polish the credibility of the new pontificate among laypeople or the wider world. And it spared the bishops any similar scrutiny.

As for purifying the hierarchy, the episcopal corollary to the solution of forming holier priests, in Benedict's view, is to appoint tougher bishops who would enforce good moral conduct and punish abusers. That approach is not likely to mollify American Catholics, however. They want to see sanctions leveled against bishops who have clearly committed purposeful errors of oversight. They know that when bishops were caught as sexual abusers themselves, as happened to a half-dozen American prelates during the crisis, they were forced to resign and given no consolation honors by the Vatican. Americans believe that those who enabled the abusers should be held just as responsible. They also know that the Vatican did not hesitate to discipline or even remove bishops whom Rome perceived as "too liberal," as happened with Seattle archbishop Raymond Hunthausen in the 1980s.

If there is no "purification of memory," as John Paul would have called it, on the sexual abuse crisis, then the preaching of a new generation of bishops appointed by Benedict will come across as nothing more than high-handed moralizing.

Moreover, American Catholics are keenly aware that for more than a generation, the Vatican under John Paul had already been promoting orthodox, supposedly hard-line, bishops—or at least that's how they acted toward their parishioners—and many of them were the very men who allowed abuse to occur. In fact, Cardinal Ratzinger, who sat on the Congregation for Bishops and was a close adviser to John Paul, had had a hand in most of those appointments. So they will wonder how naming more bishops like that, rather than collaborative prelates who will encourage transparency and cooperation with the laity, is supposed to produce a different outcome.

One of the simplest and most effective reforms would actually be a return to the long-standing tradition of having true local consultation on the appointment of bishops, a "reform" that would actually be the kind of "restoration" that appeals to Benedict's nature. "He who is to preside over all must be elected by all," said Pope Leo the Great (440–61). This local option was the praxis for much of the church's history, as priests and even laity had a say in choosing their bishops up until the nineteenth century. In fact, it was only the 1917 Code of Canon Law that finally reserved all episcopal appointments to the Roman pontiff, a critical step in the modern papalizing of Catholicism, which many see as foreshadowing a much more quiescent hierarchy. After the 1917 change, there remained a few places in Europe where local clergy were allowed a say in the selection of a new bishop, and everywhere else the accepted practice was to consult fairly broadly with local church leaders. But under John Paul even that concession to local rule was halted, and appointments were increasingly made by a few Roman power brokers, with little local input and quite often with disastrous results. The call for greater local input has drawn support across the spectrum, from retired San Francisco archbishop John R. Quinn, in his writings advocating a reform of the hierarchy, to the conservative commentator and papal biographer George Weigel.

Again, transparency and consultation, while disparaged as modern novelties, are in point of fact nothing new. "I have made it a rule, ever since the beginning of my episcopate, to make no decision merely on the strength of my own personal opinion without consulting you [priests and deacons], without the approbation of the people." Those were the words of Saint Cyprian, who was bishop of Carthage in North Africa back in the third century, a role model for Saint Augustine.

Not surprisingly, the sexual abuse scandal also highlighted demands for changes in, or at least dialogue on, church teachings on such topics as a married priesthood, women's ordination, communion for divorced and remarried Catholics, the ban on artificial birth control, and a whole range of controverted issues that have been roiling the church in the decades since Vatican II.

While these issues concern the teachings and policies of the church rather than the structure of the church, Pope Benedict seems no more amenable to changing them than was his predecessor, and maybe even less so. For Benedict, most of these issues are what constitutionalists would call settled law, that is, matters that have been chewed over and definitively ruled out by Rome. So agitating to reopen debate is merely self-interested dissent. But above all, Benedict sees the reform agenda, or "canon of criticism," as his favored biographer, Peter Seewald, puts it, as beside the point. For one thing, he views mainline Protestantism as the laboratory for all of these reform issues and contends that the ongoing struggles of many Protestant denominations demonstrate that the experiment has failed. "For it shows that being a Christian today does not stand or fall on these questions," he told Seewald in 1996. "That the resolution of these matters doesn't make the Gospel more attractive or being Christian any easier. It does not even achieve the agreement that will better hold the Church together. I believe we should finally be clear on this point, that the Church is not suffering on account of these questions."[20]

Instead, he says, Catholics must return to right belief rather than push reform agendas. In fact, he believes, reformers postpone a better future for the church by pursuing their agenda. Benedict is more than willing to wait them out rather than compromise, and now he is in a position to ensure that the church will wait them out as well. The hoped-for reforms, he has said, "will lose their urgency as soon as the Church is no longer looked upon as a final end, an end in itself, and as a place for gaining power. As soon as celibacy is once again lived convincingly out of a strong faith. As soon as we see eternal life as the goal of Christianity instead of ensconcing ourselves in a group in which one can exercise power, I am convinced that a spiritual turning point will come sometime and that these questions will lose their urgency as suddenly as they arose. After all, in the end, they are not man's real questions, either."[21]

For Benedict, another problem with focusing on visible reform is that it smacks of "taking the easy way out." True reform, he says, is an internal renewal by individual Christians that "has more to do with renouncing external power and external factors, in order to live all the more by the faith." The alternative model, which he disdains, "consists in making history more comfortable, to caricature this approach somewhat. And then things go awry, of course."[22] He laments what he sees as a self-centered church that is consumed by this idea of change, which is the opposite of the faith's task to take us outside, beyond ourselves. Today, however, Catholics "look only at ourselves; we are concerned only with ourselves; we lick our wounds; we want to construct a nice Church for ourselves and hardly see any longer that the Church doesn't exist for herself but that we have a word that has something to say to the world and that ought to be heard. . . . We are too forgetful of our real tasks."[23] For those people seeking a "nice Church," Benedict points to what are known as the "hard sayings" of Jesus in the Gospels as a much-needed counterbalance to the church of "affirmation" or "good news" (*Froh-Botschaft* in German) that many would prefer. "There are quite dramatic words of judgement in the Gospel that can really make one shudder," he told Seewald. "We ought not to stifle them. The Lord himself in the Gospel obviously sees no contradiction between the message of judgment and the good news."[24]

Benedict's reductionist view of the reform movement is a familiar approach to ideas he opposes. In Benedict's eyes, reform is cast as choosing between belief in God and belief in an institution rather than seeing a potentially positive interplay between transcendent faith and the actions of God's ordained church on earth. But his visceral rejection of the entire idea of reform in the church becomes more comprehensible given that it was formed by his experience of the drama of the Second Vatican Council and the tumult that followed.

As Benedict often notes, with great regret, the many changes spawned by the council gave the appearance of a church in permanent flux, rather than the preferred vision of the church as an unchanging edifice; it was the venerable battle cry of the ultramontanist Catholics, *ecclesia semper idem,* the never-changing church, versus the Protestant slogan of *ecclesia semper reformanda,* the ever-changing church. The reformist crowd certainly seemed to have the upper hand. Men and women religious were exchanging their distinctive (often suffocating) habits and cassocks for civilian wear, and strictures against eating meat on Fridays were going by the wayside. The church was suddenly changing a lot, and all at once. The Mass was no longer in Latin and the priest was facing the flock, who now seemed more like congregants in the Protestant churches that Catholics had once been forbidden to enter at the risk of their immortal souls. Catholics could now take communion in the hand while standing—feeding themselves, essentially—rather than on the tongue from the priest while kneeling at the altar rail, which by the by, was also being removed from the sanctuary.

All of this left Joseph Ratzinger, and many others, deeply upset, and the recent trend toward recovering some aspects of pre–Vatican II Catholic culture can, in its best manifestations, go beyond mere nostalgia to an honest desire to reconnect with that culture and with aspects of the rites and devotions that sustained it for so long. Unfortunately, much of the restorationist battle focuses on resurrecting the Tridentine Latin Mass, which is more a wedge issue for paleo-con Catholics rather than a manifestation of Catholicism's diversity or a sign of any widespread push for a Latin restoration among the faithful, or even among the bishops.

The council's teachings made it obvious that, both in principle and in the visible practices of Catholicism, the church had changed and could change, and likely would change. Before the council, Catholics tended to think that the doctrinal world was flat. Afterward, believers realized they would not sail off the edge of the moral planet if they explored church teachings a bit more adventurously, and so critical examination became the postconciliar trend.

This popular theologizing was also fostered by the council's definition of the church as the "People of God" rather than as a kind of religious monarchy or a "perfect society." The People-of-God motif had a venerable history in Christian tradition, which drew on the repeated use of communal references to Israel in the Old Testament and references to the wider Christian community in Saint Paul's epistles in the New Testament. During the Second Vatican Council, the People of God concept won out as the reigning image of the church, set above even the image of the church as the Body of Christ. As Notre Dame theologian Richard McBrien notes, the council fathers—after a dramatic debate—decided to devote an entire chapter to the People of God idea in the

Dogmatic Constitution on the Church, placing it before a chapter on the hierarchy to emphasize that "the Church is a community with a hierarchical structure rather than a hierarchical body with spiritual subjects."

"The People-of-God image reminds us that we are saved not merely as individuals but as a community and that everyone in the community—laity, religious, and clergy alike—participates in the three-fold mission of Christ as prophet, priest, and king," McBrien writes. "The image, therefore, introduces a principle of coresponsibility that some Catholics, contrary to the council itself, find threatening to the Church's traditional structure of governance."[25]

One such Catholic was Joseph Ratzinger. As a cardinal, Ratzinger lamented that "the Council's view [of the Church] has not been kept in mind by a good part of post-Conciliar theology, and has been replaced by an idea of the 'people of God' that, in not a few cases, is almost banal, reducing it to an a theological and purely sociological view."

Benedict's response to the evolutionary model of church teachings was to argue that Vatican II had been misused by proponents of reform on the one hand and, on the other hand, interpreted by ultra-orthodox Catholics as tantamount to an apostasy because it rejected specific assertions of previous popes and councils. Benedict argued that in reality Vatican II "is in the strictest continuity" with the First Vatican Council (1869–70) and with the Counter-Reformation era Council of Trent (1545–63). He declared that progressives cannot take a position in favor of Vatican II over Vatican I and Trent, and likewise that traditionalists cannot take a position in favor of Vatican I and Trent over Vatican II. "Every partisan choice destroys the whole (the very history of the Church) which can exist only as an indivisible unity."[26]

Yet Benedict's own view is also a partisan choice of sorts, in that he sees his version of the council—and that of John Paul—as "the authentic interpretation of Vatican II," an opinion that would be widely contested by other church leaders and thinkers. Underlying Benedict's absolutist stance is the desire to show that church history is a single, consistent whole, a reading that will not only enhance the truth claims of Catholicism but also warn off those who would try to change church teachings today. This avoids altogether the debate over how the church should change, or even whether it should change, and places the blame squarely on the shoulders of Catholics themselves instead of Catholic tradition. "I am convinced that the damage that we have incurred in these twenty years"—Cardinal Ratzinger was speaking in 1984—"is due, not to the 'true' Council, but to the unleashing *within* the Church of latent polemical and centrifugal forces."[27]

Two decades later, as Pope Benedict XVI, Joseph Ratzinger reprised that view in a pre-Christmas address to the Roman Curia, in which the pope compared the post–Vatican II era to Saint Basil's description of the church after the turbulent Council of Nicaea in 325—two fleets fighting a naval battle amid a terrible storm, "full of the inarticulate screams, the unintelligible noises, rising from the ceaseless agitations that divert the right rule of the doctrine of true religion." But in this address Benedict announced that the right side—his side—had now won out over what he called a "hermeneutics of discontinuity and rupture" that had "caused confusion" by preaching, with the aid of the "mass media, and also a certain sector of modern theology," that the council had changed church positions or teachings. Benedict said his own camp had embraced what he ironically called the "hermeneutics of reform" that was faithful to the true church. Their camp has "silently but more and more visibly, bore and is bearing fruit."

Benedict asserted that those who saw the council as a new course for the church invoked the "spirit" of Vatican II in order to further their progressive agenda. Under that spirit-driven approach, he said, "room is made for any whimsicality"—a widespread view that he said represented "a basic misunderstanding of the nature of a Council." In a striking passage, Benedict argued that the bishops of the council did not change anything in the church because even a council does not have such authority. He dismissed the idea of a "spirit" of the council, which could be stretched to mean anything, and instead argued that Catholics must rely solely on a close reading of the texts—the perennial fallback position of the cautious scholar fearful of coloring outside the lines.

Benedict's radical rereading of Vatican II does several things. One is to declare that ongoing debate over the council is over, and to place those who disagree with his position (which would be the vast majority of Catholics and theologians who see the council as marking an important development in church teachings and policies) definitively on the losing side. Even though Ratzinger is now pope, his declaration cannot end a debate that will continue, and indeed must take place, if the council is to be "received." Benedict's argument is also ingenious in that it ignores conservative laments that the council was a mistake or an outright failure. Benedict instead simply redefines Vatican II as something entirely different from the consensus view that it was a council of reform—thereby allowing those who disagree with the council to safely reject the parts they do not like.

But the most significant point in Benedict's address is his false dichotomy of a "rupture" and a "reform" view (now coopting the latter term for his own side). Reformers and progressives at the council, and clearly the council itself, did not see Vatican II as a break with traditional Catholicism but rather as a fulfillment of the church's perennial, pilgrim mission. Benedict's argument, instead, is at heart an attempt to argue against the very notion of development or outright change. Such an interpretation is understandably satisfying on an emotional level for someone like Benedict, who cherishes his self-image as consistent and constant across time, having been right from the start and thus right at the end. Yet Benedict's rejection of the idea of the council as one of reform and change rewrites his own long paper trail of criticism of the council for adopting reforms and changes that he did not like. And his exhortation to embrace the "texts" rather than the "spirit" of the council also runs counter to Ratzinger's notable public criticism of those very texts. Moreover, the presumption against change is intellectually dubious given the history of the church.

The reality of course is that church teachings, traditions, and laws have changed, developing and refining and sometimes undoing previous doctrines. Mandatory priestly celibacy is a canonical development of the second millennium of Christianity, for example, and Latin supplanted Greek in the first millennium, when Latin became the vernacular and church authorities realized no one understood Greek any longer. In 1215 the Fourth Lateran Council famously asserted the doctrine that *extra Ecclesiam nulla salus* (outside the Church there is no salvation), with the intention of excluding all but faithful Catholics from heaven. Nearly eight centuries later, Pope Benedict XVI, at a November 2005 public audience, told the crowd that even those without a biblical belief could be saved if they have "a spark of desire for the unknown"—a fairly clear upending of the Lateran Council's intent, and one that was made possible by Vatican II's imaginative recasting of the earlier teaching. This kind of development has taken place on all manner of topics; it has had to. In a 1445 papal bull, Eugene IV declared that circumcision "cannot possibly be observed without loss of eternal salvation," and in 1829, Pope Leo XII declared smallpox to be "a judgement of God." He said that "Whoever allows himself to be vaccinated ceases to be a child of God." Neither teaching could hold out long. In 1994, Pope John Paul II forcefully ruled virtually out of bounds any use of the death penalty, even though the Vatican itself had had a capital punishment statute on its books up until the 1960s. In his recent book *A Church That Can and Cannot Change: The Development of Catholic Moral Teaching*, John T. Noonan Jr. shows how apparently definitive church positions on slavery, usury, divorce, and religious freedom have changed.

The whole question of how church teachings change, whether they can change, what constitutes a reformable or irreformable teaching, and who has the authority to make changes, if they can be made, is justifiably one of the most controversial and perilous topics in the church today. Benedict rightly worries about the loss of a belief in absolute truths and about the prevalence of the conviction that each person can decide for himself or herself what is true, or which truth is important and which can easily be disregarded. On the other hand, surveys show that on central Christian beliefs, such as belief in the resurrection of Christ and the centrality and efficacy of the sacraments, Catholics remain remarkably united and consistent in their support.

The difficulty arises because Catholics, across the ideological spectrum, often have only a vague understanding of the various levels of church teaching, what constitutes an infallible teaching, and what can reasonably be questioned. There is little distinction made between dogma and doctrine, for example. Dogma, which only acquired its present meaning at the First Vatican Council in 1870, refers to a definitive and infallible teaching as divinely revealed in sacred scripture or tradition. Dogmas can develop in their expressions, but the underlying tenet cannot change. Typical dogmas would be the assertions in the Creed, for example, or the Assumption of Mary into heaven, which was defined by Pius XII in 1950—only the second time papal infallibility was ever invoked (after being defined by Vatican I in 1870). Doctrine, in contrast, is an official church teaching but not necessarily a dogma. In short, every dogma is a doctrine, but not every doctrine is a dogma. Doctrines are generally not infallible; they can and do evolve as the church discerns more clearly the reality of the revelation she received from Christ and the apostles in the *depositum fidei,* or deposit of faith.

To complicate matters, the magisterium, or teaching authority of the bishops, including the pope, has various levels of authority, from the ordinary magisterium propounded by a bishop or pope (non-infallible) to the extraordinary magisterium solemnly declared by a council of bishops or the pope or both (infallible) and the ordinary universal magisterium (infallible) in which a teaching is held by the entire College of Bishops as a matter of course. Moreover, magisterial teachings cannot simply be promulgated at a whim, but must comport with the *consensus fidelium,* or the sense of all the faithful. Also, according to church tradition, they must be received by the whole church, or gain the assent of the faithful, in order for them to have the final seal of authority. This process can take centuries, and usually does. While a few matters are settled—although the bans on artificial birth control and women's ordination have certainly not been received—there really is no set list of all Catholic dogmas, doctrines, traditions, and practices.

Naturally, the process of determining the weight of a given teaching once the church moves beyond the core dogmas is a freighted task, yet it is critical to a mature faith and to a truly functioning church community. (It is also a subject that merits entire volumes; for an excellent guide to discerning these issues, consult Richard R. Gaillardetz's primer on the magisterium, *By What Authority?*) Believers know instinctively that not every belief has the same import or must always be taken literally. But the effort to divine the truth so as to become a Christian who can act faithfully in the world can be so overwhelming that Catholics often take one of two easy ways out: they accept every utterance of the church—that is, the pope—as infallible (historically an extremely rare occurrence), or they behave as if individual conscience was the only guide to what to believe, irrespective of what church authorities might say.

The latter mode of thinking is an unfortunate reflex of many liberals, or disaffected Catholics, while the former avenue is an unfortunate reflex of many conservatives, such as Republican senator Rick Santorum, who was one of the über-Catholics of the American scene on the day Benedict was elected. "What you saw is an affirmation by the cardinals that the church is not going to change, even though maybe Europe and North America want it to," Santorum told CNN when asked about Ratzinger's elevation. "It is going to stay the way it has been for 2,000 years." Actually, the church has changed a lot in two thousand years, although many still prefer to imagine that Jesus was an Italian who celebrated the Tridentine Mass in Latin in a Baroque church designed by Bernini. (Santorum also did not do himself—or his fellow Catholics—any favors when he told the *New York Times Magazine*, with apparent pride, that he does not know the Bible very well: "I'm a Catholic, so I'm not a biblical scholar. I'm not someone who has verses he can pop out. That's not how I interact with the faith.")

Though Pope Benedict knows well how Catholic doctrines have evolved, he tends to view the process in an eschatalogical context, in the sense that he sees church teachings as moving toward a more complete understanding of divine revelation. Thus, undoing anything to go back, or redoing anything to move forward, would be to deviate from the God-directed pilgrimage of the church through history. That leads him to cherish the status quo, or rather the *status quo ante,* as in *before* the corruptions of the postconciliar era. "We must remain faithful to the *today* of the Church, not the *yesterday* or *tomorrow*," he has said.[28] Preserving and conserving, then, are his imperative. That imperative accomplishes two things: it universalizes a style of the faith that he finds deeply comforting, namely Central European Catholicism circa 1930, and it slows down the dizzying pace of change that gave the post–Vatican II church vertigo.

As a cardinal and prefect of the CDF with the support of John Paul, Joseph Ratzinger tried to preserve this snapshot of Catholicism in several ways. One was by clamping down on adventurous theologians. But of greater long-term import was his effort, in partnership with the pope, to greatly extend the frontiers of what are considered irreformable teachings.

One of the most prominent and contentious examples of this campaign was John Paul's 1994 apostolic letter *Ordinatio Sacerdotalis,* or On Reserving Priestly Ordination to Men Alone. The title was as clear and to the point as the unusually brief document itself—just over one thousand words to cut off one of the most intense and unsettled debates in the church. While stressing the unqualified dignity and value of women, John Paul repeated the argument that because Christ called only men as his apostles and because the church had maintained the all-male priesthood for so long, the church had no authority to ordain women as priests. Few were surprised by John Paul's decision—naturally it was vetted by Ratzinger and the CDF—but his parting line aroused consternation, because he declared that "this judgment is to be definitively held by all the Church's faithful."

The phrase "definitively held" was a novel formulation that raised as many questions as the letter was supposed to answer. As a consequence, the following year Ratzinger issued another document explaining that, yes, the pope's pronouncement "requires definitive assent" not because he, as pope and speaking *ex cathedra* from his bishop's chair, declares the all-male priesthood an infallible teaching, but because John Paul was simply pointing out "the teaching of a doctrine already possessed by the church." In other words, this was infallibility as a kind of preexisting condition.

Ratzinger also counseled John Paul to take this approach in the pope's 1995 encyclical *Evangelium Vitae,* "The Gospel of Life," in which John Paul wanted to declare infallible the teaching that abortion, euthanasia, and any direct and voluntary killing of the innocent is "always gravely immoral." The prefect advised the pope that because these teachings were universally held and taught already, that they were consequently part of the "ordinary, universal magisterium."[29] In 1998 John Paul issued another brief letter, *Ad Tuendam Fidem,* To Protect the Faith, which inserted language into the Code of Canon Law to levy penalties for dissent from a new category of "definitive teachings."[30]

In an accompanying letter that was longer than the pope's own text, Cardinal Ratzinger listed the sort of teachings that would come under this new category, such as the ban on women priests, the immorality of prostitution and fornication, and the invalidity of Anglican ordinations.

Ratzinger expressed the opinion that these bottom-line statements had brought "serenity" to Catholic consciences troubled by uncertainty and debate, but it seemed that many were more disturbed than made serene. It was not necessarily that theologians and ordinary Catholics always disagreed with the teachings themselves as much as it was their anger at the peremptory manner of the blanket, permanent condemnation of matters still under discussion or open to nuances. What had already been referred to as "creeping infallibilism" was now criticized as "galloping infallibilism" by the Redemptorist moral theologian Father Bernard Häring. The Jesuit theologian Father John Coleman called it "papal fundamentalism," and Father Richard McCormick, a moral theologian at Notre Dame, called the trend "magisterial maximalism."[31]

More than declarations from the Holy See, however, Ratzinger, now Benedict, is also concerned that debates on church teachings either not take place or, if they must, that they take place behind closed doors or in Vatican-controlled settings. As early as 1990, in his document on the proper role of theologians, Cardinal Ratzinger recognized that some theologians would still seek to challenge supposedly irreformable teachings, but he advised them to "avoid turning to the 'mass media,' but have recourse to the responsible authority, for it is not by seeking to exert the pressure of public opinion that one contributes to the clarification of doctrinal issues and renders service to the truth."

Ratzinger was motivated by a desire to halt the impression that the church was changing, or would change, an image that he felt was contributing to the erosion of belief. That impulse, rather than the goal of enforcing orthodoxy, was behind the forced departure of Father Reese from *America*. As Father Jose De Vera, the Jesuit spokesman, said after Reese's resignation, the CDF wanted the Jesuits to write articles "defending whatever position the Church has manifested, even if it is not infallible." An underlying problem with creeping infallibilism is that when church practices and even teachings do change and develop, as they must, then church leaders are left trying to explain something that they had assured believers could not happen. The effect is to erode the very authority that the church intended to shore up and to cast into doubt the truly unalterable central teachings.

Benedict was so concerned to maintain the impression of an immutable church that he was less than enthusiastic about of one of John Paul's signal initiatives, his campaign to apologize for the past sins of the church or at least the church's "sons and daughters." This "examination of conscience," what might be called a "theology of apology," reached its fullest expression with a series of public apologies read out by the pope and various curial cardinals—including Joseph Ratzinger—in St. Peter's Basilica on the first Sunday of Lent in 2000, the jubilee year. Yet the roots of John Paul's theology of apology go back to the year after his election, when the new pope told a gathering of scientists at the Vatican that he was reopening one of the Inquisition's most infamous cases—the condemnation of Galileo—not to affirm the obvious fact of the astronomer's heliocentric theory, but to foster a "loyal recognition of wrongs" by church authorities. Three years later in Madrid, the pope first referred to the "errors and excesses" of the Inquisition, and in Vienna in 1983 he apologized for the wars of religion that had scarred Christendom. With increasing regularity, he issued mea culpas to various audiences—to indigenous peoples in Santo Domingo in 1984, to Muslims in 1985, to Africans in 1986, and, most memorably, to the Jewish community at Rome's synagogue in 1986 and at several other points. He also pushed the Catholic Church further than ever in undoing the mutual anathemas leveled between Christian denominations. With the approach of the millennium, an almost mystical benchmark for the Polish pontiff, John Paul in 1994 announced a formal program of penance leading up to 2000. "Only the courageous admission of the faults and omissions of which Christians are judged to be guilty" could lead the church forward, John Paul said at a public Mass on June 13, 1994.

By 1998, when veteran Vatican correspondent Luigi Accattoli published *When a Pope Asks Forgiveness,* he cited no fewer than ninety-four occasions at which John Paul apologized for some past action of the church and its legacy in the present. With the turn of the millennium, John Paul continued his public penance. Naturally, many groups and critics viewed the pope's apologies as incomplete or a case of "too little, too late." But some of the stiffest opposition originated within the church hierarchy. At one point, Cardinal Angelo Sodano, the second-in-command at the Vatican, publicly warned the pope that "as regards a global, general examination of the past history of the church, some of the cardinals have advised extreme caution and prudence, since this is a very difficult and delicate question." One of those was reportedly Joseph Ratzinger, who a few years earlier had sharply criticized the church for "a kind of masochism and a somewhat perverse need to declare itself guilty for all the catastrophes of past history."[32]

This attitude was an expression of Benedict's personal preferences as much as of his ecclesiology. Rather than reflecting on the evolution or sins of his own past, he has always presented himself as an exemplar of faithful consistency. "It is not I who have changed, but others," as he once put it.[33] Similarly, in 1998 when Miroslav Volf, a highly regarded Protestant theologian at Yale Divinity School, published a book advocating a trinitarian but nonhierarchical understanding of the church, he sent a copy to Cardinal Ratzinger because he had drawn on Ratzinger's theology and wanted his reaction. Ratzinger thanked Volf politely, then added a characteristic filip: "You don't expect me, of course, to have changed my mind after reading it."[34]

Benedict carried this stance into his papacy, as evidenced by his meeting with Jewish leaders in the Cologne synagogue, in which he spoke neither of his own experience among the Nazis nor of the Christian legacy of anti-Judaism that contributed, at least in part, to the Nazi horrors. Benedict said only that the "insane racist ideology" of Nazism was "born of neopaganism"—a rather delimited view, given the historical record. He repeated that interpretation at the October beatification of the anti-Nazi bishop, Cardinal Clemens August von Galen, whom he praised for having the "heroic courage to defend the rights of God, of the Church and of man, which the National Socialist regime was violating in a grave and systematic way, in the name of an aberrant neo-pagan ideology." Von Galen was certainly a hero, but he also had been much more solitary a figure than he should have been among his fellow bishops. In light of his nature, it seems unlikely that Benedict will offer much in the way of penitential reflection on his record as prefect of the CDF or in the still-pressing matter of acknowledging the church's errors in the clergy sexual abuse scandal.

If Benedict is not keen on shining a light on the darker corners of the church's past, neither is he eager to spend his papacy enmeshed in public dialogues about current church debates that he considers settled.

As one of Benedict's intellectual biographers, Aidan Nichols, points out, Pope Benedict does not see dialogue at all in the way modern Catholics do, in which competing visions and claims are hashed out to reach a consensus. Rather, he sees the "dialogues" of Jesus in the Gospels as "polemics." Or, as Joseph Ratzinger wrote long before he became bishop and cardinal and then pope, "The New Testament dialogue is not (as is the Platonic) a matter of raising to the consciousness the hidden presence of spirit. Rather it is a matter of announcing to man the unthinkable, novel, free Act of God, something which cannot be drawn up out of the mental depths of man, because it announces God's unreckonable, gracious decision."[35]

Thus Benedict can meet with anyone, hold forums on any views, for the very reason that he is confident enough in his views that he is not going to be changed. He is there to present the truth—to offer what the Catholic faith offers, which his interlocutors can then accept or reject. That is their free will. In this context, ecumenical and interfaith dialogue become avenues not so much for compromise but for announcing the Catholic faith to others—and solidifying Catholic identity in wavering Catholics. In fact, in one of Cardinal Ratzinger's rare public disagreements with Pope John Paul, he expressed great displeasure—as did many conservatives at the time—with the pontiff's convocation of a grand summit of the world's religious leaders to pray at Assisi, birthplace of Saint Francis. It was a spectacular tableau and a typical John Paul gesture—but not one the cardinal appreciated. "This cannot be the model!" an indignant Ratzinger told a German newspaper at the time. A year later he said the meeting left the impression that all religions are equally valid, which is "the definitive rejection of truth." As early as 1963, Father Ratzinger's ecumenical position had already been elaborated: "'Ecumenical' should mean . . . to support the inner wholeness of faith, and thus make the separated brother aware that everything truly Christian finds shelter in the Catholic. . . . 'Ecumenical' should not mean a silence about particular truths, for fear of being out of step with other people. What is true must be spoken openly, without dissimulation. Perfect truth is an aspect of perfect love."[36] More than four decades later, as Pope Benedict XVI, he said much the same thing in his meeting with other Christian leaders in Cologne: "There can be no dialogue at the expense of truth; the dialogue must advance in charity and in truth." (Ratzinger, along with many conservatives, laid much of the blame for John Paul's splashy 1986 interfaith meeting at Assisi at the feet of the Franciscans, who they considered too liberal politically as well as ecumenically. The Vatican-friendly Italian journalist Vittorio Messori propagated urban legends that during the event the Franciscans had allowed "African animists to slaughter chickens on the altar of the basilica of Santa Chiara, and American redskins to dance in the church." The Franciscans denied the charges, but Ratzinger was not convinced. In November 2005, just a few months after his election as pope, Benedict XVI revoked an edict by Paul VI and put the great Assisi shrines under the oversight of the local bishop, a Vatican cardinal, and Italian Cardinal Camillo Ruini, one of Benedict's closest allies. It looked like payback, and it was. "The Church has a long memory," Messori told the *Independent* of London. "Joseph Ratzinger has had an account to settle with the friars of Assisi since the inter-religious meeting of 1986. Now he has fixed it.")

For Catholics, what can be frustrating about Benedict's openness to ecumenical dialogue, however, is that though he welcomes it in the context of relations with non-Catholics, he actively dissuades it inside his own house. "How can we communicate with the Lord if we don't communicate among ourselves?" Benedict said a few weeks after his election, during his visit to Bari. But that appeal, which goes to the heart of the current problems within the Catholic Church, was aimed at other Christians—the ecumenism that Benedict stated from his first day as pope would be the "primary commitment" of his pontificate, his "ambition" and "compelling duty."

Catholics see internal communication and reconciliation as at least of equal importance, but Benedict's ideological allies indicate that is a closed door. "The Nazis helped him understand the liberal mind," Father Joseph Fessio, a Jesuit and devoted former student of the pope, has said. "Liberals are as closed to genuine dialogue as fascists."[37] Or, as Cardinal Joachim Meisner of Cologne, one of Benedict's closest allies in the German hierarchy, said before World Youth Day in August 2005, "We must unambiguously stand against the spirit of the age. This means fixing a limit on endless discussions about women priests and the relaxing of celibacy. Their place must be taken by a new evangelisation of Europe."[38]

There are any number of problems with trying to shut down the church's internal debates, but two points stand out.

One point is that it goes against both church tradition and teaching. Fifteen hundred years ago, Saint Benedict, who is so beloved by the new pope, wrote that the leader of the community must always consult all the members, especially the youngest, and be willing to heed their counsel. Saint Benedict himself was echoing the advice of St. Paulinus of Nola, who a century earlier had urged, "Let us listen to what all the faithful say, because in every one of them the Spirit of God breathes." (Pope John Paul II also cited that counsel in his letter on the church in the third millennium, *Tertio Millennio Adveniente*.)

In 1859, in his essay *On Consulting the Faithful in Matters of Doctrine*, John Henry Newman, a famous convert and later cardinal of the English church, set out the importance and rationale for the hierarchy of consulting laypeople in doctrinal matters, arguing that history has shown that the people in the pews often have a better sense of the faith than the bishops. It should be remembered that Newman's essay was actually his parting shot as editor of the *Rambler*, a Catholic periodical founded in 1848 to demonstrate that Catholics were intellectually serious and independent thinkers. After a layman at the magazine was forced out for questioning a policy decision of the bishops, Newman was asked to take over in order to save the *Rambler*. Yet when he gently defended the dismissed writer in print, Newman was also asked to resign—almost a perfect foreshadowing of the *America* magazine saga. *On Consulting the Faithful in Matters of Doctrine* was Newman's last piece, unsigned, yet it prompted such severe criticism that he did not publish anything for five years.[39]

The essay was given new resonance when it was republished in 1961, just in time for the Second Vatican Council, an event so evocative of Newman's thinking that he was described by one American bishop as the "absent Council Father." Indeed, the central council constitution, *Lumen Gentium,* contained a key passage that could have been written by Newman: "The laity should disclose their needs and desires to the pastors with that liberty and confidence which befits children of God and brothers and sisters in Christ. To the extent of their knowledge, competence or authority, the laity are entitled, and indeed sometimes duty-bound, to express their opinion on matters which concern the good of the church."

To ignore that teaching and tradition today would run the risk of impoverishing the Catholic mind and returning to the dismal state that Monsignor John Tracy Ellis, the preeminent American church historian of the twentieth century, lamented in his 1955 essay in *Thought* magazine, titled "American Catholics and the Intellectual Life." In that essay Ellis decried the fact that a church with such rich intellectual traditions was so woefully short on intellectual leadership. Ellis cited clerical anti-intellectualism as the cause, but his essay triggered a debate that coincided with socioeconomic trends that produced a new generation of American Catholics who are every bit as accomplished as almost any other religious cohort in the nation. Within church institutions, as well, laypeople, rather than just clerics, now rank among the leading historians and theologians, and there are more lay ministers working in American parishes—some thirty thousand of them—than there are priests.

Today, however, the most important intellectual challenge for the church is to improve the religious education of the lay Catholics who sit in the pews every Sunday. The reality is that even as Catholics became the best and brightest in American society, they too easily parked their inquisitiveness at the church door. Catholic laypeople in many cases deepened their spirituality after Vatican II, but the nuts and bolts of theology and the magisterium, liturgy and scripture studies, church history and church governance—the tools that laypeople need to exercise their rightful authority in the church—were too often neglected as irrelevant to the "new and improved" Catholic Church. The reeducation of the Catholic laity is a priority for today's church—this is something bishops and lay leaders actually agree on—and the market is there among the laity, judging by the sales of books on theology and church history and attendance at the seminars and classes organized in the wake of the sexual abuse scandal. If the church under Benedict tries to quash or narrow that nascent intellectual exploration out of fear that it will undermine the faith, the result will be exactly the opposite. In an editorial after John Paul's death, *America* magazine warned that whoever was elected pope would have to open the church to debate rather than shut it down: "A church that cannot openly discuss issues is a church retreating into an intellectual ghetto," the editors said, in what proved a Cassandra-like prophecy.

Perhaps the greater danger, however, is the one that Cardinal Newman perceived 150 years earlier when he warned at the end of his famous essay that cutting off intellectual debate over church teachings "in the educated classes will terminate in indifference, and in the poorer in superstition."

This danger extends as well to the church's pastors, who are supposed to be leaders for the faithful rather than walking catechisms spouting text references in response to probing questions.

As *New York Times* columnist and Catholic author Peter Steinfels pointed out, the Vatican inspection of U.S. seminaries that began in late 2005 focused almost exclusively on devotional practices, preparation for chastity, and adherence to church teachings—as well as trying to single out men considered too gay for the priesthood. Of the ninety-six questions included in the guidelines for the visitation, Steinfels wrote, just two explored the intellectual potential of the future priests: "Do the seminarians show an aptitude for and dedication to intellectual work?" and "Are the seminarians capable of dialoguing, on the intellectual level, with contemporary society?"[40]

Steinfels noted that the lack of interest in the intellectual abilities of seminarians is worrisome because seminary faculty have for several years been voicing concerns about the academic formation of the priest corps. The authors of a book published in 2005, *Educating Leaders for Ministry,*[41] estimated that only 10 percent were highly qualified for educational work, that just over 50 percent were adequately qualified, and that up to 40 percent suffered from poor educational backgrounds, learning disabilities, lack of facility in English, or unfamiliarity with American culture. (The last concern is due to the growing number of foreign-born priests, some 28 percent of newly ordained priests in America.) Across all those categories, however, seminary faculty teams reported that seminarians, "regardless of native abilities and educational experiences," resist "the learning enterprise" because it threatens their "preconceived ideas about theology."

"Shouldn't such impressions, which are in fact more widely shared among Catholic seminary educators than anything having to do with homosexuality, loom large in a review of the seminaries?" Steinfels asked.

The other point to keep in mind is that whatever countermeasures the Vatican may take, they cannot stop the push for change or at least greater dialogue. Catholics want reform, they talk about reform among themselves—even if they can't read about it in Catholic periodicals—and the number of Reform-minded Catholics is growing. At a Rome café a few days after Benedict's election, I was talking with George Weigel, who was just setting off to write his own account of the new papacy, which he welcomed with fulsome praise. Weigel was happily clear about what he saw as the dead-end prospects for reform now that Benedict was pope: "The forty-year effort to compel the Catholic Church to conform to the *zeitgeist,* to tailor itself to secular modernity, is over. It's just not going to happen."

If Weigel is right, however, the Catholic Church will certainly be a smaller and spiritually poorer church. Despite the claims of some conservatives that their camp is experiencing a resurgence in orthodoxy—usually defined by their own customized parameters—the number of American Catholics wanting reforms, or simply throwing up their hands and going their own way on moral matters, is steadily increasing. According to surveys done at regular intervals over recent decades by a team of four U.S. sociologists of Catholicism, the number of Catholics who believe that celibacy should be optional for priests has risen from 63 percent in 1985 to 75 percent in 2005, and more than 80 percent prefer that priests who have left ministry to marry be allowed back. More than 60 percent would like to see women ordained (the number is slightly lower when asked whether they would like married, rather than celibate, women ordained), and nearly 58 percent of *registered parishioners* believe that "church leaders are out of touch with the laity." That alienation works both ways, as growing a majority of Catholics, especially among the young, say that they do not look to church leaders for moral guidance on matters such as abortion and birth control. And loyalty to the church, while still fairly strong, is eroding.[42]

Lay Catholics are not the only ones hoping for some flexibility. Many bishops also want to see some real openness to issues such as ordaining married men to the priesthood or allowing women to be deacons. Others want to find a way to allow divorced and remarried Catholics to take communion, which is one of the most painful and sensitive pastoral concerns of bishops around the world. In fact, these issues are not, as is often argued, the agenda of a spoiled American laity seeking to fashion a church in their own image. At the October 2005 Synod of Bishops in Rome, presided over by Pope Benedict, prelates from the developing world were outspoken, as they have been at past synods, on the need to take some action to alleviate the priest shortage, which is worse by several times in the Third World than in North America. A bishop from Honduras, for example, said he had one priest for every sixteen thousand Catholics in his diocese.

At a briefing early in the three-week meeting, a Filipino bishop, Luis Antonio G. Tagle, was blunt in assessing the crisis in his country: "Let me make a confession here. And I know our canon lawyers will get mad . . . The first Sunday after my ordination as a priest I said nine masses, and that is regular in the Philippines. . . . In the absence of the priest there is no Eucharist. We should face squarely the issue of the shortage of priests."

But while sitting next to Tagle, Cardinal Angelo Scola of Venice, a strong supporter of Benedict's election at the conclave, downplayed any shortage, saying they should talk about a better "distribution" of priests in the world and declaring that the Eucharist was a "gift, not a right or a possession" for Catholics. Many bishops at the meeting backed Tagle; others pointed out that Scola's assertion about the Eucharist was contrary to canon law, which states that the Christian faithful have a right to the spiritual goods of the church, "especially the word of God and the sacraments" (Canon 213).

Yet rather than proposing alternatives or opening the issues up to wider discussion, the bishops spent much of their time allotments focusing on devotional and liturgical matters, such as the need for more eucharistic adoration, the problems of communicants receiving the host in the hand, the apparent decline (to some) in genuflecting at Mass, and the importance of following the Mass rubrics more closely so as to prevent "abuses." One bishop suggested that the Year of the Eucharist be followed by a Year of the Sacrament of Penance to help restore "the sense of sin, which has been diminished or annulled." Another wanted to enforce a ban against eulogies during the funeral homily. Still others wanted to move the Sign of Peace to a different part of the Mass, while others sought a rule to bar the priest from moving beyond the sanctuary to greet the faithful with the Sign of Peace.

In the end, the synod wound up much as they always had during John Paul's tenure: intriguing debates at the start, then no substantive changes at the end. Even on the central mystery of the Mass, the transubstantiation of the bread and wine into the body and blood of Christ, the synod fathers agreed that the Eucharist was imperfectly understood by far too many Catholics, and yet they could not figure out how to better explain it, with many of their own explanations wandering far and wide.[43] In the fifty "propositions" presented to Pope Benedict to serve as the basis of his final exhortation, the bishops ruled out relaxing the celibacy requirement for priests—"a path not to follow," they said, even though a significant number of bishops wanted to at least explore that path. Cardinal George Pell of Australia said at a press conference after the vote approving the propositions that they should be considered a "massive restatement" of the church's celibacy rule for priests and other church traditions.

One of those other traditions was the ban against communion for divorced and civilly remarried Catholics. An initial draft proposition that referred to the bishops' empathy for the "sincere suffering" of civilly remarried Catholics was edited to drop the word "sincere." Some on the editing team cited the case of the English king, Henry VIII—who executed two of his six wives—to argue that not all civilly remarried Catholics were sincere. A statement telling the divorced that "your suffering is our suffering" was also removed, and they dropped a reference to their ban as a "sacrifice."

The synod called on pastors to preach better homilies and reaffirmed the importance of the Sunday Mass obligation for everyone. To the dismay of conservatives, the propositions did not crack down on communion for Catholic politicians who support legalized abortion, for example, reiterating Benedict's stand, which he proposed while at the CDF during the 2004 American presidential campaign, that each bishop consider "the concrete local situation" in making their determination. Likewise, restoring the Tridentine Latin Mass was a nonstarter for the bishops.

In essence, the synod wound up where it started. "I wonder why in the hell they brought us here and put us through all this, to say absolutely nothing more than what has been painfully said for decades," one bishop told John Allen of the *National Catholic Reporter*. Many U.S. Catholics might agree. The same month the synod met, a new survey showed that although more than 70 percent of Americans think the traditional family is the ideal, only 22 percent believe that divorce is a sin—and the number went up only to 30 percent among self-described traditional Catholics.[44]

One leading American participant, Atlanta archbishop Wilton Gregory, told Allen that he thought some national bishops' conferences would still want to broach with the pope the topic of ordaining married men. He also acknowledged that the final propositions against communion for divorced and remarried Catholics—an especially common problem in the United States, where divorce rates approach 50 percent—did not reflect the lingering unease among the bishops, who would like a more flexible policy. "Many of the fathers, fully knowing and accepting the teaching of the church, nevertheless came back asking, what am I going to say to these wonderful people who find themselves in an awkward situation, who want to practice their faith and be good parents and yet find themselves in this situation?" Gregory said. "How do I deal with these people who come to me every day? What do I say to my pastors who face these challenges? How can I be true to the practices of the church, but help my priests to be sensitive and compassionate in their outreach? These are wonderful Catholics who come to you and say, 'Bishop, I love my church and my faith, I was in an awful situation, I accept my responsibility, but now I've found a loving spouse and we have wonderful kids, and I want to be a practicing Catholic. Help me!' What do you say?"

Debate continued even after the synod ended. On returning to the Netherlands, Cardinal Adrianus Simonis told a Dutch television station that he wanted further study on the idea of ordaining married men. "I can see that it is not a solution [to the shortage], but you could say that in times of need, when the sacramentality of the church is at risk, it would be a possibility," Simonis said.[45] In an even more surprising twist at the synod's end, Cardinal Walter Kasper—the Vatican's chief ecumenical officer, who regularly debated church teachings with his fellow German, Cardinal Ratzinger—rejected the suggestion from Pell and others that the synod was the last word on communion for the divorced and remarried. "I can't imagine that the debate on this is closed. This is a reality and we have to at least reflect on how to respond," Kasper told a news conference. "Every bishop in Western countries knows that this is a big problem." Kasper noted that in a talk with priests the previous summer, Pope Benedict had said that church policy on remarried Catholics has resulted in "a particularly painful situation" that "must be studied." Kasper said that "this is also my position."

But Kasper did not mention that in 1993, as bishop of Rottenburg-Stuttgart, he had backed the idea of a pastoral letter saying divorced and civilly remarried German Catholics could take communion. Rome had quickly intervened and forced Kasper to reverse the policy. The Vatican official who rejected Kasper's effort was Cardinal Ratzinger.

Clearly, the Catholic Church is engaged in serious debates, at every level, on serious topics that will have critical ramifications for the future of the faith. To act as if the debates are not taking place or to quash the dialogue necessary to achieve an adequate resolution will only to make the renewal of the church that much more difficult, at least from the traditional perspective of Catholicism as a universal church that casts its nets, as Jesus commanded, into the deep.

Then again, Pope Benedict has always been bearish about the church's numerical prospects, though he would argue that his grim view is merely the perspective of an Augustinian realist who sees problems for what they are. But it is also an interesting debate—and now one of crucial import to the faith—as to whether Benedict would actually prefer to see a leaner church, a small but doctrinally compact community of believers akin to the mustard seed Jesus spoke of in the Gospels: "When it is sown in the ground, it is the smallest of all the seeds on the earth. But once it is sown, it springs up and becomes the largest of plants and puts forth large branches, so that the birds of the sky can dwell in its shade."

In an interview published in a 1996 book, aptly titled *Salt of the Earth*, then cardinal Ratzinger gave his own updated spin to Christ's words: "Maybe we are facing a new and different kind of epoch in the church's history, where Christianity will again be characterized more by the mustard seed, where it will exist in small, seemingly insignificant groups that nonetheless live an intense struggle against evil and bring good into the world—that let God in." Three years later, at the turn of the millennium, reflecting on the new world created by the end of Soviet communism that John Paul helped bring about, Cardinal Ratzinger was clear about his reading of the situation, which was far bleaker than that of the Polish pontiff: "Anyone who expected that Christianity would now become a mass movement was, of course, disappointed."

But, as he added, "Mass movements are not the only ones that bear the promise of the future within them."[46]

In fact, Benedict foresees the Catholic future in terms of the Catholic past, a church somewhere between the catacombs of imperial times and the monastic outposts of the Dark Ages. He believes that the beloved parish system, which he points out is only a few centuries old, will be downsized, and that the emergent and often controversial "movements," such as Opus Dei, the Legionaries of Christ, the Neocatechumenal Way, and Communion and Liberation, are the wave of the future. The church of the future will be more a "church in miniature," as he has put it, "cells" of believers almost like the *kibbutzim* that dotted the refounded Israel of the 1950s. The history of the Jewish people is a favorite template for Benedict. Like the "saving remnant" of the Hebrew Bible—the band of Israelites who remained faithful to God's promise to them—small groups of faithful Catholics will save the church. Similarly, Benedict sees Christians in the modern secularized West as surviving in a kind of Babylonian captivity, a circumstance that demands loyalty and obedience, and a willingness to jettison those people and structures that do not support the mission: "This movement is in full swing. Chaff and wheat must, as always, be separated in a process that involves a struggle, in accordance with the words of the Apostle, 'Do not extinguish the spirit. . . . Test everything, retain what is good.'"[47]

These views do not necessarily indicate, now that Ratzinger is pope, that some kind of purge is in store for the Catholic Church. For one thing, Benedict and his top aides seem to have revised some of their previous pessimism, arguing that Benedict's rule can usher in a "new springtime" of the faith, especially in Europe, and saying that the crowds attending papal events—crowds that Cardinal Ratzinger used to dismiss as largely irrelevant to the faith—show that he is succeeding. (While many of Benedict's supporters trumpeted the size of the crowds attending public events during his first year, they did not mention that John Paul drew much larger crowds during his early years, and at a time when there were far fewer Catholics in the world. Moreover, a sizable portion of the crowds coming to Rome in 2005 and 2006 were going to visit the tomb of John Paul rather than the audiences of Benedict. The numbers game can be a dangerous one for those trying to bolster Benedict's authority by magnifying his popular appeal.) The seductive power of seeing adoring multitudes at one's feet can understandably blur even a realist's views. Yet it is also a mistake, as Benedict knew before he became pope, to extrapolate universal truths from a narrow window onto reality.

Then again, the organized cleansing feared by many may not be necessary. Catholicism of the postconciliar era has long been afflicted with a bitter polarization that Bernard Lonergan, the distinguished Jesuit theologian and philosophical Thomist, saw coming as far back as 1967: "There is bound to be formed a solid right that is determined to live in a world that no longer exists," Lonergan wrote at the start of the postconciliar tumult. "There is bound to be formed a scattered left, captivated by now this, now that new development, exploring now this and now that new possibility. But what will count is a perhaps not numerous center, big enough to be at home in both the old and the new, painstaking enough to work out one by one the transitions to be made, strong enough to refuse half-measures and insist on complete solutions even though it has to wait."[48]

The difficulty for that vital but perhaps "not numerous" center is that, for the rest of American society, the Catholic Church has become an echo chamber dominated by the take-no-prisoners shouters of the outer fringes. "One wonders why the Christian values of charity toward one another and the American value of fair play have been abandoned," St. Paul-Minneapolis archbishop Harry J. Flynn lamented in a column during the presidential campaign, which witnessed an unprecedented level of internecine Catholic animosity. "Particularly distressing is that this uncharitable, biased and reckless substitute for what formerly was fair-minded commentary and fact-based dialogue has found its venomous way into our Catholic family."[49]

The difficulty for the Center and the Left, however, is that within the church the Catholic Right has been ascendant for so long that its partisans not only control the levers of power but are coming to define what it means to be Catholic.

As a cardinal, Joseph Ratzinger did his part to fuel the polemical atmosphere, although he could rightly say he did not create that poisonous climate nor, as a matter of conscience, could he avoid expressing his views. Yet it was also clear whose side he was on, and he was perhaps far too willing to cast the debate as one between light and darkness—between good Catholics, like himself, and bad Catholics of the left, whom he blames for both the present crisis and some of the bad behavior of "well-meaning" conservatives. "On the one hand, there are the modern circles, and we all know that for them every reform is insufficient, that they set themselves against the papacy and papal teaching," he once said. "But even the others, the 'good Catholics,' if you want to call them that, find themselves on the whole less and less comfortable in the Church. They no longer feel at home; they suffer and grieve over the fact that now the Church is no longer a place of peace where they can find refuge but is a place of constant conflicts, so that they themselves also become uncertain and begin to protest."[50]

This polarization was undermining the church before Benedict's election, in a split that runs through the college of bishops, the corps of priests, and the entire laity. Whether Benedict intends it to be so or not, his elevation only intensified the partisanship. That was clear from the moment he walked out onto the balcony of St. Peter's Basilica.

While the Catholic Left was largely shell-shocked by the conclave's outcome, the Catholic Right was, as expected, overjoyed. (The Catholic Center seemed to think Benedict was a nice enough fellow, but they still wanted John Paul.) The Jesuit Joseph Fessio, a former student of Ratzinger's and a sharp right-wing partisan, described the prospect of a Ratzinger papacy as "too good to be true," and said when he heard the news he wept for joy. Blogger Mark Shea suggested that Catholic conservatives adopt a pop anthem to announce their insider status with the new pope: "You're XVI, you're beautiful, and you're mine." Brian Saint-Paul, editor of the hard-right magazine, *Crisis,* said in his e-mail newsletter that after Benedict's election he spent "most of my waking hours dancing on my desk. . . . Can there be any question that the Holy Spirit guides the conclave? From John Paul II to Benedict XVI . . . oh, this is a good time to be Catholic." George Weigel compared Catholic progressives in the wake of Benedict's election to Japanese soldiers who fought on for years on isolated atolls, unaware that their side had lost World War II.[51] The absence of

Christian charity in such an observation is one thing; the wounds that such a vainglorious ecclesiology, wielded by church insiders, can inflict on the body of Christ are far more serious.

Joseph Ratzinger knew the dangers of such partisanship and used to inveigh against those visions of the church when he perceived them in the liberal camp. In a 1966 lecture, in the heyday of reform after Vatican II, for example, Father Ratzinger warned against the "dangerous new triumphalism" of the progressives, which he likened to "self-glorification." Yet today that same warning may be better directed to Benedict's ideological soul mates, who could take his election as cover to pursue their divisive agendas.[32]

In this partisan atmosphere, the spiritual pitfalls of Benedict's election are great for all sides. Catholics on the Left may grow harsher in their judgments, more frustrated by the lack of openness to reform, and given to the unpardonable sin of despair. The Catholic Center, which also wants to see greater dialogue, may grow disaffected or perhaps more "congregational" in their Catholicism, living their faith through a vibrant parish but with still less reference to Rome and the universality of the Catholic Church. Both of those camps would rightly argue that if the church is in crisis after nearly three decades of so-called orthodoxy, is it not time to try a different approach?

Ironically, however, the perils of the Benedictine papacy are perhaps greatest for the Catholic Right. At this moment of triumph, there is an enormous temptation to see Benedict's election as a vindication, as a final victory for their agenda, as if the church were a political party, one in which there is a definitive verdict on whose platform is the best. For several decades, the Catholic Right has enjoyed a perfect confluence of trends—a popular pope they could call their own in John Paul, along with access to the church's corridors of power and the material advantages that brings, plus a minority status within the church, which allows them to feel the comforting affirmation of the persecuted without the spiritual pain—or benefit—of actually having to suffer. Benedict has sharply criticized those who would make the church more comfortable for themselves. But he must also realize that conservatives of his ilk have been quite comfortable in the church they have created, which means that the worm of self-interest could always be behind the principled opposition to changes in the status quo.

Catholicism, like any good religion, is by its nature conservative, in that it exists to pass along the core of the faith to succeeding generations. When that religion is seen to be run by one faction, however, it is understandable, if unfortunate, that that segment comes to define the threshold of what it means to be a true believer—in this case a "good" Catholic. This perception goes to the very heart of the central debate in modern Catholicism, namely, the question of Catholic identity. With traditional Catholic culture growing ever more attenuated and the ethnic ties that kept American Catholics in particular so compact for so long now fraying, Catholics are beset more than ever by ideological campaigns to determine what it means to be a Catholic, and thereby who is a good Catholic and who is a bad Catholic. There are any number of problems with staking out Catholic identity by defining oneself "over and against" the Other, not least of which is the necessity of always and everywhere demonizing one's perceived foe, who is in reality a sister or brother in baptism. Conversely, finding the heretic in everyone else serves to elevate ourselves, in our own eyes, if not in God's.

The only proper stance, of course, is that we should all consider ourselves bad Catholics, helping each other on the winding journey to holiness. Yet members of the Catholic Right have led such a privileged existence in the church for so long, with open invitations to papal dinners and Vatican congregations, as well as seats at powerful diocesan tables in the United States, that they have too frequently come to see their own way of being Catholic as the gold standard. And they increasingly have the means to keep those with whom they disagree out of positions of influence in the church, by using communion, rather than baptism, as a kind of threshold sacrament.

This attitude mistakes subjective partisanship for a proclamation of truth, and it leads to a kind of de facto denominationalism inside the church that is the antithesis of Catholicism. Benedict is fond of quoting historian Arnold Toynbee's observation that "the destiny of a society always depends upon creative minorities," as he put it in a widely noted 2004 speech to the Italian senate. As he said at the time, Christians, too, "should conceive of themselves as such a creative minority." As Benedict's neo-con allies might put it, you go to worship with the church you have, not the church you wish you had. But what if that minority is closer to an ideological oligarchy within the church?

In any case, whether a "smaller," denominational Catholicism translates into a "purer" faith is highly debatable. Conservatives, and most commentators, tend to use overt expressions of piety as measures for fidelity, and the regularity of church attendance as a measure for a "good" Catholic. Certainly, it has been easier for self-styled orthodox Catholics to be active in the church when the welcome mat has been out for them for so long, while so many others have been dissuaded from participation for any number of sins. Yet history has shown that the worst sinners have often been the most devout Massgoers. And among everyday Catholic churchgoers—everyday sinners, like us all—polls and the rough-and-tumble of church politics show that the Catholic

Right is as selective about the magisterium as anyone. On issues ranging from birth control to the death penalty to divorce and questions of social justice and just war, the Catholic Right is a restive band of American individualists. It is a myth that a smaller cohort of so-called loyalists would somehow be reflexively faithful to Rome's every press release and thus "easy to control." Hard experience should have shown Benedict that is not the case. Besieged minorities that maintain discipline under fire splinter into factions once they reach the top of the heap, and that seems to be an iron rule for conservative-minded Catholics. Each is so convinced of his or her own rightness that they cannot brook the slightest deviation by their fellow-travelers, or they heed their own counsel so zealously that they wind up being "cafeteria Catholics" every bit as much as the most independent-minded liberal, rebuking the Vatican on one issue or another because it does not square with their chosen views.

A case in point is the rebellion of the so-called traditionalists, whose belief that Vatican II promoted heretical reforms, particularly in replacing the old Latin Mass of the Council of Trent, led them to follow the late Archbishop Marcel Lefebvre into an open schism in 1988. Thus the first schism in the church in a century came during the pontificate of the orthodox-minded John Paul, after repeated compromises and efforts, led by Cardinal Ratzinger, to keep the right-wingers in the fold. Ratzinger had always been seen by the traditionalists as sympathetic to their views, which he was, and they welcomed his election as a sign of hope for their cause to fully restore the Tridentine rite. When Benedict met with leaders of the influential splinter movement in late August, 2005 (Lefebvre died in 1991), the meeting was seen as a crucial step toward finding some kind of accommodation with the traditionalists, despite their fierce critiques of Rome, their proudly schismatic actions, and the record of their leaders' blistering comments against anyone they disagreed with, especially Jews. A further sign of Benedict's sympathy for the extreme Right was his decision to make reconciliation with the Lefebvrites the focus of his first two meetings, in February and March 2006, with the heads of all Vatican departments. That Benedict would make the traditionalist schism a major initiative of his pontificate was telling. Liberals and centrists could only wonder how it was that Benedict would bend over backward to welcome formal schismatics whereas they were shut out.

That sense of exclusion was reinforced by the news that Australia's Cardinal George Pell had asked actor-director Mel Gibson to re-create the crucifixion of Jesus in the streets of Sydney for World Youth Day in 2008. The reenactment would be similar to scenes from Gibson's blockbuster film *The Passion of the Christ*. Yet Gibson himself is a traditionalist schismatic who is harshly critical of the modern church, and even of recent popes. So it seemed unusual, to say the least, that he would be offered such an important official platform at a major Vatican-sponsored event.

To think that the Catholic Right will be mollified is a fantasy. In fact, Pope Benedict has already seen the rancor of the cafeteria conservatives emerge in his own young papacy.

Perhaps some measure of disappointment was to be expected. As a cardinal, Joseph Ratzinger was the darling of the orthodox, his trenchant observations posted like bumper stickers on their books and Web logs as they imagined how wonderful all would be with the world if only—if only—someone like Ratzinger were pope. Then, *mirabile dictu*, Ratzinger became pope. And yet the ecstasy that accompanied the "*Habemas Papam!*" of April had already cooled significantly by early winter, as Benedict was faced with the challenge of enacting prescriptions rather than diagnosing problems.

The first sign of trouble came with Benedict's appointment of Archbishop Levada as his replacement as prefect of the Congregation for the Doctrine of the Faith. Though Levada was doctrinally as by-the-book as they come—his unimaginative but perhaps unavoidable nickname was "Darth Levada"— many conservatives joined progressives in criticizing Levada's record on sexual abuse. But above all, conservatives saw Levada as unwilling to be as confrontational as Ratzinger. When Levada early on described himself as a "cocker spaniel," in joking contrast to Ratzinger's "rottweiler" reputation, conservatives did not laugh. Their chief exhibit was a 1997 episode in which Levada compromised with the City of San Francisco over a municipal law requiring all organizations receiving government funds to offer benefits for gay partners. That law would have included the archdiocese's social services agency, Catholic Charities. Rather than forfeiting $5.6 million in funding for the poor and needy, Levada negotiated a deal by which religious groups like the church would offer "spousal equivalent benefits" to anyone the employee designated in their household—gay or straight, married or unmarried. This avoided direct church support for gay partnerships, but it of course struck conservatives as a moral cave-in.

The news that Benedict would keep Archbishop Piero Marini on as his master of ceremonies, despite Marini's reputation among the orthodox as a liturgical innovator, also angered many. (The standard joke about the flammability of liturgical debates says it all: "What is the difference between a terrorist and a liturgist?" Answer: "Sometimes you can negotiate with a terrorist.") Also upsetting to the Right was the announcement that Benedict would keep

Washington cardinal Theodore McCarrick on for at least two years after he reached the mandatory retirement age of seventy-five in July 2005. McCarrick was somehow considered "soft" by the Catholic Right, perhaps because his outgoing, pastoral nature made him popular with the flock—and the media—and he had been subjected to relentless conservative attacks. So they were not at all pleased when Benedict did not send McCarrick packing. "Pope Benedict XVI becomes more of a disappointment with each passing day," wrote a contributor to Angelqueen.com, a popular conservative bulletin board. Read another: "This is the sign. Pope Benedict is the old Father Ratzinger, a liberal. His role in the Curia was a charade, maybe he had to crack down under previous Pope, but he was also liberal. Maybe he struck bargains with Cardinals to keep them on for their vote in the Conclave." Fans of Ratzinger were hoping that as Pope Benedict he would do a thorough housecleaning of the hierarchy, though just how many bishops would be left standing if the conservatives had their way was unclear.

When, at his installation Mass, Benedict personally gave communion to his friend Brother Roger Schutz, the saintly, elderly—and Protestant—founder of the ecumenical community of Taizé in France, conservatives were also nonplussed. Their surprise was muted when Brother Roger was stabbed to death four months later by a deranged woman during vespers; but it flowered again at his funeral, at which Cardinal Kasper, the president of the Vatican's council for Christian unity, presided and distributed consecrated hosts to communicants of any denomination—a scandal to many Catholics. Kasper later explained that the Vatican had developed a special practice "for the singular circumstances" of the Taizé ecumenical monastic community and the pilgrims who visit there.

Benedict's September meeting with his former friend and longtime foe, the über-liberal theologian Hans Küng, again unsettled many on the right, even though it was an encounter of personal reconciliation that expressly excluded any discussion of their differences about the church.

In short, Benedict's new view of the church—sitting as he does now, an easy target high up in the Vatican—may be quite a bit different than his view from the dark trenches of the church's partisan battles. But with the authority that comes with his new perch, however, Benedict has every opportunity, every day, to create the space necessary to bring greater peace to the church. If he is looking for inspiration in this task, he might want to look no further than his theological mentor, Saint Augustine, who is traditionally credited with the maxim that has historically defined the Catholic polity: "In essentials unity, in nonessentials diversity, in all things charity." The rub, of course, is what exactly constitute essentials and nonessentials. This is a never-ending process of discernment, but one that need not sacrifice clarity and meaning by increased participation. The boundaries between the Center and the periphery must be determined not by Roman fiats but by a vibrant church of Catholics who have been affirmed in their faith by being trusted to discern the truth as mature believers and by trusting the faith itself to be convincing. It has been so for centuries, and it can continue to be so again.

If the new pope needs a more recent model than Augustine, he may also find inspiration in his namesake, Benedict XV. That earlier Pope Benedict assumed the Throne of Saint Peter in September 1914, at a time of great turmoil, when Archduke Ferdinand had been assassinated in Sarajevo and Europe was careening toward its first world war. Anguished by the prospect of terrible violence, Benedict exerted his spiritual forces to try to bring an end to the conflict that would reshape the Western world for the next century. According to the cardinals who emerged from the 2005 conclave, the new Pope Benedict said he too saw the Europe of today—and by extension all of Western civilization—as poised at a critical juncture, where all could be lost, this time to the forces of secularization.

While that World War I analogy has been the reigning historical parallel for interpreting the papacy of Pope Benedict XVI, there is another historical link between the two popes that the new Benedict could heed—namely, the earlier Benedict's efforts to stop the raging internecine strife between Catholic Integralists, as conservatives were known then, and Modernists, as liberals of the day were known.

A century ago, as today, the feud between these two wings of the church was fierce, with the Integralists having had the upper hand for many years under Benedict's predecessor, Pius X. During his papacy, Pius X (1903–14) was unrelenting in his campaign against the Modernists, forcing priests to take an oath of loyalty and branding Modernism "the synthesis of all heresies." He encouraged a secret society, the *Sodalitium Pianum,* to pass along to the Vatican the names of anyone deemed less than loyal to the pontiff's vision, and he not only excommunicated several leading thinkers but also investigated some of the church's top cardinals.

So polarized was the church of the day that the cardinals of the 1914 conclave sought to restore some balance to Catholic life by lobbying, in a hard-fought conclave, to elect Cardinal Giacomo della Chiesa as pope. Not only did della Chiesa take an irenic name in Benedict, but his first major document as pope was the encyclical *Ad Beatissimi,* which aimed to end the conflicts within the church. In forceful terms Benedict declared that as pope "we must devote Our earnest endeavours to appease dissension and strife, of whatever character, amongst Catholics, and to prevent new dissensions arising, so that there may be unity of ideas and of action amongst all."

"As regards matters in which without harm to faith or discipline," he wrote, "there is room for divergent opinions, it is clearly the right of everyone to express and defend his own opinion. But in such discussions no expressions should be used which might constitute serious breaches of charity; let each one freely defend his own opinion, but let it be done with due moderation, so that no one should consider himself entitled to affix on those who merely do not agree with his ideas the stigma of disloyalty to faith or to discipline."

Benedict concluded with a memorable appeal to stop the uncharitable name-calling: "There is no need of adding any qualifying terms to the profession of Catholicism: it is quite enough for each one to proclaim 'Christian is my name and Catholic my surname.'"

Unfortunately, Benedict XV wasn't able to stop the Catholic infighting any more than he was able to halt World War I, but his encyclical did spare *America* magazine and the Jesuits from a suppression that was apparently looming when death suddenly claimed Pius. Today's Pope Benedict has already taken steps against *America* that do not bode well for a repeat of his namesake's peacemaking efforts, and it is perhaps beyond optimism to think that Joseph Ratzinger, in his role as Benedict XVI, will reverse the Catholic polarization of today that is so reminiscent of a century ago, and too often the fruit of Ratzinger's own decisions.

The result may be the smaller church that Joseph Ratzinger has envisioned for years, but it would be the result of a self-fulfilling prophecy rather than the greater fidelity of a saving remnant.

Conclusion

THE RULE OF
BENEDICT

When all is said and done, the defining paradox of Joseph Ratzinger's life may be that he is more memorable as a cardinal than as a pope. To a degree, that may have been the fate of any man who followed the out-sized pontificate of John Paul II. But the particular style and theology of Benedict XVI make it more likely that this polarizing cardinal will wind up as something of a papal gray eminence, a shadow role that should have been his place as the prefect of the Congregation for the Doctrine of the Faith, except that the Holy Office turned out to be the perfect media platform for his personality.

Long before becoming the Supreme Pontiff, Joseph Ratzinger dedicated his life to articulating and defending the truths of the Catholic faith, which he did to great acclaim, first as an up-and-coming theologian at the Second Vatican Council, and later as the dogged guardian of orthodoxy in Rome. Both roles were destined to gain him a wide audience, since any discussion of Truth in the modern world—especially a discussion emanating from the suspect pulpits of the Roman Catholic Church—is guaranteed to generate controversy, which is the straightest path to notoriety.

Moreover, as a cardinal, Ratzinger played the sideman to John Paul, "the best frontman the Catholic Church ever had," in rock star Bono's eulogy. And that secondary position allowed him to indulge his dual passions for public debate and church politics without thrusting him ahead of the pope or compromising his treasured virtue of self-effacement. Ratzinger was not sounding his own trumpet, he could safely argue, but just doing his job—albeit a job tailor-made to his talents and tastes. Of course, no one rises to such heights in the Catholic hierarchy without some degree of human maneuvering, and Ratzinger "was not without his own ambitions," as his longtime friend and biographer German journalist Heinz-Joachim Fischer put it.[1] Indeed, Joseph Ratzinger always managed to place himself in the path of influential church-men who could provide a career boost at critical points.

When Ratzinger was elected to the Throne of Saint Peter, however, he could no longer deflect attention so easily nor do battle so readily; now he was the chief shepherd of the flock, not the "bad cop" of the Roman Curia. Even if Ratzinger was a *panzerkardinal,* he knew as well as anyone that there could be no such thing as a *panzerpapst.* Faced with this unexpected situation, Benedict instinctually reacted in two ways: he exalted the figure of Christ, who was al-ways at the center of his piety and theology, and he emphasized the teaching office of the papacy and the basics of the faith. Both tendencies purposefully downplayed the person of the pope that had been such an integral element of John Paul's ministry, and both may be the hallmarks of Benedict's papacy.

Whether this will work to the benefit or detriment of the church may de-pend on what one expects from the church, and from the Roman pontiff.

In concrete terms, Benedict's approach translates into significantly reduced papal activism—fewer documents, fewer trips, fewer public appearances, and generally a lower profile than the church and the world had been accustomed to for the previous quarter of a century. There is simply less of the pope. With the choice of Benedict the cardinals of the conclave essentially got what they were asking for: a break from the overwhelming volume that was the papacy of John Paul at every level—in images, in words, and in the sheer intensity of his personal presence.

Because Joseph Ratzinger is not a pastoral priest by nature, his papacy, not surprisingly, stresses the educative over the emotional side of the faith; he is the professor explaining—to those who decide to attend his lectures—the subject matter as he sees it. This is not a discussion group, with inquiry leading to un-derstanding. His style is static rather than dynamic, contemplative rather than active, focused upward toward God (or toward the altar, if his revolutionary "reform of the reform" in liturgy takes hold) rather than at the faces of God's people scattered far and wide beyond the walls of the Vatican. His writings are complex but often beautiful reformulations of the fundamentals of faith. His vision is to conserve rather than create, so that, if it please God, the seed of the faith can germinate in some future era. "Every once in a while the church needs a bridge pope," as an aide to a European cardinal told me with an air of resignation in the aftermath of the conclave.

The bridge, or transitional, pope label, however, is largely a term of art in view of the advances in modern medicine, and a major question mark posed by Benedict's election are the uncertainties raised by his age and health.

Never the most vigorous of men, Benedict was the oldest cardinal elected to the papacy since Clement XII in 1730, and at seventy-eight years old he was just two years shy of the threshold at which cardinals are barred from the conclave. Clearly, his selection was another manifestation of the conclave's desire for a breather after the twenty-six-year papacy of John Paul, and perhaps an indication that they were looking ahead to the next pontificate, however discreetly.

But there are many risks to such a "transitional" scenario, including the fact that the Roman Catholic Church, which seems to have a provision for everything, has nothing comparable to the Twenty-Fifth Amendment of the U.S. Constitution to provide for an orderly succession should a pope slip into a coma or lose his mental faculties. The church's Code of Canon Law states at one point that a pope may resign, but the canon is not terribly helpful as to how the process might work. It may even complicate matters, because it is not clear if the pope can resign *to* anyone, and it stipulates that he can in no way be pushed to resign.

Should Benedict become physically incapacitated or slip into dementia, this quirk of canon law would become a full-blown crisis. Who determines when a pope is *non compos mentis*? How will a new pope be chosen if the old pope is still alive? What is to be done with the "former" pope—a term that does not even exist in church tradition. Can a pope retire? As a cardinal, Joseph Ratzinger rejected suggestions that John Paul would retire, but then later hinted that such an eventuality might be possible. No pope has retired for centuries, and only a handful have done so over the past two thousand years. But given the breakthroughs in medical treatment and the church's increasing acceptance of all forms of life support therapies, the decision will eventually force itself on the Vatican, either during this papacy or in the near future. And if Benedict has not left explicit instructions in some form of living will, his papacy could end in confusion and crisis.[2]

Of more immediate concern, however, is if Benedict, who must watch his health, becomes progressively infirm. The church has just ended a long slog watching a heroic figure gradually reduced by age and disease; an incapacitated Pope Benedict would diminish the visibility and the charismatic authority of the papacy in ways that he likely does not envision or desire. Pope John Paul II became almost larger than life as he diminished in vigor, but that was in part because of the galvanizing legacy that defined the early years of his pontificate. The grandeur of John Paul's suffering was in direct proportion to the *grandezza* of his earlier deeds.

While Pope Benedict XVI is popular enough—in modern times popes are always accorded great personal respect—he enjoys no similar reservoir of popular acclaim, nor, at nearly eighty years old, is he likely to construct a legacy the way John Paul could, given that John Paul was fifty-eight years old when he was elected. After years of caring for a nearly incapacitated John Paul, the staff of the papal household is experienced in the needs of elderly patients requiring long-term treatment, and during renovations after John Paul's death the papal apartment was fitted out as a virtual clinic complete with the latest medical equipment. Yet the prospect of an inert Benedict secluded in a Vatican hospice for years on end would likely make the church seem rudderless and vulnerable rather than heroic.

Benedict's wager is that the undeniable "beauty of the faith" will win out over any considerations of his talents or energies.

His faith in the faith was evident throughout the first year of his papacy, as he repeatedly used his sermons and speeches to stress fundamental Christian truths like the infinite grace of God and the centrality of the Resurrection. With this approach Benedict was effectively declaring that the battles on the myriad issues that alienate or inspire so many Catholics—the role of women, collaboration with the laity, hierarchical accountability, transparency and dialogue, vocations and celibacy, sexuality and birth control, and all the rest—are done and won. As Benedict's favorite biographer, German journalist Peter Seewald, said in an interview at the first anniversary of the pope's election, "He does not waste time on unproductive discussions or on questions that were decided long ago." Seewald said that while many people would continue to raise difficult questions, Benedict "wants to get past them at last, so as to highlight instead the teachings that are at the heart of the faith."[3]

Nowhere was that intention more clearly articulated than in Benedict's inaugural encyclical, *Deus Caritas Est,* or "God Is Love," released in January 2006, nine months after his election. A pope's first encyclical (one of the most authoritative documents a pope issues) is generally seen as the programmatic "mission statement," and is anticipated as the key to any new pontificate. Yet with *Deus Caritas Est,* Benedict showed that he would not move far from the contemplation of Christian truths that he set forth in his inaugural homily the previous year. There would still be no "platform," no grand ambition to change the world. This would be a pontificate of exhortation over action—theology as catechesis.

Tellingly, the pope did not address his encyclical to "all men and women of good will," as John XXIII did for the first time with *Pacem in Terris* in 1963, or as Paul VI and John Paul II subsequently did with their first encyclicals. Benedict XVI instead directed his comments to his own flock; if others wanted to take note, they were welcome to do so, he seemed to say. The encyclical's theme of Christian charity was actually bequeathed to him by his predecessor, as the document was in the works when John Paul died. Yet even as he kept John Paul's basic theme, Benedict made the encyclical wholly his own.

In the first of the encyclical's two parts, he expounded with characteristic erudition on what he considers the false division of the two concepts of love: *eros,* or erotic love, and *agape,* or spiritual love. Taking the First Letter of John as his starting point—"God is love, and he who abides in love abides in God, and God abides in him"—Benedict sought to reclaim both eros and agape from modern distortions and to show how they are intimately connected. He also wanted to rescue both forms of love from the vagaries of romantic or spiritual infatuation and ground them in a more secure and steady conceptual framework that can endure. "Love is not only a feeling; to it also belong the will and the intelligence," as the pontiff wrote in a pre-publication letter explaining the encyclical. (Aware of his tendencies to intellectualism, Benedict admitted that "the text might seem a bit difficult and theoretical." In fact, Benedict cites Plato, Aristotle, Nietzsche, Descartes, and Gassendi, among others, and he wisely used several public venues before and after the encyclical's publication to present a more accessible version of his main themes.)

In *Deus Caritas Est,* Benedict says eros is all well and good as long as it is not a submission to the divine madness of sexual pleasure, as the ancient Greeks had it: "An intoxicated and undisciplined *eros,* then, is not an ascent in 'ecstasy' towards the Divine, but a fall, a degradation of man. Evidently, *eros* needs to be disciplined and purified if it is to provide not just fleeting pleasure, but a certain foretaste of the pinnacle of our existence, of that beatitude for which our whole being yearns."

In the second part of the encyclical, Benedict extends the discussion to "love of neighbor" and the inseparable connection between Christian faith and helping the less fortunate: "If you see charity, you see the Trinity," the pope

wrote, quoting Augustine. "In a world where the name of God is sometimes associated with vengeance or even a duty of hatred and violence," he continued,
"this message is both timely and significant. For this reason, I wish in my first
Encyclical to speak of the love which God lavishes upon us and which we in
turn must share with others."

And that is what Benedict did, spending much of the 16,000-word document contemplating the history and beauty of Christian love for others—a
lyrical meditation whose tone and substance was more John Lennon than
Vladimir Lenin. How could anyone quibble with that? While often dense and
highly conceptual—this was still Joseph Ratzinger, after all—the encyclical
is less an instruction than a reflection of Benedict's stated desire to mirror
Dante's pilgrimage in the *Paradiso*, the overlooked beatific vision that ends the
Commedia.

Given the irenic topic and the depth of feeling that Benedict brought to the
subject, the initial and understandable reaction to the encyclical was, in effect,
"What's not to like?" Conservatives were pleased in that Benedict signaled, as
expected, the church's return to more purely spiritual concerns, pulling back
from campaigns for social action. Cardinal Marc Ouellet of Montreal, a close
collaborator of Benedict's for years, expressed relief that Benedict did not take
on a tough moral topic in his opening encyclical because that would have reinforced negative perceptions that many held of the pope.[4] That relief was
shared by many on the liberal side of the Catholic divide, who also seemed
happily surprised that Benedict had not used his first major platform to crack
down on some apparently wayward view or group.

Yet even in Benedict's hymn to divine love one could also discern the firm
voice of Joseph Ratzinger.

Throughout *Deus Caritas Est,* for example, Benedict takes pains to highlight individual piety as the indispensable precursor to any charitable action,
an approach which in turn seems to make social justice completely dependent
on the virtue of individual Catholics. He avoids any mention of structural sin
and collective action to remedy systemic injustice, tenets that have been hallmarks of Catholic social justice teaching—and previous papal encyclicals—
for more than a century. In a sense, Benedict, himself a paragon of continuity,
was breaking new ground by diverging from the traditions of his predecessors.
While the church "must not remain on the sidelines in the fight for justice," he
writes, the church "cannot and must not take upon herself the political battle

to bring about the most just society possible. ... A just society must be the achievement of politics, not of the Church." As he said in an explanatory letter accompanying the encyclical, "it is the task of the Church to cure reason and reinforce the will to do good."

Moreover, Benedict could not resist the temptation to conjure yet again the bogeyman of Marxism as he sought to warn believers against the lure of trying to achieve earthly justice. "Marxism had seen world revolution and its preliminaries as the panacea for the social problem: revolution and the sub-sequent collectivization of the means of production, so it was claimed, would immediately change things for the better. This illusion has vanished," he writes. He notes that classic Marxism derides charity by claiming that it subverts the cause of justice by allowing the rich to shirk their duty to work for change. "In the end, the claim that just social structures would make works of charity superfluous masks a materialist conception of man: the mistaken notion that man can live 'by bread alone' (Mt 4:4; cf. Dt 8:3)—a conviction that demeans man and ultimately disregards all that is specifically human."

Yet, as he so often does, Benedict poses an argument of absolutes, a com-forting black-and-white choice that ignores the many shadings in between and, in this case, creates a false either/or paradigm by which Christian charity is a pure ideal that must always remain apart from wider efforts to effect sys-temic change, which are inherently corrupt.

By repeatedly using Marxism as the easy foil for his conservative prefer-ences, Benedict unfortunately implies that social justice efforts are automati-cally suspect, and can only lead to socialist utopianism that would subvert the Gospel. Moreover, by associating Catholic social activism with the specter of Communism, Benedict presumes the worst about the many devoted Catholics working so faithfully for social justice. As the pope writes in one dark passage, "It is time to reaffirm the importance of prayer in the face of the activism and the growing secularism of many Christians engaged in charitable work." He cautions that church personnel "must not be inspired by ideologies aimed at improving the world, but should rather be guided by the faith which works through love." Otherwise, he warned, charitable activities can become "just another form of social assistance."

But that characterization unfairly casts a shadow on church workers and ser-vice agencies without naming names or citing instances in which he feels they have crossed the line into the vast, undefined territory that Benedict brands "secularism." His allegations in *Deus Caritas Est* constitute a broad brush that can tar the legions of men and women, lay and religious, who have often forsaken the creature comforts that Benedict has always enjoyed in order to dedicate, and sometimes sacrifice, their lives on behalf of the downtrodden, all in the name of Jesus Christ, not Karl Marx. In a speech delivered a few weeks after the encyclical's release, German archbishop Paul Josef Cordes, a longtime curialist and friend of Benedict's who reportedly wrote early drafts of the encyclical, was more explicit, and harsher, in denouncing church activists: "The large Church charity organizations have separated themselves from the Church and from their link with the bishops," said Cordes, whose Vatican council coordinates the Church's charitable institutions.[5]

For Benedict, the preferred form of charitable work would model itself on the individual acts of charity practiced in past times by religious orders of monks and nuns, or of the heroic efforts of individual saints, in particular Blessed Mother Teresa of Calcutta, who he cited three times as a paradigm for Catholics who want to address social injustice. While the holy men and women he cites are exemplars of Christian charity, stopping the discussion at their practices would reduce Catholic social justice to a one-dimensional ministry.

Moreover, although the pope obviously wants the church to steer clear of politics, the reality is that choosing to not become involved politically is itself a political choice. For example, Benedict's laissez-faire approach to economic and social justice tends to reinforce the political stands of his fellow Catholic conservatives, who prefer hands-off policies of "compassionate conservatism" that are more market-friendly and less onerous to the haves—though not necessarily helpful to the have-nots that Jesus would make his priority. Indeed, Benedict's "apolitical" view of social action almost perfectly mirrors the Bush administration's faith-based approach. As Benedict argues at one point, the state should not try to solve all social problems. Instead, the state should support church programs so that church agencies "are able to give a Christian quality to the civil agencies, too, favoring a mutual coordination that can only redound to the effectiveness of charitable service."

Another problem in Benedict's approach is that it runs the risk of the sort of inconsistency that he would normally abhor. For example, Benedict and other church leaders have no hesitation in calling on governments and political leaders to take action on issues such as abortion or bioethics or gay marriage, often aligning themselves with certain parties or supporting church political lobbying groups and producing reams of analyses to back a certain political position. Yet for the church to then remain above the fray when it comes to the morality of social and economic policies that involve the welfare of millions would seem hypocritical, and could smack of a moral relativism that values some lives and issues as greater than others. As the great Brazilian church leader, Dom Helder Camara, once lamented, "When I give food to the poor, they call me a saint. When I ask why the poor have no food, they call me a communist."

The crux of the Benedictine dilemma is that religious beliefs are not simply abstractions that stand apart from the people that profess them. It was thus at the beginning of Christianity, in the life and sayings of Jesus of Nazareth, and it is even more so today, as modern women and men rightly demand that the actions of religious leaders match up with the words they preach from the pulpit.

All of which points to a pitfall in Benedict's back-to-basics message, in particular his exaltation of Christian charity: How is a Catholic to square the irenic language of *Deus Caritas Est* with the legacy of forty years of ecclesiastical warfare that as a theologian and cardinal Benedict helped foment? Joseph Ratzinger's glowering pessimism toward the modern world, his cultivation of combative proxies and anonymous whistle-blowers (only those who shared his point of view, naturally), and the secret proceedings and sharp denunciations of those he deemed unworthy of a role in the church, are just some of the decidedly uncharitable actions that he sanctioned in a campaign that went well beyond anything required by his brief stint as head of the CDF, or his role as a theologian. And they are so contrary to the spirit and letter of *Deus Caritas Est* that one wonders what to make of the pontiff's intentions.

Benedict himself provided the most incisive explanation, telling an audience on the first anniversary of his election that his goal as pope was to be "a gentle and firm shepherd," a phrase that could be applied at many stages of his life—a mild countenance masking an uncompromising core. It is the paradox of every pope that he must balance the often conflicting impulses to be both gentle and firm. Yet Benedict seems to resolve this tension by identifying "love" and "truth" so closely as to make them indistinguishable. For Benedict, divine love finds its most complete expression in absolute truth, and thus the greatest act of love is to stand on principle.

"Truth and love are two sides of the same gift that comes from God and is preserved in the church thanks to the apostolic ministry," as the pope told an audience of thirty thousand people on a windblown April morning in St. Peter's Square nearly a year after the conclave. Taking his cue from the same epistle that undergirds *Deus Caritas Est,* Benedict noted that the First Letter of John contains the Bible's strongest exhortation to believers to love one another, but also "addresses with drastic severity those adversaries who were once members of the community, but are no longer." He said that when people do not embrace the Christian truth then it is "a precise obligation" of Christians to break with them.[6] Christian love is boundless, Benedict seems to say, but only within the confines of a carefully proscribed Christianity.

One obvious conclusion to draw from the early stages of Benedict's pontificate is that his professed desire to scale back the fixation on the person of the pope will be complicated, perhaps impossibly, by the fact that the office of the papacy remains a supersized entity, both in the current Catholic polity and in the popular imagination. As far back as that volatile year of 1968, Joseph Ratzinger himself seemed to recognize this challenge, when, in a lecture at Tübingen, he compared the ever-ascending modern papacy to a mountain climber who has reached the top of a great peak but "now finds he can't get down without breaking his neck or losing face."[7] Consequently, as much as Benedict might like to make his pontificate about the faith alone, the pope himself will always be magnified by the papacy, and Benedict's persona and outlook and priorities will inevitably color the tone and content of the Catholic mission for years, even generations, to come.

A second consideration is whether Benedict's insistent focus on the content of Christian belief will resonate with the secular world if there is no corresponding effort to renew the church itself.

At the start of Joseph Ratzinger's best-known work, *Introduction to Christianity,* he recounts a famous story from Kierkegaard, the Danish pietist whose dour outlook resonated with that of the young German priest in the late 1960s. The story (which he takes from Harvey Cox's landmark study, *The Secular City*) regards a traveling circus whose tents catch fire one day, sending the circus's clown rushing into the nearby village to get help. As the clown jumps about and yells to the townspeople to help put out the fire, the villagers take his antics as a clever performance meant to lure them to the circus. They all laugh at the demonstration, which causes the clown to grow even more desperate in his supplications, which his audience finds even more amusing—until the fire engulfed both the circus and the town.[8]

For Ratzinger, there was an obvious parallel between the clown in the story and the believer who attempts to "preach the faith amid people involved in modern life and thought"—an image of such affecting loneliness that one's heart goes out to a man who would see himself so alienated from the world. Yet one also wants to let Ratzinger know that he may not be as alone as he fears. For all of the hand-wringing over secularization and the loss of belief, modern men and women by and large do retain the *sensus fidei,* the instinct to faith, that traditional theology has always believed abides in the human heart. At least nine in ten Americans express some sort of spiritual belief, and American Catholics, those supposedly rebellious followers, are still defined by the distinctive markers of Catholic faith—belief in the resurrection of Jesus and in his real presence in the Eucharist. Even those supposedly de-Christianized Europeans have a belief of sorts, although it is often vaguely expressed or barely discerned.

The real challenge to modern people, and the signal challenge for the Catholic Church, is as much the crisis of organized religion as it is the crisis of personal faith. Benedict was absolutely correct when he told the young people gathered on the foggy field outside Cologne in August 2005 that a "do-it-yourself religion" in the end leaves us all alone. Yet the credibility of the institutional church is at such a low ebb that fewer people are willing to invest their faith in a religion that does not seem to practice the charity that it preaches, or in one whose doctrines seem incapable of responding with pastoral flexibility to the cries of "those who are poor or in any way afflicted," as so many are today, in so many different ways.

The suspicion of institutions is so widespread that it has led, among Christians, to the prevalence of a church-free faith in Jesus that often winds up in nothing more than "fideism," a belief that "faith alone" is so sufficient that community and doctrine and tradition and liturgy and ritual and anything resembling a church are nothing more than hindrances, rather than help, to true belief. Modern faith is often about believing as much as belonging, and if the Catholic Church cannot demonstrate an ability to reform itself as an organization, then the bonds of communal faith that have sustained multitudes across the generations will continue to fray.

Focusing on the church as an institution is not always a popular or energizing platform. Nor should it in any way be either the source or summit of the Catholic's journey of faith. Yes, the Catholic faith should stand on its own, and often does, in spite of the blunders of many of its ordained leaders and lay partisans. As Hilaire Belloc put it, "If any man should deny the divine origin of the Roman Church, let it be known that no mere human institution, conducted with such knavish imbecility, would have lasted a fortnight." Yet as Cardinal

Avery Dulles has observed, the church has become an obstacle to faith as much as it was once the object of faith. And with so many people today believing that the right path travels many different roads, there is less incentive to engage the constant struggle of conscience required for a Catholic to remain in the church, or for an outsider to join.

In a sense this has led both Pope Benedict and many of his erstwhile foes on the Left to an unusual point of commonality—namely that of emphasizing the contents of faith over the container of faith. Karl Rahner once said that "the Christian of the future will be a mystic or he will not exist at all," and the trend lines seem to be bearing him out.

Benedict is especially eloquent in this regard, elucidating a Christology that shimmers with the passion of his faith in Jesus. He frequently quotes the *Rule of Benedict,* the monastic guidebook of his namesake who called on his brothers to "prefer nothing to the love of Christ." So central is the figure of Christ to Benedict's spirituality, and to his gamble to restore faith to the modern world, that one can almost forget that he is the head of the largest institutional religion in history—that he is the Roman Catholic pontiff and not a Congregationalist. As Benedict said in an address to the priests of Rome a few weeks after his election, "Great theologians have tried to describe the essential ideas that make up Christianity. But in the end, the Christianity that they constructed was not convincing, because Christianity is in the first place an Event, a Person. And thus in the Person we discover the richness of what is contained."

The difficulty for the modern believer is that Benedict's Christology so closely parallels his ecclesiology. Benedict's thinking follows on the Augustinian view that the church is "the moon that does not shine with its own light, but reflects the light of Christ the sun." Thus in Benedict's Platonic cosmos, Christ is the ideal, and the church is the image of that ideal. From that perspective, one cannot change something in the reflection without distorting the original image, in this case Christ, who is God. "The discourse on the Church is a discourse on God, and only in this way is it correct," as Ratzinger once said.

As pope, Benedict continued to strike that theme. "Between Christ and the Church there is no opposition," Benedict said during a series of weekly public talks he began in March 2006. "They are inseparable." While he acknowledged that the people who make up the church are sinners, his intention was clear: to question the church is to question Christ. "Therefore, there is no way to reconcile Christ's intentions with the slogan that was fashionable a few years ago,

'Christ yes, the Church no'. The individualist Jesus is a fantasy. We cannot find Jesus without the reality that he created and through which he communicates himself," meaning the church.

In subsequent talks, Benedict made more explicit than ever his belief that the true Church is most perfectly represented by the Catholic bishops, who preserve and pronounce the truth of Christ because they are to be considered "the privileged place of the action and transmission of the Holy Spirit." As Benedict told his audience on May 10, 2006, "Through the apostolic succession, Christ comes to us: He speaks to us in the word of the apostles and their successors; he acts in the sacraments through their hands; our gaze is enveloped in his gaze and makes us feel loved, received in God's heart."

This near-total equivalency between Christ and the church—the Catholic Church, in Benedict's view, being the church par excellence—is, for one thing, a theological stretch. And because Benedict's über-hierarchical view of the church cuts off any possibility of structural reform, this ecclesiology can strike ordinary churchgoers as little more than a strategem for those vested with holy orders to avoid responsibility for the sins of the church's past or its pastoral mission for the future.

In a sense, Benedict is a low church Protestant enshrined in a high Roman Catholic ecclesiology that makes it difficult, if not impossible, to envision the kind of changes that would tempt believers to trust the church as a mediator of their faith. While liberal Catholics often dismiss the institutional church in their focus on Christ, Benedict takes the church for granted, and thinks everyone else should, too. "It is necessary to have this will to believe with the Church, to have trust that this Church—the community not only of 2,000 years of pilgrimage of the people of God, but the community that embraces heaven and earth, the community where all the righteous of all times are therefore present—that this Church enlivened by the Holy Spirit truly carries within the 'compass' of the Spirit and therefore is the true subject of faith," Benedict told the priests of Rome. "No one believes purely on his own. We always believe in and with the Church. . . . We must, in a manner of speaking, let ourselves fall into the communion of the faith, of the Church. Believing is, in itself, a Catholic act: it is a participation on this great certitude that is present in the living subject of the Church."[9]

After a generation of fighting opponents inside the church, it seems that Ratzinger—as Pope Benedict—can now take the high ground of a spiritual leader, almost the Dalai Lama of Catholicism (a development he saw coming years ago, and lamented) rather than a statesman or an evangelist or even a warrior for the faith. For now, the internal battles have been decided, and Benedict would seem to be content with whatever remnant of the church that will follow him. That passive approach is reflected in Benedict's teachings, which, despite frequent passages of beauty and profundity, do little to address the many problems pressing in on Catholicism, such as the angry polarization that tears the Body of Christ apart, the "big chill" (Luke Timothy Johnson's phrase) on theology and other intellectual pursuits, the proscribed role for women and the laity, the growing vocations crisis and the pressures on the priesthood—in short, the urgent need for internal reform to promote true renewal.

There is an endless debate between Christian "liberals" and "conservatives" on the priority of justice or charity, with liberals seen as giving pride of place to the former and conservatives to the latter. Yet, not only are the two concepts equal and inseparable, but for the Christian they are linked by an acknowledgment of one's failings in regard to both. Throughout his writings and addresses, Benedict shows little taste for self-reflection, either on his behalf or that of the church, thus continuing his aversion to the sort of introspection that is the heart of the authentic Christian witness and the spark of spiritual development.

Unfortunately, this has been a persistent shortcoming of much of the past generation of church leadership—an almost reflexive unwillingness to apply their exhortations for charity and justice in the wider world to the Catholic Church itself, with obvious and serious consequences. That seems unlikely to change much, if at all, under Benedict XVI—to the detriment of the church and also the secular world that Benedict clearly wants to affect.

Again, for all his evangelical zeal, Benedict seems to fall back on Augustine's advice to believe in order to understand, not the other way around.

Will the men and women of the contemporary world follow that exhortation to return to faith in the Catholic Church as Christ's own? Pope Benedict also likes to cite the Ignatian counsel, *sentire cum Ecclesia,* to think with the church. But that advice can be read in a communal sense of mutual exchange, rather than a one-way pledge of vertical obedience that seems to go no further than the stained-glass ceiling of the hierarchy. Without a commitment to a more open church that welcomes the gifts of all its members and recognizes all their sins—inspired by the example of its top leaders—it is more likely that Catholicism will remain in the holding pattern that has characterized its recent history, a kind of limbo that only delays the inevitable reckoning with modernity.

Benedict has declared secularism "the great challenge of our time," as he told young people during a meeting in St. Peter's Basilica shortly before the first anniversary of his election.[10] He casts this struggle with the modern world as a perilous battle with an external foe. Yet, like Jacob in the Old Testament, the pope may wake up years from now to realize that he was wrestling with an angel all along, fighting against the spirit of a faithful flock that would happily grant a blessing if asked.

In another day and age, the Catholic Church could drift along with a place-holder pope (or even two or three), buoyed as ever by the reflexive loyalty of the people in the pews. But Benedict and the church of the Second Vatican Council rightly want the laity to have a fuller life of faith than that, and the faithful are looking to the church's leadership to help provide that opportunity. Yet too much of the church's leadership still seems stuck between the comfort zone of the ancien régime and the deeper waters of the post-Constantinian era—between *ressourcement* and *aggiornamento*, not realizing that what is needed is not one or the other, but both. One cannot have an evangelical Catholicism without an evangelical pope—that is, a church and a leader that mirror in word and deed, and in pastoral presence, the Good News that Jesus incarnated.

Without that inner reform and renewal, Catholicism will undergo a de facto purification through fragmentation, rather than direct purgation. Those who feel welcomed under the Benedictine pontificate will continue to claim the mantle of orthodoxy. Those who do not will go elsewhere or, worse, go nowhere. Some will nod toward Rome on occasion but continue on in the "mental or practical schism" that Cardinal Walter Kasper warned about in his debate with Joseph Ratzinger several years before Benedict's election. "Many laypersons and priests can no longer understand universal church regulations," Kasper said, "and simply ignore them."

Perhaps the best advice for a pastor today, especially one whose high office can leave him so remote from the lives of his flock, would be to turn back to the very first word of the *Rule of Benedict,* and the guiding principle of religious obedience. "Listen," the Saint counsels, "with the ear of your heart."

NOTES

Introduction: Black Smoke, White Smoke, and Shades of Gray

1. "Crowds Cram St. Peter's Square in Expectation of New Pope," Catholic News Service (CNS), April 19, 2005.

2. Cited in John L. Allen Jr., *Conclave: The Politics, Personalities, and Process of the Next Papal Election* (New York: Image Books, 2002), p. 136.

3. Robert Mickens, "Letter from Rome," *Tablet*, September 17, 2005.

4. "Smiles, Applause, Cheers Greet Announcement of Pope's Election," CNS, April 19, 2005.

5. "Big To-Do List for an Insider," *New York Times*, April 20, 2005.

6. Quotations from Rome news conferences; "Pope Brings Own Charism, Contribution to Papacy, U.S. Cardinals Say," CNS, April 20, 2005.

Chapter One: The Shadow of the Pontiff

1. Cited by Marco Politi, "Il Papa, Orazio e la morte," *La Repubblica*, September 28, 2003; other Vatican officials confirmed that this was a favorite line of the pontiff's. He used it as well in his meditative poem on Michelangelo's *Last Judgment*, in *Roman Triptych* (Rome: Libreria Editrice Vaticana, 2003).

2. Horace's "Exegi monumentum," known as "The Poet's Monument," Book III: 30. From *Horace: The Complete Odes and Epodes*, translated by W. G. Shepherd (New York: Viking Penguin, 1986), p. 164.

3. Citations from a special commemorative issue of *U.S. News & World Report*, April 2005, p. 8.

4. See the summary of an October 2003 survey in "Catholics after the Scandal," *Commonweal*, November 19, 2004, p. 13.

5. The Eighteenth Annual Erasmus Lecture of the Institute of Religion: Public Life, given in New York City on October 25, 2004.

6. Statistics on John Paul's writings were released by the Vatican as of his twenty-sixth anniversary and cited by Zenit.org in their October 17, 2004, report. For comparisons with other popes, see Luigi Accattoli, *Pope John Paul II: The Man of the Millennium* (Boston: Pauline Books & Media, 2000), p. 118.

7. Related to the author by the former Peoria bishop, John J. Myers, now leader of the Archdiocese of Newark, New Jersey.

8. *The Place Within: The Poetry of Pope John Paul II* (New York: Random House, 1982), p. ix.

9. George Weigel, *Witness to Hope* (New York: HarperCollins, 1999), p. 304.

10. Neal Gabler, "The People's Prince," *New Republic*, August 9, 1999, p. 13.

11. "The Message of Fatima"; see www.vatican.va.

12. Joseph Ratzinger, Preface, *Introduction to Christianity* (San Francisco: Ignatius Press, 2000), p. 11.

13. From the Preamble to the "Charter for the Protection of Children and Young People"; see http://www.usccb.org/ocyp/charter.shtml.

14. "Vatican Appoints Former Boston Archbishop Head of a Rome Basilica," Associated Press, May 27, 2004.

15. Cardinal Walter Kasper, "On the Church: A Friendly Reply to Cardinal Ratzinger," *America,* April 23–30, 2001, pp. 8–14.

16. From an interview with Danneels, "Perhaps a Moment of Calm in the Church Would Be a Good Thing, to Give Us a Breather," *30Giorni,* December 2003; see http://www.30giorni.it/us/articolo.asp?id=2326.

17. "Vatican Official Wants Greater Independence for Local Churches," *Catholic World News,* December 11, 2003, citing an interview in the December 2003 edition of *Famiglia Cristiana,*

18. Cited in "The Word from Rome," *National Catholic Reporter (NCR),* December 26, 2003; see http://nationalcatholicreporter.org/word/word122603.htm.

19. *Tablet,* July 31, 2004.

20. Accattoli, *Pope John Paul II,* pp. 124–25.

21. "The Pope of the Divided Heart," *NCR,* March 4, 2005.

22. Cited in Sandro Magister, "Ruling in the Shadow of John Paul II: The Vatican Four," October 22, 2004; see http://www.chiesa.espressonline.it/dettaglio.jsp?id=19630&eng=y.

23. "Panelists Consider Direction of the Papacy under Benedict XVI," CNS, May 2, 2005.

Chapter Two: The Passion of the Pope

1. "The Word from Rome," *NCR,* August 29, 2003; see http://nationalcatholicreporter.org/word/word082903.htm.

2. Weigel, *Witness to Hope,* p. 412.

3. From the *Times of London,* cited in "Precious Suffering," *Newsweek,* February 28, 2005, p. 24.

4. "Curial Official Decries Calls for Pope's Resignation," *Catholic World News,* February 28, 2005, citing an interview in the Turin daily *La Stampa.*

5. "Precious Suffering," *Newsweek.*

6. Cited in "Voiceless, Suffering Pope Finds Powerful Nonverbal Communication," Religion News Service, March 2, 2005.

7. "End Times," *National Review Online,* February 9, 2005; see http://www.nationalreview.com/buckley/buckley200502091428.asp.

8. *La Repubblica,* Associated Press, April 5, 2005.

9. For details of papal deaths, from the amusing to the macabre, see John-Peter Pham's comprehensive description in *Heirs of the Fisherman: Behind the Scenes of Papal Death and Succession* (New York: Oxford University Press, 2004).

10. Cited in John Allen, *The Rise of Benedict XVI: The Inside Story of How the Pope Was Elected and Where He Will Take the Catholic Church* (New York: Doubleday, 2005), p. 58.

11. For an analysis of the Vatican's use of television, see Sandro Magister, "Papal Masses on TV: Benedict XVI Wants a New Director," *Chiesa,* June 10, 2005, which includes a May 21, 2005, article on the topic by Father Virgilio Fantuzzi, S.J., in *La Civiltà Cattolica.*

Chapter Three: The Ratzinger Solution

1. "Ukrainian Cardinal Urges People Not to Overdramatize Papal Election," CNS, April 6, 2005.

2. George Weigel, "A Crossroad for the Catholic Church," *Washington Post,* February 3, 2004, p. A-19.

3. For a full treatment of the history of Americans at the conclave, see Frederic J. Baumgartner, *Behind Locked Doors: A History of the Papal Elections* (New York: Palgrave/MacMillan, 2003), p. 206ff. Baumgartner's volume is a trove of conclave lore.

4. Lucio Brunelli, "Cosí eleggemmo papa Ratzinger," *Limes: Rivista Italiana di Geopolitica,* September 23, 2005, p. 296.

5. Oddi's remarks from *L'Espresso,* cited in "The Cardinals' Hotel: Not a Spot for the Bread and Water Routine That Was Used in 1271," *New York Times,* April 5, 2005, p. A-11.

6. Baumgartner, *Behind Locked Doors*, p. 211.

7. Gianni Cardinale, "Il primo incontro all'ex Sant'Uffizio," *30Giorni*, May 2005; see http://www.30giorni.it/it/articolo.asp?id=8815.

8. *The Onion*, March 2, 2005; see http://www.theonion.com/content/node/30922.

9. Address to the National Press Club of Australia, Canberra, September 21, 2005.

Chapter Four: Secrets of the Conclave

1. Pope Fabian in 236 and Pope Innocent III in 1198 were chosen this way, according to Baumgartner, *Behind Locked Doors*, pp. 4 and 34, respectively.

2. Ambrogio Piazzoni, vice prefect of the Vatican Library and author of *Storia delle elezioni pontificie* (Milan: Piemme, 2003), provided many of these fascinating details at an April 18, 2005, symposium in Rome.

3. Christopher Bellitto, "The Coming Conclave: How the Next Pope Will Be Chosen," *Commonweal*, January 16, 2004.

4. Baumgartner, *Behind Locked Doors*, pp. 209 and 221ff.

5. News conference at the Canadian College in Rome, April 21, 2005.

6. Allen, *The Rise of Benedict XVI*, p. 109.

7. Pham, *Heirs of the Fisherman*, p. 91.

8. "The Word from Rome," *NCR*, August 26, 2005; see http://nationalcatholicreporter.org/word/word082605.htm.

9. Baumgartner has an entire appendix on the history of the white smoke, titled "*Sfumata!*" It is the most comprehensive account I have found.

10. "L.A. Cardinal Says Pope Might Reform Process for Synod of Bishops," CNS, April 22, 2005.

11. Baumgartner, *Behind Locked Doors*, p. 188.

12. Cardinal Ricard María Carles in an address cited in Zenit.org, May 13, 2005; see http://www.zenit.org/english/visualizza.phtml?sid=70895; Meisner's comments to *La Razon*, a Spanish periodical, are cited in the same Zenit report.

13. Luciani was so shocked at the result that he reportedly insisted that the cardinals take another ballot, to affirm their intention; he received 102 votes. The vote tallies of the two conclaves of 1978 are reported by Francis A. Burkle-Young in *Passing the Keys: Modern Cardinals, Conclaves and the Election of the Next Pope* (Lanham, MD: Madison Books, 1999), pp. 256 and 286. The numbers have long been accepted as accurate.

14. Pham, *Heirs of the Fisherman*, p. 136.

15. "Tailor's Three Candidates for Pope: Small, Medium, Large," Religion News Service, April 14, 2005.

16. Account provided by Cardinal Theodore McCarrick in an address at the National Press Club in Washington, D.C., July 11, 2005.

17. Agence France-Presse, April 20, 2005.

18. Interview with Vatican Radio, Zenit.org, May 22, 2005; see http://www.zenit.org/english/visualizza.phtml?sid=71352.

19. Agence France-Presse, April 20, 2005.

20. Translation of an interview in *Junge Freiheit*, August 19, 2005; see http://cathcon.blogspot.com/2005/09/popes-brother-slams-cardinal-danneels.html.

21. "From Hardliner to Humble Shepherd: Pope Looks to Transform Perception," CNS, April 21, 2005.

22. Allen, *The Rise of Benedict XVI*, p. 89.

23. "Groundswell Swept Ratzinger into Office," *Los Angeles Times*, April 21, 2005, p. A-1.

24. Allen, *The Rise of Benedict XVI*, p. 100.

25. From a February 2006 speech, cited in *NCR*, March 3, 2006.

26. "The Cardinal Who Voted Yes for the EU Constitution," *Times of Malta*, June 2, 2005; see http://www.timesofmalta.com/core/article.php?id=188934.

27. To Vatican journalist Benny Lai in *Secrets of the Vatican from Pius XII to Pope Wojtyla*, cited in "Cardinals Meet Today in Secret to Elect a Pope," *New York Times*, April 18, 2005, p. A-1.

28. Interview with John Allen in *NCR*, February 24, 2006.

29. Pham, *Heirs of the Fisherman,* p. 134.

Chapter Five: A German Soul

1. Cited in Gordon A. Craig, *The Germans* (New York: Meridian, 1991), p. 15. Craig's book is a brilliant synthesis of his life's work and an excellent overall resource on things German.
2. Cited in Craig, *The Germans,* p. 84.
3. Thomas Bokenkotter, *A Concise History of the Catholic Church* (New York: Doubleday, 2004), p. 309.
4. Joseph Ratzinger, *Milestones: Memoirs, 1927–1977* (San Francisco: Ignatius Press, 1997), p. 9. All of Ratzinger's childhood memories are from *Milestones,* unless otherwise noted.
5. Cited in Aidan Nichols, O.P., *The Thought of Pope Benedict XVI: An Introduction to the Theology of Joseph Ratzinger* (London: Burns & Oates, 2005), p. 5. Nichols is the best source on Ratzinger's theology, and his treatment of Bavarian Catholicism is also excellent.
6. In Ratzinger's first book-length interview with German journalist Peter Seewald, *Salt of the Earth: The Church at the End of the Millennium* (San Francisco: Ignatius Press, 1997), p. 44. (They later collaborated on *God and the World* in 2000.)
7. *Bild am Sonntag,* October 2, 2005; translated by various news outlets.
8. Cited in John Allen, *Cardinal Ratzinger: The Vatican's Enforcer of the Faith* (New York: Continuum, 2000), p. 21. Though Allen later voiced regrets about some of his judgments in the book, it remains the best single resource on Ratzinger's life and career. I relied a great deal on Allen's work in the course of researching this book, especially on these biographical chapters, as anyone must.
9. Carlin Romano, "The Pope's Sins of Omission," *Chronicle of Higher Education,* May 13, 2005, p. 13.
10. Allen, *Enforcer,* p. 17.
11. Allen, *Enforcer,* pp. 15–16.
12. Seewald, *Salt of the Earth,* p. 51.
13. *The Ratzinger Report: An Exclusive Interview on the State of the Church* (San Francisco: Ignatius Press, 1985), pp. 166–67. Subsequently referred to as *Report*. This book, an interview with Italian journalist Vittorio Messori, was a bombshell when it appeared. Ratzinger's blunt obervations and criticisms created headlines and cemented his hard-line reputation.
14. Allen, *Enforcer,* p. 26.
15. Allen, *Enforcer,* p. 24.
16. Ratzinger, *Milestones,* p. 42.
17. *Report,* p. 167.
18. Ratzinger, *Milestones,* p. 15.
19. Cited in Romano, "The Pope's Sins of Omission," p. 13.
20. Friedrich Nietzsche, *Beyond Good and Evil* (New York: Vintage Books, 1989), pp. 178–179.
21. Seewald, *Salt of the Earth,* p. 26.

Chapter Six: Council, Crisis, and Conversion

1. Seewald, *Salt of the Earth,* p. 54.
2. "Few Marktl Residents Remember Pope as Baby, But Recall Later Years," CNS, May 4, 2005.
3. "A Future Pope Is Recalled: A Lover of Cats and Mozart, Dazzled by Church as a Boy," *New York Times,* April 22, 2005, p. A-12.
4. Cited in Richard E. Rubenstein, *Aristotle's Children: How Christians, Muslims, and Jews Rediscovered Ancient Wisdom and Illuminated the Middle Ages* (New York: Harcourt, 2003), p. 10.
5. Bokenkotter, *Concise History,* p. 312.
6. See Allen, *Enforcer,* for a fuller treatment of Ratzinger's great-uncle.
7. See the chapter "The Meaning of 'Meaning It,'" in Erik Erikson, *Young Man Luther* (New York: W.W. Norton & Company, 1958).
8. Cited in James K. A. Smith, "What God Knows: The Debate on 'Open Theism,'" *Christian Century,* July 12, 2005, p. 14.
9. Rubenstein, *Aristotle's Children,* pp. 5–6.

10. Seewald, *Salt of the Earth*, p. 66.

11. *Report*, p. 79.

12. Nichols, *Thought of Pope Benedict*, p. 43.

13. Nichols, *Thought of Pope Benedict*, p. 50.

14. William James, *Varieties of Religious Experience* (New York: Modern Library, 1994), p. 470.

15. "A Future Pope Is Recalled," p. A-12.

16. Allen, *Enforcer*, p. 54.

17. Allen, *Enforcer*, p. 46.

18. Allen, *Enforcer*, pp. 81–82.

19. Nichols, *Thought of Pope Benedict*, p. 100.

20. *Report*, p. 13.

21. Allen, *Enforcer*, p. 114.

22. Seewald, *Salt of the Earth*, p. 77.

23. Letter, *Commonweal*, June 17, 2005.

24. Allen, *Enforcer*, p. 116.

25. *Report*, p. 18.

26. Cited in Anthony Grafton, "Reading Ratzinger," *New Yorker*, July 25, 2005, p. 42.

27. Seewald, *Salt of the Earth*, p. 75.

28. Seewald, *Salt of the Earth*, p. 82.

29. Allen, *Enforcer*, p. 129.

30. Craig, *The Germans*, p. 101.

31. Allen, *Enforcer*, p. 125.

32. Seewald, *Salt of the Earth*, p. 83.

Chapter Seven: Defender of the Faith

1. Nichols, *Thought of Pope Benedict*, p. 41.

2. Seewald, *Salt of the Earth*, p. 193.

3. Seewald, *Salt of the Earth*, p. 187.

4. Stephen O'Shea, *The Perfect Heresy: The Revolutionary Life and Death of the Medieval Cathars* (New York: Walker Publishing, 2000), p. 6.

5. Allen, *Enforcer*, pp. 66–67.

6. *Report*, p. 26.

7. Cited in Father Thomas J. Reese, S.J., *Inside the Vatican: The Politics and Organization of the Catholic Church* (Boston: Harvard University Press, 1996), p. 251.

8. *La Stampa;* translated in Catholic News Agency, October 4, 2005.

9. *Report*, p. 190.

10. *Bild am Sonntag*, October 2, 2005; translated by various news outlets.

11. *Report*, p. 188.

12. Seewald, *Salt of the Earth*, pp. 132–33.

13. *Report*, p. 177.

14. Allen, *Enforcer*, p. 134.

15. For further details on the Romero saga, see Jonathan Kwitny, *Man of the Century: The Life and Times of John Paul II* (New York: Henry Holt, 1997).

16. Reese, *Inside the Vatican*, p. 253.

17. Paul Collins, *The Modern Inquisition: Seven Prominent Catholics and Their Struggles with the Vatican* (Woodstock, NY: Overlook Press, 2002), pp. 70–71.

18. Collins, *Modern Inquisition*, p. ix.

19. Reese, *Inside the Vatican*, p. 260.

20. *Report*, p. 68.

21. "In Defence of Fr. Dupuis," *Tablet*, January 16, 1999.

22. "The Word from Rome," *NCR*, January 7, 2005; see http://nationalcatholicreporter.org/word/word010705.htm.

23. Reese, *Inside the Vatican*, p. 254.

24. "'Panzerkardinal' Reflects on His Life Decisions in Autobiography," CNS, April 24, 1997.

25. *Report,* p. 21.

26. Seewald, *Salt of the Earth,* pp. 93–94.

27. Seewald, *Salt of the Earth,* p. 86.

28. Seewald, *Salt of the Earth,* p. 88–94.

29. Zenit.org, May 15, 2005; see http://www.zenit.org/english/visualizza.phtml?sid=70957.

30. Zenit.org, June 6, 2005; see http://www.zenit.org/english/visualizza.phtml?sid=72149.

31. Seewald, *Salt of the Earth,* p. 67.

32. Zenit.org, May 1, 2005; see http://www.zenit.org/english/visualizza.phtml?sid=70184.

33. Seewald, *Salt of the Earth,* p. 68.

34. A. J. P. Taylor, *Bismarck: The Man and the Statesman* (New York: Vintage, 1967), p. 12.

35. Nichols, *Thought of Pope Benedict,* pp. 241–42.

36. Sandro Magister, "Ruling in the Shadow of John Paul II: The Vatican Four," October 22, 2004; see http://www.chiesa.espressonline.it/dettaglio.jsp?id=19630&eng=y.

37. Reese, *Inside the Vatican,* p. 136.

38. Seewald, *Salt of the Earth,* p. 16.

39. *Report,* p. 44.

40. Robert Mohynihan, "Let God's Light Shine Forth," *Inside the Vatican,* August/September 2001, p. 19.

Chapter Eight: Pontifex Maximus, Pontifex Minimus

1. Sandro Magister, "The 'Reform of the Reform' Has Already Begun," *Magister,* April 28, 2005; see http://www.chiesa.espressonline.it/dettaglio.jsp?id=29626&eng=y.

2. National Press Club address, July 11, 2005.

3. "The Word from Rome," *NCR,* October 18, 2002; see http://nationalcatholicreporter.org/word/word1018.htm.

4. Andre Frossard, *Be Not Afraid: Pope John Paul II Speaks Out on His Life, His Beliefs, and His Inspiring Vision for Humanity* (New York: St. Martin's Press, 1984), pp. 25–26.

5. Hannah Arendt, *Men in Dark Times* (New York: Harcourt Brace, 1968), p. 57.

6. Interview with *Frontline* for "Pope John Paul II: The Millennial Pope," 1999.

7. September 2005 interview with *Junge Freiheit.*

8. Accattoli, *Pope John Paul II,* p. 105.

9. "Various Colleagues Say 'Church Will Come to Love' Pope Benedict XVI," CNS, April 19, 2005.

10. Martin Mosebach in an April 30, 2005 op-ed in the *New York Times.*

11. "In the Name of the Father," *New Republic,* December 26, 1994, cover story.

12. Father Richard McBrien, ed., *The HarperCollins Encyclopedia of Catholicism* (San Francisco: HarperSanFrancisco, 1995), p. 988.

13. The Laurence J. McGinley Lecture at Fordham University, New York, October 21, 2003.

14. Weigel, *Witness to Hope,* pp. 241–42.

15. Seewald, *Salt of the Earth,* p. 117.

16. Accattoli, *Pope John Paul II,* p. 114.

17. Andrea Tornielli, "Will He Stay?" *Inside the Vatican,* August/September 2005, p. 31.

18. "Out of Africa," interview with Father James Chukwuma Okoye, C.S.Sp., *U.S. Catholic,* September 2005, p. 20.

19. Seewald, *Salt of the Earth,* pp. 175–76.

20. Seewald, *Salt of the Earth,* p. 148.

21. *Report,* p. 126.

22. Father Uwe Michael Lang, "The Pope Has the Task of a Gardener," *Inside the Vatican,* August/September 2005, p. 32; the article first appeared in German in *Frankfurter Allgemeine Zeitung,* June 7, 2005.

23. *Report,* p. 129.

24. From the "Notebook" section of *Tablet,* September 24, 2005.

25. *Frontline,* September 28, 1999.

26. "Meet Benedict XVI: Shy, Orderly, Funny," *New York Times,* April 24, 2005, p. A-23.

27. "Wojtyla, as Seen by Karol," *L'Espresso,* May 14–20, 2004.

28. "The Pope and the Pussycats," MSNBC, July 13, 2005.

29. "In German Town, Benedict XVI Known for Love of Cats, Conversation," Knight Ridder, April 21, 2005.

30. "The Testimonies of Twenty-One Cardinals on the New Pope," *30Giorni*, May 2005; see http://www.30giorni.it/us/articolo.asp?id=8923.

31. "Style Secrets of the Pope's Tailor," *New York Times*, April 14, 2005, p. G-10.

32. "The Word from Rome," *NCR*, May 31, 2005; see http://nationalcatholicreporter.org/word/word053105.htm.

33. Czeslaw Milosz, *New and Collected Poems: 1931–2001* (New York: Ecco, 2003), p. 710.

Chapter Nine: Joys and Hopes, Griefs and Anxieties

1. Russell Shaw, "Opening the Church's Doors," *Our Sunday Visitor*, September 11, 2005, p. 8.

2. Joseph A. Komonchak, "Pope Benedict's Theological Vision," *Commonweal*, June 3, 2005, is one of the best summaries of Benedict's thinking.

3. Allen, *Enforcer*, p. 80.

4. Zenit.org, February 24, 2004; see http://www.zenit.org/english/visualizza.phtml?sid=48504.

5. Seewald, *Salt of the Earth*, p. 70.

6. "On Earth, as in Heaven," *Tablet*, July 9, 2005, p. 12.

7. McBrien, ed., *The HarperCollins Encyclopedia of Catholicism*, p. 964.

8. From *The True Church and the Poor*, cited in James Martin, S. J., *This Our Exile* (New York: Orbis Books, 1999), p. 40.

9. Arendt, *Men in Dark Times*, p. 66.

10. Accattoli, *Pope John Paul II*, p. 63.

11. Accattoli, *Pope John Paul II*, p. 49.

12. Accattoli, *Pope John Paul II*, p. 195.

13. "Pope Benedict XVI and World Affairs," a panel at the Pew Forum, April 29, 2005.

14. Kenneth R. Himes, O.F.M., "To Inspire and Inform," *America*, June 6, 2005, p. 7.

15. *Report*, p. 190.

16. Father Thomas D. Williams, "Seasoned Fare," *First Things*, February 1998, p. 52.

17. Seewald, *Salt of the Earth*, p. 260.

18. *Report*, p. 99.

19. Allen, *Enforcer*, p. 190ff.

20. Allen, *Enforcer*, p. 142.

21. Interviews in *Los Angeles Times*, December 31, 2005, and *Tablet*, January 14, 2006.

22. "Pope Full of Surprises, Friend Says," *Pittsburgh Post-Gazette*, October 7, 2005, p. A-6.

23. Zenit.org, August 24, 2003; see http://www.zenit.org/english/visualizza.phtml?sid=39953.

24. "The Bishops in Council," Erasmus Lecture of the Institute on Religion and Public Life, delivered October 25, 2004, and reprinted in *First Things*, April 2005.

25. "The Word from Rome," *NCR*, July 1, 2005; see http://nationalcatholicreporter.org/word/word070105.htm.

26. Peter Steinfels, "A Ban on Same-Sex Attraction and Sexual Activity Could Be a Crucial Issue for Catholics' Attitudes," *New York Times*, September 24, 2005, p. B-6.

27. National Press Club address, Canberra, Australia, September 21, 2005.

28. From unpublished answers to questions from a 1993 *Time* interview, posted by *Catholic World News*; see http://www.cwnews.com/news/viewstory.cfm?recnum=37855.

29. *Report*, p. 116.

30. Christopher Ruddy, "No Restorationist," *Commonweal*, June 3, 2005, p. 15.

Chapter Ten: America and the Battle for Catholicism

1. "Of Many Things," *America*, May 30, 2005, p. 2.

2. *In Search of an American Catholicism: A History of Religion and Culture in Tension* (New York: Oxford University Press, 2002), p. 4.

3. "CPA Members Vote Against Issuing Statement on Editor's Resignation," CNS, May 27, 2005.

4. "Editor's Ouster Worries Catholic Publications," *Boston Globe*, May 10, 2005, p. A-1.

5. E. J. Dionne Jr., "No Room for Dissent?" *Washington Post*, May 31, 2005, p. A-17.

6. "Benedict XVI on Campus," *Boston Globe,* May 16, 2005, p. A-13.

7. "Dismissal of the Editor of Jesuit Magazine *America* Is Regarded as a Signal that the New Pope Won't Tolerate Discussion from the Left; Vatican Draws Line in Sand," *Newsday,* May 16, 2005, p. A-22.

Chapter Eleven: The Counter-Reformation

1. Cited in Nichols, *Thought of Pope Benedict,* p. 132.

2. Seewald, *Salt of the Earth,* p. 123.

3. Ratzinger, *Milestones,* p. 15.

4. Seewald, *Salt of the Earth,* p. 173.

5. *Report,* p. 62.

6. Bishop Donald W. Trautman, "Our Daily Bread," *America,* October 3, 2005, p. 9.

7. Father Joseph Komonchak, "Dubious Demonizing," *Commonweal,* November 3, 2000, p. 31.

8. Seewald, *Salt of the Earth,* p. 173.

9. Ruddy, "No Restorationist."

10. *Report,* p. 53.

11. Seewald, *Salt of the Earth,* p. 271.

12. *Report,* p. 46.

13. *Report,* p. 49.

14. Zenit.org, June 6, 2005; see http://www.zenit.org/english/visualizza.phtml?sid=72149.

15. "The New Pope Benedict XVI," *Newsday,* April 21, 2005, p. A-6.

16. Interview with Evangelical Word Television Network, September 5, 2003, cited in Zenit.org, August 24, 2003; see http://www.zenit.org/english/visualizza.phtml?sid=39953.

17. Collins, *The Modern Inquisition,* p. 145.

18. "Vatican Newspaper Says Homosexual Men Not Suitable for Priesthood," CNS, November 29, 2005.

19. "California Archdiocese to Reconsider Its Adoption Policy: Its Ex-Leader Calls for Gay Parent Ban," *Boston Globe,* March 10, 2006.

20. Seewald, *Salt of the Earth,* p. 182.

21. Seewald, *Salt of the Earth,* p. 213.

22. Seewald, *Salt of the Earth,* p. 75.

23. Seewald, *Salt of the Earth,* p. 160.

24. Seewald, *Salt of the Earth,* p. 185.

25. McBrien, ed., *The HarperCollins Encyclopedia of Catholicism,* p. 985.

26. *Report,* pp. 28–31.

27. *Report,* p. 30.

28. *Report,* p. 31.

29. George Weigel, *God's Choice: Pope Benedict XVI and the Future of the Catholic Church* (New York: HarperCollins, 2005), p. 183.

30. Allen, *Enforcer,* p. 187.

31. Collins, *Modern Inquisition,* p. 234; Allen, "The Vatican's Enforcer," *NCR,* April 16, 1999, cover story.

32. *Report,* p. 159.

33. *Report,* p. 18.

34. "Changing and Changeless," *Christian Century,* May 17, 2005, p. 10.

35. Nichols, *Thought of Pope Benedict,* p. 152.

36. Nichols, *Thought of Pope Benedict,* pp. 80–81.

37. Allen, "The Vatican's Enforcer."

38. Jonathan Luxmoore, "German Cardinals Voice Priorities," *Tablet,* May 14, 2005. Luxmoore was quoting from an interview with Meisner in *Rheinischer Merkur,* a German weekly.

39. Clifford Longley, "The Bishops Saw the Role of the Laity as Being Simply to Pay, Pray, and Obey," *Tablet,* June 11, 2005.

40. Steinfels, "A Ban on Same-Sex Attraction," *New York Times,* September 24, 2005, p. B-6.

41. *Educating Leaders for Ministry: Issues and Responses* (Collegeville, MN: Liturgical Press, 2005), eds. Victor J. Klimoski, Kevin J. O'Neil, C.Ss.R., and Katarina M. Schuth, O.S.F.

42. "Survey of U.S. Catholics," *NCR*, September 30, 2005, cover story.

43. "Synod Concerned that Catholics Misunderstand Real Presence of Christ," CNS, October 19, 2005.

44. "Faith and Family in America Survey," *Religion & Ethics Newsweekly*, October 19, 2005.

45. "The Word from Rome," *NCR*, October 28, 2005; see http://nationalcatholicreporter.org/word/word102805.htm.

46. Joseph Ratzinger, *Introduction to Christianity* (San Francisco: Ignatius Press, 2000), p. 19.

47. Seewald, *Salt of the Earth*, p. 257.

48. *Collection: Papers by Bernard Lonergan, S.J.* (New York: Herder and Herder, 1967), F. E. Crowe, S.J., ed., pp. 266–67.

49. "Self-Righteousness Is Destructive and Uncharitable," *Catholic Spirit*, September 23, 2004, p. 2.

50. Seewald, *Salt of the Earth*, p. 154.

51. Weigel, *God's Choice*, p. 151.

52. *Report*, p. 13.

Conclusion: The Rule of Benedict

1. "Vatican Reporter: Pope Benedict Will Finish Work of John Paul II," *Pittsburgh Tribune-Review*, October 7, 2005, p. A-1.

2. For a full treatment of the issues surrounding papal retirement, see Father Thomas J. Reese, S.J. *Inside the Vatican* (Harvard University Press, 1996), pp. 74–76.

3. Interview from "Ich finde, der deutsche Papst macht es fantastisch," cited in *Passauer Neuen Presse*, Kath.net, April 17, 2006; see http://www.kath.net/detail.php?id=13407.

4. From a February 2006 speech, cited in *NCR*, March 3, 2006.

5. Zenit.org, March 12, 2006; see http://www.zenit.org/english/visualizza.phtml?sid=85858.

6. "Christian Community Needs Commitment to Truth, Gospel, Says Pope," CNS, April 5, 2006.

7. Ronald Modras, "In His Own Footsteps: Benedict XVI: From Professor to Pontiff," *Commonweal*, April 21, 2006, p. 15.

8. Ratzinger, *Introduction to Christianity*, p. 39.

9. Question-and-answer session with the clergy of Rome on March 2, 2006, translated by Zenit.org; see http://www.zenit.org/english/visualizza.phtml?sid=86573.

10. "Secularism Is Greatest Challenge, Pope Tells Youth," *Catholic World News*, April 7, 2006; see http://www.cwnews.com/news/viewstory.cfm?recnum=43442.

INDEX

ACKNOWLEDGMENTS

Writing a book can become such a consuming endeavor that the personal and the professional start to overlap, something that in my experience has always been a great benefit. Good friends become sharp-eyed readers, and sharp-eyed editors become good friends. Both brought different perspectives that enriched this manuscript, and my life, and both deserve enormous thanks.

I am grateful to the folks at HarperSanFrancisco for continuing to provide a home for my work, and a platform for the writing of a wonderful array of authors in the field of religion and spirituality. Mark Tauber and Mickey Maudlin have been especially supportive, as have the indefatigable Kris Ashley and my publicist, Maria Meneses. Lisa Zuniga's patience and keen attention in copyediting rescued me from all sorts of lapses. Above all, I would like to thank my editor, Roger Freet, who got behind this project and pushed it to a successful conclusion. Roger's editing skills and consistent encouragement were indispensable.

Friends were as generous as ever with their support and prayers, and I can't thank them enough. In Rome, Alessandra Angelini and Alessandro Di Marco provided lodging and every possible assistance during the conclave. A host of clergy and lay friends in and around the Vatican were especially helpful; it is wiser, as ever, not to cite them all by name.

Among my colleagues in the writing life, I would single out for thanks Grant Gallicho and Tim Reidy at *Commonweal* for taking valuable time to read the manuscript and provide typically smart critiques. Father James Martin, S.J., at *America*, offered spiritual insights and his gift with words, both of which would do Saint Ignatius of Loyola proud. Since I last thanked him,

Rocco Palmo has made a great debut in the blogosphere and in print, and his analyses continued to point out new avenues for my work.

One of the pleasures of this project was the chance to reconnect with old friends and make new ones. Liam Kelly, now working on behalf of the Benedictine community at Ampleforth Abbey, and Patricia Hardcastle, now his wife, were very generous in pointing out my shortcomings and providing research and leads that strengthened the book at several points. Dr. John Block, my professor at Furman University all too long ago, was kind enough to remind me of some of the lessons of German history that I had forgotten. At Kean University, church historian, fellow writer, and good friend Christopher M. Bellitto saved me from sins of commission and omission.

As always, I made the final call on all judgments herein, and any errors are my responsibility alone.

My expanding family—from my parents to my siblings and in-laws and the rest of tribe—remains a source of joy and support. At the heart of it all is my wife, Josephine, who every day reminds me of the many graces of God. And there has been no greater blessing in our lives, or sign of faith in the future, than the birth of our daughter, Stella, who arrived like a party-crashing Muse midway through the writing of this book, on July 31, 2005, the Feast of Saint Ignatius. God bless her. *Ad Majorem Dei Gloriam.*